CHICAGO

HEART AND SOUL OF AMERICA

▲ ALAN KLEHR

URBAN
TAPESTRY
SERIES

TOWERY
PUBLISHING, INC.

CHICAGO

HEART AND SOUL

BY NORMAN MARK AND KERRY ROBERTSON

CHICAGO

OF AMERICA

Art Direction by Brian Groppe

LIBRARY OF CONGRESS CATALOGING-IN-PUBLICATION DATA

Mark, Norman.
    Chicago : heart and soul of America / by Norman Mark and Kerry Robertson ; art direction by Brian Groppe.
        p.   cm. — (Urban tapestry series)
    Includes index.
    ISBN 1-881096-53-X (alk. paper)
    1. Chicago (Ill.)—Civilization.   2. Chicago (Ill.)—Pictorial works. 3. Business enterprises—Illinois—Chicago.   4. Chicago (Ill.)—Economic conditions.   I. Robertson, Kerry, 1964-
II. Title.   III. Series.
F548.52.M35 1998
977.3'11—dc21   97-51957
                                                   CIP

Towery Publishing, Inc.
1835 Union Avenue
Memphis, TN 38104

PUBLISHER:	J. Robert Towery
EXECUTIVE PUBLISHER:	Jenny McDowell
NATIONAL SALES MANAGER:	Stephen Hung
REGIONAL SALES MANAGER:	Michele Sylvestro
MARKETING DIRECTOR:	Carol Culpepper
PROJECT DIRECTORS:	Andrea Glazier, Henry Hintermeister, Mindy Levine, Don Neason, Brett Sechrest, Paul Withington
EXECUTIVE EDITOR:	David B. Dawson
MANAGING EDITOR:	Michael C. James
SENIOR EDITORS:	Lynn Conlee, Carlisle Hacker
EDITOR/PROJECT MANAGER:	Lori Bond
STAFF EDITORS:	Mary Jane Adams, Jana Files, Susan Hesson, Brian Johnston
ASSISTANT EDITORS:	Pat McRaven, Jennifer C. Pyron, Allison Ring
PROFILE WRITER:	Deborah Leigh Wood
EDITORIAL CONTRIBUTOR:	Mark Schuman
PROFILE DESIGNERS:	Laurie Beck, Kelley Pratt, Ann Ward
DIGITAL COLOR SUPERVISOR:	Brenda Pattat
DIGITAL COLOR TECHNICIANS:	Darin Ipema, Jack Griffith, Jason Moak
PRODUCTION RESOURCES MANAGER:	Dave Dunlap Jr.
PRODUCTION ASSISTANTS:	Geoffrey Ellis, Enrique Espinosa, Robin McGehee
PRINT COORDINATOR:	Beverly Timmons

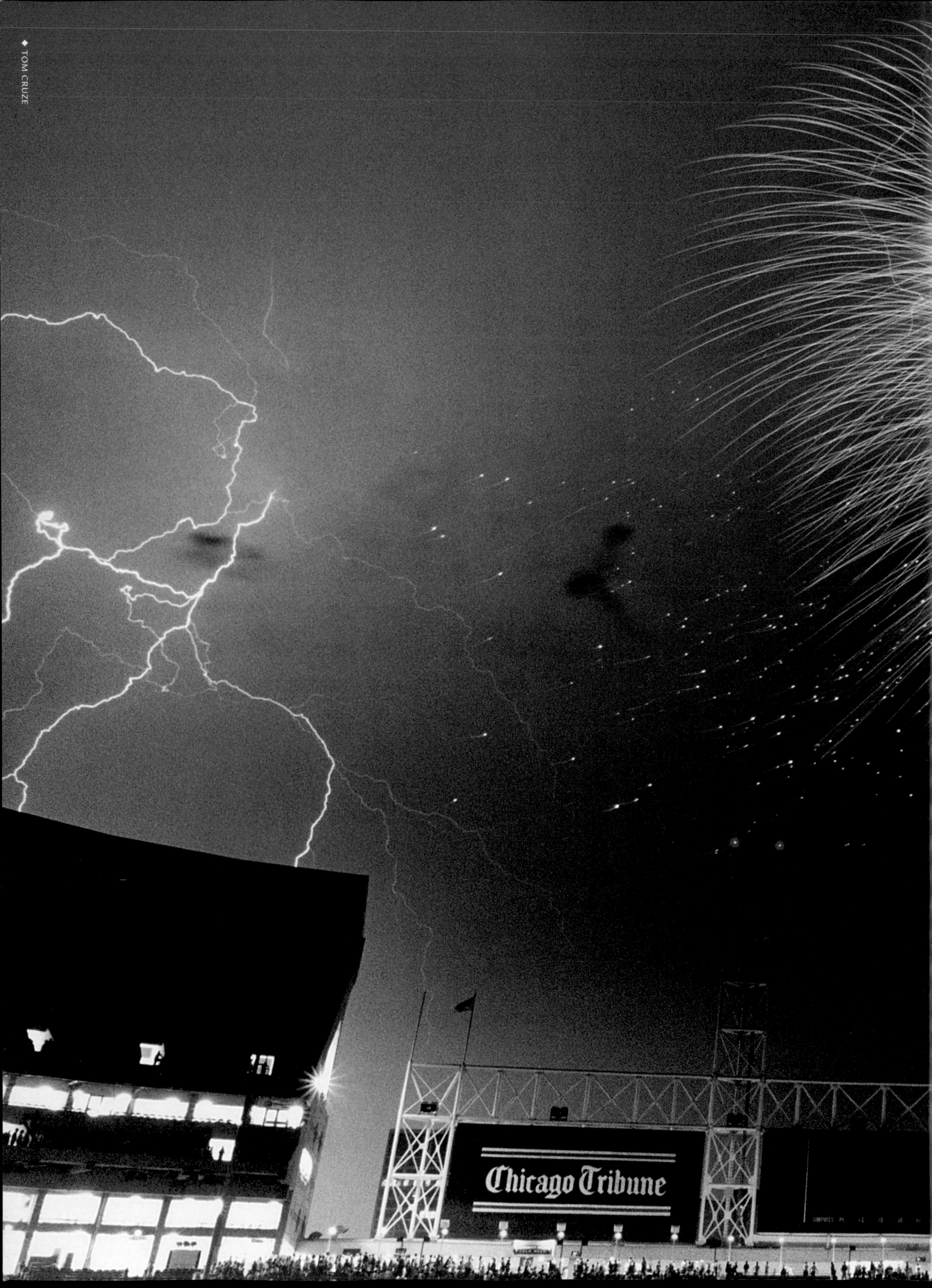

◆ TOM CRUZE

GATE 4
ACCESS ONLY
FOR
WILL CALL
&
VALET PARKING
GUESTS

ALL OTHERS ACCESS
GATE 6 & 3

GATE
ACCESS O
FOR
WILL CA
&
VALET PAR
GUEST

ALL OTHERS
GATE 6&

MICHAEL JORDAN

**M**OMENTS BEFORE THE SECOND ACT OF A CHICAGO BAL-LET PERFORMANCE, A ROLY-POLY, MIDDLE-AGED MAN WAS LITERALLY BOUNCING IN HIS SEAT. "IT'S A WORLD PREMIERE. AND A WORLD PREMIERE IS A DANCE THAT'S NEVER BEEN SEEN BEFORE," HE ENERGETICALLY

informed everyone in the balcony.

Then he pushed his right arm and forefinger high into the air above his head, stood, and began chanting, "We're Number One. We're Number One."

It was an amazing moment. Here was a ballet fan as involved in being "Number One" as any Bulls, Bears, Hawks, Sox, or Cubs rooter. That enthusiast embodies the essence of being a Chicagoan.

Chicago is the city that loves to be Number One above all things. Drive down any street and you'll see signs boasting about the city's best hot dog or the Number One ribs in town. One North Side establishment even proclaims that it sells the best scones in the world.

Chicagoans love to talk about having the Number One best professional basketball team in the universe (da Bulls) or the Number One historically worst professional baseball team (the Cubs). We point with pride at our Number One best buildings, symphony orchestra, restaurants, work ethic, hot dogs, Greek food, and pizzas.

We'll even take credit for having the worst politicians, weather, and mail delivery. In fact, about the only area in which Chicagoans are embarrassed by our Number One status is our gangsterism. Ask about Capone and most Chicagoans will quickly change the subject.

The first open-heart surgery (by Dr. Daniel Hale Williams) was performed in Chicago. The fire pole was invented here, as were the ice-cream sundae and Mickey Finn knockout drops. The first sustained nuclear reaction happened in Chicago, which was also home to the first panda in captivity. Locals even claim the creation of the ultimate French dish, the crêpe suzette, and the ultimate Greek recipe, flaming saganaki.

But my Number One reason for loving Chicago is the people. Real Chicagoans are both tougher and softer, friendlier when it comes to giving directions, and somewhat better at telling the truth than people in most other cities.

Chicagoans are also funnier. Of course, an extreme range of

▶ RAY F. HILLSTROM / HILLSTROM STOCK PHOTOGRAPHY

weather inspires most natives to develop a delicious sense of the absurd. Perhaps that's why Chicago is the home of Second City, the renowned improvisational troupe that has served as a farm club for so many famous actors and comedians.

A lot of our cynicism stems from the fact that so many of our most respected politicians regularly take long vacations in prison. An old Chicago definition of a good politician is one who "stays bought"—one who accepts a bribe and then actually does what he promised to do. One politician

recently went to jail after being tape recorded expressing delight at the peach-colored panties worn by his underage mistress. Reading such stories in the morning papers teaches Chicagoans to laugh. Or cry. ☞

A CITY KNOWN FOR ITS thriving performing arts scene, Chicago offers the ultimate in theatrics of every sort, from the more traditional tragedy and comedy to the high-flying choreography of a well-known athlete frozen in time. Exploding over Comiskey Park during a White Sox game, fireworks of the celestial and man-made varieties add their own drama to the evening sky (PAGES 6 AND 7).

HICAGOANS PROUDLY CLAIM STEVE ALLEN, BENNY GOODMAN, AND ERNEST HEMINGWAY, WHO ALL CAME FROM THE AREA, AS WELL AS ARCHITECT FRANK LLOYD WRIGHT, WHO GOT HIS START HERE. ■ SOME OF MY FAVORITE CURRENT CHICAGOANS (AND IT WOULD BE IMPOSSIBLE TO OFFER A COMPLETE LIST)

HICAGOANS HAVE ALWAYS been a feisty bunch, from Mayor "Long John" Wentworth, who scared the electorate into voting for him back in the 1860s (BOTTOM LEFT), to Mayor Richard J. Daley, who in more recent years invited critics of his son to pucker up (PAGES 10 AND 11). Today's citizens demonstrate their own brand of enthusiasm, as they throw their support behind the stars and stripes.

include movie critic Roger Ebert, one of the world's great storytellers; Michael Jordan, who truly defies gravity; Oprah Winfrey, who knows when to take the high road; Bob Djahanguiri, who is almost single-handedly reviving smoky music in Middle America by hiring singers for his cafés; Ray Nordstrand, who made WFMT the best classical FM station in the country; and my father, who continues to write a living love story to my mother years after her death.

But my Number One favorite historic Chicagoan has to be the mayor who fired the entire police force—and the crime rate went down!

"Long John" Wentworth is the one responsible for that action, which occurred at 1:40 a.m. on

March 26, 1861. The city was without its captain, six lieutenants, and 50 patrolmen for the next nine hours, during which time there were only two robberies. That qualified as nearly crime-free for a city of about 100,000 residents.

The mayor stood six feet six inches, weighed more than 300 pounds, drank nearly a quart of brandy most days of his life, and once tore down an entire neighborhood just because it offended him. But perhaps Long John's finest moment occurred when he introduced Edward Albert—later King Edward VII of England—to the citizens of Chicago. The entire city was in a tizzy about meeting its first royal visitor, and all eyes were straining toward the Prince of Wales. As the two men stepped onto the balcony atop City Hall,

Long John made an unforgettable introduction: "Prince, here are the boys. Boys, here is the prince."

Long John also once delivered what poet Carl Sandburg called "the shortest and most terrifying stump speech ever heard in Illinois." Speaking to the large and raucous crowd that had gathered outside the courthouse, Long John shouted, "You damned fools . . . You can either vote for me . . . or you can go to hell!"

Politicians who tell off the Chicago electorate are another local tradition. About a century later, Mayor Richard J. Daley was asked embarrassing questions about his son's qualifications for a city contract. Ironically, Daley increased his own popularity with his memorable answer: "You can kiss my ass." ☞

IN ORDER TO UNDERSTAND CHICAGOANS, IT IS IMPORTANT TO REMEMBER THAT NO ONE IN HIS OR HER RIGHT MIND EVER CAME HERE FOR THE CLIMATE. ONE ANCIENT JOKE IS ABOUT A WINTER'S DAY WHEN IT WAS SO COLD IN CHICAGO THAT A POLITICIAN WAS SEEN WITH HIS HANDS IN HIS OWN POCKETS FOR A CHANGE. ■ CHICAGO BEGAN AS A

swamp, and continued as a cesspool of disease that was only somewhat alleviated when the flow of the Chicago River was reversed in 1900, giving the city another claim to Number One: Reversing the flow of that river remains among the engineering marvels of the world.

People basically came—and still come—to Chicago to make money. One of my favorite local entrepreneurs is Captain George Wellington Streeter, who—more than a century ago—held off the Chicago police department and the forces of good society for more than three decades so he could sell beer on Sundays.

"Cap" Streeter, who once claimed that he had been in business with Jesse James, stranded his steamboat, the *Reutan*, on a sandbar north of the entrance to the Chicago River on July 11, 1886. The sandbar grew because Cap allowed builders who were constructing North Side mansions to dump whatever they wanted there. Soon he had created 186 acres. "Found land," he called it. "An eyesore"

▲ TOM CRUZE

was the most charitable reaction of his wealthy neighbors.

Those rich folks thought they finally had the goods on their nemesis when he was arrested for shooting at a Chicago police officer. But Cap's lawyer, a very clever former slave, won his client's freedom by proving that Chicago had no law against shooting *at* a police officer. You had to actually wound the cop before you could be charged with a crime. (The city changed the law after the attorney discovered the loophole.)

In 1918, some 32 years after he

arrived, the tough, irascible, independent Cap Streeter was finally defeated, but not by cops, deputies, or gunslingers. It took a judge to throw him off his found land.

Cap operated a hot dog stand on Navy Pier until his death in 1921 at age 84. His land, which he sold for $1 per lot and which is now worth more than $3 billion, included everything east of Michigan Avenue from the river to Oak Street. It now holds the Hancock Center, CBS Television, hospitals, offices, and expensive high-rise apartments. ☞

THERE ARE PLENTY OF reasons why people come to Chicago, but the weather usually isn't one of them. Still, life goes on, no matter how far the mercury plummets (TOP AND OPPOSITE).

SINCE THE CITY'S EARLIEST days, the local police force has helped keep the peace (LEFT), but they met their match when Captain George Wellington "Cap" Streeter came to town (RIGHT). All Cap wanted to do was squat on a Lake Michigan beach and sell beer on Sundays, and he fought off Chicago's finest for more than three decades trying to do just that.

◄ CHICAGO HISTORICAL SOCIETY / CHARLES R. CLARK

◄ CHICAGO HISTORICAL SOCIETY #DN-000325 / CHICAGO DAILY NEWS

cannot be guaranteed.

Known far (and very wide) as the fattest madam in town, Gentle Annie set her cap for Cap Hyman, a renowned gambler of the bachelor persuasion. She wanted wedded bliss, but he was comfortable in single hitch.

So Gentle Annie took matters into her own hands. She entered Cap's downtown gambling establishment and crossed the entire main floor—with no one daring to stop her because her eyes said she was a woman on a mission. She then stomped up the stairs to Cap's second-floor offices and went in without so much as a "May I disturb you?"

Grabbing Cap by his lapels, Gentle Annie threw him off his sofa and kicked him down the stairs while expertly brandishing a whip. With the whip cracking and flicking nearly all parts of Cap's hide, Annie chased her love through the mix of shocked gam-

blers, out the door, and up the street to the amusement of on-lookers and journalists.

Less than six weeks later, Gentle Annie married Cap Hyman and, by all accounts, they lived happily ever after. It was an example of a determined Chicago woman challenging a force of nature—and winning.

There were times, however, when determination wasn't enough. Mrs. Edith Rockefeller McCormick died in her Drake Hotel suite in 1932, still hoping her ex-husband, Harold, might come back to her—even though their marriage had ended in 1913. He never did.

Having had his name linked with any number of other women, Harold had chosen an operatic diva named Ganna Walska over returning to his former wife. And in the summer of 1922, before their proposed nuptials, Harold checked into Wesley Memorial Hospital for a secret operation by Dr. Victor

D. Lespinasse, the one who said, "A man is as old as his glands." Newspapers speculated that the glands of a younger man had been transplanted into Harold McCormick so as to make him fit for the rigors of wedded bliss with Miss Walska.

This led to much giggling, even in the best of circles, and the following ditty began making the rounds of society's drawing rooms:

Under the spreading chestnut tree,
The village smithy stands.
The smith a gloomy man is he;
McCormick has his glands.

Although we have no information on the results of the operation, alas, the marriage was not a success. When the couple divorced, Ganna Walska got $6 million, a fourth of Harold's International Harvester holdings.

In the annals of Chicago di-

CHICAGO IS A PEDESTRIAN'S town, where hurried businesspeople share the busy sidewalks with shoppers and curious tourists.

vorces, the April 1889 court case involving Caroline Louise and Leslie Carter would take the prize as the Number One most fascinating. She sued him, he sued her, and the newspapers of the day did not stint on the steamy details.

The *Chicago Times* noted, "Her hair was the color of an August stubble field and her lips red and inviting." The *Chicago Tribune* revealed that, on the first day of the trial, Mrs. Carter was "fashionably attired in a rich, tight-fitting walking suit of black that showed her mature figure to excellent advantage. Through a flimsy black veil, her complexion seemed matchless."

The proceedings got so explicit that the judge announced a minimum age limit of 35 for those attending the trial. Later, he changed his mind, thundering from the bench, "An old curiosity monger is quite as reprehensible as a young curiosity monger. We must check the spread of immorality among the old and the decrepit." With that, he opened the trial to anyone over age 21.

Although Mrs. Carter had been accused of many infidelities, the five-week trial ended when the jury found her guilty of adultery with only one man. An actor,

he was hissed six times that week when he appeared on a Chicago stage in *Antony and Cleopatra*.

Another strong woman was Mrs. Potter Palmer, who ruled Chicago society in the 1890s as the wife of one of the richest men on the planet. Mr. Palmer made a fortune in a dry goods store that he sold to a kid from Massachusetts named Marshall Field.

Bertha Palmer's Number One most memorably triumphant moment was the result of a snub by Her Royal Highness, the Infanta Eulalia of Spain. During the 1893

World's Columbian Exposition, the Infanta arrived late at a reception in her honor, left early, and rejected an opportunity to meet Mrs. Palmer because she was merely the "wife of an innkeeper."

Bertha Palmer did not forget. Six years later, when she was invited to a reception for the Infanta in Paris, Mrs. Palmer refused, saying, "I cannot meet this bibulous representative of a degenerate monarch." So there. ☛

OMEN OF THE WINDY City boast a long history in law enforcement, dating back to 1893 when Marie Owens became the first female to be granted the power to arrest. Although they may not look the part, these courageous members of Chicago's police force, pictured in 1914, did their share to keep the city streets safe.

HE 1893 EXPOSITION—WHICH CELEBRATED THE 400TH ANNIVERSARY OF CHRISTOPHER COLUMBUS' ARRIVAL ON THE CONTINENT, BUT OPENED A YEAR LATE—WAS FAMOUS FOR HAVING THE FIRST FERRIS WHEEL IN AMERICA (ANOTHER NUMBER ONE) AND FOR GIVING CHICAGO THE NICKNAME

"Windy City." Chicagoans boasted so much while trying to land that 1893 fair that Charles A. Dana wrote in the *New York Sun*, "Don't pay attention to the nonsensical claims of that windy city." From that point on, Chicagoans have been proud of their "wind."

We also rightly boast about our architecture. When I look around Chicago, I see amazing buildings grouped in a soaring skyline. But the ones I love the most are where the best human stories originated.

For instance, whenever I walk by the Allerton Hotel at Michigan and Huron, I begin humming "Chestnuts roasting on an open fire." That's because in 1946, Mel Tormé came to this rather nondescript hotel to write the beloved *Christmas Song*.

Or, at 209 South LaSalle is the Rookery, a building enclosing a magnificent winding staircase that looks to me like an architect's version of a nautilus shell. It is here that a character named John W. "Bet-a-Million" Gates held his famous whist and bridge games that would last throughout the weekend. Imagine betting $100,000 on a bridge hand and you'll have some idea of the way Bet-a-Million gambled.

I once met a 92-year-old man in a wheelchair who said that he had spent a portion of his boyhood as a runner for Bet-a-Million. Gates, he remembered, helped create the Steel Wire Trust, which eventually became U.S. Steel. Gates was sure it would be the biggest deal of his life, bringing together all the manufacturers of steel wire under one large, powerful, and rich company.

After spending a good long time wheeling and dealing, on the eve of the creation of the trust, Gates was omitted from the board of directors. He angrily barged into financier J.P. Morgan's office and, after a good deal of shouting and pounding on the wealthy man's desk, asked if he was cut out of the final deal "merely because I do in public what you men do behind closed doors." Then, Morgan allegedly fixed Gates with a cold stare of disapproval and advised, "Young man, that's what doors are for."

My favorite corner in the entire city is at Michigan and

Wacker because it is the site of an entire library of stories. Fort Dearborn, Chicago's first military settlement, was here until it was evacuated on August 15, 1812. Nearly everyone who left the fort on that day was massacred. Standing on that corner is a reminder that living in Chicago has never been easy.

The Michigan Avenue Bridge at Wacker is one of the Chicago River's 43 drawbridges that are raised and lowered about 30,000 times a year. Through the decades, Chicago's bridges have been a reminder that the city can sometimes rival Paris in beauty.

But the bridges can also be seriously controversial. The Clark Street Bridge was once raised to prevent the German population living on the north side of the Chicago River from storming the Courthouse and City Hall on the south side. This incident occurred in 1855 after a pro-American

◀ RAY F. HILLSTROM / HILLSTROM STOCK PHOTOGRAPHY

◀ HOWARD E. ANDE

◀ HOWARD E. ANDE

A VIEW DOWN NORTH Michigan Avenue at night reveals a city on the move (PAGES 22 AND 23). Known as the Magnificent Mile, the famed boulevard is Chicago's premier business and shopping address, hosting such stores as Neiman Marcus and Cartier, not to mention such well-known skyscrapers as the Wrigley Building and the Tribune Tower.

mayor, who belonged to the aptly named Know Nothing Party, decreed that beer gardens must be closed on Sundays. His order solely affected *German* beer gardens and not American saloons, which sold only whiskey. After the Germans voiced their displeasure during the Lager Beer Riots, the Know Nothings disappeared from Chicago politics. The lesson: Never get between a German and his Sunday beer.

I love looking at the Wrigley Building at night when the spotlights shine on this old, cathedral-like building that still serves as the headquarters of the renowned chewing gum company. The Wrigley Building is a monument to man's desire to perpetually chew something, and it houses a terrific story of determination and luck.

William Wrigley Jr. may have been thrown out of the eighth grade, but when he died in 1932, his estate was worth more than $200 million. He began his life in business with only $35 in his pocket, and he was selling soap instead of gum. If you bought enough soap from him, he'd throw in some baking soda as a

premium. When the baking soda became more popular than the soap, he became a baking soda salesman who then gave away gum to his favorite customers. When they loved the gum more than the baking soda, an empire was born. The lesson: Listen to your customers. They just may be right.

To the west of the Wrigley Building is the gray metal Chicago Sun-Times Building that was once home to the 102-year-old *Chicago Daily News*. The paper ceased publication on March 4, 1978, and when the last edition came up from the pressroom, there was not a dry eye among all the tough newspaper reporters there. And that included Mike Royko, the Pulitzer Prize-winning columnist who got his start with that paper.

A little farther north on Michigan Avenue is the Tribune Tower. Back in 1923, the *Chicago Tribune* held a competition to design its headquarters, but built the runner-up rather than the

winner, which was deemed too modern for the staid old *Trib*.

If you look at the building, there are several Gothic flying buttresses that have been sort of stuck on top. One famed Chicago architect cursed the design and put an image forever in my mind when he said that those buttresses make the building look like it is being attacked by an eight-legged spider. You know what? They do.

The *Chicago Tribune*, which supported Lincoln's nomination for president in return for the right to name the city's postmaster general and get better rates for delivery of the newspaper, has usually been conservative. It is said that one *Tribune* publisher, upset with the way a particular state had voted in an election, came into the building one morning and ordered a star removed from the U.S. flag hanging there. Ah, the power of the press mogul! ☞

BIG, BIGGER, BIGGEST: Chicago is an architectural treasure chest, where earthly desires scrape the sky, where brick, concrete, and steel fantasies caress the clouds. The city's gradual—and spectacular—reach for the heavens culminated with the 1974 completion of the Sears Tower—the world's tallest building until it was surpassed in 1997.

▲ RAY F. HILLSTROM / HILLSTROM STOCK PHOTOGRAPHY

▲ HOWARD E. ANDE

▲ RAY F. HILLSTROM / HILLSTROM STOCK PHOTOGRAPHY

 N ADDITION TO DARING AND MAGNIFICENT BUILDINGS, CHICAGO BOASTS A UNITED NATIONS OF NEIGHBORHOODS. IT ONLY TAKES A HALF HOUR'S AUTOMOBILE RIDE TO SAMPLE THE CULTURES OF GREECE, ENGLAND, AFRICA, CHINA, SWEDEN, VIETNAM, POLAND, IRELAND, CHINA, THAILAND, AND A DOZEN OTHER FOREIGN PLACES—

 WEALTH OF ETHNIC and religious backgrounds find diverse expression in the City of Neighborhoods, from an orthodox Jew walking along Devon Avenue (PAGE 26) to a Swedish beauty turning heads amid a portable skyline (PAGE 27). For those who love lasagna and Luigi, the Taste of the Heart of Italy festival offers food, live music, and fun (BELOW).

all without ever leaving the city.

Historically, many of Chicago's newcomers have first settled along Milwaukee Avenue on the Near North Side. Mike Royko once wrote: "In time Milwaukee Avenue became probably the most colorful street in Chicago. Its south end became a haven for immigrants and a streetcar ride was a short tour of Europe. The street sliced through Little Italy, Little Poland, Germany, and Scandinavia. A person who walked the length of the street could hear the words 'stick 'em up' in half a dozen languages."

As far as I'm concerned, no trip to Chicago is complete without enjoying our ethnic diversity. For instance, I love to visit Greektown, which is centered just west of the Loop around Halsted and Jackson. My personal favorite is the Greek Islands Restaurant, at 200 South Halsted, where I have never had a bad meal or a less-than-fascinating evening.

Nearby, at 130 South Halsted, is Pegasus, which features rooftop dining and a mating-for-life service. Harriet Papastratakos, an energetic matchmaker for lonely members of the Greek commu-

nity, schedules first dates at Pegasus. Either the restaurant or Harriet (or both) seems to cast quite a spell: More than 5,000 marriages have been arranged there, with only two divorces—and one of those couples got married despite Harriet's warning that they were not meant for each other.

Over at 2446 North Lincoln, the Red Lion Pub is as British as any tavern in London (except for the ease of getting ice in mixed drinks). But the real stories of this watering hole come from the owner, John Cordwell, an architect who was a bombardier, navigator,

RON SCHRAMM

and copilot in the British Air Force in World War II. He will reluctantly talk about the three and a half years he spent as a prisoner of war in Stalag Luft Number 3. *The Great Escape*, starring Steve McQueen, told the story of the 76 men who tunneled out of that prison. Cordwell gets very quiet when he speaks about how few survived the escape.

Cordwell is a little happier talking about the many ghosts that inhabit the Red Lion. (That seems to be a requirement for a pub, doesn't it?) He says that spirits have tapped customers on the shoulder and disappeared when they turned around. The ghosts may very well be there—or they may be a good indication that a customer has drunk enough and it's time to go home.

Within the city, we have the Number One most unusual fast-food restaurant in the world—the

VEN FAST FOOD TAKES A unique turn in Chicago, home to the rock and roll McDonald's (TOP). In addition to a life-size Beatles sculpture, the popular joint showcases a perfect 1959 Corvette and a jukebox that plays such favorites as Chuck Berry and Dion and the Belmonts. In nearby Des Plaines is the McDonald's Museum, a former restaurant that now houses company memorabilia and artifacts (PAGES 30 AND 31).

rock and roll McDonald's. It's at Clark and Ontario, and it has life-size statues of the Beatles, dressed in Nehru jackets, forever walking across the road. The booths include framed pictures of Elvis, James Dean, John Lennon, and Marilyn Monroe, and the jukebox

features 1950s tunes so you can have a Big Mac and sing along with "It's my party and I'll cry if I want to," although I don't suggest doing it when your mouth's full. ☞

McDonald's

M

HA

We ha

**T**HE WONDERS OF CHICAGO ARE NOT MERELY CONFINED TO THE CITY LIMITS. JUST OUTSIDE THE CITY IN OAK BROOK IS THE HEADQUARTERS OF McDONALD'S, WHICH ALSO HOUSES HAMBURGER UNIVERSITY, WHERE OWNERS AND MANAGERS ARE TRAINED IN THE MICKEY D'S CREDO. ■ IN SUB-

urban Oak Park are the Frank Lloyd Wright Home and Studio, many Wright-designed houses, and the architect's Unity Temple. A visit to Oak Park, which was also the birthplace of Ernest Hemingway, is an ideal way to encounter genius (but don't ask about the outrageous extramarital affair that drove Wright out of town in 1909).

We also have an important city/suburb competition between the huge, fee-charging, beautiful Brookfield Zoo in the suburbs and the smaller, free, magnificently refurbished Lincoln Park Zoo in the city. Then there's the eternal

battle between suburban Northwestern University, with its beautiful coeds, football, and high academic achievement, and the city-centered, anti-football University of Chicago, which has ever increasing numbers of Nobel Prize winners. My advice: Visit them all.

You can't call Chicago lovely, but it *is* beautiful. You can't say it's happy, but it *is* toddlin'. We're very sophisticated, boasting the most vital theatrical community in America, but we're naive to the point that we're still shocked whenever another politician we trust gets indicted. A deeply religious town that tolerates sinners,

Chicago combines all that is awe inspiring and a lot of what is awful about America.

Chicagoans pride themselves on loyalty—especially to political parties and to people. I've gone to the same barber and dentist to hear the same jokes for years.

Chicagoans love their sports teams, neighborhood bars, politicians, skyline, museums, theaters, restaurants, parks, lakefront, and enough of their neighbors to allow the whole thing to work pretty well as a city—a mighty metropolis that's Number One in more ways than we can count. ✏

AMERICA'S DREAMS—AND a legendary highway— begin in Chicago. What better way to see it all than atop a double-decker bus?

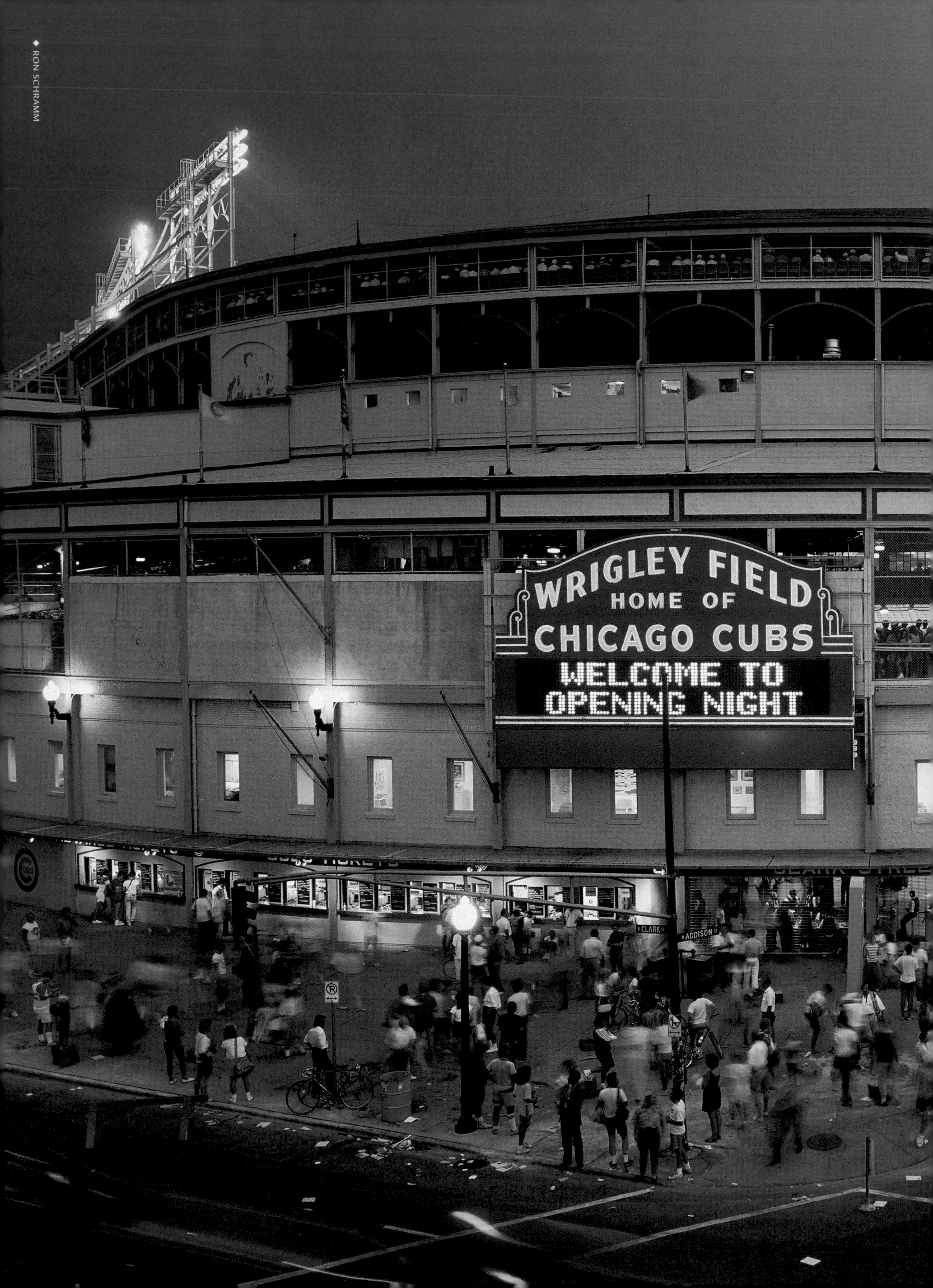
WRIGLEY FIELD
HOME OF
CHICAGO CUBS
WELCOME TO
OPENING NIGHT
CLARK ST
ADDISON ST

◆ RON SCHRAMM

CHICAGO LIGHTS UP AFTER dark, from the Skyline Stage and 190-foot Ferris wheel at Navy Pier (TOP) to the iconic Water Tower, a proud survivor of the Great Fire of 1871 (BOTTOM). Wrigley Field turned on its lights for the first time on August 8, 1988 (PAGES 34 AND 35). An infamous moment for traditionalists, it marked the Cubs' first night game at the stadium and ended 72 years of daytime play. While evening baseball hasn't seemed to help the hapless Cubs, it surely has improved television revenues.

HICAGO MAY BE LOCATED on Lake Michigan, but it's very much a river town. The city's majestic skyscrapers tower over the Chicago River, which is spanned by some 43 drawbridges (PAGES 38-41).

HEART AND SOUL OF AMERICA

C H I C A G O

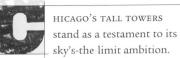

 NY WAY YOU LOOK AT IT, Chicago's architecture is among the most innovative and impressive in existence. The city's undying will to reach ever higher has resulted in three of the world's tallest buildings.

THOUGH IT'S NOT A JOB
for the faint of heart,
working atop the 97-story
John Hancock Tower carries with it
some obvious perks—one of which is
a tremendous panoramic view.

ATTERNS OF DAILY LIFE: A brave fellow tries his hand at the "balance beam" (OPPOSITE), while traffic intersects artfully at State and Ontario streets (ABOVE).

CHICAGO

I N CHICAGO, THE SUBWAY IS more than just a means of transportation. It's also a great place to hear the latest underground sounds.

CHICAGO OFFERS PLENTY of ways to get from point A to point B. If riding the rail's your game, then find your way to the Illinois Central station south of downtown (TOP) or the Amtrak train yard on Canal Street (OPPOSITE). But if you'd rather take to the skies, head to O'Hare International Airport, where the United Airlines tunnel greets passengers with a shifting light show and music by Gershwin (BOTTOM).

Customer Service Center
♪ Telephones

Concourse B E F
Gates C1–C19
Baggage Claim
Terminal 1 2 3 4

Gate C20

C20

C H I C A G O

HE WORLD'S BUSIEST airport, O'Hare International (OPPOSITE) was named for Edward "Butch" O'Hare, a WWII navy pilot who received the Medal of Honor for shooting down five Japanese bombers and crippling a sixth during his rescue of the aircraft carrier *Lexington.*

The modern-day McCormick Place, which was rebuilt in 1971 after a 1967 fire razed the structure, recently completed a nearly $1 billion expansion (LEFT). With 1.3 million square feet of contiguous exhibit space and more than 2.2 million total square feet, it is the largest convention center in the United States.

ORGANIC FOOD PAVILION

HICAGO OFFERS A VERI-table gallery of exciting public sculpture. Within a few blocks of each other are Jean Dubuffet's fiberglass *Monument with Standing Beast* outside the James R. Thompson State of Illinois Center (TOP); Marc Chagall's 70-foot-long mosaic, *Les Quatre Saisons*, at the First National Bank Building Plaza (CENTER); and Nita K. Sunderland's *Ruins III*, erected in 1978 in the Dirksen Federal Building Plaza (BOTTOM).

More than just a building, the Helmut Jahn-designed James R. Thompson Center is itself a work of art. Detractors maintain that the exterior of the ultramodern structure in Chicago's Loop resembles Darth Vader's helmet, but almost everyone agrees that the 7.9 million-cubic-foot atrium is nothing less than spectacular (OPPOSITE).

 HE MASTERS HAVE TRULY made their mark on Chicago's outdoor spaces, including (CLOCKWISE FROM TOP LEFT) Alexander Calder's 50-ton *Flamingo*, Jerry Peart's colorful *Splash*, Claes Oldenburg's metal *Batcolumn*, and Joan Miró's 39-foot-tall *Chicago*. Perhaps the city's best-known public piece is the one without a name. Completed by Picasso in 1967, it is the highlight of Daley Center Plaza (OPPOSITE). Locals often debate whether the work depicts a woman's head, the face of an Afghan hound, or the artist's second wife, but whatever it is, Chicagoans love it dearly.

▲ RON SCHRAMM

THE WORLD-FAMOUS ART Institute of Chicago has renewed, reinvented, and revitalized itself in recent years. The beloved museum, with its important holdings and creative displays, is a must-see on any Chicago visit.

 MULTICULTURAL CITY where world religions flourish, Chicago has no shortage of beautiful churches, temples, and mosques.

I N CHICAGO, PLACES OF WOR-
ship combine the serenity of
faith with the ornamentation
of elegant architectural details and
luminescent stained-glass windows.

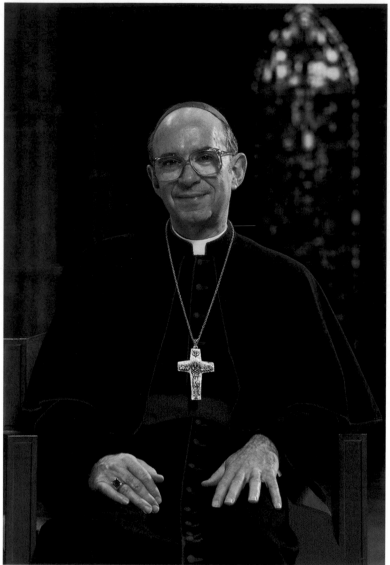

 MONG THE CITY'S BEST-known houses of worship is the Holy Name Cathedral on North State Street (BOTTOM RIGHT). For nearly a century, the church has hung from its ceiling the *galeros*, or hats, that once belonged to officials of the city's Roman Catholic Archdiocese. In December 1996, the *galero* of Joseph Cardinal Bernardin, Chicago's archbishop for more than a decade, was raised to honor the popular religious leader following his death (LEFT).

ERNARDIN OCCUPIED the grand archbishop's residence at State Parkway and North Avenue (TOP LEFT) from his papal appointment in 1982 until his death. He was much loved by Chicago's 2.3 million Catholics, and his funeral was attended by thousands (BOTTOM LEFT).

When Pope John Paul II came to town in 1979, more than 200,000 people flocked to his three-hour mass in Grant Park (RIGHT). The service was the largest mass ever celebrated in the city, and some locals feared that the concrete-walled underground garages might actually collapse beneath the weight of the crowd.

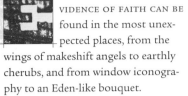

VIDENCE OF FAITH CAN BE found in the most unexpected places, from the wings of makeshift angels to earthly cherubs, and from window iconography to an Eden-like bouquet.

ON ST. PATRICK'S DAY, everyone in Chicago is a little bit Irish. Thousands of paraders and spectators congregate on Dearborn Street, where the centerline is painted the color of the day. Even the ordinarily green-hued river gets more Irish during the festivities (PAGES 76 AND 77).

ROY CAJERO

▲ KEVIN O. MOONEY

N ORNATE RELIEF ON the Cook County Building and Chicago's city seal on parade remind us of the pomp and circumstance of government. The city's official slogan, *Urbs in Horto*, means "city in a garden" and was adopted in 1833.

 STUDY IN POLITICAL diversity: Chicago's governmental leaders have made an indelible mark on the city's past, as well as its future. Three recent mayors include (FROM TOP) Richard M. Daley (1989-), Eugene Sawyer (1987-1989), and Jane Byrne (1979-1983).

T HE WINDY CITY HAS a tradition of hosting political conventions that goes back to 1860, when the Republicans nominated a tall, shy Illinois fellow named Abraham Lincoln for president. In 1996, Chicago's United Center was the site of the Democratic National Convention (TOP), which selected Bill Clinton to be the party's candidate for reelection.

KAREN I. HIRSCH

CHICAGOANS YOUNG AND old show their patriotic stripes at local Fourth of July celebrations, but the pride in being an American shines brightest as a group of immigrants take the oath to become U.S. citizens (BOTTOM).

CHICAGOANS DON'T NEED a national holiday to throw a party. Nearly every ethnic group in the city has an annual parade celebrating their heritage, and in 1996, locals of every stripe lined up to welcome World Cup soccer when it came to town (OPPOSITE TOP).

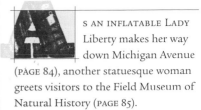

S AN INFLATABLE LADY Liberty makes her way down Michigan Avenue (PAGE 84), another statuesque woman greets visitors to the Field Museum of Natural History (PAGE 85).

OR MORE THAN A CEN-
tury, the Field Museum
has been educating—and
entertaining—folks with its authentic,
impressive, and oftentimes enormous
exhibits. The facility's more than 20
million specimens will soon be joined
by Sue, the Tyrannosaurus rex skel-
eton acquired by the museum in 1997
for $8.3 million, the highest price ever
paid for a fossil.

The Field Museum's interest in
paleontology appears to have spilled
into the local art world. This eye-
catching sculpture reminds viewers of
a time when dinosaurs and mastodons
roamed the earth (OPPOSITE).

THE ANNUAL CHICAGO Air and Water Show, the oldest and largest free event of its kind, has thrilled local audiences since 1958. The two-day extravaganza draws some 2 million people, not to mention such high-flying daredevils as the U.S. Navy's Blue Angels (TOP RIGHT).

CHICAGO REMEMBERS ITS military and political heroes with myriad ceremonies, reenactments, and memorials.

Buried in the Rosehill Cemetery are Major General Thomas Ransom and many other soldiers who fought in the Civil War (ABOVE).

LIFE, DEATH, AND BEYOND: Henry Moore's *Nuclear Energy*, a haunting, 12-foot bronze sculpture on the grounds of the University of Chicago, marks the spot where the first self-sustained nuclear reaction occurred in 1942; Lorado Taft's *Eternal Silence* stands guard near the entrance to Chicago's Graceland Cemetery; and an angelic figure offers hope for peace in the afterlife.

 VER HEIGHTENING THEIR consciousness, Chicagoans have listened to the teachings of Maharishi Mahesh Yogi (LEFT), supported the veterans of a controversial war (TOP RIGHT), and meditated with poet Allen Ginsberg at a sit-in during the 1968 Democratic National Convention (BOTTOM RIGHT).

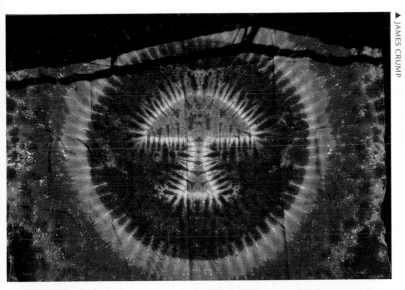

OVER THE YEARS, THE CITY'S rock scene has ebbed and flowed, but true-blue—and tie-dyed—fanatics have never lost their groove. Two local groups lighting up the stage today are Yum-Yum, fronted by Chris Holmes (BOTTOM LEFT), and Ministry (RIGHT).

ROM DARING DRESS TO colorful coiffure, Chicago-ans have a spectacular sense of style. Actors Todd Schaner and Robert Bouwman make their own fashion statement in the long-running comedic play, *The Tiff and Mom Show*, which features a booze-infested bimbo from Berwyn and her over-weight daughter (BOTTOM LEFT).

NCE HIDDEN, ATTACKED, and harassed, Chicago's gay and lesbian community is now visible and politically powerful. Each spring, the city's Gay Pride Parade draws thousands of participants and onlookers, including Mayor Richard M. Daley, who marched in 1989 in honor of gay rights.

CLOWNING AROUND: A familiar redhead waves to the crowd at the World Cup Parade (TOP LEFT); a costumed rodeo jester gets tough at a Mexican *charriada* (TOP RIGHT); a demure lady demonstrates her offbeat idea of beauty (BOTTOM RIGHT); and Dorals drummer Kriss Bataille poses in honor of the group's song *Rodeo Clown* (OPPOSITE).

No one knows the fine art of face painting and performing better than master mime Marcel Marceau, who has made frequent visits to Chicago (BOTTOM LEFT).

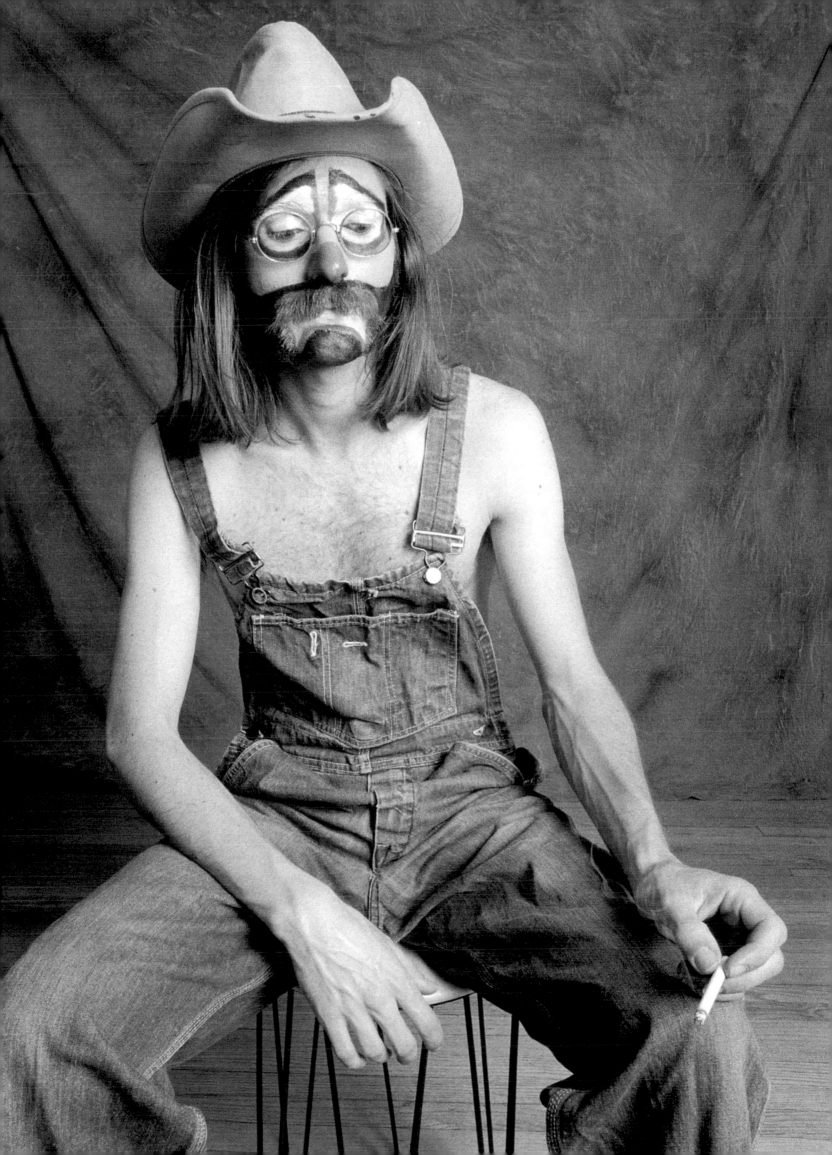

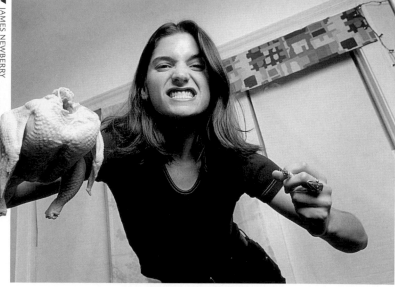

HE WINDY CITY HAS turned out more than its share of stage hounds, including performance artist Abby Schacner, who's no chicken in front of an audience (TOP RIGHT). Since the Second City opened its doors back in 1959, founder Bernie Sahlins (LEFT) and his famed improv company have trained generations of performers and too many *Saturday Night Live* cast members to mention.

CHICAGO NATIVE WILLIAM "Upski" Wimsatt, author of *Bomb the Suburbs: Graffiti, Freight-Hopping, Race, and the Search for Hip-Hop's Moral Center*, waits on the mail.

WHILE LIVE ZEBRAS CAN only be found at the zoo, their likeness seems to turn up all over town.

HEART AND SOUL OF AMERICA

 ITH ALMOST 200 AC-
tive troupes, Chicago's
theater scene is often
considered more vital than New York
City's. The famed Steppenwolf Theatre Company, which presented 1992's
standout *The Song of Jacob Zulu* (ABOVE),
consistently sends hit productions to
Broadway and actors to Hollywood.

JAZZ IS ALIVE AND WELL IN Chicago, thanks in part to talented singer Geraldine de Haas. The creator of Jazz Unites, a nonprofit organization that recently announced plans to build a local jazz museum, de Haas has also been a driving force behind such popular programs as the annual Duke Ellington birthday concert and Jazz Fest at the South Shore Cultural Center.

T MAY BE ONLY ONE BLOCK long, but Oak Street is the center of fashion in Chicago. Designer dresses and the world's most expensive perfume can be found along this boulevard, which includes such fine shops as Ultimo, Sonia Rykiel, and Armani.

STYLE CHICAGO-STYLE: Among the highlights of the city's fashion scene are Jil Sander, an upscale shop on Oak Street (TOP), and BABS Designs, whose founder Barbara Bates went from being a secretary noted for her fashion flair to heading her own business (BOTTOM).

I AM WOMAN: FROM GILDED statues and snazzy hood ornaments to wall murals and a papier-mâché mannequin, Chicago has plenty of ideas about beauty.

THERE'S MORE THAN ONE way to a person's heart, but your best bet is still with candies and other tasty treats. Singer-songwriter Syd Straw, who has developed a following among Chicago audiences, appears to agree (BOTTOM).

 OTHING SAYS CHICAGO quite like the Superdawg drive-in—opened in 1948 and still serving 1950s-style hot dogs—unless it's a real-life "blues brother," posing with his trademark shades and harmonica outside the Heart of Chicago Motel.

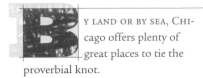

BY LAND OR BY SEA, Chicago offers plenty of great places to tie the proverbial knot.

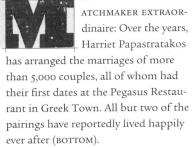

MATCHMAKER EXTRAORdinaire: Over the years, Harriet Papastratakos has arranged the marriages of more than 5,000 couples, all of whom had their first dates at the Pegasus Restaurant in Greek Town. All but two of the pairings have reportedly lived happily ever after (BOTTOM).

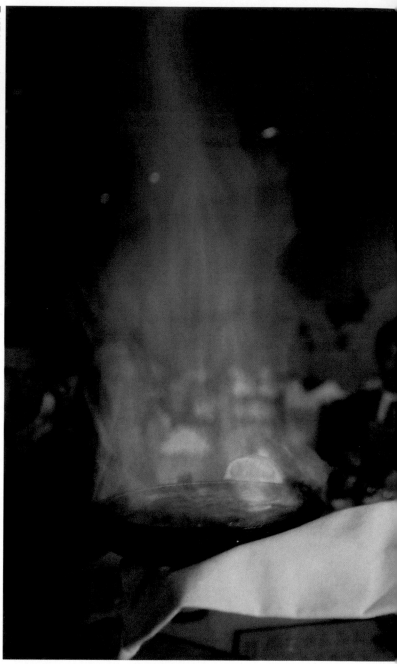

HICAGO MAY BE BEST KNOWN for its deep-dish pizza, but the city offers a virtual United Nations of culinary options, from Thai, African-American, and Indian cuisine to Caribbean, French, and German delights. Located on West Wacker Drive, Catch Thirty Five specializes in seafood with an Asian flair (OPPOSITE LEFT). Nix serves Pacific Rim cuisine from its charming location in the Regal Knickerbocker Hotel (TOP RIGHT). And Pegasus has made a name for itself as one of the city's best Greek restaurants (CENTER AND BOTTOM RIGHT).

C LAIMS OF THE "WORLD'S best" may pepper Chicago's restaurant scene, but it's the Billy Goat Tavern & Grill on North Michigan Avenue that has earned true notoriety. The popular joint gave rise to a *Saturday Night Live* skit, which had people nationwide saying "cheezborger, cheezborger." And back in 1945, when owner William Sianis and his goat, Savonia, were denied entrance to the World Series (in which the Cubs were playing), Sianis pronounced that the team wouldn't appear in another World Series until his beloved pet was allowed back in the game. Unfortunately for the Cubs, the curse appears to have worked.

▲ JANET CENTURY

WHETHER YOUR CRAVing is for tacos and burritos, spicy Italian beef, or typical diner fare from the Lincoln Restaurant, Chicago can oblige. Of course, there's no better way to top off a meal than a treat from the Good Humor man.

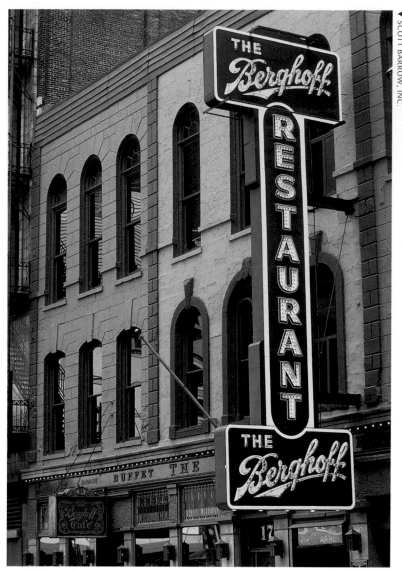

THE ENORMOUS BERGHOFF Restaurant, an Adams Street fixture for more than a century, is known for its great beer, delicious rye bread, and traditional German dishes that are among the best in the world. A relative new-comer, Harry Caray's, named for one of Chicago's most boisterous sports-casters, dishes out generous portions of loud enthusiasm with its Italian-American fare. Most people agree, however, that mom still serves the best plate of food around.

 lfresco Chicago: On warm evenings, locals vie for that coveted outdoor table, whether their tastes run toward haute cuisine or cold beer and deep-dish pizza. Dining under the stars was once discouraged in the city, but today, the delightful summer experience is alive and well, and dozens of restaurants have expanded onto the sidewalks.

VIEW OF THE SKYLINE
from south of the
center city's Loop—
so named because the elevated trains
encircle the area—reveals the beauty
of Chicago at night (PAGES 120 AND 121).

▶ VITO PA-MISANO

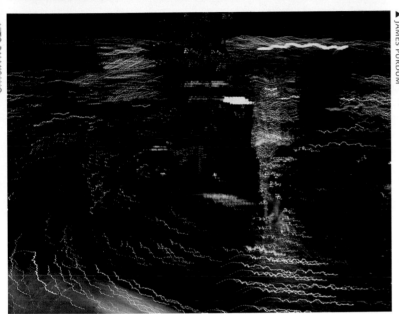

▶ JAMES PURDUM

 HICAGO MAY NOT HAVE invented jazz, but locals have welcomed the genre— and the cocktail culture it inspired with open arms. From the sweet sounds of Maynard Ferguson (OPPOSITE) to the last, lonely riff before closing time (BOTTOM RIGHT), the city swirls with the spirit of this uniquely American art form.

THE BLUES MIGRATED to Chicago during the 1930s, and ever since, the city has been in love with this distinctive musical form. The annual Blues Festival is testament to the community's undying devotion to the soulful genre and its practitioners, including Koko Taylor (BOTTOM RIGHT) and Buddy Guy (OPPOSITE, BOTTOM LEFT).

HEART AND SOUL OF AMERICA

THE WINDY CITY'S GOT THE blues, from Rosa's on the West Side to B.L.U.E.S. on the North Side. Known as the patriarch of post-World War II Chicago blues, all-time great Muddy Waters (TOP LEFT) was inducted into the Blues Foundation's Hall of Fame in 1980.

MARTY PEREZ

DISCO NEVER DIED IN Chicago, and ballroom dancing is alive and still counting the beat. The city also claims to have the best polka music in the world, and several local bands have the Grammys to prove it.

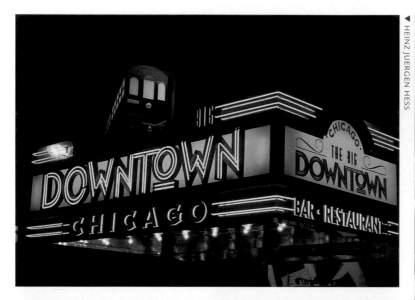

T'S NEARLY IMPOSSIBLE TO FOR-get where you are in Chicago, a city that's home to The Big Downtown, a new restaurant located in the Palmer House Hilton (TOP), and the Beaux Arts Chicago Theatre, opened in 1921 on North State Street (CENTER). Why, there's even a long-running musical named after the city: Based on Maurine Dallas Watkins' play *Chicago*, first performed in 1926, today's Tony Award-winning adaptation opened on Broadway in 1975 and has been pleasing audiences ever since (BOTTOM).

 HE LOCAL THEATER COM-
munity knows how to
take care of its own. In
1996, when popular monologist and performance artist Cheryl Trykv (RIGHT) went public with her fight against cancer, the Steppenwolf Theatre held a benefit to raise money for her battle.

FTER FALLING ON HARD times, the Chicago Theatre was brought back to life in 1986 with a gala reopening that featured Frank Sinatra singing "My Kind of Town." The Disney organization now packs the patrons in at the old movie palace with crowd- and critic-pleasing musicals.

 S ONE OF THE WINDY City's leading directors, Robert Falls of the Goodman Theater has achieved critical acclaim for the productions he has taken to Broadway and to Dublin, Ireland (LEFT). With Falls in charge, the Goodman won a Tony Award in 1992 for best regional theater.

Once the main building of the Chicago Public Library, built in 1897, the Chicago Cultural Center is today a theater, dance, performance, and lecture space. The structure is noted for its beautiful Carrara marble staircases and the elegant mosaics that adorn Preston Bradley Hall on the third floor (RIGHT).

CHICAGO HAS SEEN MORE than its share of celebrities over the years, including actor Marlon Brando, pictured here at his family home in suburban Chicago in 1951 (TOP). Oliver Stone, director of *Platoon* and *Wall Street*, and Studs Terkel, local chronicler of working America, converse during the Chicago International Film Festival (CENTER). Returning to his roots, actor John Malkovich portrayed John Wilmot in the 1996 production of *The Libertine* at the Steppenwolf Theatre, a venue he helped establish (BOTTOM).

ARY SINISE IS ANOTHER Steppenwolf veteran who has achieved fame in Hollywood (TOP). Among his most memorable roles, Sinise played a Vietnam veteran in *Forrest Gump*, an astronaut in *Apollo 13*, and Harry Truman in a cable TV movie.

William Shakespeare may not have made it to Chicago, but his plays certainly have. In fact, locals are so enamored of the brilliant bard that they created the Shakespeare Garden on the western edge of Lincoln Park (BOTTOM). The botanical refuge features plants and flowers that are mentioned in the master's works.

WILLIAM
SHAKESPEARE
1564-1616

HE CHICAGO SYMPHONY Orchestra has taken its place among the world's great performing arts organizations, thanks in part to such talents as prin-cipal guest conductor Pierre Boulez (BOTTOM LEFT) and violinist Heidi Turner (RIGHT). The orchestra, which traces its origins to 1891, has earned more than 50 Grammy Awards throughout its history.

In 1997, comedian Jay Leno served as master of ceremonies for CNA Financial Corp.'s 100th-anniversary celebration (TOP LEFT). No stranger to the Windy City, Leno has twice taken his late-night talk show on the road to broadcast from Chicago, where he loves the Italian beef sandwiches.

The Oprah Winfrey Show

MEDIA MONTAGE: While there are plenty of opportunities to watch movies and TV shows being created in Chicago, one local establish- ment lets you get in on the act. At the Museum of Broadcast Communi- cations, newscaster wanna-bes can live out their fantasies at a miniature television studio (BOTTOM LEFT).

HICAGO COMES ALIVE
when the sun goes down,
and local diners, drive-ins,
and shops find colorful ways to light
up the sky. Second Century Neon in
Brookfield even sells neon novelties
so residents can add their own bit
of color to the evening landscape
(BOTTOM LEFT).

CRUISERS

Salt & Pepper
DINER

BURGERS • HOT DOGS
SHAKES • ICE CREAM

We may not be Detroit, but we certainly love our cars, from authentic antiques to intricately carved interpretations.

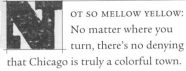OT SO MELLOW YELLOW:
No matter where you
turn, there's no denying
that Chicago is truly a colorful town.

BEGUN AS A PUSHCART produce market in the mid-1800s, the Maxwell Street Market was once the home to an eclectic assortment of unique goods and people. In its heyday, it offered blues, shoes, and more, not to mention a merchant whose trained chicken would dance when enough money was left on the pavement. During a particularly long, cold Chicago winter, however, the merchant was forced to eat his act.

ARD TIMES HAVE LONG been a part of life in the big city, but these Far South Side kids were all smiles as they made the most of a lazy afternoon back in 1961 (TOP). In modern-day Chicago, the Pacific Garden Mission lends a helping hand to those battling drug and alcohol addictions (BOTTOM).

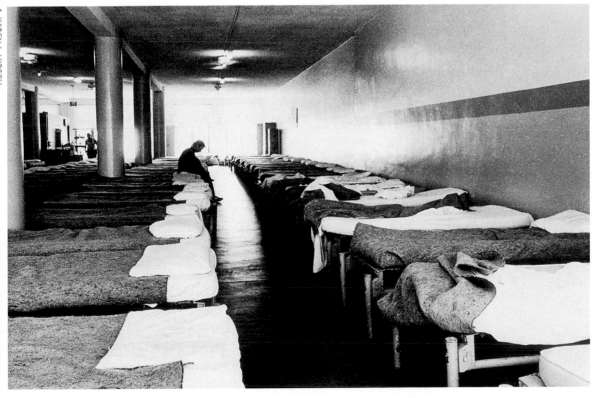

SHRINES OF THE TIMES: Latino families pay homage to their ancestors with this Day of the Dead Altar at the Mexican Fine Arts Museum (TOP), and a local fan of all things Hollywood finds an eye-catching way to honor his favorite entertainers (OPPOSITE TOP).

N CHICAGO, THE CREATIVE juices are always flowing. Mexican-American playwright and performance artist Pablo Helguera is the author of *The Palace (And Other Pilsen Ghost Stories)* and *Jurua* (LEFT). John Harriman demonstrates his acting ability in John Covert's movie *Waiting for the Man* (BOTTOM RIGHT). And independent filmmaker Jim Sikora (OPPOSITE) scored a hit in 1994 with *Walls in the City*, which featured David Yow, front man for Chicago rock band Jesus Lizard (TOP RIGHT).

 UILDING AND REBUILDING:
A group of suburbanites
protest the start of a new
housing development (TOP LEFT), while
a tornado victim wishes for her old
residence (TOP RIGHT).

REEN AROUND THE GILLS: Barb Wruck Thometz depicts the title character in *The Skriker*, a British play given its Chicago premiere by the Defiant Theater Company (ABOVE); Frankenstein challenges miniature-golf aficionados to make a hole in one (OPPOSITE, BOTTOM RIGHT); and a couple of painters wonder if they have anything left for the building (OPPOSITE, BOTTOM LEFT).

EVERAL CHICAGO BANDS
have earned a strong fol-
lowing in their hometown,
including Number One Cup, whose
song "Divebomb" has made waves
on local radio (TOP), and the Flying
Luttenbachers, whose drummer,
Weasel Walter, helped form the group
in 1992 (OPPOSITE BOTTOM). One of
the most famous names to come out
of the Windy City in recent years is
the Smashing Pumpkins, headliners
of the Lollapalooza tour in 1994
(OPPOSITE TOP). Moving from Smashing Pumpkins to smashing piñatas,
these kids find the beat and go for
the candy (BOTTOM).

 JUMBLE OF JACK-O'-
lanterns sends a scary
message during Hallow-
een at Lincoln Park.

CHICAGO IS STILL HOST TO the heaviest of industries, from steel mills to manu-facturing plants to scrap yards.

ON'T THESE GUYS KNOW that you fight the fire before you take the group portrait? Fortunately, this blaze in Libertyville was intentional.

WITH THE ONSET OF autumn and winter come such weekend chores as burning leaves and plowing snow. But with the right attitude, both activities can be enjoyable.

HE ARCTIC MAKES ITS
way to Chicago during
the winter months, when
flourishes of ice and snow truly become
works of art.

ITH WINTERTIME activities like skiing, skating, and sledding to distract them, locals just might forget how cold it is. The Blackhawks, on the other hand, live for the weather to turn frosty, signaling the start of another hockey season. A powerful force in the National Hockey League's Central Division, the team has won the coveted Stanley Cup three times during its history.

OMETIMES THE BEST WAY to beat the snow is just to enjoy it—in this case by cutting your own Christmas tree and "flocking" it the old-fashioned way.

HICAGO DECKS ITS HALLS (and streets and just about everything else) each Christmas, complete with friendly Santas, heralding trumpets, and the Lincoln Park Zoo's spectacular Festival of Lights.

CHICAGO HAS ALWAYS BEEN a town that loves Christmas, and locals go to great lengths to celebrate the season. In fact, Chicago's holiday spirit is so infectious that it inspired Mel Tormé to write *The Christmas Song* while he was staying at the Allerton Hotel in 1946.

YEARS AGO, CHRISTMAS IN Chicago meant the arrival of the *Rouse Simmons*, or "Christmas Tree Ship," a lumber schooner captained by Herman Schuenemann that delivered freshly cut pine trees to the Windy City from Michigan and Minnesota. Today, the holidays mean shopping, shopping, and more shopping. Department stores along State Street and Michigan Avenue combine lights and decorations with the bustle and cheer of searching for the perfect gift.

T'S POSSIBLE TO BE OF GOOD cheer, even when winter hits Chicago. While a couple of figurines at the University of Chicago huddle against the snow, a carriage ride brings warm romance to any season.

HICAGO HOTELS HAVE played host to their share of unforgettable events. Financier J. Pierpont Morgan supposedly fell into one hotel fountain after imbibing too much, while another local inn was the site of the original "smoke-filled room," where a cabal of politicians conspired in 1920 to make Warren G. Harding president. Today, the grandeur of the city's historic hotels is exemplified by their restored interiors, from the elegant lobbies of the Regal Knickerbocker (TOP LEFT), the Chicago Hilton and Towers (TOP RIGHT), and the Drake (BOTTOM LEFT) to the 16th-floor mosaic swimming pool of the Moorish-flavored Hotel Inter-Continental Chicago (BOTTOM RIGHT) and the delightful English decor of the Talbott (OPPOSITE).

THE RESTORER AND THE restored: Lido Lippi, who consulted on the restoration of the Sistine Chapel in Rome, is a fine-art conservator and the director of Chicago's Florence Art Conservation (ABOVE). In 1989, Lippi was involved in a $125 million transformation of the Hotel Inter-Continental, which opened in 1929 as the Medinah Athletic Club (OPPOSITE). Over the course of the project, he helped refurbish 37 murals and duplicated eight oil landscapes that had been lost.

WHILE CHICAGO'S BUR-
geoning Asian popula-
tion is centered around
Chinatown on the South Side (OPPO-
SITE RIGHT) and Little Saigon on the
North Side (LEFT), members of the
community are scattered throughout
the city. Most consider American culture very attractive, but they still find
plenty of ways to celebrate their
unique heritage.

PATTERNED AFTER THE Latona Basin in the gardens of Louis XIV's palace at Versailles, Buckingham Fountain in Grant Park is one of the most beautiful and romantic spots in the city (PAGES 174 AND 175). In keeping with the local tradition of one-upmanship, though, Chicago's version is twice as big as the French original.

J UST NORTH OF THE LINCOLN Park Zoo is Saint-Gaudens' *Storks at Play*, affectionately called the Bates Fountain. Considered one of Chicago's "happiest" attractions, it's been splashing the bronze figures of three boys, three storks, and three squirting fish since 1887.

 MID THE CONCRETE AND steel that is modern-day Chicago, locals haven't forgotten Mother Nature. An urban canvas that's been transformed into a slice of paradise (BOTTOM) rivals the verdant parkland that envelops this mystic figure (TOP).

CCUPYING MORE THAN 300 acres along Chicago's lakefront, Grant Park offers breathtaking vistas and exquisite blossoms, not to mention the renowned Art Institute and Buckingham Fountain. While many U.S. cities have devoted their most scenic stretches of land to commercial and residential use, Chicago has reserved much of its undeveloped land for parks, beaches, and other public spaces.

KAREN I. HIRSCH

HOWARD E. ANDE

STEVE BAKER

ALTHOUGH LIVE HORSES no longer fill the city's streets, when it comes to equestrian statues, Chicago has herds of them. Ulysses S. Grant and his mount stand guard in Lincoln Park (OPPOSITE LEFT), and Civil War General Philip Sheridan forever ambles at Fort Sheridan (OPPOSITE, TOP RIGHT). Dedicated in 1929, Ivan Mestrovic's famous warrior statues bookend downtown's Congress Plaza (TOP LEFT), and Cyrus Edwin Dallin's *A Signal of Peace* sends an important message to visitors in Lincoln Park (RIGHT).

HICAGO BELONGED TO Native Americans until August 18, 1835, when the Pottawatomies left town forever. Their final war dance through the city so frightened onlookers that one man wrote, "Their muscles stood out in great hard knots. . . . Their tomahawks and clubs were thrown and brandished in every direction . . . and with every step and every gesture they utter the most frightful yells in every imaginable key and note." Today, Chicagoans recall the region's Native American heritage during such events as the annual canoe race on the Des Plaines River.

N NEARBY NAPERVILLE, THE Naper Settlement re-creates daily life during the 19th century as Chicago made its transformation from a frontier town into a bustling American city. A village of historic buildings, complete with guides in period costume, the settlement features such educational highlights as a typical 1830s log house (OPPOSITE TOP) and the Copenhagen School-house, the last remaining one-room school in the area (TOP).

N AN EFFORT TO PRESERVE THE area's natural beauty despite its large urban setting, Chicago maintains thousands of acres of parks and woodlands. Indeed, it is a city enveloped by and involved in nature.

CHICAGO

THE REGION'S RICH PRAIRIE soil was critical to Chicago's development. Not only did the surrounding farmland spur the transportation hub that would become the Windy City, but the flat midwestern landscape also greatly influenced the designs of Frank Lloyd Wright and other architects.

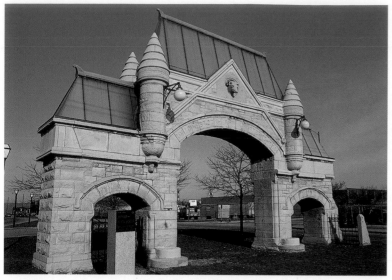

ISTORIC ARCHES AND doors are the gateways to old Chicago: A stone entrance, featuring an image of the 1878 winner of the American Fat Stock Show, is about all that remains of the once vast Chicago Stockyards (TOP LEFT); the original Chicago Stock Exchange building welcomed traders from 1894 until 1972, when it was torn down and its impressive archway was moved to the Art Institute (TOP RIGHT); and the entry to the art deco Laramie State Bank features various images of industry and thrift (OPPOSITE). Not to be outdone, several other historic structures in the Loop demonstrate the mastery of metalworkers over the years (BOTTOM).

CELEBRATION OF EARLY
Chicago history awaits
visitors to the landmark
Marquette Building. In addition to
vividly detailed reliefs (BOTTOM), the
interior features colorful mosaics that
depict Native Americans greeting
Father Jacques Marquette, a Jesuit
missionary who, in 1673, became the
first European to visit the Chicago area
(TOP). Marquette left a poignant note
about his attempts at friendship: "In
vain I showed the calumet to explain
that we had not come as enemies."

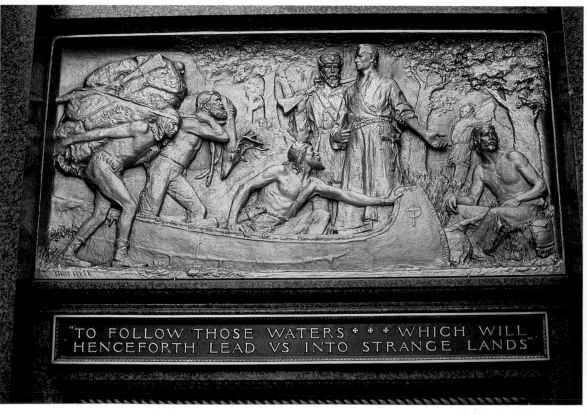

"TO FOLLOW THOSE WATERS * * * WHICH WILL
HENCEFORTH LEAD VS INTO STRANGE LANDS"

N 1977, THE HUGE TRADING room of the old Chicago Stock Exchange building, which had been demolished five years earlier, was rebuilt within the Art Institute as an elegant banquet hall (TOP). Today, the challenge of playing the stock market lives on at the Windy City's numerous active exchanges, where modern-day traders reflect century-old concerns as they watch the current numbers—and fortunes—rise and fall (BOTTOM).

T HE FLOOR OF THE CHICA-
go Board of Trade, where
the prices of wheat, soy-
beans, corn, oats, silver, gold, plywood,
and mortgage-backed certificates are
determined, is a madhouse of purpose-
ful activity during trading hours. But
when the day is done, a sea of crumpled
opportunities is all that's left.

HICAGO'S GRAND PAST IS preserved in countless historic homes, including the Henry Hobson Richardson-designed Glessner House, which was widely criticized for its prisonlike, virtually windowless facade (PAGE 194), and the 19th-century brick row houses of the Jackson Boulevard Historic District, which achieved landmark status in 1976 (PAGE 195).

CHICAGO'S DISTINCTIVE facades create a nostalgic urban collage, from the light-hued stone of this historic home-turned-law-office (OPPOSITE LEFT) to another grand building across from Lincoln Park (OPPOSITE, TOP RIGHT). The Carson Pirie Scott & Co. department store on State Street is both an architectural landmark and a testimony to family business in 19th-century Chicago (OPPOSITE, BOTTOM RIGHT); in fact, Samuel Carson married John T. Pirie's sister, and Pirie married Carson's sister, effectively sealing the bond between the company's founding families. Built to last in 1891, the graceful Monadnock Building features masonry-bearing walls that are six feet thick at the base (LEFT).

ORIGINALLY CALLED HUB-
bard Trail, State Street
got promoted to "that
great street" as dozens of department
stores, including the original Marshall
Field's, put down roots along the boulevard. Pictured here around the turn
of the 20th century, the famous thor-
oughfare experienced a down cycle in
the 1980s after becoming a pedestrian
mall, but hit an upswing again when it
reopened to automotive traffic in 1996.

 EAUTY IN THE DETAILS: Scrolling decorations, retrieved from a parochial school before its demolition, seem to yearn for the eternal (TOP), while adornments on the Wrigley Building demonstrate the Spanish influence on this famous structure (BOTTOM).

CHICAGO

THE GRACEFUL STAIRWAY and indoor fire escape of the gently refined Rookery resemble a nautilus shell. The building, which got its name because its predecessor on the site attracted so many pigeons, was the setting for local financier John W. "Bet-a-Million" Gates' weekly, high-stakes whist games in the early 1900s.

 HE CLOCK IS ALWAYS ticking in Chicago, where there are seldom enough hours in the day to complete our many grand plans.

RAY F. HILLSTROM / HILLSTROM STOCK PHOTOGRAPHY

IRE ESCAPES FORM SAFETY patterns on the urban landscape. While Chicago's old water towers stand watch (OPPO-SITE), the historic Fisher Building maintains its presence in the Loop (CENTER). Printer's Row, where the upwardly mobile now live, was once home to the presses that imprinted the nation's paper products (RIGHT).

 36-FOOT-TALL, 70-FOOT-long sculpture (TOP) adorns the Harold Washington Library Center, named after Chicago's first African-American mayor. Built in 1991, the $145 million structure is the largest municipal library in the nation and is home to the Chicago Blues Archives, the Jazz/Blues/Gospel Hall of Fame, and the Balaban and Katz Theater Orchestra Collection. Located on the top floor is the Winter Garden hall, which is used for literary dinners and other special events (BOTTOM).

HEART AND SOUL OF AMERICA

O N A WING AND A PRAYER: From a "flighty" gargoyle at the University of Chicago (OPPOSITE TOP) to a beautifully carved sculpture in Washington Park (TOP), Chicagoans have a flair for the fanciful. Even less mythical figures can fly in a Logan Square mural (OPPOSITE BOTTOM) and a tile mosaic near City Hall (BOTTOM).

FIRE IMAGERY FIGURES prominently in local art, from the metallic blaze at the State of Illinois Center (OPPOSITE) to a stylized torch at the Red Light Asian restaurant (LEFT). Recalling how fire has played a prominent role in local history, Egon Weiner's *Pillar of Fire* marks the spot where the disastrous blaze of 1871 supposedly began in Mrs. Catherine O'Leary's barn (RIGHT). Recent historians and investigators have actually exonerated O'Leary and are now pointing their accusing fingers at her neighbor, Daniel "Peg Leg" Sullivan, as the culprit who started the fire that killed 300 people, made 100,000 homeless, and destroyed a third of the city.

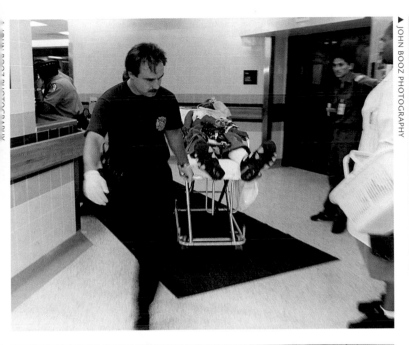

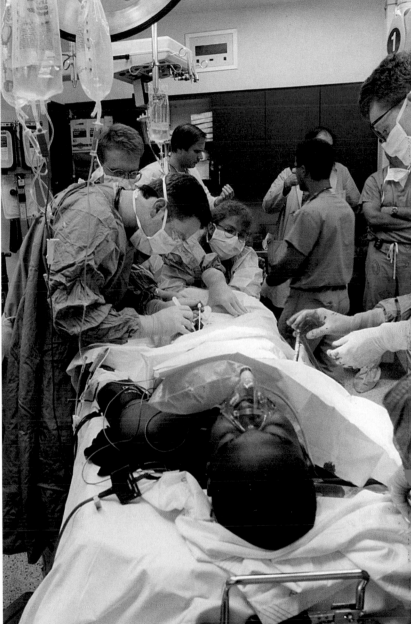

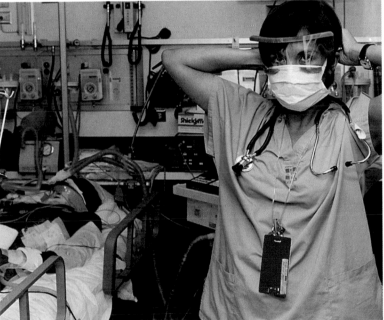

 HICAGO IS JUSTLY FAMOUS for its health care facilities, including the University of Chicago Hospital, which was ranked 13th in the nation in a 1997 *U.S. News & World Report* article (OPPOSITE). Cook County Hospital, whose emergency room is one of the largest and busiest in the world (ABOVE), has even caught the eyes of Hollywood. The heroic efforts of the facility's emergency-ward doctors, who serve approximately 160,000 patients annually, helped inspire the hit television series *ER*, which is set at the distinguished hospital.

CHICAGO

UDWIG MIES VAN DER Rohe's less-is-more philosophy is carried out in the unembellished S.R. Crown Hall on the Illinois Institute of Technology campus (TOP), the Farnsworth House in nearby Plano (OPPOSITE BOTTOM), and even his gravesite in Graceland Cemetery (BOTTOM). The Chicago architect's many brilliant commissions, including the One and Two Illinois Centers, the Dirksen Federal Building, and the Lake Shore Drive Apartments, truly changed the style of modern architecture.

PERHAPS CHICAGO'S MOST famous architect was Frank Lloyd Wright, who lived in suburban Oak Park from 1889 to 1909. The long, low roof lines of the Robie House at the University of Chicago (TOP) epitomize Wright's Prairie School of architecture, but contrary to popular rumors, he never ordered Mrs. Robie to wear horizontally striped dresses to complement the lines of the home.

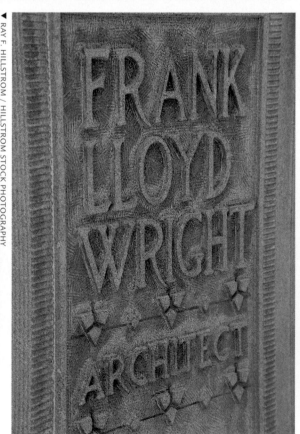

RAY F. HILLSTROM / HILLSTROM STOCK PHOTOGRAPHY

RANK LLOYD WRIGHT LEFT many examples of his farsighted architectural vision in the Chicago area, including the relatively modern-looking Nathan G. Moore House, which sits amid old-fashioned, lavishly decorated homes built during the same period (TOP). In 1974, the National Trust for Historic Preservation began a 12-year, $2.2 million effort to restore Wright's Oak Park home and studio, starting with his stylish dining room (BOTTOM). Today, the estate is open to the public.

J

UST BEYOND THE BUSTLE and intense business activ- of the Loop are quiet, tree- lined neighborhoods, where lawn care and home maintenance are paramount. At Alta Vista Terrace, patterned after an avenue in London, 20 different facades repeat in mirror image on the opposite side of the street (TOP).

HE PULLMAN HISTORIC
District was a commu-
nity divided in 1894, when
workers' demands for more than seven
cents a week in wages led to one of the
longest and most vicious labor strikes
in American history (OPPOSITE BOTTOM).
No matter what their differences were
in the past, however, Chicago neighborhoods today unite in patriotism
on the Fourth of July (BOTTOM).

HERE'S NO BETTER WAY to enjoy a warm spring day than to spend it in the great outdoors, whether you're playing soccer before a dramatic skyline backdrop, running the bases at Grant Park, or strolling around Wicker Park with a good friend.

CHICAGO

HICAGO'S SPORTS FANS ARE
known for their undying
loyalty, even though it's
been greatly tested by the city's two
professional baseball teams, the Cubs
and the White Sox. Win or lose, sup-
porters of both clubs love to drink
beer, eat hot dogs, and watch their
guys play ball.

LTHOUGH AN ALL-Chicago World Series seems nearly impossible these days—the Cubs and the Sox very rarely appear in the fall classic—a precise pitch or a home-run hit always excites the crowd with championship-worthy baseball.

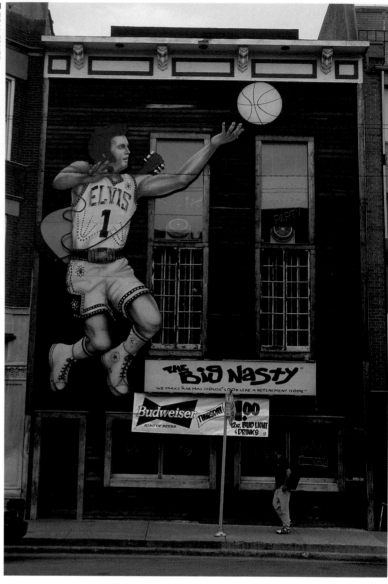

THANKS TO THE WORLD-champion Chicago Bulls, rapture for roundball starts early in the Windy City and seems to infect just about everyone. Local youngsters pattern their game after defensive dynamo Scottie Pippen (LEFT) and the gravity-defying Michael Jordan, whose deft dunking ability has been deified in Nike's ubiquitous Air Jordan logo (RIGHT).

CHICAGO BULLS BASKETBALL is fast, tough, and relentless, and—thanks to Dennis Rodman, who changes his hair color as often as his uniform—it grows more interesting every day. While Rodman is an expert at grabbing rebounds, his attempts at scoring points sometimes fall a bit short (BOTTOM RIGHT). Instead, he and the rest of the world take notes from Michael Jordan, the master of basketball ballet (BOTTOM LEFT).

 HERE'S ALMOST NEVER an empty seat for a Bulls home game at the United Center, where Michael Jordan, Coach Phil Jackson, and Scottie Pippen, the men most responsible for the team's five NBA championships, have a courtside summit.

T HE CHICAGO BULLS ARE truly an international sensation, and local fans, storefront mannequins, and even the "ladies" at the Museum of Science and Industry show their support for the home team. In 1996, nearly 250,000 people gathered in Grant Park to celebrate the Bulls' victory over the Seattle SuperSonics in the NBA finals.

 HEN THE DUNKING is done, it's Michael time. Golfing is one relaxing way His Airness gets his mind off his hoop dreams.

▲ ALAN KLEHR

▲ VITO PALMISANO

DUFFERS, DIVOTS, AND DA hat: Chicago boasts a number of public golf courses downtown and in city parks along the lakefront, providing an inexpensive way to enjoy the sport without the high fees and membership requirements of private country clubs.

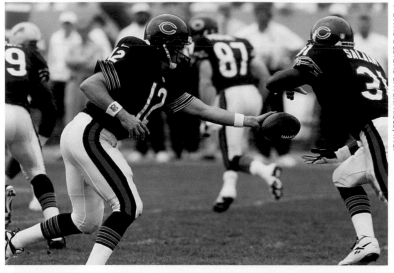

WITH PLENTY OF HAND-offs, hustle, hassle, and harassment, the Chicago Bears often deliver exciting football. The team plays its home games at Soldier Field, which, built in 1924, is one of the league's oldest stadiums (OPPOSITE TOP).

JIM McMAHON
FOOTBALL

T HE BEARS GAVE FANS A taste of glory and football immortality in 1986 when they won the Super Bowl with a 46 to 10 rout of the New England Patriots. That famed Chicago team under the leadership of Coach Mike Ditka (BOTTOM LEFT) and quarterback Jim McMahon, whose handprints are preserved at the entrance to a local sporting goods store (BOTTOM RIGHT)— will go down as one of the best in NFL history.

CHICAGO IS A CITY THAT produces champions. Here, a boxer learns too late to watch out for a quick left jab at the Windy City Gym, where former heavyweight champion Muhammad Ali understood that lesson as well as any fighter in history.

▶ JAMES NEWBERRY

▶ DANIEL KURINA

CHICAGO PRIDES ITSELF ON being streetwise. A mural in a local stereo shop offers one artist's idea of a bad attitude (TOP LEFT), while a production of Nelson Algren's *Never Come Morning* demonstrates that the Chicago writer packed a punch of his own (TOP RIGHT). In the real world, Guardian Angels patrol the subway (BOTTOM LEFT), and the Pink Angels stand watch over the gay and lesbian community (BOTTOM RIGHT).

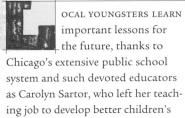

OCAL YOUNGSTERS LEARN important lessons for the future, thanks to Chicago's extensive public school system and such devoted educators as Carolyn Sartor, who left her teaching job to develop better children's programming for television (TOP).

C HICAGO'S CHILDREN ARE looking toward the future, and there's almost no greater vantage point than atop Dad's shoulders or from Mom's comforting arms.

JANET CENTURY

ANTONIO PEREZ

TOM CRUZE

WHEN SCHOOL'S OUT, local youngsters enjoy plenty of playtime. These high schoolers learn that all education is not confined to the classroom as they go for grit, grime, and glory in a tug-of-war (OPPOSITE TOP). In search of some good, clean fun, one young lady finds that, in the summer heat, wetter is better (TOP), and other students of life make a big splash with curious onlookers (BOTTOM).

WHILE A COUPLE OF KIDS show off the buddy system inner-tube-style (TOP), visitors to Chicago's John G. Shedd Aquarium offer their own version of water safety as they view a live shark from *outside* the tank (BOTTOM).

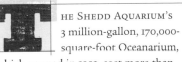 HE SHEDD AQUARIUM'S 3 million-gallon, 170,000-square-foot Oceanarium, which opened in 1991, cost more than $40 million to build and is now the main attraction at the world's largest indoor aquarium (TOP). Inside, visitors can see beluga whales, white-sided dolphins, and countless other aquatic creatures. At the 200-acre Brookfield Zoo, the ocean's most intelligent creatures put on spectacular shows each day for audiences of up to 2,000 (BOTTOM).

WITH LAKE MICHIGAN in Chicago's front yard, the waterfront becomes a vital part of nearly everyone's life. A portion of the city's considerable sailboat fleet await their captains in Monroe Harbor (TOP), while folks and fowl take to the water in Lincoln Park and compete for the title of best paddler (BOTTOM).

 VERY DOG HAS HIS DAY, AND if he's lucky, he'll spend it in the great outdoors.

CHICAGO'S FIELD MUSEUM, on Lake Shore Drive, features world-renowned collections of Tibetan and Native American artifacts, panda pelts, meteors, totem poles, and dinosaur bones, not to mention a Pawnee earth lodge, an Egyptian tomb, a Maori house, a Tahitian market, a jade display, and countless other fascinating exhibits.

 ENRY MOORE'S WORK- ing sundial, titled *Man Enters the Cosmos*, leads the way to the Adler Planetarium, which has been bringing the universe within reach since it opened in 1930. A fast-paced, multimedia show precedes visits to the facility's Sky Theater, where nearly all the stars in the heavens can be reproduced.

THE SPRAWLING, NEOCLAS-sical Museum of Science and Industry was designed in 1892 to house the Palace of Fine Arts for the 1893 Columbian Exposition (TOP). Reopened as a museum in 1933, it presents a wide array of interesting items, including model trains, hatching chicks, the world's smallest bible, a captured World War II submarine, a coal mine, a walk-in model of the human heart, and a passenger jet that's suspended from the ceiling above the main floor.

 OUNDED IN 1856, THE CHI-cago Historical Society is itself a thing of history. The niches along the stairway at the building's entrance are chock-full of unusual memorabilia, including a 1910 sign advertising Dr. William's Pink Pills for Pale People and a Dad's Root Beer sign from 1950 (OPPOSITE BOTTOM). To accommodate the Pioneer, a loco-motive that was retired in 1874, the Historical Society floor had to be reinforced, a wall removed, and the roof opened so a crane could lower the 12-ton train into place (BOTTOM).

OCATED JUST WEST OF THE city, the Brookfield Zoo presents a magnificent collection of animals from across the globe. In Tropic World—a spectacular man-made rain forest featuring the free-swinging animals of Africa, Asia, and South America—birds fly, monkeys climb, and anteaters explore. Simulated thunderstorms even occur at various points throughout the exhibit, but these spectators don't seem to mind; the walkway through this wilderness provides some shelter from the rain.

HE WINDY CITY embraces all creatures great and small, imaginary and real. The recently opened Warner Bros. Studio Store proves that plenty of folks are Daffy about Sylvester. Elsewhere, a resident of the Lincoln Park Zoo offers his seal of approval on a sunny day, a costumed canine puts his best face forward, and a pleased-as-punch polar bear and a proud penguin embrace sweet home, Chicago.

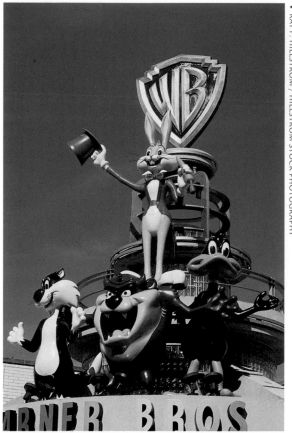

RAY F. HILLSTROM / HILLSTROM STOCK PHOTOGRAPHY

KAREN I. HIRSCH

KAREN I. HIRSCH

NEARLY EVERY WEEKEND during the summer, Grant Park welcomes yet another festival, including celebrations of jazz, gospel, and Latin American music. The biggest and most popular of these lakefront fests is Taste of Chicago, which invites thousands of people to gather near Buckingham Fountain to sample the local cuisine and enjoy plenty of music and other entertainment.

N AVY PIER, WHICH JUTS into Lake Michigan, was originally built in 1916 as a port facility for commercial shipping. Recently, the old pier was replaced with a spectacular fun zone that includes an IMAX theater, indoor botanical gardens, kiosks for shopping, curious sculptures, plenty of food and drink, and a giant Ferris wheel that offers spectacular skyline views.

▶ RAY F. HILLSTROM / HILLSTROM STOCK PHOTOGRAPHY

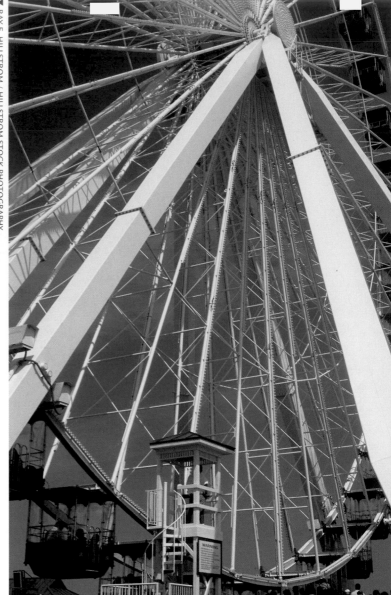

OCAL SAILORS LOVE TO take advantage of breezy days on the lake, whether they're out for a pleasure cruise (OPPO-SITE) or gearing up for the annual race from Chicago to northern Michigan's Mackinaw Island (BOTTOM RIGHT). Captain Bob Marthai stands proudly at the helm of his 145-foot *Windy*, the first four-masted schooner built since 1921 and the only boat of its kind on the Great Lakes (LEFT). For those who prefer to take in the scene from on high, the Navy Pier's 15-story Ferris wheel offers a stunning perspective (TOP RIGHT).

C H I C A G O

 **T**HERE'S NOTHING BETTER than a summer's day on Lake Michigan, where colorful sails, snapping flags, and cool breezes greet you at every turn.

BOATS FROM AROUND THE region gather at the Chicago Yacht Club before the three-day Chicago-to-Mackinaw race. Although weather on Lake Michigan can quickly change and produce dangerous wave conditions, avid sailors agree that the thrill of competition always outweighs the risk.

RUFFIAN
CHICAGO

WINDY
CHICAGO

N WARMER MONTHS, THE LAKE becomes Chicago's playground, and these boats won't likely remain in dry dock for long (TOP LEFT). While some folks are content to soak up the sun near the shore, others can't wait to test their mettle on the open waters.

SAILING IS NOT ALWAYS THE main event on Lake Michigan. Sometimes, the show moves beneath the surface, where divers can explore the area's sunken treasures.

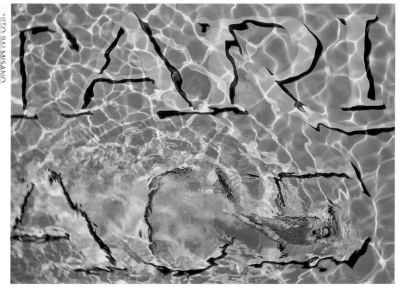

LTHOUGH THE BEACHES of Lake Michigan are free and open to all, swimming is sometimes prohibited— and usually for good reason. Never

fear: Locals can find lots of other outlets, including the crystal-clear waters of Ontario Place, a luxury high-rise on the Near North Side (BOTTOM LEFT).

No matter the season, this mermaid never strays far from the water, thanks to her enviable spot on the prow of the *Buccaneer* party boat (RIGHT).

HICAGO BEACHES CERtainly offer solitude in the winter, but they're far from deserted in the summer, as throngs of sun worshipers make their way to the shore. Although these bathing beauties will have to wait a season or two for snow angels, it looks like the sand variety suits them just fine.

 UBLIC BEACHES RUN nearly the entire length of Chicago's lakefront— good news for wanna-be architects and youngsters anxious to get their feet wet. All the while, the gentle waves are enough to wash away anyone's troubles.

ISITORS TO THE CITY'S
lakefront are often met
with unexpected delights,
from a graceful flock of seagulls to an
impromptu game of chess.

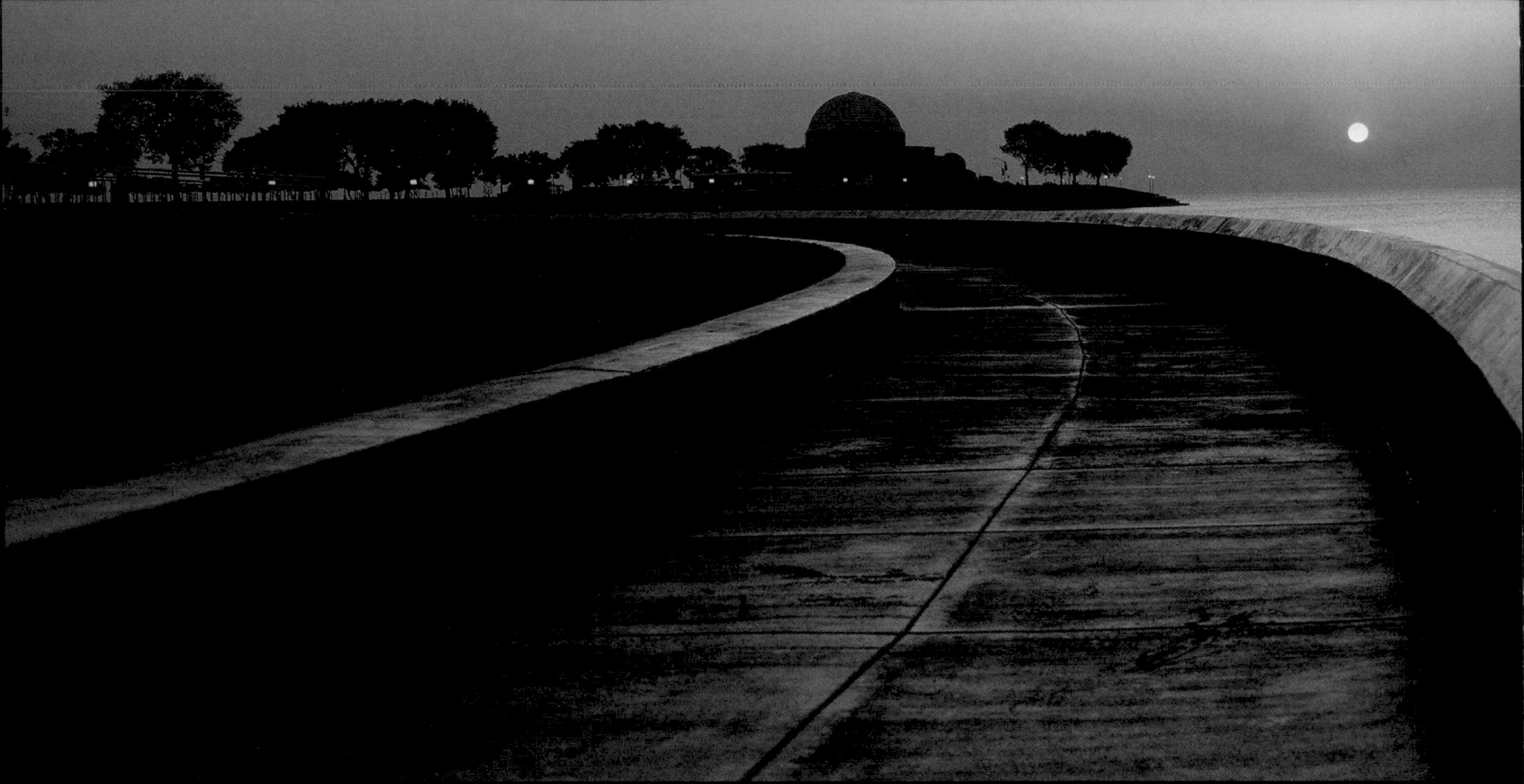
VITO PALMISANO

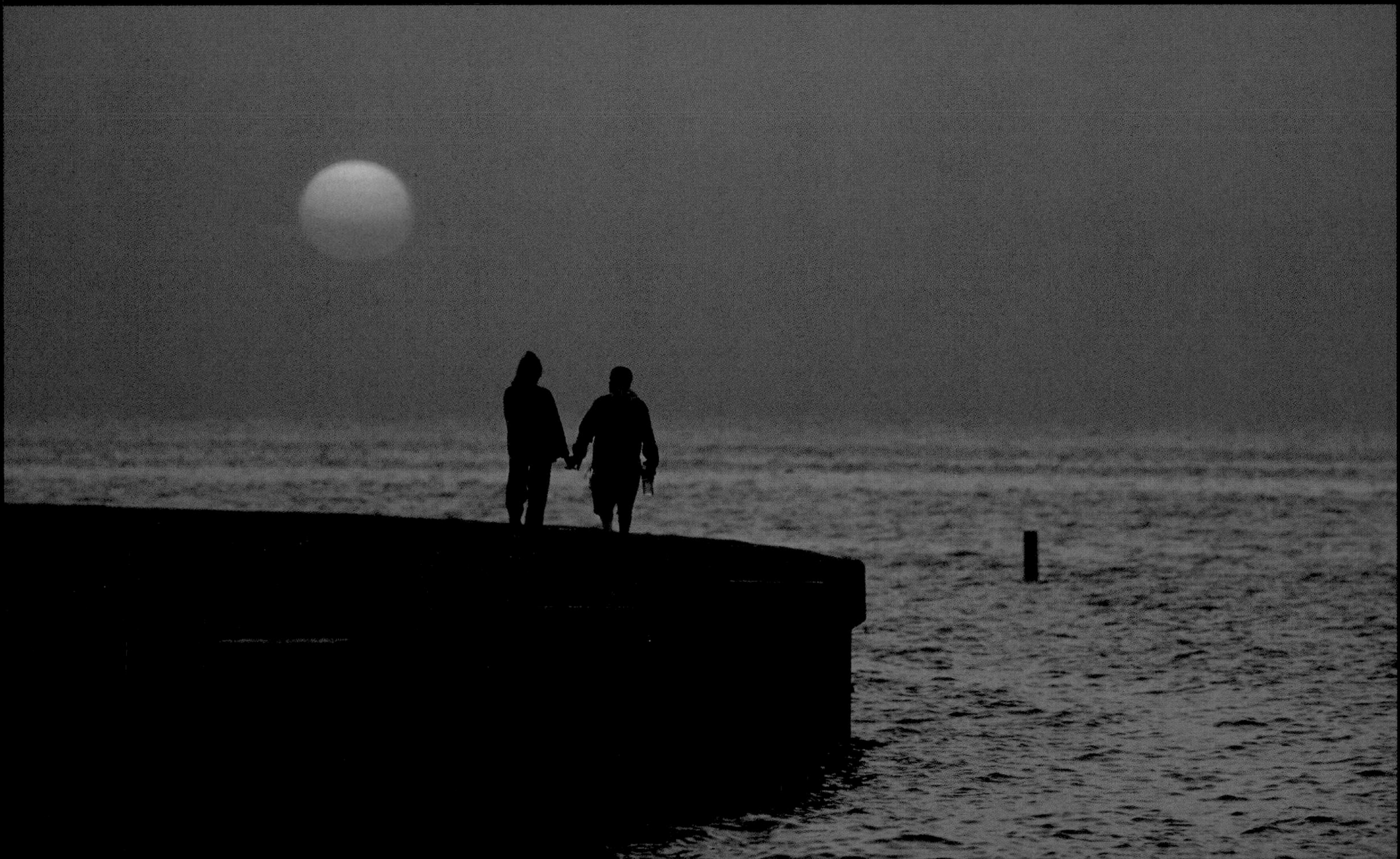
KEVIN O. MOONEY

WORDLESS WONDERS:
A spectacular sunrise
over Lake Michigan
presents a softly changing light show
for runners, lovers, photographers,
and other early risers.

HEN MOTHER NATURE
paints the sky over
Lake Michigan, it's
easy to forget the thriving commercial
and cultural center that rises from the
shoreline and spreads its influence
across the nation and around the world.

 HE LAKE HAS ALWAYS been a valuable commercial resource for Greater Chicago, and area steel mills continue to rely on the vast waterway to transport such precious cargo as ore and fossil fuel.

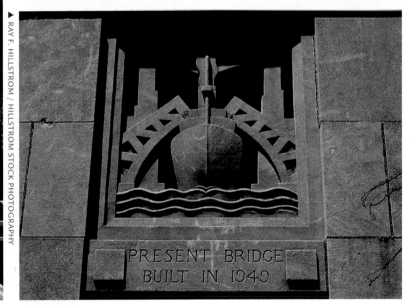

PRESENT BRIDGE
BUILT IN 1949

DOZENS OF SPANS, INCLUD-ing more than 40 draw-bridges, traverse the Chicago River. Critical to the north/ south flow of pedestrian and automo-tive traffic, many of these bridges are also noted for their beauty and historic significance.

C H I C A G O

NO MATTER THE SPORT, Chicagoans love to put their athletic prowess to the test: Swimmers take to Lake Michigan despite its often chilly temperature, cyclers race through the University of Chicago campus, and runners demonstrate their own fancy footwork.

C H I C A G O

DEDICATED IN 1989, THE 125-foot-long Centennial Fountain commemorates 100 years of water-quality improvements in the Windy City. For 10 minutes each hour, the granite fountain pumps nearly 20,000 gallons of water in an 80-foot arc across the Chicago River.

CHICAGO

T HE CHICAGO RIVER carves a path through the heart of the city, providing a beautiful setting for boaters, strollers, and other water watchers.

In 1900, to curb the epidemics that once plagued the swampy city, the flow of the river was permanently reversed in an engineering feat that remains impressive to this day.

A SCULPTURE BY LOCAL
artist Phil Schuster
depicts one of downtown
Chicago's most beautiful areas: where
the Michigan Avenue Bridge crosses
the Chicago River in view of the Wrigley
Building and the Tribune Tower.

I'T'S ONLY FITTING THAT A QUAR-
tet of classical columns should
welcome visitors to Greektown,
a community just outside the Loop
where the life spirit is always energetic,
the wine always flows, and the food
inspires shouts of "Opaa!"

 ILHOUETTES OF CHICAGO:
Elaborate rooftops frame
a city on the rise.

ROBERT MORRIS · GEORGE WASHINGTON · HAYM SALOMON

CHICAGO IS NO STRANGER to traffic jams, but a band of colorful equestrians are sure to turn heads as they relive the Middle Ages (BOTTOM). Cars and people also fill busy Michigan Avenue and its bridge, which features four ornate pylons depicting such local historic events as the Fort Dearborn Massacre of 1812 (OPPOSITE).

N OUTDOOR MURAL titled *The First Impression*, gracing a Printers' Row building in the South Loop, reminds modern-day tenants of the neighborhood's hardworking origins (TOP).

Elsewhere, Paul Bunyan promotes business in a suburban lumberyard (BOTTOM LEFT), and a trio of city workers pose for the camera with their tool of the trade (BOTTOM RIGHT).

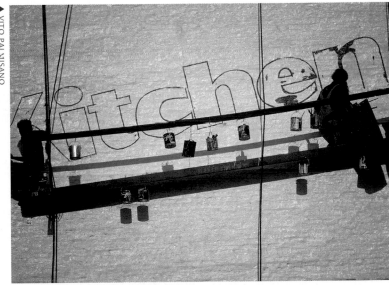

HERE'S NO DENYING THAT Chicago is a city hard at work, and one down-town building even commemorates that heritage with a unique bas-relief (TOP LEFT).

L OCALS LOVE TO SAY THERE are really only two seasons in Chicago: winter and construction. Above ground or below, the sights and sounds of hard work pervade city life in every season.

OME OF THE TOUGHEST IN the business, Chicago police take their motto "to serve and protect" very seriously. But there's also a softer side to many of the city's cops, especially when they're watching over children or finding friends in traffic.

S THEY ROLL OFF THE assembly line, cars of every make and model are ready to tackle the open road. Unfortunately for Chicago drivers, there are a few forces at work to slow things down (PAGES 304-307).

HE DETRITUS OF CITY LIFE takes its toll in Chicago, where curbside attractions are sometimes a reflection of bad parking decisions, rather than sophisticated urban planning. Anyone seen a taxi?

HEART AND SOUL OF AMERICA

CHICAGO MAY MARK THE end of historic Route 66, but it's also where a world of fun and excitement begins, and what better way to start a tour of the city than with a chauffeured ride, courtesy of a cabbie with character.

▲ RON SCHRAMM

 T THE END OF THE workweek, thousands of locals escape the stresses of daily life and head south on the Chicago Skyway, the fastest route into the dunes of Indiana and Michigan.

ELSON ALGREN, IN *Chicago: City on the Make*, speaks to the duality of his hometown: "Chicago . . . forever keeps two faces, one for winners and one for losers; one for hustlers and one for squares." Today, Algren's statement still rings true, as this midwestern metropolis reaffirms its role as the heart and soul of America.

HEART AND SOUL OF AMERICA

CHICAGO

PROFILES IN EXCELLENCE

A LOOK AT THE CORPORATIONS, BUSINESSES, PROFESSIONAL GROUPS, AND COMMUNITY SERVICE ORGANIZATIONS THAT HAVE MADE THIS BOOK POSSIBLE. THEIR STORIES— OFFERING AN INFORMAL CHRONICLE OF THE LOCAL BUSINESS COMMUNITY—ARE ARRANGED ACCORDING TO THE DATE THEY WERE ESTABLISHED IN CHICAGO.

A. M. CASTLE & CO. ■ ABC RAIL PRODUCTS CORPORATION ■ ALLSCRIPTS ■ ALTHEIMER & GRAY ■ AMERICAN AIRLINES ■ AMERITECH CORPORATION ■ AMOCO CORPORATION ■ ANDERSEN CONSULTING ■ AON CORPORATION ■ ATF, INC. ■ BANC ONE CORPORATION ■ BANK OF AMERICA ■ BARTON INCORPORATED ■ BAXTER INTERNATIONAL INC. ■ BLOCK STEEL CORPORATION ■ BOOK COVERS INC. ■ BOZELL WORLDWIDE ■ BRITISH AIRWAYS ■ BROOKFIELD FARMS ■ CAPITOL CONSTRUCTION GROUP, INC. ■ CDW COMPUTER CENTERS ■ CENTERPOINT PROPERTIES ■ CHERNIN'S SHOES, INC. ■ THE CHICAGO BOARD OF OPTIONS EXCHANGE ■ CHICAGO BOARD OF TRADE ■ CHICAGO STOCK EXCHANGE ■ CHICAGO TRANSIT AUTHORITY ■ CHICAGO TUBE & IRON ■ CHICAGO WHITE METAL CASTING, INC. ■ CITY COLLEGES OF CHICAGO ■ COLUMBIA PIPE & SUPPLY CO. ■ CONSOER TOWNSEND ENVIRODYNE ENGINEERS, INC. ■ CORPORATE TRAVEL MANAGEMENT GROUP, INC. (CTMG) ■ CRANE CARTON COMPANY ■ DDB NEEDHAM CHICAGO ■ DRAFTWORLDWIDE ■ DYNACIRCUITS MANUFACTURING COMPANY ■ ED MINIAT, INC. ■ EDELMAN PUBLIC RELATIONS WORLDWIDE ■ ESI ■ THE FAIRMONT HOTELS ■ FAVORITE BRANDS INTERNATIONAL ■ FIRSTAR BANK OF ILLINOIS ■ FLUOR DANIEL, INC. ■ FOLLET CORPORATION ■ FRANKEL & CO. ■ GIORDANO'S ENTERPRISES, INC. ■ GRAYCOR ■ HABITAT CORPORATE SUITES NETWORK, LLC ■ HARZA ENGINEERING COMPANY ■ HEYMAN CORPORATION/CHILDREN'S APPAREL GROUP ■ HOME RUN INN ■ HYATT REGENCY CHICAGO IN ILLINOIS CENTER ■ ILLINOVA ENERGY PARTNERS ■ INLAND STEEL INDUSTRIES, INC. ■ THE INTERNATIONAL ASSOCIATION OF LIONS CLUBS ■ JOHN O. BUTLER COMPANY ■ JORDAN INDUSTRIES, INC. ■ LAI ■ LASALLE NATIONAL CORPORATION ■ MARKETING INNOVATORS INTERNATIONAL INC. ■ MAY & SPEH, INC. ■ MCL COMPANIES ■ MERCY HEALTH SYSTEM ■ METRON STEEL ■ MI-JACK PRODUCTS, INC. ■ NALCO CHEMICAL COMPANY ■ NATIONAL FUTURES ASSOCIATION ■ NATIONAL RESTAURANT ASSOCIATION ■ NORRELL CORPORATION ■ OAKWOOD CORPORATE HOUSING ■ PHOENIX DUFF & PHELPS CORPORATION ■ PODOLSKY NORTHSTAR REALTY PARTNERS, LLC ■ QUALITY SCREW & NUT CO. ■ QUERREY & HARROW, LTD. ■ QUIXOTE CORPORATION ■ ROSS & HARDIES ■ RUDNICK & WOLFE ■ RUSH-PRESBYTERIAN-ST. LUKE'S MEDICAL CENTER ■ RUSSELL REYNOLDS ASSOCIATES ■ RUST-OLEUM CORPORATION ■ S&C ELECTRIC COMPANY ■ SARA LEE CORPORATION ■ SCHUMACHER ELECTRIC CORP. ■ SUNDANCE HOMES INC. ■ TECHNOLOGY SOLUTIONS COMPANY ■ TELLA TOOL & MANUFACTURING CO. ■ TMB INDUSTRIES ■ TRANSO ENVELOPE COMPANY LLC ■ UGN INCORPORATED ■ UNITED AIRLINES ■ UNIVERSITY OF ILLINOIS AT CHICAGO MEDICAL CENTER ■ US CAN COMPANY ■ WESTIN RIVER NORTH ■ WGN TV ■ WILLIAM BLAIR & CO.

CHICAGO
1837 - 1929

1837	RUSH-PRESBYTERIAN-ST. LUKE'S MEDICAL CENTER
1848	CHICAGO BOARD OF TRADE
1852	MERCY HEALTH SYSTEM
1873	FOLLET CORPORATION
1882	CHICAGO STOCK EXCHANGE
1882	UNIVERSITY OF ILLINOIS AT CHICAGO MEDICAL CENTER
1889	AMOCO CORPORATION
1890	A. M. CASTLE & CO.
1893	INLAND STEEL INDUSTRIES, INC.
1902	ED MINIAT, INC.
1902	FLUOR DANIEL, INC.
1902	ROSS & HARDIES
1904	TRANSO ENVELOPE COMPANY LLC
1907	CHERNIN'S SHOES, INC.
1911	CITY COLLEGES OF CHICAGO
1911	S&C ELECTRIC COMPANY
1914	CHICAGO TUBE & IRON
1914	HEYMAN CORPORATION/CHILDREN'S APPAREL GROUP
1915	ALTHEIMER & GRAY
1917	THE INTERNATIONAL ASSOCIATION OF LIONS CLUBS
1919	CONSOER TOWNSEND ENVIRODYNE ENGINEERS, INC.
1919	HOME RUN INN
1920	HARZA ENGINEERING COMPANY
1921	GRAYCOR
1923	JOHN O. BUTLER COMPANY
1925	DDB NEEDHAM CHICAGO
1926	AMERICAN AIRLINES
1927	LASALLE NATIONAL CORPORATION
1927	NATIONAL RESTAURANT ASSOCIATION
1927	UNITED AIRLINES
1928	NALCO CHEMICAL COMPANY

USH-PRESBYTERIAN-ST. LUKE'S MEDICAL CENTER HAS ROOTS GOING BACK TO 1837, WITH THE CHARTERING OF RUSH MEDICAL COLLEGE AND THE SUBSEQUENT FOUNDING OF TWO OF THE CITY'S OLDEST HOSPITALS. TODAY AT RUSH, BASIC AND CLINICAL RESEARCH SUPPORTS THE PATIENT-centered care, the latest in medical practices and technology, and the up-to-date facilities that combine to provide premier health care.

Located on Chicago's Near West Side, Rush draws patients from throughout Greater Chicago. For certain specialty services, like those of the Rush Transplant Programs and the Rush Children's Hospital, patients come from far beyond the metropolitan area, including overseas.

Rush-Presbyterian-St. Luke's Medical Center includes Presbyterian-St. Luke's Hospital for acute care, Rush Children's Hospital, and the Johnston R. Bowman Health Center for the Elderly. Rush also houses seven centers of clinical excellence known as the Rush Institutes, dozens of specialty programs, and Rush University, with colleges of medicine, nursing, allied health, and biomedical sciences, and a student body of more than 1,400.

The medical center serves as the major referral center and founding member of an eight-member hospital system, the Rush System for Health, reaching some 2 million people in the metropolitan area. Nearly half of the university's 3,350 faculty practice at member hospitals: Rush North Shore Medical Center (Skokie), Rush-Copley Medical Center (Aurora), Illinois Masonic Medical Center (Chicago), Holy Family Medical Center (Des Plaines), Oak Park Hospital (Oak Park), Lake Forest Hospital (Lake Forest), and Riverside HealthCare (Kankakee). The system also provides home health and hospice services, and has a managed care program through a partnership between Rush-Presbyterian-St. Luke's Medical Center and the Prudential Insurance Company.

In addition to the Rush System for Health, Rush maintains a comprehensive teaching affiliation with its neighbor, Cook County Hospital.

ORIGINS AND A VISION

r. Daniel Brainard was only 24 years old when he founded Rush Medical College in 1837, two days before the City of Chicago received its own charter. By 1850, the college was the nation's 10th-largest medical school. Rush moved from downtown to the West Side after

Clockwise from top left: Rush-Presbyterian-St.Luke's Medical Center has consistently been ranked by *U.S. News & World Report* as one of the nation's best hospitals for complex specialty care.

Rush Children's Hospital provides a full range of medical, surgical, and psychiatric services for newborns through teens.

More than 600 Rush residents and fellows are pursuing postgraduate training in 22 clinical departments.

◄ MARK BATTRELL

▼▼ DAVID JOEL

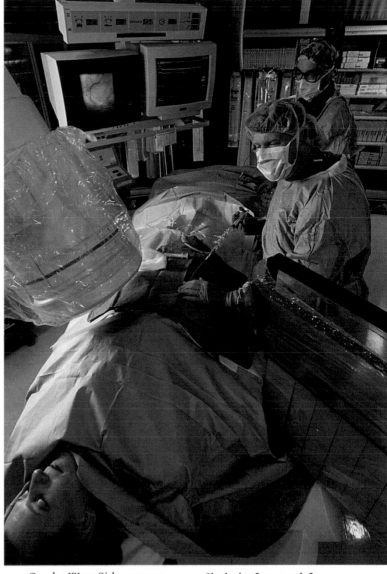

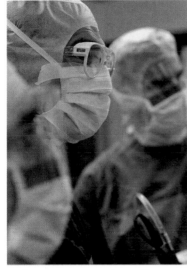

the great Chicago fire. Its faculty convinced local Presbyterians to build a teaching hospital, and Presbyterian Hospital opened in 1883. By the turn of the century, Rush was the nation's largest medical school, and its faculty were leaders of American medicine; they helped organize the American Medical Association and were instrumental in the drive to create national standards for medical education.

World War II forced the college to close in 1942, but its faculty maintained the charter and continued to see patients and teach at Presbyterian. In 1956, Presbyterian Hospital and nearby St. Luke's Hospital (founded in 1864) merged. The vision of then President Dr. James Campbell led to the reopening of Rush Medical College in 1971 and the establishment of Rush University with a network of four affiliated hospitals.

Today, many Rush University graduates work at member hospitals of the Rush System for Health. The system's original goals—to improve quality of care in community settings and access to specialty care—have been largely achieved.

CUTTING-EDGE CARE CLOSE TO HOME

ush-Presbyterian-St. Luke's and the Rush System for Health strive to offer patients the highest-quality care close to home. Key to this approach have been the Rush Institutes, which bring new research findings to outpatient settings and a team approach to diagnosing and treating serious illnesses.

Today, the Rush Heart Institute, the Rush Cancer Institute, and the Rush Institute for Mental Well-Being see patients at system hospitals as well as on the main campus. The Rush Heart Institute is also linked electronically with Rush-Copley, so that some testing can be done in Aurora and interpreted by specialists on the main campus. The Rush Arthritis and Orthopedics Institute and the Rush Neuroscience Institute are working to expand their city-based programs.

Other institutes are focused on improving the way health care is delivered. The Rush Institute on Healthy Aging has launched an ambitious program to train professionals in a team approach to caring for the elderly. And the Rush Primary Care Institute is linking community-based practitioners with the main campus and with each other via a computer network.

On the West Side campus, there are more than 600 residents and fellows in postgraduate training, rotating between Rush, Cook County, and system hospitals. Their presence spurs ongoing attempts to improve patient care. Many new technologies are available to Rush patients as a result of research, including implant devices to treat neurological illnesses like Parkinson's disease and epilepsy, less invasive surgical techniques for heart disease, and new forms of cancer treatment.

"We have a legacy of innovation from those who have preceded us," notes Dr. Leo M. Henikoff, president and CEO since 1984. "Their legacy is being invested in continued innovation, through the Rush Institutes and through the growth of the Rush System. There will be significant challenges to health care in the future. We are not just preparing for this future. We are working hard to shape it, with an emphasis always on what's best for the patient."

Clockwise from top left:
Rush University faculty are engaged in more than 2,300 active research projects supported by $45 million in external funding.

Cutting-edge treatments are the hallmark of the Rush Institutes, the medical center's seven centers of excellence for clinical care and research.

The medical center's 1,450 attending physicians care for more than 31,000 inpatients and see 800,000 patients in their offices each year.

THE CHICAGO BOARD OF TRADE (CBOT), THE WORLD'S OLD-EST AND LARGEST FUTURES AND OPTIONS EXCHANGE, WAS FOUNDED IN 1848 BY 82 MERCHANTS SEEKING TO ESTABLISH A CENTRAL MARKETPLACE TO STABILIZE CHAOTIC GRAIN MARKETS. A DARING INNOVATION THEN, THE CBOT HAS

vastly expanded that bold move into a 150-year tradition of inno-vation and progress, today employ-ing approximately 800 people and serving more than 3,600 mem-bers and countless market users worldwide.

GLOBAL LEADER THROUGH INNOVATION

s a global leader, the Chicago Board of Trade and its subsid-iary, the MidAmerica Commodity Exchange, provide markets for hedgers and investors seeking to minimize price risk and maximize profit opportunity. Through the tried and proven system of the open outcry auction market style of trading, buyers and sellers trade in pits on three floors, and dis-cover prices for various agricul-tural and financial futures and options contracts. This system is supported by the soundness and integrity of the exchange's own proven method of self-regulation and the trade matching of the Board of Trade Clearing Corp., the only institution of its kind to receive a Triple-A rating from Standard & Poor's, the established credit rating service.

One of the exchange's most recent successes came in June 1997, when Dow Jones & Company granted the CBOT permission to trade futures and futures-option instruments on its century-old and world-renowned Dow Jones Industrial Average Index. With this development, the Chicago Board of Trade expanded its diversified product mix into the market for equity futures and futures options.

Additionally, during the 1990s, the CBOT inaugurated its Project A® electronic trading system for the worldwide trading of the ex-change's financial and agricultural futures and options when the CBOT pit trading is closed. This system has proved to be an unqualified success and has been developed into a system permitting CBOT members to trade from their com-puters at home.

HEALTHY GROWTH

s market volume at the CBOT has grown and set records, the exchange has met the demand for more efficient service to its mem-bers and customers by building the world's largest trading facility, a $182 million, 60,000-square-foot floor that opened on February 18,

The Chicago Board of Trade provides markets for hedgers and investors seeking to minimize price risk and maximize profit opportunity. Through the tried and proven system of the open outcry auction market style of trading, buyers and sellers trade in pits on three floors, and discover prices for various agricultural and financial fu-tures and options contracts.

1997. This new facility features a state-of-the-art electronic order processing system and the capability to expand the floor still further to accommodate new products. Previously, in 1982, the exchange built a 32,000 square-foot agricultural trading floor.

A laboratory for new ideas and new technologies, the CBOT began in 1848 with the development of forward, and then standardized, futures contracts. In its role as industry leader, the CBOT advanced to the initial development of financial (interest-rate) futures in 1975; options on futures in 1982; and subsequently, in the 1990s, the Chicago Board Brokerage for the trading of cash government securities. Product innovation also led to the creation of flexible, yield-curve, and inflation-indexed financial instruments; catastrophe insurance options; and clean air emission allowance auctions.

Financial Giant in Chicago

A 1997 landmark study conducted by the Risk Management Center of Chicago called the CBOT an "engine of growth and opportunity for Chicago." According to the study, the city's four exchanges account for more than $35 billion of margin deposits in local banks. Jobs created due to trading in securities and commodities boomed 13.9 percent over the last decade, compared with 9 percent in the Chicago economy as a whole.

The Chicago exchanges also accounted for 151,000 new nonfinancial jobs in the last decade. According to the model used by the Federal Reserve Board, for every 100 new securities and commodities jobs, Chicago gains 173 new nonfinancial jobs in areas such as health care, retail, and management services. With the volume of the Chicago exchanges growing by 45 percent from 1987 to 1995, the continued success of the Chicago Board of Trade and the city of Chicago is firmly in place.

An Architectural Symbol

Since 1930, the Board of Trade has been headquartered on West Jackson Boulevard, anchoring

Designed by Holabird and Root, the 45-story Chicago Board of Trade building on West Jackson Boulevard is an art deco beacon in a city renowned for its fine architecture. The structure is appropriately topped by a 30-foot-plus cast aluminum statue of Ceres, the Roman goddess of grain, reflecting the organization's roots in agriculture.

Chicago's financial district. Designed by Holabird and Root, the 45-story Chicago Board of Trade building is an art deco beacon in a city renowned for its fine architecture. The structure is appropriately topped by a 30-foot-plus cast aluminum statue of Ceres, the Roman goddess of grain, reflecting the organization's roots in agriculture.

In 1982, Helmut Jahn designed an annex to the 1930 building to house the 32,000-square-foot agricultural trading floor. And in 1997, the CBOT opened its record-size, 60,000-square-foot financial trading floor, the work of project architects Fujikawa Johnson & Associates, Inc.; general contractors Morse Diesel McHugh Joint Venture; and design builder Stein & Co.

With additional innovations under development, the Chicago Board of Trade continues to hold true to its roots as an agricultural exchange, with its sights set high and far into the 21st century. The CBOT plans to expand and extend the progress that began with those original 82 merchants a century and a half ago.

MERCY, CHICAGO'S FIRST HOSPITAL, CONTINUES AS A VITAL FORCE ON CHICAGO'S SOUTH AND SOUTHWEST SIDES. THOUGH MEDICINE HAS DRAMATICALLY CHANGED SINCE 1846 WHEN FIVE SISTERS OF MERCY TRAVELED FROM PITTSBURGH TO WHAT WAS THEN A frontier town, the dedication and commitment to the Chicago community has not changed. When the sisters landed, they found a town plagued by yearly outbreaks of cholera, typhoid, and smallpox. Today, Mercy Health System fights cancer, diabetes, heart disease, and AIDS, to name only a few ills that plague modern society.

PIONEERING SPIRIT

When the Sisters of Mercy arrived in Chicago, the city was only nine years old. In their first makeshift convent at Madison Street and Michigan Avenue, it was not uncommon for the sisters to awaken on winter mornings under bedclothes dusted with snow. Nonetheless, they began immediately to visit the sick, and within a year, they started nursing at a temporary hospital set up at the Tippecanoe Inn. This pioneering spirit led to an official charter for Mercy Hospital in 1852 and to the tradition of providing innovative and excellent care.

STILL LEADING THE WAY

After nearly a century and a half of service to Chicago, Mercy remains at the forefront of quality health care. The system's 477-bed, teaching hospital anchors a network of health care facilities serving diverse communities and ethnic groups in Chicago and its surrounding suburbs. Mercy enjoys a medical staff of more than 500 physicians who represent 35 specialties and subspecialties.

Mercy has played a leading role in medical education from the day it opened its doors. The medical center has a major teaching affiliation with the University of Illinois at Chicago Medical School and with St. Xavier University's School of Nursing. Mercy also educates allied health professionals representing 32 disciplines.

WORKING WITH LOCAL BUSINESSES

Each year through the MercyWORKS program, Mercy helps 45,000 injured employees return to work. By closely interacting with company representatives, the multidisciplinary team has reduced clients' average number of injury-loss workdays to fewer than four. Mercy also helps clients avoid injury through its Industrial Services component. Through this program, trained specialists analyze injury data and tailor prevention programs to the needs of the company. MercyWORKS' work-hardening program helps injured employees, such as bricklayers, build their strength and learn proper performance tech-

Mercy Hospital, Chicago (top)

Neurologist Michael Jerva, M.D., (left) and cardiovascular surgeon, Robert Gazior, M.D., work together to repair a spinal injury near a patient's heart (bottom).

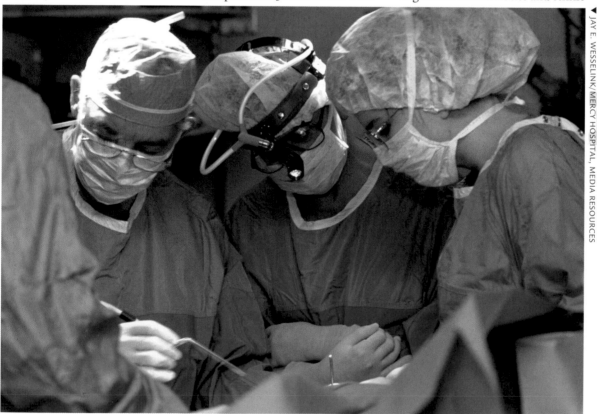

niques, so they can return to work without risking further injury. MercyWORKS also offers pre-employment physicals, drug and alcohol screening, and pulmonary function testing. Among its 2,500 clients are the United Parcel Service, Amtrak, and Ameritech.

FOCUSING ON WELLNESS

Mercy's community service and wellness programs promote physical, emotional, social, and spiritual well-being for Chicagoans of all ages and races. The Give Kids a Chance program provides the medical care and social services high-risk parents need to deliver and rear healthy, happy youngsters. The school nurse program teaches healthful lifestyle wellness education through local schools. The Health Professionals for the Future gives high school students first-hand exposure to career opportunities in health care. House Calls provides in-home physician care for the homebound elderly, while people recuperating from surgery or extended illness are assisted through Home Health services.

The Diabetes Treatment Center at Mercy provides education, so patients may effectively manage the disease. Through Mercy's innovative Less Stress program, patients with high blood pressure, cholesterol imbalances, or diabetes can learn to combine medication with non-drug therapies to control cardiac risk factors and improve their quality of life. The Adolescent Health program helps inner-city youngsters facing gang affiliations, early pregnancy, neglect, and drug abuse.

CARDIAC CARE

Mercy's cardiac care program offers a full gamut of services that range from prevention to rehabilitation. The first aim is to find heart disease before it claims or damages a life through the Quality Stress Analysis program. Using portable diagnostic equipment, the team travels to health fairs, visits companies that sponsor wellness programs, and takes appointments in the downtown office in the lobby of the Insurance Exchange Building at 175 West Jackson Boulevard. Those

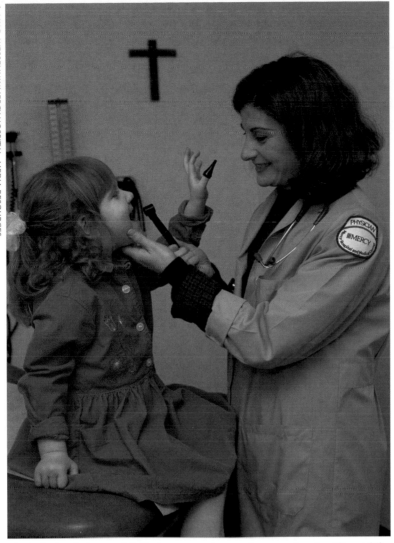

▶ JAY E. WESSELINK/MERCY HOSPITAL, MEDIA RESOURCES

identified as being at risk for heart disease are advised to see their physicians, so they can learn what lifestyle changes to make now to prevent heart disease later.

Today, coronary artery blockage doesn't require that all patients undergo open-heart surgery. Mercy's skilled interventional cardiology team can locate and remove blockage without major surgery. Mercy's team can also place stents to help keep arteries open.

Along with interventional cardiology, Mercy's cardiovascular surgeons work on many rare and unique cardiac conditions as well as routine procedures, such as coronary bypass surgery and reparation of valves. A relatively new and less invasive bypass procedure is called mini-coronary artery bypass surgery. For those whose arrhythmia—irregular heartbeat—can't be corrected by medication, Mercy's electrophysiologist can fit them with either a pacemaker or an internal cardiac defibrillator.

Recovering and returning to a full and productive life requires

With a winning smile, pediatrician Lyna Massih, M.D., gains the trust of her young patients.

that patients make significant lifestyle changes. Mercy helps cardiac patients with this by offering emotional support, education, and an exercise regimen through its 12-week cardiac conditioning program. In the program, patients meet three times a week for hourlong sessions designed to strengthen their hearts, so they can resume their normal activities. Patients begin exercising while hooked up to portable telemetry monitors. As they build strength and endurance, they also meet with a dietitian who helps them develop heart-healthy diets. The program aims to help patients alter their lifestyles by exercising and eating right so that they can reduce their risk for another cardiac event.

THE SPIRIT OF MERCY

Health care has changed radically since Chicago's first hospital was founded, but the spirit of Mercy remains the same: Minister to all with dignity and respect.

EIGHBORHOODS ARE A VERY IMPORTANT PART OF LIFE IN ANY URBAN CENTER. SINCE 1976, MCL COMPANIES HAS CONTRIBUTED TO THE DEVELOPMENT OF CHICAGO'S WELL-LOVED ENVIRONS BY BUILDING NEW NEIGHBORHOODS IN URBAN AREAS, REJUVENATING DECAYING RESIDENTIAL AND retail properties, and revitalizing public housing.

Led by President and CEO Daniel E. McLean, MCL specializes in market research, project management, sales and marketing, engineering construction, pricing and budgeting, management support, and accounting. MCL's efforts in urban planning and revitalization have been recognized through numerous awards, including the Professional Builder Award for Urban Revitalization, Chicago Developer of the Year, Builder of the Year, Best City Development, Pillar of the Industry Award, and nine Sammy Awards for marketing and advertising. In September 1997, McLean was inducted into the Chicago Association of Realtors Hall of Fame. MCL was also chosen to build the home of Mayor Richard M. Daley.

URBAN EXPERTS

The Residences at Central Station is one of MCL's most innovative urban neighborhoods. The property was developed on the former Illinois Central railroad track right-of-way. The development, which runs to the north of McCormick Place and the south of Chicago's Loop, has revitalized the Near South Side and helped establish a sense of stability for the area.

As a specialist in urban planning, MCL is redeveloping public housing at the Henry Horner Replacement Homes, Near West Side and Cabrini Green, Near North Side. By integrating new public housing with market rate units, MCL is helping to create thriving mixed-income communities.

Current projects are also ongoing in Chicago's Streeterville and Old Town neighborhoods. New residential developments include the Embassy Club, Dearborn Park II, Residences at Central Station, Pointe at Lincoln Park, Oak Club, Cornell Square, Old Town Square, Homes of Mohawk North, and Altgeld Club.

HISTORIC DEVELOPMENTS

In July 1997, MCL announced plans for a new neighborhood to be built along the north bank of the Chicago River.

Since 1976, MCL Companies has contributed to the development of Chicago's well-loved environs by building new neighborhoods in urban areas, rejuvenating decaying residential and retail properties, and revitalizing public housing.

Bordered by Grand Avenue, Columbus Drive, Lake Shore Drive, and the river, this vibrant, 13-acre district, named River East, "will have the appeal of the waterfronts and the energy of an urban center. This will be the place to live and work or to visit for dining, recreation, and shopping," remarked McLean during the unveiling of the plans. With a history older than Chicago itself, the River East property reflects the importance of the river and lakefront for commerce, recreation, aesthetics, and community appeal.

The River East development is MCL's largest undertaking to date. Scheduled for completion within 10 years at an estimated cost of $1 billion, River East will transform current structures, parking lots, and vacant land into 2,000 condominiums, rental apartments, town houses, two hotels, riverfront walkways, parks, stores, a restaurant, and a 24-screen cinema complex. The ambitious project will complete the link between the vitality of Michigan Avenue and the recreation of Navy Pier, opening up a scenic stretch of Chicago's lakefront.

MCL purchased the River East property in April 1997 from the Chicago Dock & Canal Trust, which has owned the property since 1857. Chicago's first mayor, William B. Ogden, founded Chicago Dock & Canal, and sought to develop the tract and the surrounding 23 acres into a trade center for the fledgling city. With the help of his attorney, Abraham Lincoln, Ogden established the company and a vibrant waterfront community, including a bustling port, warehouses, and factory space. The North Pier Terminal building, completed in 1905, was then the largest combined warehouse and docking facility in the world.

MCL's River East project is backed by a group of prominent Chicagoans with a common desire to create livable neighborhoods in urban areas of Chicago. These private investors include Richard Duchossois, owner of the Arlington International Racecourse; Dean Buntrock, former chairman of Waste Management Inc.; Patrick Ryan, chairman of AON Corp.; John Melk, a former Waste Management executive;

and Peer Pederson of Pederson & Haupt, among others.

A COMMUNITY THAT WORKS

In addition to his leadership at MCL, McLean is involved in the Chicago community through various charitable concerns. He is vice president and a board member of the Steppenwolf Theatre Company, and is trustee to the Adler Planetarium. He serves as director of the Burnham Park Planning Board, is a member of the Lincoln Park Builders' Club of Chicago, and is active in fundraising activities for Ronald McDonald House.

McLean envisions communities in places where other developers fail to see potential. By implementing projects in offbeat locations, he creates viable living space where it didn't exist before. Since 1984, MCL's sales have totaled more than $500 million, with $250 million worth of development currently in progress, not including the River East project. MCL is moving in productive and profitable directions, and will continue to create livable neighborhoods for Chicago residents.

The River East development is MCL's largest undertaking to date. Scheduled for completion within 10 years at an estimated cost of $1 billion, River East will transform current structures, parking lots, and vacant land into 2,000 condominiums, rental apartments, town houses, two hotels, riverfront walkways, parks, stores, a restaurant, and a 24-screen cinema complex.

COMPANIES ABLE TO SURVIVE OVER TIME SHARE AN IMPORTANT CHARACTERISTIC: THE ABILITY TO LEARN, ADAPT, AND LEAD. THAT IS THE STORY OF FOLLETT CORPORATION. WHAT STARTED IN 1873 AS A SINGLE STORE SELLING USED TEXTBOOKS TO EDUCATORS, TODAY IS THE NATION'S PREMIER PROVIDER

of products and services to the education marketplace.

Beginning with C.W. Follett, the Follett family has steadily grown the business, expanding and changing to meet the needs of students, educators, and institutions. Follett products and services now impact the lives of one-third of American students and countless more around the world. Follett Corporation is still privately owned and operated by the third and fourth generations of Follett family members. Com-

posed now of seven specialized, individual, autonomous divisions, Follett Corporation generates more than $1 billion in revenues annually and employs more than 8,000 associates.

Follett Corporation is dedicated to excellence in serving the educational community with products and services that enhance the educational process and experience. In the United States, the company helps shape the course of learning in all 50 states, impacting more

than 110,000 elementary and high schools and more than 3,000 college and university campuses. Internationally, Follett reaches more than 60 countries.

Whether the learner is a child embarking on his first day in kindergarten, a young woman starting her college career at the University of Notre Dame, or an adult searching the African Art Index of the Smithsonian Institution, Follett is there—sometimes right up front, sometimes behind the scenes—providing experience and new technology to help educators worldwide.

"We are working hard to position Follett as a leader in creating innovative, effective solutions for the education marketplace," says Richard Traut, Follett Corporation chairman. "As the world moves toward digital delivery of information, we continue to focus on the changing needs of our customers, looking to the future and building on the success of our past."

THE CORNERSTONES

Follett's longevity and success derive from a set of cornerstone principles that motivate all its business decisions: The customer comes first; people are the key to success; ethical behavior is required; innovation is necessary; building on strengths is indispensable; and profits are essential.

The company's dedication to these principles has generated an unparalleled breadth and depth of services and products. So in addition to traditional educational services like book distribution, the various Follett business units apply cutting-edge technology and management solutions to meet the unique needs of the company's different customer sets.

Customers include bookstores, university and school system administrators, district-level planners,

Bookstore retailing has changed dramatically since Follett opened its early store in Chicago. The new Folle²tt [energy squared] store at the University of Illinois at Champaign-Urbana is a 22,000-square-foot, three-story retail environment offering curriculum-centered merchandising "worlds," a two-story video "cyberwall," an in-store cafe, internet computer stations, publishing services, music, software, and books.

Follett College Stores is the largest operator of college and university bookstores in the United States and Canada.

technologists, publishers, librarians, parents, professors, students, and government agencies. Each customer has a singular set of concerns for which Follett helps develop the best solution.

Follett College Stores manages more than 550 college and university bookstores in 46 states and Canada. Follett Campus Resources markets used college textbooks and automated retail management systems to college and university bookstores. Follett Collegiate Graphics, through its Custom Academic Publishing Company affiliate, uses the latest technology to obtain copyright clearance and to reproduce and distribute intellectual property in the form of custom course materials. Follett Library Resources distributes books and other information services to school and public libraries. Follett Educational Services provides used textbooks and new workbooks for elementary and high school students. Follett Software Company is the leader in the automation of school libraries and the use of technology to access library collections. The company's Library Systems and Services provides collaborative outsourcing services to libraries.

"Though each business unit serves unique needs, the strength of Follett Corporation is its presence across the entire educational

Automated retailing and inventory tracking systems from Follett help bookstores and libraries manage their increasingly demanding needs.

market," says Kenneth Hull, Follett Corporation president. "Follett is focused on customer service, quality products and services, and solutions for the needs of education and educators."

FOLLETT PEOPLE: A CULTURE OF SERVICE

ustomers say that the Follett name is synonymous with customer service. Follett account managers and executives are in the field every day to ensure that the customer is being heard, understood, and served. Relationships are built on respect and integrity, and fostered by communication. Follett keeps the lines to customers open through activities like focus groups, consulting boards, seminars, Internet list-serv user groups, product training programs, professional development programs, and involvement in national symposia and conferences. Whether face-to-face, over the phone, or through direct electronic communication, Follett listens, learns, and responds to its customers.

Networking is an essential component of Follett's mission. It begins with each Follett business unit and culminates with the customer. New and emerging technologies enable Follett to connect students, teachers, classrooms, libraries, and school districts to a multitude of resources worldwide. Likewise, electronic connectivity makes doing business with Follett easier and more cost effective.

Information is the raw material of education, and it can take many forms. Whether in book form or through the use of the latest technology, Follett is pioneering frontiers to ensure that the education marketplace can capitalize on the best and latest information distribution systems.

Solutions for Elementary and Secondary Schools

In the elementary and high school market, Follett Software Company, Follett Library Resources, and Follett Educational Services provide resources that support and expand the missions of their customers.

Follett Software Company leads the industry in the development of automated systems that enable librarians to better manage and circulate their collections. Follett Software products also enable librarians and educators to integrate research skills into the curriculum, teaching students and other users how to use electronic media in the information gathering process. These products motivate students to analyze, filter, and synthesize information—a critical skill in an age of information explosion.

Delivering information to school libraries is Follett Library Resources' sole concern. Through attention to traditional materials and expansion into new electronic arenas, Follett Library Resources is now the leading wholesaler of books, CD-ROMs, and audiovisual materials to elementary and high school libraries.

As a one-stop service for books and resource materials, Follett Library Resources enables libraries to develop and manage their collections through a series of computer-based ordering methods. A staff of professional librarians is on hand to address customer concerns and needs.

Relationships with more than 35,000 customers attest to Follett

Follett pioneered the book reconditioning process that extends the lives of used textbooks and guarantees that students receive instructional materials of the highest quality.

Educational Services' success in providing used textbooks and other instructional materials to elementary and high schools.

To help schools manage their resources to maximize benefit, Follett Educational Services has developed services that lengthen the life and usefulness of textbooks. Recent innovations include an electronic system that links field reps and customers to Follett Educational Services' home office systems, and a comprehensive software program that enables school administrations to track textbook inventories accurately and efficiently.

SOLUTIONS FOR HIGHER EDUCATION

Colleges, universities, and federal institutions turn to four Follett divisions as partners in managing growth and change: Follett College Stores, Follett Campus Resources, Follett Collegiate Graphics, and Library Systems and Services.

Follett College Stores is the largest operator of college and university bookstores in the United States and Canada. As experts in the privatization of educational services, colleges and universities turn to Follett College Stores to help them improve the quality and cost-effectiveness of their bookstore operations.

The hallmarks of Follett College Stores bookstores include ready availability of all required new and used textbooks throughout the year; access to more used textbooks than any other bookstore operator; computerized inventory control systems that improve profitability and operational efficiency; and a comprehensive academic general book department.

Follett College Stores is on technology's cutting edge through innovative retailing concepts on the Internet. Web sites for institutions like Rutgers University and the University of Illinois enable students, faculty, and alumni to order course materials and merchandise on-line.

Follett Campus Resources has made itself indispensable to customers by providing the highest levels of quality in used college textbook services, information systems, and consulting.

Follett Campus Resources goes far beyond the cornerstone operations of selling and buying back used textbooks. It partners with college stores to reach beyond their four walls by integrating sophisticated computer-based retail management systems into the campus information infrastructure, and by designing software solutions that optimize productivity and maximize profitability.

Custom course materials are some of the fastest-growing product categories in today's college stores. Follett Collegiate Graphics, through its Custom Academic Publishing Company unit, works with educators, publishers, and campus stores to create affordable course materials specially tailored to the needs of students and professors.

Custom Academic Publishing Company is leading the way in legal and ethical custom course materials creation and distribution. These capabilities are enhanced by the company's order information

and ordering capabilities accessible through the Internet.

Library Systems and Services is a leading provider of library outsourcing services in the United States. Institutions like the Department of Energy and the Library of Congress, as well as large public library systems like that in Riverside County, California, rely on the company to enhance their management capabilities through enhanced access to electronic resources and library science expertise.

LEADING IN A WORLD OF CHANGE

New technologies, new business units, new alliances, and new ideas continue to add strength and focus to our mission," says Traut. "With a world of change ahead of us, we continue to adapt our strengths to meet the needs of our customers. Through partnering with our customers, we will remain leaders in our fields."

Follett's culture of service and commitment to complete customer satisfaction have formed the company's cornerstone since its founding more than a century ago.

HEN THE PEOPLE OF ILLINOIS NEED HEALTH AND HEALING, THEIR SOURCE IS THE UNIVERSITY OF ILLINOIS AT CHICAGO (UIC) MEDICAL CENTER. FROM ITS BEGINNINGS, UIC MEDICAL CENTER HAS PIONEERED RESEARCH AND TECHNOLOGY, INTER-

disciplinary training for health professionals, and high-quality care. It has distinguished itself with commitment to excellence and community. The Center is the hub of clinical activity within the UIC Health Sciences Center, the world's largest and most comprehensive academic health science center.

Since 1994, *U.S. News & World Report* has ranked UIC Medical Center among the nation's leading hospitals, and ranked it first among Chicago hospitals in neurology and ophthalmology in 1996. Another affirmation came from the Joint Commission on Accreditation of Healthcare Organizations, which gave the hospital and 29 ambulatory care clinics a summary rating of 93 percent, with a nearly perfect ranking for the ambulatory care center.

The UIC Medical Center serves local residents as a community hospital with more than 40 clinics and an academic medical center serving the Illinois region and the world. Located on Chicago's Near West Side, the Center—UIC Hospital, UIC Clinics, and the UIC Physician Group—sees more than 400,000 patient visits annually. The Health Services Center includes

six colleges: medicine (the largest in the nation), nursing, pharmacy, school of public health, dentistry, and associated health professions. As a state institution, UIC Medical Center and the College of Medicine are responsible for training health professionals in both urban and rural settings on its campuses in Chicago, Champaign-Urbana, Peoria, and Rockford.

RESEARCHING THE FUTURE

hroughout its history, UIC Medical Center has taken major strides in research, from pioneering magnetic resonance imaging, EEG

technology, and treatments for epilepsy to leading-edge clinical-imaging trials of ProstaScint, a new diagnostic tool to detect prostate cancer. Researchers have also completed a groundbreaking study and national trial of hydroxyurea, a cancer drug, for treating pain associated with sickle-cell anemia. UIC specialists are studying depression in head trauma patients, using xenon-enhanced CT scans, the only such technology in the Midwest. Another neurological technique being pioneered is the use of laser-formed polymers in skull reconstruction. This research makes UIC Medical Center a place in

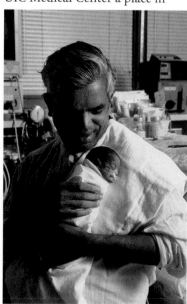

which causes are discovered and where cures are taught to the world.

The world-renowned faculty at UIC Medical Center uses innovative teaching methods and clinical training to give pre- and postgraduate students the knowledge and tools for solving today's challenging health problems. UIC Medical Center trains people from all over the state, many of whom stay and practice in Illinois.

From its early beginnings, UIC Medical Center has used innovative programs to prevent and treat disease. The Eye and Ear Infirmary, founded in 1858, houses the only eye trauma center in Illinois and is the site of the world's first glaucoma clinic.

The Craniofacial Center, the first in North America, is a comprehensive, interdisciplinary center for patients with craniofacial anomalies. UIC also houses the only comprehensive, family-centered AIDS program in Illinois. The multidisciplinary team believes that infectious disease psychologically affects entire families, and therefore, each member requires treatment and counseling. UIC Medical Center staff members are leaders in research and technology, yet they realize that this means nothing without the compassion to help people become whole again.

A Worldwide Community

UIC shows its community commitment through the Great Cities Initiative. The initiative provides transportation; education; safety; and health care training, assistance, and service through more than 250 community outreach programs, community groups, and school systems. The Mile Square Health Center provides access to affordable health care. Mile Square has been one of the largest federally funded U.S. community health care centers. Nurses and health advocates from Mile Square's REACH program provide in-home pre- and postnatal care and train women to go back to their communities to train other women. First lady Hillary Rodham Clinton congratulated the REACH team for their efforts during a 1996 visit. Mile Square also has opened a model school-based health clinic in a Chicago public school.

UIC Medical Center runs the clinic at O'Hare International Airport. Staffed by physicians, the clinic is used by travelers and employees for emergencies, occupational therapy, screenings, and back-to-work programs. Other world outreach programs from UIC Medical Center are continuing in North Africa, Bolivia, Taiwan, Guatemala, and the Republic of Uzbekistan. These programs include intense clinical care, craniofacial surgery, neonatology, instruction, and development.

As UIC Medical Center continues to develop, it is making plans for an off-campus primary care facility, for the widening of the primary care network, and to become a larger player in the managed care market. As it always has, the center will continue to upgrade its physical plant, which includes the construction of a new outpatient care center, add innovative programs, and recruit top names in health care as it reaffirms its commitment as the source of health and healing to all of the people of Illinois.

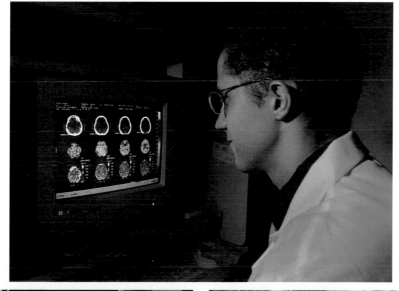

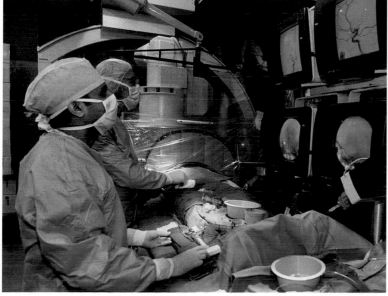

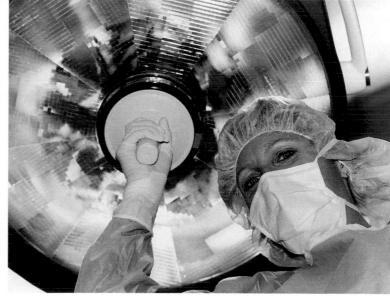

THE FOUNDERS OF THE CHICAGO STOCK EXCHANGE WOULD NO DOUBT BE AMAZED IF THEY COULD WITNESS TODAY'S COMPUTERIZED, TECHNOLOGICALLY SOPHISTICATED WHIRL OF ACTIVITY ON THE FLOOR OF WHAT HAS BECOME THE SECOND-LARGEST STOCK EXCHANGE IN THE UNITED STATES.

The original Chicago Stock Exchange (CHX), founded in 1882, traded 134 stocks and bonds, most of them regional issues such as Chicago Gas, Light & Coke Co. (now Peoples Gas). Following World War II, the market for securities expanded and, in 1949, the Chicago Stock Exchange merged with exchanges in St. Louis, Minneapolis-St. Paul, and Cleveland, Ohio, to form the Midwest Stock Exchange. The New Orleans Stock Exchange merged with the Midwest 10 years later.

In 1993, the Exchange renamed itself the Chicago Stock Exchange to reflect Chicago's growing worldwide reputation as an international trade center, trading some 4,000 stocks daily from its headquarters on South LaSalle Street.

CUTTING-EDGE TECHNOLOGY

Today's high-tech exchange floor, filled with state-of-the-art computer systems, bears little resemblance to the old noisy, ticker-strewn pits filled with traders. "We consider ourselves to be at the very cutting edge in terms of technology," explains Riva Hemond, spokesperson for the Exchange.

"Most of our traders sit at computers. It's very quiet, compared with the open outcry system used at other exchanges."

The Chicago Stock Exchange revolutionized the way stock orders were executed in 1985 when an automated trading system was implemented. This new development established the Exchange as a technological leader, a reputation that continues today. The CHX needs to be prepared for whatever the market may bring. Therefore, the Exchange is constantly upgrading its trading systems and volume capabilities. This is especially important in today's ever changing marketplace where volume continues to grow. The CHX's reputation as a technological leader is worldwide. The Exchange has been involved in the design and implementation of new trading systems in other exchanges around the world, including Amsterdam, Tel Aviv, Athens, Bangkok, Quito, Manila, and Johannesburg.

KEEPING IT IN CHICAGO

Chicago, home of four exchanges, has become a strong force in the U.S. economy. Chicago is known as the city where individuals and institutions can come to buy or sell their portfolio holdings, whether they invest in stocks, options, commodities, or futures. The Chicago Stock Exchange has contributed to this city's becoming an economic force by offering the highest quality of execution and customer service to brokerage firms. "We've significantly increased our market share as compared to our competitors," Hemond says. "Our technology and ability to execute trades efficiently and cost effectively have allowed us to provide our customers with the highest-quality execution at the lowest cost."

But the Exchange isn't just satisfied with serving its customers. The Chicago Stock Exchange also extends its hand to the community through a variety of charitable endeavors, among them the Greater Chicago Food Depository, annual toy and food drives, and the Boy Scouts of America.

The Chicago Stock Exchange plans to continue upgrading and expanding its technological capabilities, keeping it in the forefront of its industry, while still providing personal, professional, and customer-driven services for brokerage firms and their customers.

Today's high-tech exchange floor, filled with state-of-the-art computer systems, bears little resemblance to the old noisy, ticker-strewn pits filled with traders. The Chicago Stock Exchange revolutionized the way stock orders were executed in 1985 when an automated trading system was implemented. This new development established the Exchange as a technological leader.

luor Daniel, Inc. has been a Chicago institution for nearly 100 years. A leading presence in the international engineering, construction, environmental, and diversified services field, the company today boasts more than 80 offices and 50,000 employees worldwide.

Based in Irvine, California, Fluor Daniel traces its Chicago roots to 1902 and a firm called H.M. Byllesby and Company, whose founder once worked with Thomas Edison. The company later evolved into Pioneer Engineer and Service Company, becoming a subsidiary of Fluor Corporation in 1974. Fluor Daniel was created in 1986 when the Fluor Corporation purchased Daniel International. The merger resulted in a company that is a benchmark of quality, innovation, and consistency in successful project delivery.

Client satisfaction is a primary goal at Fluor Daniel. The company serves more clients in more industries and more locations than any of its competitors. As much as 81 percent of its business comes from repeat clients. Fluor Daniel's Chicago clients include Abbott Laboratories, Amoco, Bethlehem Steel, the City of Chicago's 911 facility, GE Plastics, Nabisco, Northern Indiana Public Service Company, Northfield Labs, and Stepan.

Fluor Daniel Chicago provides a full-service engineering center

with state-of-the-art communications, design, printing, computing, and general office services. A special feature offered by the company is the Multi-Projects Task Force. Originating in the Chicago office, this team offers one-stop shopping to clients through a central organization established for multi-project execution. Providing shared resources and facilities, as well as a full range of engineering disciplines, Fluor Daniel gives its clients

a cost-effective approach to engineering projects.

Fluor Daniel employs total quality management (TQM) in an effort to improve the quality and effectiveness of its projects and operations. The company's corporate TQM program, called Continuous Performance Improvement (CPI), provides a disciplined framework that encourages and empowers management and employees to constantly improve their work environment and work processes.

Civic responsibility is also a high priority for employees. Many participate in activities such as National Engineers Week, which includes visits to local grade schools; United Way; United Blood Services blood-donor programs; Toys for Tots; Lindblom High School's Adopt-A-High-School Program; Business Opportunity Fair for Minority Owned Companies; and MERC—Minority Economic Resource Corp.

The goal of Fluor Daniel Chicago is to complete tasks "better, faster, cheaper, and safer" than the competition. By fostering a work environment that challenges, enriches, and rewards each individual, the company meets that goal and, in the process, delivers satisfaction to its clients.

From its Chicago offices on South Riverside Plaza, Fluor Daniel offers a full range of engineering and construction services for virtually every industry and government sector.

T O DISCUSS THE AMOCO CORPORATION IS TO REVIEW MORE THAN A CENTURY OF AMERICAN BUSINESS AND SOCIAL HISTORY. FROM ITS BEGINNINGS AS PART OF THE FAMOUS STANDARD OIL TRUST TO ITS PRESENT STATE AS ONE OF THE WORLD'S MOST PROMINENT ENERGY ENTERPRISES,

Amoco has matched technological know-how with long-range vision, prudence with risk taking, and managerial and financial acumen with a maverick spirit that breaks new ground whenever necessary.

A RECORD-BREAKING HISTORY

H uman ingenuity, as well as a strong and ongoing technological orientation, is the succinct secret to Amoco's success. Both have been evident since the company's earliest years, when John D. Rockefeller and his associates decided to clear a sandy marsh along Lake Michigan's Indiana shore and build a refinery to serve the expanding Midwest market for Standard Oil Trust's petroleum products. The Trust, incorporated in Indiana as Standard Oil Company on June 18, 1889, was selling 88 percent of all the kerosene and gasoline in its midwestern territory by 1911. Cutthroat pricing was an important part of that stunning growth, but so was Standard's policy of providing free tank-wagon deliveries to its far-flung rural customers.

As Standard's Midwest operations prospered, however, government antitrust activity was moving into high gear. After its court-ordered dissolution in 1911, Standard found itself restricted to just nine midwestern states in which it was allowed to make and sell petroleum products. The company wasted no time in starting a complex array of mergers, acquisitions, and groundbreaking technical developments that led to the growth of a far-flung empire that has since weathered numerous economic storms.

The result is today's Amoco Corporation: a three-sector giant in exploration and production of petroleum products, their refinement and marketing, and the manufacture and sale of chemicals used to make everything from paint to polyester. The exploration and production sector is North America's largest producer of natural gas, an aggressive overseas explorer, and a producer of both gas and oil. The petroleum products sector boasts America's largest-capacity refinery, as well as thousands of miles of pipeline connecting its five refineries with supplies of crude and refined oil, gas, and carbon dioxide. The refineries together can process more than 1 million barrels of crude oil per day. And the company's chemicals sector leads worldwide in production of half a dozen substances humankind couldn't do without.

ANCHORED IN CHICAGO

A ll this flows from the Amoco Building, a slender, elegant skyscraper that evokes the image of a tower atop an oil well. Overlooking Chicago's splendid lakefront, this downtown landmark holds the company's world headquarters, from which are man-

Amoco has matched technological know-how with long-range vision, prudence with risk taking, and managerial and financial acumen with a maverick spirit that breaks new ground whenever necessary.

Today's Amoco stays consumer focused in many ways, including the company's co-branded alliance with McDonald's, which allows one-stop shopping for gas, sundries, and dinner.

aged assets totaling more than $32 billion and revenues exceeding $36 billion. Keeping it all running smoothly are some 41,000 employees worldwide. Other Amoco facilities in the area include an office complex in suburban Oak Brook, Joliet Chemical to the southwest, Naperville Research to the west, and Standard Oil's original Midwest location—the refinery in Whiting, Indiana, not far across the state line to the east, right along the lakeshore.

Certainly Amoco is among the city's most prominent companies, and the nation's as well—but that isn't just because of its size. Amoco is known as a good citizen, too, and has created a foundation that grants millions of dollars each year to improve community life and education, especially in math, science, and technology and engineering. Numbered among America's top 20 corporate foundations, the Amoco Foundation is active in 28 countries and about 250 U.S. cities. Amoco employees are active, too, with volunteer commitments backed by the company to leverage more good for each dollar. Even retirees are encouraged to help; and help they do, donating the equivalent of about $2 million in volunteer services yearly.

Amoco's short-range future is as ambitious as anything in the company's long history. Within the next five years, Amoco plans

to increase its production of gas and oil by an impressive 25 percent, partly through bringing new fields on-line and partly by improving operations at existing properties. "Meanwhile," says Chairman H. Laurence Fuller, "in chemicals, we expect to begin reaping the benefits of our recent capacity additions as markets for our key products strengthen." And in a move that testifies to management's belief in the company, Amoco has been repurchasing its stock on the open market.

Also in Amoco's future are new ways to bring together products and consumers. The company's products are rated as tops in quality by consumers, so what's needed is more convenience. One success-

ful strategy is convenience retailing, which places stores within service stations. A new twist on the same idea that appears to be just as promising is Amoco's co-branded alliance with McDonald's, which takes the concept a step further by installing a McDonald's within the service station. Now, consumers can stop just once for gas, sundries, and dinner.

Giving consumers one more reason to choose Amoco is what the company has understood from its earliest days, when horses hauled Standard Oil's tank wagons of home heating oil over miles of country road. Then, as now, customers wanted the best and they wanted it to be convenient; and, just as it did then, Amoco delivers.

N INETEEN YEARS AFTER THE GREAT CHICAGO FIRE OF 1871, ALFRED M. CASTLE SAW THAT STEEL WOULD BE NEEDED TO REBUILD THE CITY. TO MAKE IT READILY AVAILABLE, HE BEGAN TO DISTRIBUTE STEEL PRODUCTS TO CUSTOMERS THAT WERE TOO SMALL TO BUY DIRECTLY FROM THE

foundries on the East Coast. With his partner, William B. Simpson, Castle built good relationships with the eastern steel foundries, developed customers in Chicago and San Francisco, and formed a business structure that has stood the test of time.

"What we try to do is build value over time. That's not always going to translate into quarter-to-quarter growth," explains Michael Simpson, chairman of the board of A. M. Castle & Co. "Instead, by design, we focus on opportunities that will build lasting value for both customers and shareholders."

Castle still delivers. Prospects for long-term growth have been firmly established through the company's wide customer base of industrial companies and the introduction of advanced materials management concepts. What began in Chicago has swept across the United States and into Canada, Mexico, and the United Kingdom.

Starting out with horseshoes, rims, and steel strips for farm-implement repair, Castle has branched out to serve literally hundreds of manufacturers—everything from aerospace, bearings, and oil field equipment to hand and machine tools, health care, and recreation. Castle's focus has expanded, but its principles have not changed.

A UNIQUE QUALITY PROCESS

F rom its early plant near Goose Island to its main location today in Franklin Park, Castle has performed with quality and integrity for more than a century. The early optimism and business savvy of a young Chicagoan in the late 1800s have grown into an international franchise that focuses on customers. Castle is a committed agent of change, and strives for high performance standards and integrity. Quality is a key element in customer and supplier relation-

ships, and is essential to all aspects of the company's manufacturing and distribution business.

Castle's twin towers logo illustrates its dual commitment to building value for both customers and shareholders. This strategy has defined product and service offerings; driven investments in new processes, technologies, and equipment; and inspired employees to stretch themselves.

"Castle was the first major metals distributor to implement a quality process. After 17 years, the process is more vibrant than ever," says President and CEO Richard Mork. Castle was the first service center in the industry to achieve certification from the International Organization for Standardization (ISO). All of the company's operating facilities have now achieved this certification.

A corresponding aspect of the quality process is the strategic partnership program. "In 1982, we

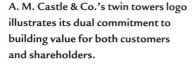

A. M. Castle & Co.'s twin towers logo illustrates its dual commitment to building value for both customers and shareholders.

From its main location in Franklin Park, the company provides highly engineered materials and value-added processing services to a broad range of industrial companies within the $600 billion durable-equipment sector.

pioneered the concept of integrated supply management in our industry," Mork says. "We are currently working with a number of customers to help them take that next step toward a customized and comprehensive service program."

Perhaps the best confirmation of the value these strategic partnerships afford Castle's customers is their growth as a percentage of the company's total business. From less than 5 percent of sales in the mid-1980s, these programs today represent approximately 50 percent of its specialty metals business, the equivalent of a 35 percent compound annual growth rate.

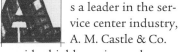

THE BENEFITS OF DIVERSITY

As a leader in the service center industry, A. M. Castle & Co. provides highly engineered materials and value-added processing services to a broad range of industrial companies within the $600 billion durable-equipment sector. Its customer base includes many Fortune 500 companies and thousands of medium- and small-sized companies across the full spectrum of metals-using industries. In its core metals specialty business, Castle is North America's largest industrial distributor of nickel

alloys; aluminum; titanium; copper; brass; and carbon, alloy, and stainless steel. These metals are available in bar, plate, sheet, and tube form.

Castle made its first move beyond specialty metals with the 1995 acquisition of Total Plastics, Inc. (TPI), a distributor of value-added industrial plastics. With TPI, Castle saw an opportunity to leverage the same marketing and distribution strategies into another highly engineered material with a strong, value-added focus. Today, Castle and its affiliated companies operate in 41 North American locations. Other new ventures include the distributor Keystone Tube and

the joint venture of Castle de Mexico in Monterrey and Kreher Steel, a national volume distributor based in Melrose Park.

This historical expansion has produced a well-diversified company. The beauty of this strategy is a portfolio of growth potential and a highly varied range of industries, customers, and geographic markets that can moderate cyclical fluctuations in any industry segment or market.

"Diversity gives us strength. When one division or product is slow, others keep us busy," Mork says. Independent ownership is another of Castle's strengths. Unlike many competitors, it is not a conglomerate and is not owned by the mills. Its only business is materials distribution.

A. M. Castle & Co. aims to be the market leader in its core metals products, and the supplier of choice to its domestic and international customer base. With a strong employee foundation, this conservative company intends to maintain its world-class quality process.

"Sales is a team effort and everyone in our organization participates. Employees are trained to outthink, outwork, and outhustle the competition to ensure that our customers' expectations are met on time, every time," Mork says.

Through selective acquisitions that complement its business focus and culture, A. M. Castle & Co. intends to remain close to distribution, including plastics and metals, and to continue development of materials management services and programs that will enhance its value to its customers.

From its main location in Franklin Park, the company provides highly engineered materials and value-added processing services to a broad range of industrial companies within the $600 billion durable-equipment sector.

All of Castle's processes, technologies, and equipment are geared toward quality. In the company's Hammond, Indiana, plant, water is sprayed from all directions on the rotating bar during the quenching process (left), ultra-straight bars exit from the tempering furnace (center), and both ends of the single bar are then saw cut (right).

AMONG THE 28 MILLION PEOPLE WHO VISITED CHICAGO'S COLUMBIAN EXPOSITION IN 1893 WERE TWO CINCINNAT-IANS, JOSEPH BLOCK AND HIS SON PHILIP. THE BLOCKS HAD COME NOT ONLY TO SEE THE SIGHTS, BUT ALSO TO TAKE CARE OF BUSINESS: CHICAGO STEEL WORKS, A steel mill in Chicago Heights, had shut down, and owed a sizable debt to the Blocks' firm, the Block-Pollack Company.

At the time, the steel industry was on the rise. The first steel-framed skyscraper had been built in Chicago just eight years before, steel track railroads encircled the growing city, and area farmers were harvesting with new steel implements. The 1893 World's Fair in Chicago introduced a vision of the future to the world and brought the founders of Inland Steel together for the first time.

In October 1893, Joseph and Philip Block met with six Chicago businessmen: William Adams, George Jones, Elias Colbert, Frank Wells, Joseph Porter, and John Thomas. Jones suggested a name, and on October 30, 1893, the Inland Steel Company was incorporated. By January 16, 1894, the company had a new mill up and running, and in its first year, Inland Steel sold 5,500 tons of steel for a profit of $8,000.

More than a century later, Inland Steel Industries, Inc. is the sixth-largest steel company in the United States and the proud parent of 12 divisions, joint ventures, and businesses around the world. In 1996, under CEO Robert J. Darnall, Inland shipped 5.1 million tons of steel and had an operating profit of more than $1.6 million.

100 YEARS OF GROWTH

Inland grew through hard work, investment in new plants and related industries, and innovations in the steel-making process that have led to lighter, stronger cars and tougher appliances. The company began building the Indiana Harbor Works on 50 acres of wasteland in East Chicago in 1901; today, the Harbor Works is a massive complex sprawling over 1,900 acres of landfill jutting into Lake Michigan.

As one of the industrial giants of the 20th century, Inland Steel developed the Ledloy line of bar steel in 1939 and accelerated steel production by 100 percent during World War II, which helped the Allied forces catch up to and eventually surpass the production volume of the Nazis. In a letter to P.D. Block, Winston Churchill wrote, ". . . One of the principal reasons for our success will be your marvelous Ledloy steel which has doubled the output of every lathe in the British Empire."

The company added to its sales capabilities in 1935 by purchasing Joseph T. Ryerson & Son,

JON MILLER © HEDRICH BLESSING

Inland Steel Industries is based in the Inland Steel Building at 30 West Monroe Street, a Chicago architectural landmark (top).

Automated torch cutting prepares parts for further processing by a customer of Joseph T. Ryerson & Son Inc. Ryerson's Chicago service center at 16th and Rockwell is part of a network of more than 60 sites operated in the United States and Mexico by Ryerson Tull Inc., now a separate company whose stock is 87 percent owned by Inland Steel Industries (bottom).

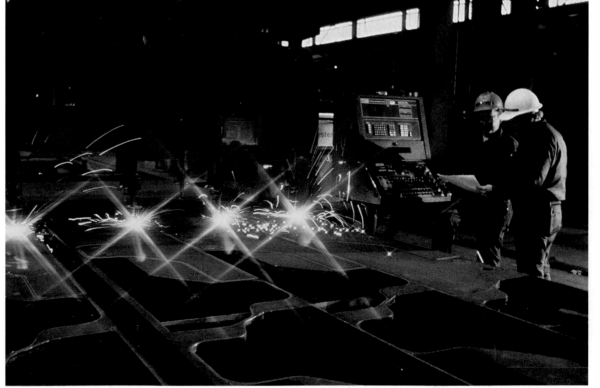

a leading distributor to smaller steel buyers. An independent company under the Inland banner, Ryerson purchased another service company in 1992, J.M. Tull of Atlanta, in order to expand its shipping capabilities to the East Coast. Today this company, Ryerson Tull, Inc., is 87 percent owned by Inland and is in the vanguard of Inland's international expansion. In 1996, Ryerson Tull opened offices in China and India.

Much of the steel Ryerson Tull distributes is from the Harbor Works, as well as at the company's other Indiana operations, I/N Tek and I/N Kote. Both facilities were constructed in the 1990s and are joint ventures with Japan's Nippon Steel. "These new facilities are cutting-edge, fast, beautiful, high quality, and incredibly clean and quiet," says Ann Zastrow, manager of investor and public relations. The difference in the types of steel manufactured by Inland today and those made at the turn of the century is equally significant.

A Century of Progress

One reason for Inland's success was the Block family, which contributed its values to the company's leadership. These principles were codified by Joseph L. Block in 1953, and include promoting from within, rewarding employees amply, promoting good works in the community, and conducting business in an ethical manner.

For example, because the early steelmaking process was dangerous to workers, the company set up an emergency clinic with a full-time doctor in 1908. A safety program, one of the first in the industry, was instituted in 1911. The company sponsored its first annual picnic for all employees in 1910. In 1919, P.D. and L.E. Block instituted the steel industry's first eight-hour day, without cutting wages. Employees were treated with respect, and applicants from 42 countries found their way to the Harbor Works' gates.

According to Zastrow, "It's not surprising to find whole families working here. It's amazing; we have aunts, uncles, cousins, brothers—several generations. The original principles of the Blocks are still in place at Inland.

"Our commitment to diversity sets us apart from many heavy industrial companies," Zastrow adds. "Inland has better representation by women and minorities at higher levels in the organization than in many industrial companies."

The Inland Steel Building at 30 West Monroe Street in Chicago is an architectural landmark that set a new standard for office construction when it opened in 1958. It was the first new office building constructed in downtown Chicago after the Great Depression, and it stands today as a steel and glass affirmation of Inland's commitment to the city. From Chicago to Asia, Inland has become a world family, setting standards for the steel industry and for corporations in every industry.

A worker tests the metallurgy of a heat of steel at Inland Steel's Indiana Harbor Works in East Chicago, which covers more than 1,900 acres and can produce up to 6 million tons of raw steel annually (left).

Automated guided vehicles carry coils of steel between destinations at I/N Tek's plant in New Carlisle, Indiana. I/N Tek operates the world's most advanced cold-rolling mill, producing flat-rolled sheet for the most demanding automotive and appliance customers. I/N Tek and the adjacent I/N Kote galvanizing plant are joint ventures between Inland Steel Co. and Nippon Steel Corp. of Japan (right).

T THE TURN OF THE 20TH CENTURY, THE FIRST SKYSCRAP-
ERS HEFTED INTO THE SKY IN DOWNTOWN CHICAGO, A
LITTLE CITY THAT SOON WOULD GROW LARGE. IT WAS A
FORTUNATE TIME FOR A HARDWORKING YOUNG IMMIGRANT
TO ARRIVE IN SEARCH OF A BETTER LIFE. AS A NEWCOMER

from Lithuania, Michael Miniat felt the energy and optimism of the prairie capital. He told friends he would raise a family and build a business there. Miniat's was a little idea, but it too would grow large.

Today, Ed Miniat, Inc. is the result of his efforts. The Chicago-based meat processing and distribution company has grown into a $150 million business with two facilities, including a 73,000-square-foot, state-of-the-art processing plant built in 1995.

THE MINIAT LEGACY

ichael Miniat started small, worked hard, and kept an eye on the future. He rented a room on Chicago's South Side and eventually married the landlady's daughter. In time, he started the family that has nurtured the business through four generations of growth and evolution.

"He bought a horse and wagon and started delivering meat from the Chicago stockyards to neigh-

borhood mom-and-pop grocery stores," recalls Michael's grandson, Ron Miniat, now chairman of the board of Ed Miniat, Inc.

By the 1920s, Michael's son Ed had started work on the truck alongside his father. "After Michael died, my older brother, Ed Jr., and I also worked on the truck, and then I got a truck of my own," says Ron Miniat.

But the years following World War II saw the emergence of supermarkets, which began to displace the Miniats' mom-and-pop customers. Faced with one of the early challenges of the ever changing food industry, the Miniats had to decide on a direction to refocus their business. The company leased a plant and began buying dressed carcass beef from the stockyards to distribute to supermarkets and other accounts, some of which became national in scope.

The stockyards were a Chicago landmark. In their heyday, workers processed 18 million head of livestock a year. By the early 1970s, however, transportation costs and

other factors would usher in the stockyards' demise. When the stockyards finally shut down, the Miniats had devised a solution.

A NEW DIRECTION

e purchased the South Chicago Packing Company in 1972 for its edible rendering operation," Ron Miniat explains. "Before long, we constructed our shortening operation, and then, around 1979, we started cooking the meat ourselves."

Miniat's cooked meats became fast-selling items, embraced by customers of the national supermarket chains that had become the company's major customers. Led by Michael, the fourth generation in the business, the company began providing delicatessen meats and other cooked meats for an increasingly convenience-oriented public.

"Things really took off," says David, the current company president. But more changes were on the horizon.

Ed Miniat, Inc.'s cooked meat operation is located in this state-of-the-art facility in South Holland.

Michael, who still serves on the company's board of directors, stepped back from the family business and turned to work as a cattle rancher in Colorado. David, meanwhile, built Ed Miniat, Inc. into a frozen food business. In the late 1970s, a large national entrée manufacturer began outsourcing cooked items to the company. "Since then, we've become one of the major suppliers to the frozen food industry," David says.

About this time, the company became heavily involved in providing foodservice companies with prepared products—combining meat, vegetables, and sauce in a convenient, reheatable pouch designed to client specifications by Miniat's modern research and development operation.

Hundreds of new Miniat products, too numerous to list, grew from the company's foodservice segment. "We simply support the customer's needs," says David. "The real challenge is to change with the times."

CHICAGO PRIDE

Through the shifts and curves of the marketplace, Ed Miniat, Inc. has found one area of its business unwavering. The family credits much of the company's strength to a loyal and dedicated workforce, now numbering around 300. "Many of our employees have been with us for 30 or 35 years," says David "Our employees are the reason we've stayed in the Chicago area."

"The employees here sense the commitment to the business that this family has exemplified,"

says Chuck Nalon, Ed Miniat, Inc.'s director of sales and marketing. "I think they feel at home here and cared for."

The company has given back to the community that helped it grow. Heavy involvement with the Juvenile Diabetes Foundation, and a 20-year relationship with Misericordia, a local institution that provides education, training, and housing to handicapped and developmentally disabled children, are points of family pride.

Facing a crossroad every 20 or 30 years, Ed Miniat, Inc. has always adapted. For the Miniat family, the plants and the people who work there ensure a bright future for the company. Still, when the business climate changes—as it invariably does—the company will be ready, just as it has been for nearly a century.

When Michael Miniat started the journey with his horse-drawn cart, the end of the road was nowhere in sight.

Clockwise from top left: Miniat's world-class product research and development lab is staffed with trained, responsive food technology specialists.

Miniat's shortening, oils, and rendering plant is located on West 38th Street.

Hundreds of new prepared products have originated in Miniat's foodservice division, including one that combines meat, vegetables, and sauce in a convenient reheatable pouch.

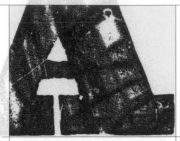

MONG CHICAGO'S MOST PRESTIGIOUS LAW FIRMS, ROSS & HARDIES WAS FOUNDED IN 1902, WHEN AMERICA'S INDUSTRIAL REVOLUTION WAS IN FULL SWING. AT THAT TIME, THE DEVELOPMENT AND DISTRIBUTION OF ENERGY WERE CRITICAL TO THE SUCCESSFUL GROWTH OF THE NATION.

The firm's founding partners recognized this need and focused much of their legal expertise on the consolidation of various regional gas distribution companies into what was to become an industry giant and long-standing client, The Peoples Gas Light & Coke Company.

THE FIRM'S GROWTH AND DEVELOPMENT

s the legal needs of business have expanded throughout the century, Ross & Hardies has continued to respond by adding specific areas of expertise to serve its diversified client base. The firm has added expertise in the laws relating to securities and finance, antitrust, real estate and land use, products liability, labor and employment discrimination, estate planning, telecommunications, tax and employee benefits, government contracts, environmental regulations, health care, intellectual property, customs and trade, and international business transactions. Senior Vice President and General Counsel of Daka International Inc. Charles W. Redepenning Jr. addresses the firm's diversity: "I think Ross & Hardies has a lot of depth. If one attorney lacks expertise, or is not available, they can get someone else."

Today, almost 100 years after its inception, Ross & Hardies is a full-service business law firm. Clients range from large multinationals to privately held businesses and individuals. These clients reflect an impressive panoply of enterprises, from traditional manufacturing to 21st-century computer technologies.

Headquartered in Chicago, on seven floors of the architecturally significant Stone Container Building, Ross & Hardies maintains additional offices in key business, financial, and governmental centers. The firm's practice, however, is not limited by office location. To meet the needs of those they serve, Ross & Hardies attorneys are regularly involved in business transactions, litigation, and counseling around the globe.

A UNIQUE APPROACH TO LEGAL SERVICES

hroughout its history, Ross & Hardies has enjoyed a reputation not only for providing high-quality legal services, but also for training attorneys to be responsive to the particular business needs and objectives of their clients. "I needed someone at two in the morning," says Vice President of

Clockwise from top:

Ross & Hardies is a results-oriented firm that gets deals done on time and with added value.

Attorneys for the firm regularly appear in courtrooms throughout the country.

Ross & Hardies is headquartered in Chicago and has offices in New York City, New Jersey, and Washington, D.C., which employ approximately 425 individuals.

Hinsdale Health Systems Thomas J. Williams. "The firm that came to mind was Ross & Hardies. I knew they could handle it. I was able to get this lawyer out of bed and into the office. I've worked with a dozen significant law firms, and I've never had that kind of responsiveness."

At Ross & Hardies, innovative, creative thinking is highly prized. Close, personal contact is required. President and CEO of ArcVentures, Inc. Marie E. Sinioris says: "They don't look at you as a project, but as a relationship. They bring a lot of knowledge and present it in a very candid, forthright way. They don't mislead you into self-serving alternatives."

In what many consider to be an era of "over lawyering," Ross & Hardies' attorneys are widely regarded as problem solvers whose focus is on achieving practical, effective results—regardless of the forum. "Ross & Hardies is good at resolving problems and finding solutions," says President of Medical Specialists, Inc. Dr. Alexander A. Stemer.

DEDICATION TO THE PROFESSION AND COMMUNITY

Ross & Hardies' attorneys are also dedicated to serving and improving the legal profession. Throughout its distinguished history, members of the firm have served in government posts as well as on state and federal court committees. They have provided

leadership in local, national, and international bar associations.

In addition, Ross & Hardies' attorneys have routinely donated their time and expertise to a myriad of professional organizations. Not only do members of the firm teach law at institutes of higher education, but they also lecture to business groups and write articles for a variety of publications.

The culture at Ross & Hardies places great emphasis on collegiality. Staff and professionals are all considered critical parts of the same team. To foster this special sense of camaraderie, the firm regularly schedules family picnics, holiday parties, quarterly socials, and impromptu events to which all are invited.

In the same way, professionals and staff work closely together on charitable projects and in community organizations. In this regard, the firm prides itself on being in the forefront of leadership in the legal community, as well as on being a part of the social and cultural fabric of the city.

One example of this leadership is the firm's sponsorship of the Bamileke League, a girls' softball team whose members come from the Cabrini-Green housing project. Ross & Hardies' attorneys and staff coach the team and provide members with academic tutoring assistance. The firm provides the girls with equipment, uniforms, and insurance.

The Chicago Challenge is another unique project in which

Ross & Hardies is involved. The Challenge identifies academically talented inner-city youngsters and sends them to private schools where they can develop their skills. The program works with children of all ages—from preschool through high school. Donations from area businesses pay for everything from tuition to field trips. Ross & Hardies' members and staff contribute legal and administrative work pro bono.

A LOOK FORWARD

Ross & Hardies is a firm that believes in investing in the future—whether by educating promising Chicago children or by expanding the reach of its practice to meet its clients' growing needs. It is a firm whose members are proud of their distinguished past and look forward to the challenges and opportunities that await them in the new century.

Clockwise from top left:
Ross & Hardies' attorneys use a teamwork approach in representing clients around the world.

The firm is committed to providing cost-effective legal services through the use of modern technology and training.

A comprehensive collection of 60,000 volumes, including many rare tomes; CD-ROMs; on-line services; and the Internet provide clients with up-to-date information.

CONSIDER THE SIMPLE ENVELOPE. IN TODAY'S HIGHLY COMPETITIVE DIRECT-MAIL ENVIRONMENT, IT'S NOT SO SIMPLE ANYMORE. CUSTOMERS MAY REQUIRE A UNIQUE TRANSPARENT WINDOW, A SPECIAL PAPER OR PERFORATION, A SPECIAL KIND OF GUMMING, A CUSTOM TINT, OR ANY ONE OF A COUNTLESS

number of shapes, sizes, paper grades, and styles.

Whatever the request, Transo Envelope Company can fill it. The Chicago-based company has been turning envelope problems into selling solutions for more than 90 years, and it is now one of the largest full-service envelope manufacturers in the Midwest, producing millions of envelopes daily. Seventy percent of that volume is focused on direct-mail products.

"Chicago has the largest concentration of companies in the direct-mail industry in the United States," says President and Chief Executive Officer Bob Blanke. "Transo is uniquely positioned to service this market. It is large enough to match the economies of scale of much larger companies, yet small enough to be much more responsive than its large, public, multiplant competitors in this demanding market."

Transo Envelope Company has invested heavily in state-of-the-art computerized prepress equipment, offering customers quick processing and customized graphics.

FLEXIBILITY IS THE KEY

 lexibility and responsiveness are key to the company's success," Blanke says. "Due to the emphasis on direct mail, Transo recognizes the time constraints that accompany this product segment. The company is committed to a scheduling system that allows for production flexibility, priority treatment of orders, and quick turnaround time."

A new estimating system, state-of-the-art prepress capability, and an efficient preventive maintenance program also contribute to an on-time delivery record unmatched in the envelope industry. In the past three years, Transo has not had one major customer terminate service for reasons related to quality or service.

Innovation is another key at Transo, which operates out of a 100,000-square-foot facility. The transparent envelope windows featured on bills and direct mailings were invented by Transo in 1904. BiPak envelopes—used by the financial industry to mail annual reports and proxy statements in the same package—were developed by Transo in the 1950s.

Transo's commitment to quick service in the Chicago area is enhanced by its ability to control the shipping and delivery process.

Transo has been an innovator in other areas, as well. The company was among the first in the industry to use spectrophotometers for color matching. Further contributing to Transo's success are environmentally friendly processes and a constant striving for new product development and graphic innovation.

The bottom line at Transo is simple, says Mike Fox, vice president of sales: "No matter what type of envelope you need, we're ready to provide it." To back up that promise, Transo uses the most advanced technology in the industry, investing more than $10 million into its machinery, including a variety of wet and dry offset presses, and special American- and German-made folding equipment that operates 24 hours a day.

Transo clients get another promise, too. It's called QIP: Quality Improvement Process, and it's a pledge by all employees to provide quality, efficiency, and customer satisfaction.

In this process, teams of hourly and salaried personnel are set up to address major tasks or problem areas. "This has proven to be a very workable system for continuous improvement, and Transo and its customers have benefited greatly from it," says Blanke.

SAFETY LEADER

One success story from the nine-year-old QIP is the company safety program. Since 1990, Transo has been awarded Industry Safety Leader by the Envelope Manufacturer's Association every year. "Only one other envelope manufacturing company in the United States can claim this record," says Blanke.

The company has 150 full-time employees, 105 being union personnel. National sales offices are located in the New York and Los Angeles metro areas. And Transo has developed partnership relationships with many of its suppliers, particularly with several Chicago-area lithographic printers. All members of the sales and management team hold Postal Partner Certificates, indicating certified knowledge of the rules governing mailing specifications dictated by the U.S. Postal Service.

Transo was owned by the Arvey Corporation, which was operated by the Regenstein family, until 1987, when it was purchased by International Paper Company. Since 1994, Transo has been privately owned.

Transo will continue to modernize its plant and equipment, focusing primarily on new equipment utilizing digital programmable technology in the production of envelopes. The company is also hoping to grow domestically through strategic acquisitions within its field.

"Despite the continuing technological attacks on our mature product line, Transo is proud of its ability to change with customers' demands and prosper," Blanke concludes. "Transo's culture is one in which we strive to anticipate the effect of technological changes and seek out those customers who appear well positioned to respond and grow as a result."

Transo has the latest technology in both die-cut and web-fed envelope folding equipment.

The company offers a wide range of products for the direct-mail, financial services, and annual report markets.

CHERNIN'S SHOES, INC.

OSE AND HARRIS CHERNIN WERE STRUGGLING IMMIGRANTS FROM RUSSIA, STREET PEDDLERS OF OLD SHOES WHO WERE JUST TRYING TO MAKE A LIVING, WHEN THEY OPENED THEIR FIRST SHOE STORE AT 606 ROOSEVELT ROAD IN 1907. THE STORE STARTED AS A WHOLESALER OF MEN'S WORN AND defective shoes from the factory, supplied primarily by the Florsheim Corporation.

Over the years, Chernin's has grown to become a retailer of new shoes for men, women, and children. Twice—in 1994 and 1996—*Footwear News* named Chernin's Independent Shoe Retailer of the Year in America. Today, there are 15 Chernin's shoe stores in the Chicago area, including six outlets. In addition, the company, which currently has 900 employees, has plans to expand out of state.

A CHICAGO LANDMARK

he flagship Chernin's store on Roosevelt Road is a landmark. It still draws faithful customers—Chicago-area residents, as well as tens of thousands of visitors to the city every year. It counts among its clients four generations of customers. Celebrities who have shopped at Chernin's include Bob Hope, Bette Midler, Jack Nicholson, Mike Ditka, Muhammad Ali, John Malkovich, Walter Payton, Tony Bennett, and Mike Tyson.

The Roosevelt Road location lays claim to being the highest-grossing shoe store per square foot in the United States and boasts the largest selection—approximately 100,000 pairs of shoes—of any independent shoe store in Chicago. Like the other Chernin's locations, the flagship store, which employs 150, also carries handbags, hosiery, men's belts, socks, and shoe care products.

A $1 million renovation completed in fall 1996 features the Chicago Historical Wall depicting Chicago fashion and footwear in the last 90 years, and the Sports Wall of Fame, which displays shoes collected and autographed by the likes of Michael Jordan and Shaquille O'Neal. The store also is home to one of the few waterfall displays in the nation built by Timberland to showcase its shoes in retail stores.

How does Chernin's, a privately held business, stand its ground against the big, national discount chains? Selection, service, and value, according to Chairman and CEO Steve Larrick.

"We try to be on the cutting edge of fashion. Our inventory is this season's most popular merchandise," Larrick says. "We pride ourselves on having the largest selection of any store in America. We have a huge range of sizes for men, women, and children in dress, casual, and athletic footwear. Our competitive prices, legendary service, and numerous special events generate incredible customer loyalty."

SERVICE AND TRAINING

hernin's also operates a thriving mail-order business, attracting customers throughout the United States and abroad by delivering the best possible service. Visitors who shop the store on trips to Chicago are often so impressed by the service and selection that they become loyal mail-order customers.

The Chernin's store in Lincoln Park—one of 15 in the Chicago area—opened in 1991.

"Our sales force is the best trained in the shoe industry and in high demand," Larrick says. "People try to steal them all the time. They're our greatest asset besides our shoes. Some of our staff have been here for 25 years or more. It's normal for someone to have 10 to 15 years of service at Chernin's, which far exceeds retail industry norms."

Chernin's salesclerks undergo extensive training at the company's University of Shoeology, where classes are held on the proper fitting of shoes, shoe comfort, style, and shoe technology, as well as customer service skills. Salespeople take continuing education courses, and attend weekly meetings and vendor-conducted seminars.

Harris and Rose Chernin no doubt would be pleased and surprised at the technological turn Chernin's has taken to keep pace with the marketplace. Through a sophisticated inventory management system, stock is automatically replenished. A relational database provides the company with considerable segmentation data for targeted marketing programs. Through targeted advertising, families with young children are mailed a flyer announcing a sale on children's shoes, while men with a predilection for $250 dress shoes receive an announcement of a sale or special event relevant to their tastes.

All customers are invited to be members of Club Chernin's, the company's frequent shopper reward program. The club helps build loyalty, Larrick says, noting that the company's best customers are dual-earner families with children and household incomes of $50,000 and greater.

Chernin's continues to make changes to enhance corporate efficiency and increase market share. That means being able to claim fifth-generation customers—customers who think Chernin's when they think shoes.

Harris Chernin, a Russian immigrant (kneeling), opened his first shoe store at 606 West Roosevelt as a wholesaler of men's worn and defective shoes from the factory. The shop is a Chicago landmark today.

In the fall of 1996, the original Chernin's store underwent a $1 million renovation. This photograph, taken during a reception to honor vendors and introduce them to the newly remodeled store, depicts the old and new neon signs as they appear at night on the building's facade.

COMMUNITY ACTIVITIES

Chernin's Shoes is connected to its birthplace in ways other than commerce: The company is a key contributor to various Chicago-area charities, particularly those involving children. Chernin's shoe stores throughout the area sponsor Little League, soccer, and other sports teams.

The company's biggest community project so far has been its financial contribution toward the construction of the New Duncan YMCA Chernin's Shoes Center for the Arts, to be housed in the Duncan YMCA. This West Side facility, which was completed in fall 1997, includes a 206-seat theater with a production shop, recording studio, video lab, computer lab, workshops, classrooms, and dance studio.

Although Chernin's Shoes has plans to expand outside the Midwest, its commitment to the community makes clear the company's firm grounding in its Chicago roots.

OUR YEARS BEFORE CARL SANDBURG CALLED HIS TOWN "THE CITY OF BIG SHOULDERS," 32 STUDENTS SEEKING HIGHER EDUCATION BEGAN THEIR STUDIES AT CHICAGO'S FIRST CITY COLLEGE. BY THE TIME SANDBURG HAD PENNED THE FAMOUS LINE IN HIS POEM "CHICAGO," TEACHERS AT THE SCHOOL

were already accustomed to helping the growing ranks of their mostly working-class students develop something else: broad minds.

Each year, the City Colleges of Chicago (CCC), a system of seven dynamic institutions of higher learning, serves some 200,000 students from all walks of life. More than 50,000 are enrolled in college credit courses, while others pursue continuing education, English as a second language, or precollegiate studies. Most offerings are on the college campuses, but many people take courses broadcast over

WYCC-TV, Channel 20, the system's Public Broadcasting station, or broadcast via satellite to military bases as far away as Europe and the Middle East under government contracts.

Stories of successful City Colleges alumni are as varied as the people of Chicago. The city's first African-American mayor, Harold Washington, was an alumnus, while Arthur Goldberg graduated from the City Colleges on his way to becoming a justice of the Supreme Court. Both actor Dennis Franz, who plays a detective on the televi-

sion series, *NYPD Blue*, and the late, great newspaper columnist Mike Royko attended City Colleges. There are thousands of less prominent graduates, of course: women and men, sometimes of modest backgrounds, who have become doctors, Internet designers, nurses, electricians, shop owners, and chefs.

The City Colleges are open admission institutions, welcoming all adults seeking to improve their knowledge and skills. Comprehensive testing ensures that students are placed in courses appropriate to their current levels of reading, writing, and mathematics.

The colleges' mission statement speaks to its purpose: "The City Colleges of Chicago, an institution of higher education, will provide opportunities for all students to enhance their knowledge and skills by offering superior, affordable, comprehensive educational programs and services."

Harold Washington College, located in Chicago's Loop district, offers a myriad of business-related courses. Pictured here are students in a Meeting/ Convention Planning class (top).

Opened in 1993, this new building at Wright College North campus features one of City Colleges of Chicago's most recently completed facilities (bottom).

FOR THE PEOPLE

 hicago's first City College, now named Malcolm X College, was established on the Near West Side to serve a population of largely first-generation European immigrants. The school flourished until the Great Depression, when a budget crisis temporarily forced its closure in 1933.

The subsequent efforts of students, faculty members, labor leaders, and Progressives, such as the renowned lawyer Clarence Darrow and Hull House founder Jane Addams, rallied city leaders to reopen the school the next year. While arguing why the college "had to endure," Darrow articulated the essential philosophy of all the City Colleges. They are, he said, "for the people."

Each of the system's seven colleges started small, usually with a handful of students gathered into high school classrooms after

Truman College, on the Far North Side, houses the award-winning theater Pegasus Players.

sunset. Demand for classes, however, became insistent. The growth of Richard J. Daley College on Chicago's Southwest Side is just one example. Founded in 1960, the college held its first classes at Bogan High School, enrolling about 1,000 students at the high school. As enrollment grew, the college spread east along 79th Street. Next, the college was housed in a group of buildings on 14 acres of a former prairie. Finally, in 1981, a $26 million building was dedicated, and today Daley College serves a student body of 20,000.

In the mid-1990s, the City Colleges system completed its building program with the construction of Wright College North, the Humboldt Park Vocational Education Center, and the West Side Technical Institute. Each college now has its own campus, and six of the seven colleges feature satellite learning or technical centers. A $44 million capital renovation campaign approved by the City Colleges board in 1997 is spreading new technology to all locations, providing new laboratories, automated libraries, and Internet access for students and faculty.

BEYOND THE CLASSROOM

The advent of a technologically advanced school system has helped the City Colleges of Chicago reach out to legions of new students.

WYCC-TV is the City Colleges' award-winning educational television station, which reaches more than 750,000 households weekly. The station's high viewership increases steadily and places the City Colleges at the forefront of an effective program known as direct instruction. Broadcasting out of Daley College, the station brings quality educational programming to the entire Chicago region.

About 65 percent of the on-air programming consists of telecourses that enable some 8,000 students to earn college credits at home each year. WYCC also airs quality entertainment from the Public Broadcasting Service, and locally produced series and specials. Among the station's highly acclaimed programs are *Educate!*, which recently won a Chicago Bar Association award for a program on race relations, and *Absolute Artistry*. In 1997, the station won its first Emmy award for a coproduced special titled *Sing n' Sign with Gaia*.

The City Colleges system has extended its reach even beyond the signal range of WYCC by becoming a major source of interactive college classes for American military personnel around the world. Standing before a camera in any one of 14 interactive studios in Chicago, a City Colleges teacher communicates live with soldiers stationed as far away as the Sinai Desert, or even to war zones such

West Side Technical Institute, the newest CCC facility and a satellite of Daley College, was erected in 1996 to serve as a vocational center for the West Side and Southwest Side.

as Bosnia. Closer to home, students at one City College now may also choose to attend live video lectures conducted at sister campuses elsewhere in the city, eliminating the need to travel across town for class.

The City Colleges' Web site (http://www.ccc.edu) went on-line in 1996, and attracts 30,000 to 40,000 responses each week. Students working on-line—in facilities such as the gleaming new computer rotunda at Wright College North—may now access computerized tutoring systems or use an on-line library, which provides virtually instant interaction with dozens of reference sources.

Educational results at the City Colleges of Chicago have improved through a recent standardization of admissions and academic requirements at all seven colleges. As a component of the schools' open admissions policy, entering students may now also use a free, precredit program tailored for students who need extra academic help before they can qualify for associate degree studies.

But it's not all work at the City Colleges of Chicago. A theater-in-residence program sponsors eagerly awaited productions with African-American themes at Malcolm X College; Wright College hosts Kids Company performances for school groups; and the celebrated Pegasus Players, whose home is at Truman College, sponsor an annual competition for high school playwrights, holding performances of the winning plays.

ACCESSIBLE AND UNIQUE

he seven City Colleges of Chicago are conveniently located throughout the metropolitan area, with each reflecting the character and cultural diversity of its neighborhood. The schools are funded through the local college district, through tuition, and with federal and state monies.

The basics at all seven schools include a high-quality associate degree program, which prepares students for transfer to four-year institutions; occupational programs; developmental and remedial programs to prepare students

for college-level work; and adult basic education programs that cover literacy, GED preparation, and English as a second language. Yet each college also offers its own unique and distinctive programs, which together greatly expand the system's overall educational breadth.

Daley College, located on the Southwest Side, offers a nationally recognized associate degree program in manufacturing technology, coordinated with the Illinois Institute of Technology. It also provides accelerated weekend courses in math, the sciences, and English. Daley's satellite, the West Side Technical Institute, was completed in 1996, and is a dynamic vocational job training facility that has become a keystone in the redevelopment of Chicago's southwest and western corridors.

Kennedy-King College, on the South Side, operates a nationally renowned graphic communications program; a unique dental hygiene program in partnership with the University of Illinois at Chicago College of Dentistry; an accredited registered nursing program; and a nationally praised culinary arts course at the Washburne Trade School. The culinary arts program has an 80-year tradition in Chicago that encourages a hands-on instructional approach with extensive laboratory training. The teaching style

pays off. The *Chicago Sun-Times* recently said typical graduates choose from an average of 10 job offers.

Malcolm X College leads the Chicago region in health care technology training, with state-of-the-art laboratories for nursing, radiography, medical laboratory technology, pharmacy technology, respiratory therapy, and mortuary science. The two year Physician's Assistant Program is unique in the region. Some 98 percent of the college's health graduates find immediate employment, often prior to graduation.

Olive-Harvey College, on Chicago's Southeast Side, provides training in pre-engineering and health certificate programs in phlebotomy, pharmacy technology, and physical therapy. The college's Regional Small Business Development Center on East 111th Street aids small-business people by providing basic business counseling services, business analysis, and workforce training programs.

In the melting pot that is the North Side's Uptown neighborhood, Harry S Truman College offers nationally accredited programs in business, nursing, automotive technology, and health information technology. A full schedule of weekend classes is also offered at Truman, which serves students from a veritable United

Horticulture students at West Side Tech learn about floriculture, plant landscaping, and grounds maintenance in their own greenhouse.

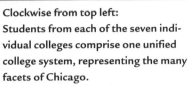

Nations of 110 countries, speaking more than 50 languages.

Harold Washington College, in Chicago's central Loop district, operates international associate degree programs for 9,500 students on military bases around the world in conjunction with three colleges in England. Other programs unique to the school include actuarial science, hotel/motel management, meeting and convention planning, and courses in travel and tourism.

Wilbur Wright College, on the Northwest Side, offers customized, short-term, intensive training courses at the request of Chicago-area businesses and industry, as well as leading radiography, business, bank training, and environmental studies programs. Wright's new campus, with a half-million square feet of space, was completed in 1993. The flagship building is a gleaming, 85-foot pyramid, which houses a 516-terminal computer center, a library, and faculty offices. Six foreign language sequences and a premier counseling center boast articulation agreements with leading four-year institutions in the Chicago area and distinguish Wright's place in regional education.

Also affiliated with the school is Wright's satellite learning facility, the Humboldt Park Vocational Education Center, completed in 1994. Career education programs offered at this site have provided training to more than 12,000 students seeking better jobs.

COMMUNITY OUTREACH

The City Colleges of Chicago have no ivory towers. Instead, the system offers many practical ways to strengthen the urban community, one life at a time.

The Opportunities Program, for example, helps single parents move off welfare by partnering with companies that offer meaningful jobs. Partnerships with the Chicago Public Schools pave the way into college-level course work from inner-city schools. Still other programs, such as the Local Area Network Program at Malcolm X College, finish the process by linking graduates to jobs within their specialties.

The City Colleges system has also employed its Executive Development Program to directly improve the quality of city management in Chicago. Working with City Hall, mid-level managers in local government are trained in teamwork, time management, cooperative problem solving, and other management skills.

The leadership of City Colleges knows that constant economic and workplace change means that the City Colleges cannot stand on past accomplishments. A newly established board for the City Colleges of Chicago Foundation is working to build outside financial support for the district's quality initiatives. The new district strategic plan, developed following focus groups, community meetings, and interviews with civic, educational, cultural, and governmental leaders, is reestablishing district priorities for 1998 through 2003.

The City Colleges of Chicago system takes pride in providing education to a diverse population. Seventy-five percent of its students are minorities, and 73 percent attend school on a part-time basis—often hitting the books between work, caring for children, or managing a household. For more than four generations, the City Colleges of Chicago have been a port of entry to the working world for these busy students, fulfilling the role assigned so long ago by Clarence Darrow as "the people's college."

Clockwise from top left:
Students from each of the seven individual colleges comprise one unified college system, representing the many facets of Chicago.

Culinary students at Washburne Trade School, a Kennedy-King College satellite, learn hands-on in this lab for pastry, cakes, and desserts.

TV and film actor Dennis Franz, a Wright College alumnus, is one of many celebrities who attended the City Colleges

▲ MICHAEL YARISH

THE SPACIOUS, BEAUTIFULLY KEPT GROUNDS—SOME 45 ACRES OF THEM—ARE THE FIRST HINT THAT S&C ELECTRIC COMPANY IS DIFFERENT. ALL ALONG ITS BORDERS, THIS EXPANSIVE CITY CORNER IS LANDSCAPED AS METICULOUSLY AS ANY SUBURBAN ENCLAVE. AT HOLIDAY TIME, ITS TREES

are adorned with thousands of colorful lights; all summer long, its flowers bloom brightly as its lawns are watered, trimmed, and nurtured.

Indoors, too, the site looks unlike what one might expect of a manufacturing plant. S&C makes high-voltage switching and protection products, and offers engineering, laboratory, and field services. Yet a walk through the well-tended buildings evokes the squeaky-clean air of a high-tech business. In one area, machinists at computerized tools produce gleaming parts for fuses and switches; in another, workers install components in forest-green, metal enclosures that channel electricity into apartment complexes and business parks. Farther on, blue-smocked workers assemble S&C's own circuit boards.

S&C's industrial complex was assembled over a 50-year period in the North Side neighborhood of Rogers Park. The corporate offices and other buildings feature abundant landscaping and matching color schemes.

FROM EDISON TO INDEPENDENCE

To see how S&C grew from its origins to today's facility on the far North Side, it's necessary to go back to Thomas Alva Edison himself and the earliest days of providing electric power to America's cities. In Chicago, the electric company was Commonwealth Edison, and it was run by Samuel Insull.

"Samuel Insull was secretary to Edison for years," explains John R. Conrad, S&C's 81-year-old chairman. "When he went into business supplying electricity, his vision was that the power supply should be generated centrally and distributed to the point of use. This was copied by other companies, and his engineers became very much in demand."

Conrad continues, "One of those engineers was my father, Nicholas J. Conrad. Insull at that time encouraged his employees to patent their own inventions and reap the profits from them. My father and a colleague invented the first high-voltage fuse that actually worked, back in 1911. By the 1920s, its use was firmly entrenched in the United States, the United Kingdom, Germany, and Japan."

The idea behind that first fuse and subsequent S&C products, was simple enough, Conrad says. "When you want to stop the flow of power, you have to create a gap in its path," he explains. "When you pull a light switch at home, the air gap stops the conductivity

S&C Chairman John Conrad (left) and President and Chief Executive Officer John Estey have carefully nurtured a company culture that includes strong employee benefits and top-quality workmanship.

and power stops flowing. This is fine at low voltage, but it isn't enough at high voltage because the electricity will jump across the gap like a lightning bolt."

S&C's Liquid Power Fuse quenched that arc in a bath of nonconducting fluid. "My father needed a glass tube that could go from hot to cold without shattering," Conrad says. "He got in touch with the Corning Glass Company to see if it had something that was not vulnerable to thermal shock. Well, Corning's work for us led to the first Pyrex."

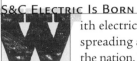

S&C Electric Is Born

With electric use spreading across the nation, Nicholas Conrad and silent partner Edmund O. Schweitzer soon outgrew their "factory"—three rented rooms— and moved to a small building in what was then a bedroom community, Ravenswood, and is today a gentrifying residential neighborhood. "Schweitzer kept his day job at Commonwealth Edison, but my father left the utility, which made Insull very angry," Conrad says with a smile. "He didn't mind his people collecting for their inventions, but he did mind their leaving."

While S&C's engineers have brought out many other new products, the S&C Liquid Power Fuse survived for 87 years. The last one was made in 1997, having been superseded by another fuse invention.

Though the company was successful, Nicholas Conrad's poor health, combined with the chronic differences he and Schweitzer experienced, led to the sale of the company in 1930 to a Milwaukee-based manufacturer, Cutler-Hammer. At the same time, young John Conrad was attending college and starting work in the dynamic new airline industry, in which he stayed busy through World War II.

The Conrad family reacquired S&C in 1945, just in time to serve a pent-up postwar demand for electricity. "Many of the new technologies were electricity driven, so we had plenty of opportunity," Conrad recalls. "We tried to pick up more capacity in our old neighborhood of Ravenswood, but we couldn't find it there."

At that time, many companies were leaving the city for suburban industrial parks, "but we were very aware that we'd lose our experienced

Clockwise from top:
The company's innovative circuit-switcher is used by utilities at electrical substations like this one at Hoover Dam on the Colorado River.

S&C's fully integrated factory fabricates most parts on-site to create products that are often unique in the industry.

Craftsmanship has always been the key to S&C product quality. Today, extensive training programs maintain top skills among S&C employees.

workforce if we moved," Conrad continues. "Our male workforce was mostly European craftsmen, usually living in Ravenswood. The white-collar staffing, largely made up of divorced mothers raising children, also lived nearby. None of these people would want to go to the suburbs."

S&C's solution was an overgrown victory garden: "Ten acres all the way up on Ridge Boulevard in Rogers Park," Conrad says. "It was way more land than we needed, and I felt we could only afford to buy six acres. Dad thought I was wrong, and he personally bought the other four. Several years later, I ended up buying the land from him. He paid 55 cents a square foot, but he sold it to me for $2 a square foot."

In the 1950s and 60s, as S&C created a stream of new products to switch and protect high-voltage systems, the company was growing so fast that John Conrad once again faced the question of expansion. Again he chose the city, this time taking advantage of the plant's location along train tracks that once brought lumber, coal, and dairy products to small companies nearby. One by one, S&C bought and demolished old docks and buildings, sometimes buying a parcel simply to rid the area of old, eyesore buildings, such as an abandoned dry-cleaning plant that had been crumbling for years. When new buildings went up, they were of cream-colored brick and "S&C green" siding. Slowly, a unified industrial complex emerged behind trees and flowers along Ridge Boulevard.

Today's Company

Inside the plant, a gleaming mosaic version of S&C's original trademark greets visitors to the corporate offices. "That was on the outside of our original building," Conrad says. Beyond lies one of the company's Product Demonstration Centers, a walk-in catalog of S&C products where enormous fuses, switches, and new electronic equipment are on display for prospective customers who want a demonstration.

Among these products is one created to interrupt the flow of power at utility substations. "We invented it and called it a circuit-switcher, because it works differently than a circuit breaker," Conrad says. "We decided *not* to register the name, because we wanted it to become the generic term for this device." The strategy worked. Since its 1959 debut, the S&C circuit-switcher has carved a new niche in the industry—and has been a solid S&C performer.

"The innards of our products are largely made here," Conrad says. "Moreover, with respect to these huge fuses—we're the only company in the world that manufactures them. And as our alternative to porcelain insulators, we produce a polymer insulator, Cypoxy, on site in our newest building."

Neither automation nor dissatisfaction has reduced S&C's workforce: Nearly half of the company's 1,500-plus employees have been there for more than a decade. The Quarter Century Club has more than 400 members, each with 25 years or more of service to S&C. And second-generation employees are increasingly common.

The company makes such loyalty worthwhile. Pay scales exceed industry averages, employee outings and sports leagues are a tradition, and the entire plant

Engineering offices and chemical and analytical laboratories are part of the Rogers Park complex. Inside the building above is a scanning electron microscope and other sophisticated equipment.

shuts down every year for a paid week off between Christmas and New Year's. "It makes more sense than trying to operate with so many people on vacation," says Conrad. "And it gives people time to be with their families."

COMMUNITY MINDED

S&C's benevolence extends to the larger community through company support for local cultural and educational efforts. "We've always made a policy of supporting worthy causes," Conrad says, noting contributions not only to local museums and zoos, but also to downtown theater and music venues and to nearby public schools.

In terms of growth, the company's sights are fixed firmly on the future. Conrad over the last few years has passed day-to-day responsibilities to S&C President and CEO John Estey, who in turn has assembled a team of experienced executives to move the company forward. International sales are a major focus, as are new products and partnerships with other suppliers in the fast-changing electrical equipment industry. Thanks to a well-conceived plan to maintain the company's core philosophies, S&C will remain privately held by Conrad's three daughters and S&C's top leaders.

"There's no question we have to go global," Conrad says. Back in 1953, S&C established a Canadian subsidiary near Toronto, but today "global" means more than just going next door. "In the 1970s, it was the Arab countries that were developing at a rapid pace; today it is countries like Brazil," Conrad says. "We're looking at opportunities all over the world."

S&C recently opened two new sales area support offices in the Philippines and Australia, while continuing major investments at the Chicago headquarters. Today, S&C Electric is the product of two generations' devotion to hard work and high standards, and the city it calls home. It's a purely Chicago story that anyone, anywhere, can admire.

Clockwise from top left: Modern machine tools and new manufacturing techniques help S&C maintain competitiveness in a fast-changing industry.

Utilities and large power users rely on the S&C metal-enclosed switchgear to provide high-voltage protection and switching. This 12-bay lineup serves the Excalibur Hotel in Las Vegas.

S&C uses computer-aided design to speed the design process for its custom products, then downloads manufacturing information to computer-controlled machine tools.

Testing facilities include this high-voltage laboratory, where engineers and technicians simulate conditions such as lightning strikes.

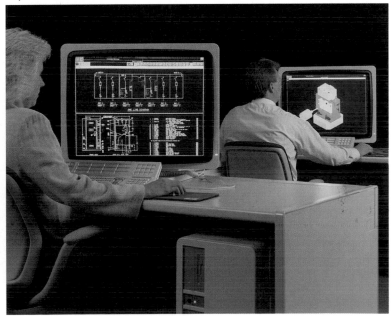

HAT DO A NUCLEAR POWER PLANT IN KOREA, THE PATRIOT MISSILE PROJECT IN THE MIDDLE EAST, A PETROCHEMICAL PLANT IN NEW ZEALAND, THE DISNEY EMPIRE, SHEDD AQUARIUM, UNITED CENTER, AND JUST ABOUT EVERY MAJOR DOWNTOWN CHICAGO

skyscraper have in common? All have been supplied steel products by the Chicago Tube & Iron Company (CT&I). For sport, you can throw NBA backboards, hockey goals, and football goalposts into that mix, too.

CT&I was founded in 1914 in Chicago's Back of the Yards, where it purchased and then distributed tubing and steel products by horse and wagon. Today, while logging $150 million in annual national and international sales, the closely held corporation is engaged in the sale, distribution, and fabrication of mechanical tubing, pipe, valves, fittings, stainless, aluminum, boiler tubing, and cold finished bar. The company also provides cutting,

threading, grooving, swaging, cold and hot bending, and code welding, as well as value-added services such as inventory management.

CT&I still operates in the Back of the Yards, where its 12 warehouses cover three city blocks. But that's not the extent of it. CT&I now consists of seven subsidiaries, each with its own office and warehouse facilities, located throughout the Midwest, with more than a million square feet of warehousing, processing, and storage areas.

And there's more to come, promises President and Chief Operating Officer Donald McNeeley. CT&I has embarked on what it calls Project 2000, a plan to expand into a number of new locations. By the end of 1998, the company expects to open two new divisions, one in Des Moines, Iowa, and one in Louisville, Kentucky. Further, it anticipates completing the market research for a possible site in Toledo. In addition to its two divisions in Chicago, CT&I has locations in St. Paul and Duluth, Minnesota; Milwaukee, Wisconsin; Milan, Illinois; and Indianapolis, Indiana. The two newest facilities are expected to generate another $20 million to $30 million in annual sales.

More important, the company expects to continue fundamentally repositioning itself in the market. "Historically, our company has sold steel," explains McNeeley. "Today, we are processing 30 percent of what we sell, up from 10 to 12 percent a decade ago. Our expectation for the future is that, into the next millennium, we will be processing 60 to 70 percent of what we sell."

PROFIT IS THE NAME OF THE GAME

cNeeley is just as clear about CT&I's corporate philosophy. "We are devout capitalists," he says. "Our objective is profit—the pure, unadulterated pursuit of ethical profit.

"In business, profit is the ball. In baseball, if you take your eye off the ball you're going to strike out. It's the same in business. The moment management tries to take its eye off the ball, when they dilute their focus on profit, they put the company at risk and mitigate their obligation to shareholders. We're in business to make money, and we have no compunction about that."

Clockwise from top:
CT&I President Donald R. McNeeley (left) and Chairman Robert B. Haigh are proud of the company's profitable success as it approaches the 21st century.

One of CT&I's 425 dedicated employees completes a precision TIG welding procedure.

Today, the Corporate/Chicago division still operates in the Back of the Yards, where its 12 warehouses now cover three city blocks.

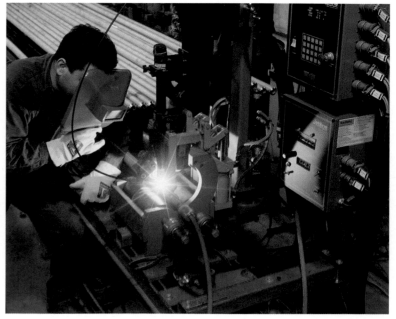

And profit it has. Through two world wars, the Great Depression, and 14 recessions, CT&I has posted profits every year.

McNeeley is quick to credit an ongoing conservative fiscal policy begun in the company's early years by Herbert Haigh, then president and principal of the company. According to Robert Haigh, current chairman, chief executive officer, and grandson of the founder, "The concept is simple: Limit the amount of money you borrow, and never expand, increase inventory, or purchase unless the project can be fully funded by internal monies." Consequently, the company has avoided the mass layoffs that have plagued so many others.

CT&I has been good to employees in other ways, too. In 1942, it instituted a then-rare profit-sharing program. In addition, the company now offers a 401(k) program with a 20 percent employer match. Employees are encouraged to continue their education and seek college degrees through a 100 percent tuition reimbursement program. Education is so important at CT&I that it has acquired facilities and is developing the cirriculum for its own internal learning center. The company has a long history of promoting from within, including the placement of women in sales, management, and the boardroom. Corporate charitable donations and performance bonuses are also a part of the profit picture.

In turn, the company's progressive attitude toward its workforce, currently numbering 425, has reaped the highly prized, intangible reward of employee loyalty. Second- and third-generation workers are commonplace. The average tenure is 12.5 years, impressive by industry standards. Together with their dependents, 2,000 individuals rely directly upon CT&I. "In this day and age, when employee loyalty has become passé, we have worked hard to preserve loyalty," says McNeeley, who holds a doctorate in economics and is an adjunct professor in the Department of Management at DePaul University where he teaches in the MBA program.

Diversification Is Key

hen Herbert Haigh died in 1963, he was succeeded by his son, John, who recognized the importance of diversifying product lines and expanding operations. Throughout his 25-year term at the helm, a series of geographic and product expansions occurred.

John Haigh retired in 1981 and was succeeded by his son, Robert. Robert Haigh and McNeeley—his partner of 25 years—integrated a strategic financial orientation. They furthered the ethics and integrity of their predecessors, forged domestic and international alliances, and implemented financial expertise and accountability throughout the organization. In the spirit of portfolio theory, related products and services were incorporated into the company's already vast offerings. During the 1990s, every subsidiary experienced a facility expansion as well as significant equipment and capability upgrades. "With a visionary board of directors and supportive shareholders, we are able to reinvest a significant percentage of our earnings into our future," offers McNeeley.

"We started laying the groundwork in 1990 for Project 2000," says McNeeley, again stressing the company's profit motive. "In the future, our dynamic organization will make the successful transition from selling steel to selling parts that happen to be made from steel. I want to sell our customers finished or semifinished parts, not the raw steel."

As Project 2000 shifts into high gear, CT&I is well positioned for future success. Young by upper management standards, McNeeley and Haigh have many years ahead. They are seasoned leaders, having assumed control of CT&I in 1981. And they are quick to credit a series of mentors and a competent board of directors for their success. With its solid history, its strong corporate goals, its commitment to its employees, and its loyalty to both customers and suppliers, Chicago Tube and Iron Company will be reaping the rewards of its profits for many years to come.

CT&I offers specialty pipe fabrication services for its international customer base.

Among the company's services are cutting, threading, grooving, swagging, cold and hot bending (below), and code welding.

EYMAN DISTRIBUTING CO. WAS FOUNDED BY H.D. HEYMAN IN 1914 WITH A $200 INVESTMENT. AT THE TIME, HE WAS A 21-YEAR-OLD RUSSIAN IMMIGRANT. THE COMPANY BEGAN AS A WHOLESALE DISTRIBUTOR OF HOSIERY AND UNDERWEAR PRODUCTS SOLD TO

retail stores throughout the midwestern United States.

Heyman Distributing Co. was originally located at 107 Market Street. In 1928, the company moved to 200 Market Street (now Wacker Drive) and, in 1933, relocated again to 301 West Adams (now one of the Sears Tower corners). In 1965, H.D. Heyman's son Leonard, then executive vice president, moved the company to its first one-story distribution operation on North Kimball Avenue, just off the Kennedy Expressway, and changed the name of the company to Heyman Corporation.

Changing Its Industry

n 1928, Heyman Distributing Co. completed what many in the apparel business believe was the first distribution agreement between a national manufacturer and a distributor when P.H. Hanes Knitting Company awarded it regional exclusiv-

ity for Hanes products. In turn, Heyman agreed to drop all other competing knit products that it carried.

The move turned out to be a historic deal for Hanes, Heyman, and other wholesale distributors across the United States, which then struck similar deals with Hanes. P.H. Hanes Knitting Company was started in 1914, the same year as Heyman, and the two companies grew over the years as P.H. Hanes Knitting became Hanes Underwear Company. When the other side of the Hanes family started Hanes Hosiery Company, it extended exclusive regional rights to Heyman for its products, as well.

H.D. Heyman's vision in 1928 that "brands build business" took the company from one of many jobbers of unbranded hosiery and underwear products to the pinnacle of professionally run wholesale distribution of nationally marketed brands. The move also made Heyman into one of the largest businesses of its type in the apparel field from 1928 to 1988.

Along the way, H.D. Heyman brought in two key sales partners, as well as adding two sons-in-law and his own son to the management team at the company. Together, they successfully managed the business through World War II and through the booming postwar

H.D. Heyman and son Leonard enjoy a family gathering during the 1960s (left).

H.D. Heyman founded the Heyman Distributing Co. in 1914 with a $200 investment. The company began as a wholesale distributor of hosiery and underwear products sold to retail stores throughout the midwestern United States. The company's headquarters stood at the corner of Franklin and Adams from 1933 to 1965, where the Sears Tower stands today (right).

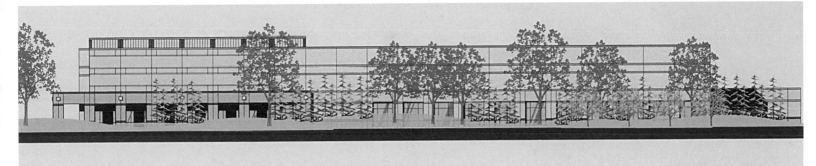

375 NORTH FAIRWAY DRIVE

era into the 1970s. During the immediate postwar period, the company added a third crown to the Hanes distribution line by striking a deal with the Buster Brown Company.

GROWING THROUGH ACQUISITIONS

eonard J. Heyman, H.D.'s son, joined the company in 1957. While his father was ever the marketer, Leonard Heyman moved the company to a state-of-the-art, one-story distribution center, and set Heyman Corporation as a model of wholesale distribution in the apparel field.

Leonard's other legacy was as a leveraged buyout (LBO) artist during the 1960s and 1970s, prior to the time when leveraged buyouts were the norm. Through his leadership, the company completed 18 LBOs during this period, resulting in increased sales, elimination of competition, and expansion from two distribution centers (in Minneapolis and Chicago) to additional operations in Grand Rapids, Michigan; Milwaukee, Wisconsin; and Des Moines, Iowa. The company also began its first direct importing operation under Leonard Heyman, a move that eventually led to the current worldwide sourcing operations of the company.

Hard times hit the company between 1980 and 1986. An eroding customer base accelerated as the apparel industry largely became a direct-selling industry. Manufacturers sold increasingly fewer goods through their wholesale distribution channels, and the company struggled to survive as 1985 came to a close.

At the end of 1985, Leonard Heyman turned the decision making over to his two sons, Larry and Michael Heyman. The third generation of Heymans—grandsons of the founder—knew they had to take the company beyond its regional markets and into a national one.

MOVING TO NATIONAL MARKETS

ithin a 12-month period, the Heyman brothers discontinued all products that could not pass their litmus test for future viability. They secured a national market by licensing the exclusive right to manufacture and distribute OshKosh B'gosh socks to OshKosh B'gosh retailers across the United States. The bold moves reduced $25 million of unprofitable sales to $9 million in solid sales.

The beginning of licensing high profile brand names and designing, sourcing, and bringing those products to market came in 1988 with what would become the first series of licenses for OshKosh B'gosh. During the next five years, the licenses came to include socks, underwear, headwear, sleepwear, and winter accessories products.

Thus, the third generation of Heymans accomplished the first turnaround in the company's history by significantly altering its role as a buyer of others' finished products to that of a designer and sourcing contractor in factories around the world. Heyman now manufactures a growing array of children's apparel and accessories.

In 1994, Larry Heyman became president of the company as his brother left to pursue other interests. Sales had returned to the $25 million range.

Under Larry's direction, the company has experienced another significant growth leap as licensed products have expanded into multiple agreements with the Walt Disney Company for a number of Mickey Mouse and Winnie-the-Pooh products, as well as agreements for Warner Brothers' Baby Looney Tunes, United Media's Peanuts, and Nickelodeon/MTV's Rugrats.

Today, the company's products include socks, underwear, headwear, winter accessories, backpacks, sleepwear, layette (newborn-infant apparel, washcloths, bibs, receiving blankets, and towels), and most recently, playwear for the first time.

Such remarkable growth fueled the company's move in 1998 to a brand-new, 140,000-square-foot corporate park facility in Vernon Hills, just north of Chicago. With annual sales projected at approximately $50 million, Heyman Corporation will continue leading the way in the apparel industry.

Heyman's explosive growth during the 1980s and 1990s fueled its recent move to a brand-new, 140,000-square-foot corporate park facility in Vernon Hills, just north of Chicago (top).

Larry Heyman, CEO, guided the company through an explosive growth period through multiple licensed-product agreements with the Walt Disney Company, Warner Bros., United Media, and Nickelodeon/MTV (bottom).

ROM OFFICES HIGH ATOP THE NORTH TOWER OF THE CHICAGO MERCANTILE EXCHANGE, THE LAW FIRM OF ALTHEIMER & GRAY HAS A WONDERFUL VIEW OF THE SKYLINE IT HAS HELPED DEVELOP. THROUGH REAL ESTATE AND INTERNATIONAL LAW, AMONG OTHER AREAS OF PRACTICE, THIS

high-profile group is dramatically changing the landscape of Chicago, both literally and figuratively.

Founded in 1915, Altheimer & Gray is a premier, full-service law firm with a solid base in Chicago and a global profile. Its cutting-edge philosophy is consistent with the growth and entrepreneurial spirit of its hometown. Altheimer & Gray, like Chicago, is a principal hub for ever widening international growth.

The diversity of the organization's lawyers reflects both its domestic commitments and its international focus. The home office has grown from 30 lawyers in the mid-1970s to more than 175 today, and the firm now boasts more than 230 lawyers worldwide, including 12 European partners and seven overseas offices. A Washington, D.C., office strategically places Altheimer & Gray at the seat of national government and international affairs, as do its overseas offices in Shanghai, Warsaw, Prague, Kyiv, Bratislava, Istanbul, and Bucharest.

A Well-Rounded Practice

ltheimer & Gray has seven major practice groups: litigation, intellectual property, tax, government, real estate, corporate, and international law. In the area of litigation, the firm's senior attorneys include a number of superior litigators, while its intellectual property group represents prominent international and domestic clients around the world.

The government law unit of Altheimer & Gray works in zoning, land use, planning, municipal finance, and related matters in the Midwest, in Washington, D.C., and throughout the country. This group has worked as bond counsel for the McCormick Place expansion, and negotiated financing for the development of O'Hare Interna-

tional Airport, Navy Pier, and Illinois Center—some of the largest planned-use developments in the United States.

Altheimer & Gray's real estate group focuses on the leisure industry, developers, investment funds, banks, and real estate investment trusts (REITs), real estate pension funds, and architectural, engineering, and construction firms from Chicago to Shanghai. In the 1920s, the firm represented the Albert Pick Hotels, one of the nation's first hotel chains. It now represents more domestic and international hotel groups than any other U.S.

law firm, including Hilton Hotels, which maintains five-star properties in Istanbul and Hong Kong. Altheimer & Gray also leads the global marketplace in REIT consulting, a billion-dollar component of the hotel industry.

Another dynamic part of the firm's practice is corporate mergers and acquisitions. Altheimer & Gray began leveraged-buyout activities in the early 1980s and has worked to refine the process ever since. In the last 10 years, the group has engaged in more than 50 buyout transactions annually, including acting as lead counsel

From offices high atop the North Tower of the Chicago Mercantile Exchange, the law firm of Altheimer & Gray has a wonderful view of the skyline it has helped to develop.

in the $3.8 billion management buyout of Montgomery Ward from Mobil Corp. It also represents more than 15 funds and groups that specialize in buyouts.

Altheimer & Gray represents many major multinational corporations, Fortune 100 companies, and international financial institutions, including Gillette, Levi Strauss, Teledanmark, Philip Morris, Motorola, the Polish government, the European Bank for Reconstruction and Development, and the World Bank. With 20 years of solid experience behind the Iron Curtain, the firm was the first to establish an office in Poland after Eastern Europe was opened to outsiders. It has subsequently become one of the biggest law firms in Central and Eastern Europe. Since the mid-1980s, Altheimer & Gray has been a pioneer in China. It is one of 12 major U.S. firms holding a license from the Chinese Ministry of Justice, where more than 200 competitors sought a license, and is among only three major U.S. firms in Shanghai.

LOCAL PRESENCE

On a local level, Altheimer & Gray is involved in many civic programs. Partners are committed to the Chicago Sister City Program, where they are active on various boards, and several are members of the boards of the Ravinia Festival and the Lyric Opera of Chicago. As a major patron of Chicago Cares, a principal clearinghouse for programs focused on meeting the needs of residents in the Chicago metropolitan area, Altheimer & Gray donates office space to young professionals involved in this outreach.

In addition, the firm's partners have held many responsible positions in the community, including serving as president of the Chicago Bar Association and the new Chicago Reform School Board, and as former chief of staff for Mayor Richard Daley. On a national scale, several Altheimer & Gray lawyers have been White House aides and one was a speech writer for President George Bush. All affirm the organization's dedication to community responsibility.

The attorneys at Altheimer & Gray have traditionally committed their time and skills to pro bono legal services for the welfare of others. In that regard, Altheimer & Gray lawyers have been involved in a wide variety of pro bono matters ranging from simple legal services to litigation of nationally recognized civil rights cases such as *Ramos v. Kraft*, an unprecedented fair housing and hate crime case. For that reason, Altheimer & Gray attorneys have been recognized for their service through such honors as the Fair Housing Award of the Chicago Commissioner of Human Relations in 1996, and, in 1997, the Abraham Lincoln Marovitz Civil Rights Award presented by the Anti-Defamation League.

Based on the vision of a strong global marketplace in the 21st century and beyond, Altheimer & Gray has built a strategy for the future. As businesses continue to grow beyond their local roots and adopt an international perspective, law firms will likewise have to adapt to the changing landscape. Altheimer & Gray has seen this future early on, and has laid a solid groundwork of domestic and international building blocks to position itself as a top global law firm.

Altheimer & Gray is one of only three major U.S. law firms to be awarded a license from the Chinese Ministry of Justice to open a law office in Shanghai (left).

Altheimer & Gray's Prague office, viewed from the Vltava River, is located at the Charles Bridge (right).

IN 1917, MELVIN JONES, AN INSURANCE SALESMAN WHO HAD GROWN UP IN AN ARMY FAMILY IN FRONTIER ARIZONA, BELIEVED SOCIETY DESERVED MORE FROM THOSE WHO PROSPERED. WITH THE BACKING OF THE BUSINESS CIRCLE OF CHICAGO AND OTHER BUSINESS CLUBS AROUND THE NATION, HE FORMED A CLUB THAT WOULD GROW INTO the largest service club organization in the world, with nearly 1.5 million members in 43,500 clubs.

And thus, the years of public service for the International Association of Lions Clubs began with a businessman's simple vision of a better world.

CRUSADE AGAINST DARKNESS

Though now world renowned for its extraordinary services for the blind and visually impaired, the association did not adopt that mission until challenged by Helen Keller at the international convention in 1925. The blind and deaf author challenged the organization to become "knights of the blind in the crusade against darkness." The Lions clubs took up the task and, in the ensuing years, have become the foremost organization in service to the blind.

In 1940, Lions in Buffalo opened the organization's first eye bank, taking advantage of emerging technology in the field of corneal transplants. "Today, the organization operates 70—the majority of the world's eye banks," says Patrick Cannon, manager of the public relations and production division for Lions Clubs International.

In 1990, Lions took a major step in establishing SightFirst, a $145 million global initiative to rid the world of preventable and reversible blindness. The unprecedented program joins leading blindness prevention experts, blindness organizations, governments, and Lions volunteers in a team effort to find long-term solutions to eye problems, to train eye care professionals, and to promote treatment and public education.

Without such intervention programs as SightFirst, the World Health Organization estimates the number of blind people in the world could double from 40 million to 80 million in fewer than 25 years. Among the organization's current projects is a program to prevent "river blindness" in equatorial Africa, where a parasite that thrives in wet, humid areas attacks the eyes and causes blindness. Drug therapy, however, will prevent the loss of sight, and Lions Clubs International intends to ensure the supply of curative drugs to the region. A major partner in this effort is the Carter Center. Former President Jimmy Carter is a long-time Lions member.

In early 1997, the Lions surpassed the 1 million mark in number of cataract surgeries made possible through SightFirst. Each year the organization helps provide 600,000 free glaucoma screenings and 25,000 corneal transplants. Lions clubs also supply thousands of people each year with free eye care, eyeglasses, braille writers, large-print texts, white canes, and guide dogs.

EXTENDING ITS SERVICES

While sight-related services remain a primary focus for the clubs, the association's service work extends far beyond. "We are getting more into youth pro-

Clockwise from top:
During a break from their convention in 1919, Lions club members gathered in front of the Art Institute to mark the occasion by visiting this Chicago landmark.

Reminders of the "international" in Lions Clubs International abound at its headquarters. This garden was installed and is still maintained through the generosity of the Lions of Japan.

The organization's headquarters in Oak Brook, Illinois, is the administrative center for nearly 1.5 million Lions in more than 43,500 clubs around the world.

grams," Cannon notes. Lions clubs have formed 5,500 Leo clubs, or service organizations for youths, around the globe.

Additionally, Lions clubs are partners in the Lions-Quest program, a comprehensive series of curricula that teach decision-making skills, conflict resolution skills, and drug awareness. In its various phases, Lions-Quest offers course work for children in all grades from kindergarten through high school. The program also includes extensive teacher training. The most widely used program of its kind, Lions-Quest is currently being employed in 30 countries.

Individual Lions clubs aren't restricted to association programs, however. "We encourage the clubs not to limit their activities to what we do," Cannon says. "We try to have the clubs periodically look at their communities and see what needs to be done locally."

Membership in local Lions clubs is by invitation, but the groups are not exclusive. "The qualifications are easy: You must be of legal age, and be of good character and reputation," Cannon says. "We look for people who reflect the community—business-people, doctors, dentists, attorneys—a really wide variety. We have a lot of teachers, as well as some retired people, who are cherished as members because they have a little more time to give."

In addition to President Carter, Cannon estimates that roughly 10 to 15 percent of the members of Congress are Lions, as are a former premier of Japan and many other eminent world citizens. But then, so is basketball legend Larry Bird.

In 1987, Lions clubs opened their membership to women. "Women joined almost immediately," Cannon says. "We now have

120,000 women members, and the number of new women members keeps going up every year."

The International Association of Lions Clubs plans for continued growth. Cannon says, "We never think there are enough Lions. A country without a Lion is a challenge for us." Today, Lions clubs operate in 185 countries. The association just entered into a five-year agreement with the People's Republic of China to start a SightFirst-funded cataract program. "Our hope is that, down the road, the Chinese government will let us form clubs," Cannon notes.

But the group's more immediate goal is to continue its honorable fight against blindness. "Our goal is to eliminate preventable and reversible blindness," Cannon says. "Once we feel we have accomplished all we can, we will be looking for a new challenge. We always say that our motto—We Serve—says it all, but what our organization comes down to is just caring, humanitarian service."

Clockwise from top left:
Lions, kids, and camps go together around the world. In Australia, youngsters with diabetes have fun at camp while learning to control their disease.

In the Philippines, used eyeglasses find a recipient. This elderly woman could not afford eyeglasses on her limited income.

The SightFirst Program aims to eliminate preventable and reversible blindness around the world. In Indonesia, a woman who recently underwent cataract surgery receives a postoperative kit to aid in her recovery.

Lions sponsor Leo clubs for young people. Here, a group of Leos drop off used eyeglasses as a part of a recycling effort in conjunction with LensCrafters.

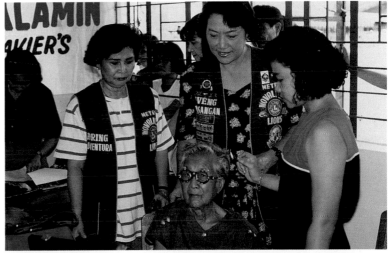

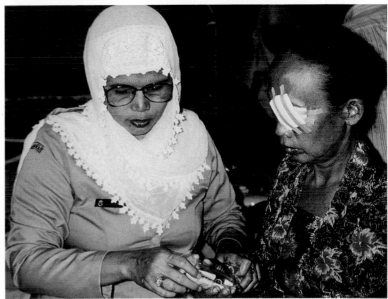

ONSOER TOWNSEND ENVIRODYNE ENGINEERS, INC. (CTE) IS A FULL-SERVICE CONSULTING FIRM BUILT ON THE PRINCIPLE FIRST PROMOTED BY ITS FOUNDER, A.W. CONSOER: "ENGINEERING THAT ISN'T OF THE HIGHEST QUALITY IS VERY EXPENSIVE." FROM ITS HEADQUARTERS IN CHICAGO, CTE HAS, FOR NEARLY

80 years, had a profound impact on the nation's infrastructure through the development of innovative engineering solutions for airport, transit, and highway improvements as well as water, wastewater, and hazardous waste treatment systems.

The largest civil engineering firm in Chicago, CTE has 300 employees based locally and more than 700 nationwide. In 1997, *Engineering News Record* ranked CTE 66th among the top 500 U.S. design firms, and in the top 20 in the fields of transportation and water and wastewater treatment. In addition to its Chicago operations, CTE maintains 26 offices throughout the United States with regional operation centers in New York City; Nashville; and Orange, California.

CTE is recognized nationally for its expertise in aviation, surface transportation, and water and wastewater treatment systems. Ongoing projects include the reconstruction of the Grand Central Terminal in New York City and the rehabilitation design and construction management for the Stevenson Expressway (I-55) in Chicago. On the environmental front, the firm is managing the $700 million Overflow Abatement Program in Nashville, and is assisting with the lead and asbestos remediation program for the Chicago Public Schools. Past projects include the design and construction management of major public works programs throughout the United States in the areas of highways, bridges, rail transit and railroads, flood control, water systems, wastewater treatment, and hazardous waste remediation.

master plans, airside and landside design, and environmental services. Nationwide, CTE has been responsible for planning, design, and construction management for nearly 200 airports. Locally, CTE has continued to be active at O'Hare and Midway airports since the early 1950s. The company's experience includes everything from drainage studies and paving improvements to the management of the $2 billion O'Hare Development Program.

In addition to CTE's longstanding work at O'Hare and Midway, the company is preparing a master plan for improvements at Seattle-Tacoma International Airport and Portland International Airport, and the re-use of El Toro Airbase in Orange County, California, for commercial air traffic.

SURFACE TRANSPORTATION

o infrastructure is complete without a well-planned, -built, and -maintained surface transportation system. CTE is well rounded in all aspects of rail or highway planning, design, and construction. The range of services includes system planning, feasibility studies, corridor analysis and location stud-

Clockwise from top:
CTE worked on a $24.5 million, two-year planning, design, and construction process culminating in the gracious streetscape revitalization of State Street, Chicago's premier historic shopping district.

CTE served as a consultant to the Regional Transportation Authority in the development of a new personal rapid transit system.

For more than 40 years, CTE has done ongoing planning and engineering support for O'Hare International Airport.

AVIATION SERVICES

he comprehensive aviation services provided by CTE represent the finest in multidisciplinary problem solving, including airport

PETER J. SCHULTZ

ies, environmental assessments, and impact statements for proposed rail transit and highway improvements. Nationally, the firm has worked on such projects as the biennial inspection of the Brooklyn Bridge; the Environmental Impact Statement for the Transportation Corridors Agency in Orange County, California; and the redecking of the Triborough Bridge in New York.

Locally, the firm has served as the general engineering consultant to the Illinois Toll Highway Authority since 1954. CTE has also been engaged as a consultant to the Illinois Department of Transportation for virtually every Interstate rehabilitation program undertaken by the Department in the last 15 years. This tenure began with the reconstruction of the Circle Interchange in 1981 and has continued through the Eisenhower, Dan Ryan, Kennedy, and Stevenson expressways in Chicago.

On the transit engineering side, CTE has been active in all types of systems design and construction from rapid rail transit with the Chicago Transit Authority (CTA) to commuter rail (Metra), light rail, high-speed rail, automated people movers, and advanced personal rapid transit (PRT), where the company currently serves as consultant to the Regional Transportation Authority for the development of a new technology.

Testament to CTE's ability to manage major improvement programs is the recently completed rehabilitation of the Green Line for the CTA. As program managers, CTE worked with the CTA to plan and manage this $400

million rehabilitation project. The project was designed and constructed while the line was removed from service. In just 27 months, the line was completely rehabilitated and revenue service was restored on a faster, safer system. This project has been recognized both locally and nationally for excellence in engineering by the American Society of Civil Engineers, the Consulting Engineers Council, and the Chicago Building Congress.

ENVIRONMENTAL SYSTEMS

ince its founding, CTE has continued to be on the cutting edge of the development of solutions to water treatment and wastewater treatment technologies. From the onset, CTE was involved with the planning, design, and construction management of the Metropolitan Water Reclamation District of Greater Chicago (MWRDGC) Tunnel and Reservoir Project (TARP). Today, CTE continues to assist the MWRDGC with the design of improvements to their Stickney Wastewater Treatment Plant, one of the world's largest.

With respect to water resource projects, the firm is currently engaged in the planning and design of a Lake Michigan cutoff wall and pump station at the mouth of the Chicago River that will limit leakage of lake water into the Chicago River and improve compliance with the Supreme Court's Lake Michigan Water Allocation Agreements.

In the field of hazardous waste management, CTE has continued to serve as a consultant to the Chicago Public Schools system to assist

it with the abatement of lead and asbestos as part of its Children First capital improvements program. This program involves improvements to more than 90 schools citywide, providing a safer, more attractive learning environment.

Key to CTE's success with environmental projects is the ability to plan and implement restoration and management programs that are cost-effective solutions and can be executed in a thorough and discreet manner.

SERVICE AND STANDARDS EQUAL LONGEVITY

Consoer's vision of success for CTE Engineers called for the firm to "perform top-quality work in a professional manner, keep staff aware of professional advances, be cognizant of changes in clients' needs, and operate as a profitable business." The company remains true to that mission today, and enjoys a repeat business rate of more than 70 percent. Client needs are addressed at predetermined project stages: clients and staff discuss progress and problem solving in a workshop format, ensuring that concerns are met and that the project is not impeded.

CTE takes great pride in its longevity and quality. "We attribute our longevity to the principles established by our founder: top-quality work, legendary client service, professional development opportunities for staff, and sound financial practices," says CTE President and CEO Robert Fischer. These principles have built the firm foundation on which CTE Engineers stands poised for the future.

CTE helped devise the Tunnel and Reservoir Project (TARP), one of the world's largest pollution control systems (left).

CTE designed a method to reduce or control the high flows, and developed a system for meeting biological loads entering the Knollwood Wastewater Treatment Plant (right).

OME RUN INN IS A CLASSIC AMERICAN SUCCESS STORY. IT IS THE TALE OF AN IMMIGRANT FAMILY ARRIVING IN CHICAGO WITH LITTLE BUT HOPE AND THE WILLINGNESS TO WORK LONG AND HARD. THE FAMILY STARTS A BUSINESS, WORKS AT IT NIGHT AND DAY, AND SEES THE BUSINESS

begin to prosper. As the years pass, succeeding generations of the family work and learn, waiting their turn to step up to the plate. In this story, the result is a real Home Run.

Decades ago, when the winning hit from a neighborhood baseball game shattered the front window of their tavern, Mary and Vincent

Grittani christened their business Home Run Inn. At first, it was strictly a shot-and-beer joint—no food was served. When Prohibition arrived, Home Run Inn adapted, temporarily becoming an ice-cream parlor.

In 1942, Nick Perrino married Loretta Grittani. After World War II, Nick, like thousands of other

World War II soldiers returning to civilian life, needed a way to support his family. So in 1947, Nick and his mother-in-law, Mary Grittani, formed a partnership, and together they developed a pizza recipe. Customers flocked to Home Run Inn for the pizza—and they're still coming, more than 50 years later, to savor the legendary taste.

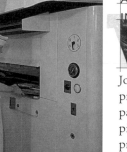

AN INSTITUTION IN A PIZZA CAPITAL

e pride ourselves on being a Chicago institution," says Joe Perrino, the third-generation president responsible for the company's impressive growth. "Our pizza is not like the big chains' products. Everything we use is top quality. We make a thin-bottomed crust, stretched by hand and crimped at the edge, to keep the toppings from sliding off."

Home Run Inn uses a special aging process in producing the

Founder Nick Perrino (center) works on his famous Home Run Inn pizza in the kitchen of his restaurant, circa 1960.

The original Home Run Inn got its name when the winning hit from a neighborhood baseball game shattered its front window.

dough for its crusts, and it makes quite a bit more today than the founders could have ever envisioned. The ingredients that make up a premium Home Run Inn pizza—whether the fresh or frozen version—are produced under strict quality control guidelines by the company at its huge, new, state-of-the-art USDA-monitored commissary and frozen pizza production facility in suburban Woodridge.

A Premium Product at a Fair Price

When Joe's father, Nick, first introduced frozen pizza back in the late 1950s, it was produced right in the original 31st Street restaurant on Chicago's Southwest Side. As the reputation of the original pizza spread and demand increased, a frozen pizza factory was built in Chicago. When leadership of the company passed from Nick to Joe, the pace of change picked up. Loyal customers were moving farther from the city, so Home Run Inn moved along with them, adding restaurants in Darien and Arlington Heights. Its customer base continued to grow, and the company responded with Home Run Inn Pizza Express restaurants located in the suburbs of Orland Park, Westmont, Melrose Park, and Arlington Heights.

The pace of change continues to quicken, and the company is poised to respond, blending technology and tradition. As another

Home Run Inn's corporate offices and frozen food plant are located in Woodridge.

Home Run Inn President Joe Perrino keeps the business going today along with sisters Lucretia Costello (left) and Marilyn Carlson (right), and mother, Laura Perrino.

generation comes on board, Joe Perrino remains focused on the same ideals. "Our company has prospered by providing our customers with a premium product at a fair price," says Perrino. "We've gone from a mom-and-pop operation to one that sends memos. It's a difficult transition, and our people are key. Training is important, but there's more to it than just that. I want to hear new ideas; I constantly asked my dad why he did things the way he did, and I want to hear that from my kids."

As he talks about his company, Perrino's determination and dedication become evident. "Home Run Inn values loyalty, and I want Home Run Inn to be a great place to eat and a great place to work. I want satisfied customers, happy employees, and a fair profit at the end of the day."

O N April 13, 1992, more than 250 million gallons of Chicago River water poured into the basements of buildings in Chicago's downtown Loop area, causing massive damage, power outages, and evacuation of the buildings. The flood was so devastating that

Governor Jim Edgar declared Chicago a disaster area. Virtually shutting down the Loop for weeks, the flood was the result of a breach in the tunnel walls below the north branch of the Chicago River at Kinzie Street. The 98-year-old freight tunnel system was connected to many downtown buildings and had been used to carry cargo, mail, and coal in the past. Harza Engineering Company came to the city's rescue, designing a system of 29 permanent bulkheads to isolate all 11 river crossings from the rest of the tunnel system, preventing future flooding.

Leroy F. "L.F." Harza would be proud, and probably not surprised, at the performance of the company he founded in 1920. Through his insight and direction, Harza Engineering has grown from a firm that specialized in river projects and hydroelectric engineering to a company that assists private enterprises and governmental agencies throughout the world in the

development of land, water, and energy resources.

"The Chicago flood recovery plan is just one example of how we fulfill our mission of working in partnership with clients to achieve innovative and environmentally sound solutions," says Richard Meagher, Harza chairman.

FOLLOWING THE COMPANY'S SUCCESS

H arza Engineering's success can be traced back to the high standards and philosophy employed by Harza and his mentor, Daniel W. Mead, head of the department of civil engineering at the University of Wisconsin. Mead believed that dams and power plants should be designed by experts who work directly with the owner of the facility.

Beginning his own career in 1912, Harza headed out to Portland, Oregon, an area with abundant water sources, hills, and mountains

in which to build dams. Few dams were being built at that time, however, and Harza's vision was ahead of the marketplace.

Returning to the Midwest, Harza worked for a construction company that built dams and hydroelectric plants for the Chicago-based Insull Utilities Group. His association with brothers Samuel and Martin Insull, who headed the utilities empire, paved the way for launching his own company in Chicago, a location Harza deemed ideal due to the city's central location.

Harza Engineering made steady progress until the Great Depression. The firm landed on its feet in the early 1930s, when it was awarded the Loup River Public Power District project in Nebraska.

In the following years, as the company has expanded its business, it has steadily built up its workforce, organizing employees into a flexible matrix of departments and

Mayor Richard M. Daley comments about the effects of the Chicago flood of 1992, for which Harza Engineering designed a recovery plan.

projects geared to making the most of its talent. After World War II, Dick Harza, L.F.'s son, began to establish the firm's presence internationally in the hydroelectric development industry. A plan for the hydroelectric development of the Lempa River in El Salvador began in 1947, marking the company's first overseas assignment. Harza Engineering remained cutting-edge, as in 1956, when it began using computer technology to design dams. Today, it employs the most sophisticated computer technology in all areas of operation.

A COMPETITIVE EDGE

Currently under the leadership of President and CEO, Refaat A. Abdel-Malek, Harza Engineering employs 750 people, with half of the employees working in the Chicago headquarters. Other offices are located in Los Angeles, Oakland, Salinas, and San Diego, California; Utica, New York; Bellevue, Washington; Portland, Oregon; and São Paolo, Brazil.

Domestically and internationally, Harza Engineering has worked on some of the most prestigious and important projects in the world. In the United States, it designed the largest pumped-storage project in the world with the Bath County Pumped-Storage Project. It also developed the first high thin-arch concrete dam in the United States for the Mossyrock Development in Washington State. Also in Washington, Harza designed the largest salmon hatchery in the world.

Internationally, Harza's projects have been among some of the largest in history. The company has been involved in projects in more than 90 countries. The Guri Hydroelectric Project in Venezuela is the largest hydroelectric plant in the world; Harza provided design and construction management services for this tremendous project. The firm continues to serve its first overseas client, Comisión Hydroélectrica del Rio Lempa (CEL), with which it started working 50 years ago. Harza was also the designer of the highest rock-fill dams in the world at the time of completion: Derbendi Khan Dam in Iraq and Ambuklao Dam in the Philippines.

This complete mainstream tunnel shaft is an example of the firm's ability to provide superior services in land, water, and energy resources development (top).

Harza Engineering designed bulkheads such as this one to prevent future flooding in downtown Chicago (bottom).

Another example of how Harza stays on top of the cutting edge is by tapping into the private power sector. The company has participated in various roles in the private development of hydroelectric plants. This pursuit of the private power market shows Harza's expertise in not only meeting, but anticipating the needs of its clients.

Harza's competitive edge lies primarily in its pursuit of the best employees and in its strategy of making inroads in emerging markets, according to Meagher. The fact that the company has a high employee retention rate and has been awarded some of the most prestigious and important commissions in the world attests to its success in those areas.

Finding creative solutions to the challenges of its diverse clients is one of Harza Engineering's objectives. As much as the company has grown, it remains committed to its founder's goal of operating an independent, profitable company, wholly owned by its professional employees and dedicated to providing superior services in land, water, and energy resources development.

OR MORE THAN 75 YEARS, GRAYCOR HAS TACKLED COMPLEX CONSTRUCTION PROJECTS THAT REQUIRE A FULL AND INTEGRATED COMPLEMENT OF SERVICES. TODAY, THIS LEADING NORTH AMERICAN BUILDER CONSTRUCTS A WIDE VARIETY OF COMMERCIAL, INDUSTRIAL, HEALTH CARE, AND INSTITUTIONAL

facilities, in addition to providing specialized maintenance services to Fortune 500 industrial corporations.

This broad-based approach has earned Graycor a place on the *Crain's Chicago Business* list of the city's fastest-growing private companies. "Our business growth reflects the rock-solid belief that hard jobs make us stronger and help us meet our clients' needs more effectively through comprehensive construction services," says Melvin Gray, the company's chairman and CEO.

ROARK JOHNSON

Clockwise from top:
Since 1921, Graycor has been a family-owned and -operated enterprise. Today's family members include (from left) Steven Gray, vice president and secretary; Melvin Gray, chairman and CEO; and Matthew Gray, vice president.

Ford Motor Company, which contracted with Graycor for an addition to its Chicago assembly plant, awarded the company the coveted Q1 Quality Award.

Graycor's larger construction projects have included a 2.7 million-square-foot retail, hotel, residential, and office complex at 900 North Michigan Avenue.

FROM CLEANING TO CONSTRUCTION

n 1921, company founder Edward Gray moved his cleaning business, specializing in building exteriors and windows, from St. Louis to Chicago, where he saw tremendous opportunities in construction and industry. He steered the business into a new direction and renamed it the Chicago Concrete Breaking Company. Soon, the new enterprise won a contract to remove a railroad retaining wall in Grant Park—without disrupting train traffic. The project's success led the company to adopt the slogan

"Wanted—a hard job." During the 1930s, the company created new methods and machines to break slag and waste materials in steel mills. Over the next decade, Chicago Concrete Breaking Company continued to develop new technology for the steel industry.

Renamed the Edward Gray Corporation in 1957, the company moved to south Chicago and added construction of industrial and commercial facilities to its growing list of services. By the end of the 1970s, the company had evolved into a full-scale construction and industrial services organization, initiated state-of-the-art comput-

erized cost-control and planning systems, and successfully completed construction projects across the nation.

In 1982, the organization acquired Inland Construction Company, which had broad experience in commercial construction. A decade later, the company, firmly established as one of the nation's largest general contractors, moved its headquarters to Homewood, maintaining shop facilities in Chicago. Celebrating its 75th anniversary in 1996, the company united all its divisions under the name Graycor.

PROGRESSIVE THINKING

raycor is a proven leader in construction and maintenance. Through a keen understanding of project requirements, based on long years of experience, the company develops effective solutions to maintain efficient project controls. Strongly enforced quality standards begin with top management and are upheld companywide. As testimony to Graycor's quality commitment, Ford Motor Company has presented the company with the coveted Q1 Quality Award, signifying compliance with the stringent ISO 9000 criteria estab-

MCSHANE-FLEMING STUDIOS, BRIAN FRITZ

MICHAEL GUSTAFSON

lished by the International Organization for Standardization, as well as a proven commitment to continuous improvement.

Melvin Gray, named 1997 Construction Person of the Year by the Chicago Building Congress, emphasizes the importance of building lasting client relationships: "We believe long-term relationships are among a company's most valuable assets—even more valuable, though less visible, than the tangible assets on the balance sheet. Much of what we do is aimed at developing and nurturing those continuing alliances."

On-site safety also takes a high priority at Graycor. "Nothing is more important than safety—not production, not sales, not profit," Gray says. Clients, employees, and subcontractors know that the company guarantees their well-being on work sites. To educate employees about risks and safety measures, Graycor instituted a Zero Injuries Program that has become an industry standard. This systematic approach ensures that safety goals are met through management commitment and continuous training.

Additionally, Graycor's leadership in technology and networking provides a competitive edge in the industry. Computerized project management gives supervisors immediate access to essential data needed to coordinate operations for maximum safety, efficiency, and value. All work sites have a computer link to Graycor headquarters, and field superintendents are equipped with laptop computers. By enabling swift communication and information access, Graycor maintains exceptional project control.

Graycor takes pride in its history of technological development. Always striving to improve business and to bring new and better services to customers, Graycor plans to continue to further widen its geographic range and enhance its client relationships. Integrity, financial strength, and stability—combined with a commitment to quality, safety, and tight project control—have contributed to Graycor's tradition of excellence and will continue its advance into the future.

MICHAEL GUSTAFSON

From top:

As early as 1929, Graycor—going by the name Chicago Concrete Breaking Company—led the way in its industry, as typified by this modern-for-its-time concrete breaking equipment.

Graycor's projects, such as this U.S. Steel facility in Gary, Indiana, have made it a leading North American builder.

The beautiful Steppenwolf Theatre, home of the world-renowned Steppenwolf Theatre Company, was yet another Graycor project.

RUSSELL PHILL PS PHOTOGRAPHY

ECHNOLOGY HAS RADICALLY ALTERED THE WAY PEOPLE LIVE, EVEN IN SEEMINGLY SIMPLE WAYS. CONSIDER THE TOOTHBRUSH. A TOOL THAT MOST AMERICANS USE AT THE BEGINNING AND END OF EVERY DAY WAS NOT MUCH MORE THAN A CURIO UNTIL 1923, WHEN IT WAS REINVENTED

by Chicago periodontist Dr. John O. Butler.

Until that time, toothbrushes were designed mainly to provide basic teeth cleaning. Though rudimentary toothbrushes have existed for thousands of years (the ancient Sumerians used them), when Butler presented his two-row, 12-tuft, wide-handled toothbrush, it was the first ever designed to reach below the gum line and to the teeth in the back of the mouth. Butler's breakthrough solved an ancient problem that had caused distress throughout history, and also marked the beginning of an era of cleaner, healthier teeth and gums. It virtually launched the oral care industry and, at the same time, the John O. Butler Company.

Ten years after Butler introduced his innovative toothbrush, competitors began marketing similar products, yet he always stayed a step ahead of them. Continuing to improve on his original toothbrush, he developed specially treated nylon bristle tips and colored handles so that family members could tell their toothbrushes apart. Butler was a man with a mission—he lectured on oral care while single-handedly selling his products and

running the company for 23 years. Consequently, Butler became known throughout the dental care community as the father of the modern-day toothbrush—a status that still lives on.

BUTLER G•U•M® TODAY

Today, Butler would barely recognize his company. In 1981, it moved from offices among the towering buildings on Lake Shore Drive to an industrial park planted amid the bungalows and ranch houses of Chicago's northwest side. While Butler ran his operation alone, offices and manufacturing plants in Chicago and suburban Elgin now buzz with more than 500 employees, producing oral care products 24 hours a day. Butler marketed his products only to dental professionals. Today, the John O. Butler Company sells a myriad of oral care products to dental professionals and consumers in 60 countries around the world.

The Butler G•U•M® series is the most extensive line of toothbrushes in the oral care industry, offering more than 30 different types of toothbrushes designed for a variety of oral conditions.

The dome-trim-style brush was created to meet the needs of most people, while specialized end tuft brushes, with seven bristle tufts on a little circle of plastic, are useful for areas requiring more detail. The company manufactures a variety of other dental products as well, including interdental products, floss, stimulators, and toothpaste; and its focus continues to be on new product innovations.

Until the 1980s, Butler products were sold only in pharmacies, but that is changing. Now the company is elbowing its way onto supermarket and mass merchandiser shelves. Unlike its competitors, who are diversified consumer product conglomerates, Butler specializes in oral care only and offers the broadest array of preventive care products in the industry.

The force behind Butler's aggressive growth goals today is Sunstar Inc., a Japanese manufacturer of health-related consumer products and the number one manufacturer and seller of oral care products in Japan. Sunstar purchased the John O. Butler Company in 1988. Its CEO, Hiroo Kaneda, is a kindred spirit of Butler's, dedicating himself and

Butler products are used worldwide by consumers and dental professionals.

his company to improving oral health globally.

A Better World through Better Health

It was the John O. Butler Company's orientation with the dental professional and its unsurpassed reputation for quality products that interested Kaneda; and, like Dr. Butler, Kaneda is not content to rest on past accomplishments. He wants to use Sunstar and Butler (its wholly owned subsidiary) to build a better world by improving the overall health of individuals.

Kaneda's hypothesis is that total body health originates in the mouth. In other words, oral health is organically related to systemic health. To that end, Sunstar hosts international symposia for dental and medical researchers to collaborate and share their findings. At the 1997 symposium held at the Dental School of the University of North Carolina, compelling evidence was presented, indicating that heart disease and low birth weight are related to periodontal disease.

A global concern for health and beauty is inherent in all of the companies in the Sunstar circle. Sunstar also manufactures hair care and cosmetic products, nutritional foods, and environmentally friendly construction materials. Sunstar's concern for health and well-being extends to its employees, as well.

"At Butler, employees are regarded as the company's greatest asset," says Butler President Mike Bava, "and it shows in several respects: The atmosphere is very friendly and family-like; the working environment is attractive, safe, and clean; and in its history, Butler has never had a layoff." In turn, Butler employees volunteer their time outside the company, participating in the American Heart Walk and raising funds for public television.

While awareness of Butler in the dental industry is very high, Butler products have remained the dental industry's best-kept secret commercially. Unlike most other oral care products manufacturers, Butler did not have a big advertising budget until 1997, when it launched its first national TV commercial featuring the slogan, "Butler—No One Has a Better Dental Record."

"We have been a small player with a strong profile," says Bava. That profile is much larger now than when Butler first approached dental care professionals with his newly developed toothbrush. As Sunstar and Butler pursue the mission of further improving dental health for all, the John O. Butler Company continues to prove that one man can make a difference in the lives of many.

Butler toothbrush handles are molded (left) and their bristles attached (right) on state-of-the-art equipment at its Chicago facility.

ANYONE FAMILIAR WITH THE JINGLES "LIKE A GOOD NEIGH-BOR, STATE FARM IS THERE" OR "YOU DESERVE A BREAK TODAY AT McDONALD'S" IS FAMILIAR WITH DDB NEEDHAM CHICAGO. IT'S THE AGENCY BEHIND "TWO ALL-BEEF PATTIES, SPECIAL SAUCE, LETTUCE, CHEESE,

pickles, onions on a sesame seed bun" and "I love you, man" for Bud Light. From its inception, this inventive advertising agency has delivered daringly creative and effective advertising to loyal clients and a receptive public. The Needham Agency became DDB Needham in a 1986 merger with Doyle Dane Bernbach in New York. The two agencies were drawn together by their common commitment to creative excellence.

From the beginning, the Needham Agency pioneered new concepts in the advertising field, including sponsorship of the first commercial radio broadcast of a professional baseball game. The year was 1928 at Chicago's Wrigley Field. Later, in 1935, the agency literally invented the forerunner of today's sitcom when it developed a new format for a radio show that became known as *Fibber McGee and Molly*. The program introduced a new and clever way of presenting commercials integrated into the script with the stars themselves doing the selling. It was a first.

Today, DDB Needham boasts U.S. billings of more than $5.1 billion and the distinction of being named the largest ad agency in the country in 1996. The worldwide organization has more than 200 offices in 86 countries around the world and more than 11,000 employees. It is part of Omnicom, the second-largest advertising agency holding company in the world. DDB Needham Chicago handles sales promotion, direct marketing, database management, retail, event and sports marketing, and public relations, and produces all aspects of advertising and marketing.

DDB Needham Chicago represents the largest single business unit of DDB Needham Worldwide, with 625 employees recently relocated to new offices in the Amoco building at 200 East Randolph Drive. "The Chicago office is the heart of our organization; it has a unique spiritual quality that creates a worldwide creative force," says Alan Pilkington, chairman of DDB Needham Chicago.

"You can't have better results without a better idea, and it isn't a better idea unless it generates better results. At DDB Needham Chicago, creativity is everybody's business; we expect it from everywhere in the agency," says Alan Pilkington, chairman, DDB Needham Chicago (right).

State Farm Insurance has been an agency client for more than 50 years (left).

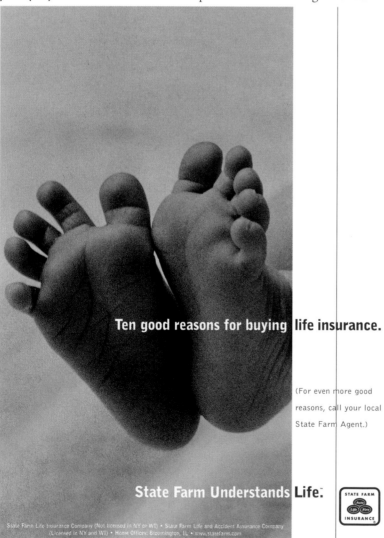

Ten good reasons for buying life insurance.

(For even more good reasons, call your local State Farm Agent.)

State Farm Understands Life.

State Farm Life Insurance Company (Not licensed in NY or WI) • State Farm Life and Accident Assurance Company (Licensed in NY and WI) • Home Offices: Bloomington, IL • www.statefarm.com

Playtex apparel divisions; Sargento Foods; State Farm Insurance; Tyson Foods; Westin Hotels & Resorts; and Wilson Sporting Goods.

In keeping with its list of top-rated clients, the company has entered into an exciting new arrangement with filmmaker Spike Lee. Spearheaded by DDB Needham Chicago, Spike DDB represents an alliance between Madison Avenue and Hollywood. The partnership creates marketing and advertising geared toward the urban market and its set of unique concerns. Lee serves as the urban expert, chairman, and creative director; DDB Needham provides strategic and media expertise.

Groundbreaking ideas such as Spike DDB fit right into DDB Needham's philosophy of "Better Ideas Better Results." As Pilkington explains, "You can't have better results without a better idea, and it isn't a better idea unless it generates better results. At DDB Needham Chicago, creativity is everybody's business; we expect it from everywhere in the agency."

Even DDB Needham's internal structure varies from the norm: all areas of the company, not just the creative groups, are segmented into team-based clusters to deliver the best idea to get the best results. These cluster groups are usually

BETTER IDEAS BETTER RESULTS

The client list at DDB Needham Chicago reads like a who's who of businesses, many based in the Midwest, including Anheuser-Busch; Morgan Stanley, Dean Witter, Discover & Co.; General Mills; Hamilton Beach; Heinz U.S.A.; Helene Curtis; McDonald's; Montgomery Ward; Morton Salt; Sara Lee Corporation's L'eggs and

found only in smaller companies and are considered unconventional by many larger businesses; but for DDB Needham, the unconventional works.

Another agency idea that produces better results is DDB Needham's ongoing relationship with its employees. "We take great care in giving our people a working environment that stimulates creativity in a way that shows we care for them as individuals," Pilkington says. The company's multicultural employee base encompasses youth, experience, creativity, and longevity, with many employees staying with the agency for as long as 30 years.

"We think nourishing talent is a really important part of what we do," Pilkington adds. "And talent is the one resource that an

agency must have. While it is renewable, it is rare, hard to identify, and only moderately useful in its raw state. So whenever we discover it, we like to give it a sunny climate and hope that it takes root with us and grows."

AWARD-WINNING RESULTS

DB Needham has taken its talents further into global advertising to service its clients worldwide with one of the strongest global networks. Currently, it has a focus on South America, northern Asia, and eastern Europe. It is expanding in the interactive arena, using the Internet and other cutting-edge technology in exciting ways.

DDB Needham has received many awards for its creative work, including 82 Effie awards for ad-

vertising effectiveness and numerous Cannes awards for creativity. Between 1986 and 1996, DDB Needham was the most honored worldwide network in the creative field, earning more than 116 awards. The agency received a Gold Lion award at Cannes in 1996, and in 1997 won gold awards in the Addys and the Chicago Film Festival competition. DDB Needham's most significant industry recognition in recent years was in 1995, when it was selected Agency of the Year by *Advertising Age* magazine.

While expanding its global presence, DDB Needham is also dedicated to the local community. The agency provides pro bono services to many worthwhile causes, including the Brookfield Zoo, the American Cancer Society, and the Washington, D.C.-based Defenders of Wildlife. The company is also active in national and local community organizations and programs, providing financing and resources to the Off the Street Club, Public Allies, and YMCA.

The creative philosophy behind DDB Needham comes from one of its founders, Maurice Needham, who said, "There is really no advertising problem that cannot be solved by bright people if they trust one another and are daring and tough." This sentiment is displayed every day by the creative minds at DDB Needham; it is a belief that has stood the agency in good stead for more than 70 years, and that will serve it well for many years to come.

Discover Card is now celebrating its 10th year as a DDB Needham client (top).

DDB Needham serves McDonald's in 44 global markets and is the fast-food giant's lead agency in the United States (bottom).

did somebody say [M]? ™

Clockwise from top left: Advertising for Budweiser, King of Beers, won a Cannes Gold Lion in the 1996 competition. It is the number-one-selling beer in the world.

DDB Needham created new advertising for Helene Curtis' Finesse hair care.

Jason Alexander and Rold Gold Pretzels come in for a Super Bowl landing. Rold Gold is the number one pretzel brand.

Wheaties and Michael Jordan have been a duo since 1987.

"I love you, man" for Bud Light added talk value to the advertising for the number-one-selling light beer in the world.

O THE MORE THAN 12,000 CHICAGO-BASED EMPLOYEES OF AMERICAN AIRLINES AND ITS REGIONAL AIRLINE PARTNER, AMERICAN EAGLE, "WE MEAN BUSINESS IN CHICAGO" IS MORE THAN JUST A SLOGAN. IT'S A 70-YEAR COMMITMENT TO PROVIDING EXCELLENT SERVICE TO THE MILLIONS OF passengers who travel through O'Hare International each year.

A LONG LIST OF FIRSTS

April 15, 1926, marked the beginning of a series of firsts for American Airlines in Chicago. On that day in aviation's infancy, a young pilot named Charles Lindbergh flew mail aboard a single-engine biplane from Chicago to St. Louis for Robertson Aircraft Corporation, which grew to become American Airlines. A little more than a year later, Lindbergh made his historic transatlantic flight from New York to Paris.

American made history again in 1955 when its Flight 715 from Detroit was the first scheduled passenger plane to land at what was then the new O'Hare Airport. In 1959, American introduced the first jet service to Chicago, and American was the first carrier to create a mid-continent Gateway to the World hub at O'Hare when it began a daily nonstop flight from Chicago to Frankfurt in 1985. By the mid 1990s, American was the premier carrier to Europe from Chicago. American provides daily international service to London's Heathrow Airport, Birmingham, Brussels, Frankfurt, Glasgow (seasonal), Manchester, Paris, Milan, Stockholm, and Zurich.

Domestically, American and American Eagle offer nearly 1,000 flights to and from O'Hare each business day, with extensive service to New York's LaGuardia Airport, Newark, Boston, Atlanta, Dallas,

Clockwise from top:
American Airlines traces its Chicago roots to 1926. Today, American and its commuter line, American Eagle, employ more than 12,000 personnel in Chicago.

Since O'Hare was designated as a hub in 1982, American has spent more than $500 million on upgrades and expansion projects at its facility there.

Since the mid-1990s, American has been the premier carrier to Europe from Chicago. American provides daily international service to London's Heathrow Airport, Birmingham, Brussels, Frankfurt, Glasgow (seasonal), Manchester, Paris, Milan, Stockholm, and Zurich.

Clockwise from top left:
Domestically, American and American
Eagle offer nearly 1,000 flights to
and from O'Hare each business day,
with extensive service to New York's
LaGuardia Airport, Newark, Boston,
Washington National, Atlanta, Dallas,
Denver, Minneapolis-St. Paul, Los
Angeles, and San Francisco.

American and American Eagle employees are dedicated to providing the
personal attention and service that
are expected from the airline that
"Means Business in Chicago."

The Admirals Club, established in
1939, was the first VIP lounge created
by an airline to accommodate leisure
and business travelers on layovers
between flights, and is synonymous
with comfort and elegance at major
airports around the world.

Located in the Admirals Club complex
between Terminal 3's H and K concourses is the unique Executive Center
with 19 fully equipped conference rooms.
The rooms can function as a branch
office for business travelers needing
a quiet place to hold meetings or
make presentations.

Washington National, Denver, Minneapolis-St. Paul, Los Angeles, and San Francisco.

VIP AMENITIES

In 1939, American became the first airline to establish a VIP lounge to accommodate leisure and business travelers on layovers between flights. Today, American's Admirals Club is synonymous with comfort and elegance at the world's major airports. The 33,000-square-foot Admirals Club at O'Hare is the largest VIP lounge in the world.

Also located in the Admirals Club complex between Terminal 3's H and K concourses is the unique Executive Center with 19 fully equipped conference rooms. The rooms can function as a branch office for business travelers needing a quiet place to hold meetings or make presentations.

The Executive Center, opened in 1991, is just one example of the improvements that American Airlines has undertaken since O'Hare was designated as a hub in 1982. Since then, American has spent more than $500 million on upgrades and expansion projects at its O'Hare facility.

American's commitment to the city is not limited to its O'Hare operations. The airline also supports major institutions, including the Lyric Opera of Chicago, the Goodman Theatre, the Museum of Contemporary Art, and the Museum of Broadcast Communications. American also has been an active sponsor of Chicago's Neighborhood Festivals and the North American Challenge Cup/ Independence Cup race for sailors with disabilities.

WORLD-CLASS EMPLOYEES

A world-class city such as Chicago deserves world-class service from an airline. And American Airlines not only is committed to providing the greatest choice and convenience in air travel at O'Hare, but also is committed to providing personalized service—making sure passengers feel welcome when they check in, and relaxed and comfortable when they fly. Each of the more than 12,000 Chicago-based American and American Eagle employees is dedicated to providing the attention and service that are expected from the airline that "Means Business in Chicago."

ROFITS AND LOSSES, ASSETS AND LIABILITIES, THE YEAR'S SUCCESSES AND WHAT LIES AHEAD—SUCH ARE THE COMPONENTS OF ANNUAL REPORTS, THE MESSAGE OF ACCOMPLISHMENT AND IMAGE A COMPANY WANTS TO PRESENT TO THE WORLD. INDEED, THIS INFORMATION AND MORE DOES

appear in annual reports issued by LaSalle National Corporation, parent company of The LaSalle Banks.

The conventional information recounting the achievements and innovations of the LaSalle corporation is impressive—establishment of the Rembrandt family of mutual funds, the CashPro+ for Windows computerized cash-management system for commercial customers, and the Affordable Mortgage Program. Capital partnerships expanded as the bank ascended to the number one position nationwide in commercial mortgage-backed security trusteeships.

But this company's 1995 annual report told another story through its photographs. Wood paneling, shiny vaults, and dark-suited businessmen are scarce, almost absent. Instead, nearly every picture in the report is of a LaSalle employee working for the community.

Community Service, Chicago Style

he annual report contains a photo of ABN AMRO North America Inc. Chairman and CEO Harrison Tempest, bundled up for chilly lakefront weather at the March of Dimes WalkAmerica fund-raiser. Norman Bobins, shown reading to a classroom of young children, is president of LaSalle National Corporation and a man who could choose to spend his time making deals over lunch or on the golf course. Instead he works unpaid, often thankless hours as a trustee of the Chicago School Reform Board.

The impulse to do good is hardly confined to top management. Throughout the report, other employees are shown pitching in and helping out. On the cover are singers in the LaSalle-sponsored Do-It-Yourself *Messiah*, a supporter pouring orange juice for runners in a LaSalle Banks Chicago Marathon, a handyman working on housing for the poor, and a little boy listening with an inquisitive smile to a teaching aide's explanation of an intriguing idea.

All of them, and hundreds of others, are part of the LaSalle corporate culture, which calls on everyone to work beyond work.

"This organization doesn't just give lip service to serving the community," says Jocelyn Hamlar, first vice president for communications. "We roll up our sleeves and pitch in. We always send a really big team to Urban Plunge, a program in which companies get together

ABN AMRO North America Inc. Chairman and CEO Harrison Tempest leads the bank's efforts in a March of Dimes WalkAmerica fund-raiser.

to paint seniors' homes. We have an internal program that promotes our officers' working on not-for-profit boards; we encourage and celebrate that, and we internally promote the causes of those organizations. In addition to the standard giving, our employees *really* get involved."

Unwavering Character

LaSalle's character goes back to its earliest days. "LaSalle and Exchange Bank, which LaSalle acquired in 1990, were both relatively strong throughout the Great Depression," Hamlar explains. "Both developed a reputation for being there, not just trying to make a quick buck,

but working for the long term. That's fundamental to the character and personality of the bank."

And it affects everything the bank does. "We build our advertising, public relations, and marketing programs around our customers," she explains. "We stress our flexibility, the success of our retail and commercial customers, and service, which means using a lot of our frontline people. Our tellers and other customer service people are wonderful; we get mail from customers thanking them for their help and attitude. But in an ad campaign we worked on recently, we were concerned that maybe we were over-promising on our willingness to do whatever the customer needs. We

didn't want our employees to not relate to the campaign, so we did an internal survey. The researchers said that not only was the campaign fine, . . . they had never interviewed a bunch of people who were so happy about where they work."

LaSalle's parent corporation, the Netherlands-based international giant ABN AMRO Bank NV, is the world's 15th-largest bank, a global enterprise whose numbers show its impressive size and scope. ABN AMRO operates offices on six continents, where some 73,000 employees administer capital exceeding $25.7 billion, and $398 billion in assets. ABN AMRO has more than 1,800 locations in more than 71 countries.

LaSalle is the proud sponsor of Chicago's Do-It-Yourself *Messiah*.

The North America portion of ABN AMRO is no less impressive, comprising more than 350 locations, 16,000 employees, and $106 billion in assets. European American Bank, a New York-based ABN AMRO affiliate, represents $10 billion of those assets. In Chicago, LaSalle National Corporation is a holding company for two banks, including LaSalle National Bank, with assets beyond $19 billion. Another $11.4 billion comes from LaSalle Bank FSB, the state's largest thrift.

With pockets this deep, ABN AMRO clearly can do whatever is needed for its customers. "We pretty much offer everything to everybody," says Hamlar. "In the North American subsidiaries, our services range from ATMs all the way up through corporate financing for companies with more than $250 million in sales. Demographically, there is not a group we do not service. Geographically, in the

The LaSalle corporate culture extends beyond the workplace.

Chicago area, you'd be hard-pressed to find an area we're not in."

SUCCESSFUL MERGERS

LaSalle's extensive reach is partly the result of 10 mergers in as many years, starting several years after its own acquisition by ABN AMRO in 1979. The Hartford Plaza Bank, Bank of Lisle, and W.N. Lane Interfinancial were the first, followed by the important merger in 1990 of the Exchange Bancorp into LaSalle National Bank.

In 1992, LaSalle's parent acquired a Chicago stalwart, Talman Home Federal Savings and Loan Association. This South Side institution helped countless families, many of them less than a generation removed from another country, to realize the American dream of owning a home—whether a multiunit apartment building for housing the extended family while generating

rental revenue, or a single-family, Chicago-style bungalow, complete with garage and backyard. Now as then, the dream continues to thrive at LaSalle Home Mortgage Corporation, the largest single provider of home mortgages in the state of Illinois.

ABN AMRO has continued to acquire through the 1990s, adding to its ranks the Cragin Federal Savings Bank, the Illinois offices of Savings of America, CNBC Bancorp., and others. "We've grown in capability with each acquisition," Hamlar says. "Each has added something to our service mix. Talman and Cragin, which we acquired in the early 1990s, were the largest S&Ls in the area. Comerica Bank Illinois took us into the northern suburbs. We've acquired Standard Federal Bank in Michigan, which really broadens our area, and The Chicago Corporation, now known as ABN AMRO Inc., which is a very

LaSalle's James Wynsma surveys a low-income housing site developed through the support of the bank.

well-known and highly respected investment banking firm."

WORKING WITH CHICAGO

long with that greater reach and expansion of capabilities, LaSalle Bank can point with pride to another indicator of success: 10 straight years of increased earnings. There can be little dispute that LaSalle is justified in taking as its slogan The Bank That Works—but can it be coincidence that Chicago's own slogan is The City That Works?

"Strictly unintentional," Hamlar laughs. "It simply means that we get it done. As we started spreading capabilities, though, it took on an additional angle. Now, what we want to convey is not only that we work hard, but that the system works for the customer."

Intentional or not, evoking the Chicago connection is meaningful; it is a source of pleasure and pride throughout the bank. "I think everyone here has a good sense of a strong, capable Chicago," Hamlar says. "The economy here has been consistently strong; even when the rest of the country is not doing so well, Chicago has managed to ride out recessions."

One result of Chicago's relatively healthy economy is that the local construction industry stays

relatively healthy, too. LaSalle nurtures that vital sector of the local economy with its own lending division, which works specifically with general contractors throughout the Midwest. Closer to home, the bank supports city neighborhoods with services to small businesses in the Hispanic neighborhoods of Pilsen and Little Village, as well as housing loans to community organizations in Austin and on the Near West Side.

Its careful nurturing of the city beyond downtown demonstrates LaSalle's understanding of Chicago's unique character. "Chicago is very much an international hub," Hamlar explains, "but it's also a city of neighborhoods, which is very important to us. If I were to say one tangible thing about our being

here and staying here, it would be that Chicago is a world-class city."

ABN AMRO appears to agree. With offices everywhere from Boston to Bangkok, Moscow to Miami, this is an institution that knows all about world-class cities. And of the 15 North American offices ABN AMRO operates, including those in Los Angeles, New York, Mexico City, and Toronto, the company chose Chicago as its regional headquarters for all of North America, including Canada and Mexico.

"We're awfully proud to have that honor over New York and all the other possibilities," Hamlar says. "Of course, we do feel it's the right choice."

And for the many residents of Chicago, LaSalle Bank has proved to be the right choice, as well.

LaSalle employees spruce up inner city housing through the Urban Plunge program.

WITH TODAY'S HECTIC SCHEDULES, MORE AND MORE AMERICANS ARE CHOOSING TO EAT OUT. BUT EVEN WITH MORE PEOPLE DINING AWAY FROM HOME, THE RESTAURANT BUSINESS REMAINS INTENSELY COMPETITIVE. THAT MEANS THERE IS AN EVER INCREASING

need for the National Restaurant Association (NRA), an organization committed to helping its members stay on top of their industry.

With more than 32,000 members representing more than 170,000 food service outlets, the NRA is the leading national trade association for the restaurant and hospitality industry. The association works to promote the ideals and interests of its members, the employers of 9 million individuals throughout the United States.

Founded in Kansas City in 1919, the association moved to Chicago in 1927, where its head-quarters remained for more than 50 years. As the industry grew and evolved, so did the importance of legislative and regulatory issues affecting restaurant owners. In order to be a more effective voice for its members, the association purchased a building in 1979 and established its present headquarters in Washington, D.C. The NRA's function of representing the interests of its members takes place from its Washington office, where lobbying and informational efforts originate. The organization maintains its convention office in Chicago.

THE SHOW

What members think of first when they think of the NRA, though, is probably its largest event, known simply as the Show. More precisely, it is the annual NRA Restaurant-Hotel-Motel Show, the largest and most complete hospitality trade show in North America. For the 1997 Show, 1,950 exhibitors set up their wares across 1.2 million square feet of space in the giant McCormick Place convention center. Attendance at the five-day extravaganza reached 104,000, including 10,000 international buyers representing 98 countries.

Starting in 1924, all but 15 of the NRA Shows have been held in Chicago. And the hospitality industry has been meeting at the NRA Show in Chicago continuously since 1950, when it was staged at Navy Pier. The NRA Show was then among the first events to move into the original McCormick Place when it was completed in 1961. Following a devastating fire in 1967, which destroyed the convention center, the Show was forced to move temporarily to the International Amphitheater until McCormick Place was rebuilt and reopened in 1971. The Show occupied virtually every square foot of that building until 1986, when the first McCormick Place expansion was completed. In May 1997, the Show moved into the most recent expansion of the complex, which created the largest one-level exhibit floor in the country, with more than 840,000 square feet of space in the South Hall alone.

"Without a doubt, the annual NRA Show is the place to see what's new in the industry. It's where new trends often become apparent—where new product lines are launched and new technology is unveiled," says Herman Cain, the NRA's president and CEO. In addition to every conceivable product and service

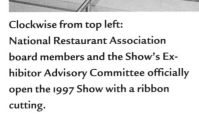

Clockwise from top left:
National Restaurant Association board members and the Show's Exhibitor Advisory Committee officially open the 1997 Show with a ribbon cutting.

Chicago Mayor Richard M. Daley visits with association staff at the NRA membership exhibit.

McCormick Place South Exhibit floor is larger than 17 football fields combined.

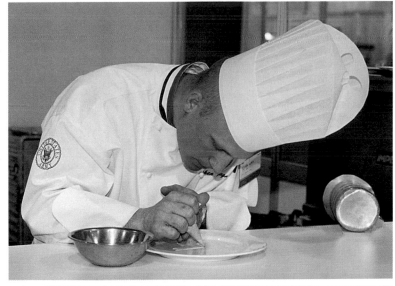

the industry has to offer, there are outstanding educational programs, culinary competitions, and social events. The NRA also has a long history of treating Show attendees to some of the biggest and most distinguished names in business, the arts, and politics, ranging from Bob Dole to Maya Angelou to Tom Peters to Ted Koppel to Norman Schwarzkopf and Colin Powell. In fact, three of the keynote speakers at the Show's opening day programs have been former chief executives of the United States—Presidents Gerald Ford, Ronald Reagan, and George Bush.

Tools of the Trade

In addition to the annual Show, the NRA uses several publications as educational tools. *Restaurants USA* is a monthly trade magazine that keeps members apprised of issues, problems, and solutions in such important areas as food trends, management

techniques, food-related health matters, and advertising and promotion. Even the important but elusive question of what to name a new restaurant is tackled in these pages. *Washington Weekly* is another vital publication produced by the NRA that provides timely updates and points of view on legislative and regulatory matters affecting the restaurant industry. *Washington Weekly* also supplies valuable how-to compliance advice to members on a wide range of legal and taxation issues.

The Ideal Location

Chicago is commonly referred to as the Convention Capital of America because it hosts more top trade shows than any other city in the country. One obvious reason is the McCormick Place complex itself. Another is the abundance of first-class hotels in the city. There are nearly 26,000 hotel rooms

in the downtown area alone. Not only is Chicago a great place to do business, but it also is the most central, most accessible city in the country. Averaging more than 110 arrivals and departures nearly every hour, no airport in the world has more daily nonstop flights than O'Hare International Airport. Just as important is the fact that Chicago is such a great restaurant town. Dining out is one of the most popular pastimes in the city and there is a wonderful mix of restaurants, each with its own unique ethnic flavor. What's more, there is a terrific blend of the old and new. There are restaurants in Chicago that have been in the same family for generations, as well as an ever changing wave of new establishments featuring the latest in cuisine and design trends. With practically every nationality and cuisine represented, the restaurant business in Chicago truly reflects the city's melting pot history.

Clockwise from top left:
Former Senator Bob Dole, the latest in a long line of internationally known speakers at the NRA Show, addresses members at the 1997 opening day program.

A member of the U.S. Army Culinary Team displays concentration and artistry in creating a plate for judging in the Professional Chefs Competition.

Attendees make their way through the Grand Concourse at the start of the Show.

CEO and President Herman Cain greets two of the nearly 10,000 international visitors to the Show.

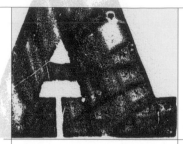

GLOBAL AIRLINE WITH STRONG CHICAGO ROOTS, TODAY'S UNITED AIRLINES IS RISING TO THE CHALLENGE OF THE NEXT CENTURY BY LISTENING TO ITS CUSTOMERS AND MEETING THEIR NEEDS. UNITED IS THE WORLD'S LARGEST AIRLINE, OPERATING SOME 2,300 FLIGHTS PER DAY,

carrying nearly 224,000 passengers to 139 destinations in 30 countries and two U.S. territories. United serves both the business and the leisure traveler, as well as cargo service markets, on five continents. In addition, United is one of the world's largest international carriers, flying nearly 9 million travelers on 70,000 international flights per year.

The airline is one of the largest companies in Illinois, with revenues of more than $16 billion. With its worldwide headquarters in nearby Elk Grove Township, United operates its largest hub from Chicago's O'Hare International Airport. Some 3,000 employees work at United's headquarters location, while the company's O'Hare International Airport staff is made up of more than 11,000 employees who service more than 440 flights daily. In total, United employs more than 90,000 people worldwide.

In many ways, United has made its mark on its home city, but perhaps nowhere is the company better represented than through its award-winning terminal designed by world-renowned, Chicago-based architect Helmut Jahn. Connect-

ing United to O'Hare, the 48-gate terminal has high ceilings, natural light, and an underground people mover that features piped-in music and Michael Hayden's fascinating light sculpture. Hayden's 800-foot sculpture is formed with more than a mile of colorful neon tubes that flicker on and off in a sequential pattern that flows from hot to cold and light to dark.

AVIATION HISTORY

For more than 70 years, United has had a history of leadership and innovations that include the world's first flight attendant service in 1930, the first airline flight kitchen in 1936, the first nonstop coast-to-coast U.S. flight in 1955, and the first nationwide automated reservations system in 1971.

United Airlines first took off in 1926 as Varney Air Lines, a mail carrier in the Pacific Northwest.

In 1927, Chicago became the key midpoint for travel between San Francisco and New York for the carriers National Air Transport and Boeing Air Transport. In the 1930s, these airlines, along with Pacific Air Transport and Varney, combined to become United. Chicago has also always been a major center for railroads and, therefore, freight cargo; today, United has the best hub-and-spoke route system in the industry. O'Hare, Denver, San Francisco, and Washington Dulles international airports are the airline's major hubs.

United operates an industry-leading flight training center in Denver and the world's largest aircraft maintenance facilities in San Francisco and Indianapolis. United's largest regional reservations office is located in Chicago, close to O'Hare. This $25 million, 120,000-square-foot facility is equipped with nearly 1,000 work-

United is the world's largest airline, operating some 2,300 flights per day, carrying nearly 224,000 passengers to 139 destinations in 30 countries and two U.S. territories (left).

For more than 70 years, United has had a history of leadership and innovations that include the world's first flight attendant service in 1930, the first airline flight kitchen in 1936, the first nonstop coast-to-coast U.S. flight in 1955, and the first nationwide automated reservations system in 1971 (right).

Nowhere is the company better represented than through its award-winning terminal designed by world-renowned, Chicago-based architect Helmut Jahn. Connecting United to O'Hare, the 48-gate terminal has high ceilings, natural light, and an underground people mover.

A global airline with strong Chicago roots, today's United Airlines is rising to the challenge of the next century by listening to its customers and meeting their needs.

stations and has the capacity to handle more than 7,000 calls per hour.

In 1990, United became the first commercial carrier to use satellite data communications in flight, allowing air traffic controllers and pilots to know where planes are at all times, even over the Pacific Ocean. This clear, quick, and uninterrupted communication is done directly between the cockpit and ground controllers, and is used instead of radio signals.

United Airlines is proud of its safety record and is a carrier known throughout the industry for making air traffic safer. Ongoing efforts include the develop-ment of safety programs that have been adopted by other carriers, such as wind-shear training for pilots, human factors or teamwork training, air-to-ground radio navigation, and deicing.

Customer Satisfaction

uring an exhaustive air traveler study, United discovered that the U.S. airline industry was failing to meet the expectations and needs of its customers. In response, United developed a customer-driven initiative that would revolutionize its service and the industry. In addition to the basic elements of safety, reli-ability, and competitive prices, United's core customer-satisfaction philosophy includes providing genuine attention to each traveler's needs, offering comfort as the minimum experience and enjoy-ment as the ideal; global access; reward and recognition; and can-dor and responsibility.

In 1994, employees took own-ership of United; today, employees own 55 percent of United's stock. The Employee Stock Ownership Program is an incentive for all employees to provide the best ser-vice and to meet the needs of the customer.

Community Involvement

United plays an active role in the Chicago community. Through its department of civic affairs, the airline is involved in Adopt-a-School and school mentor programs, and is the opening-night sponsor of the Ravinia Festival.

United's plan for the future includes an expansion of its global market through alliances with other carriers. By continuing to develop good and consistent international service, United can fulfill its mis-sion to be recognized worldwide as the airline of choice. Guided by its customer satisfaction phi-losophy, United Airlines is ready to enter the next century.

alco Chemical Company, the largest marketer of water treatment and industrial process chemicals in the world, traces its Chicago roots to 1928. That year, two local businessmen—Herbert A. Kern of Chicago Chemical Company and P. Wilson Evans of

Aluminate Sales Corporation—joined forces to create the National Aluminate Corporation.

The company's first product was sodium aluminate, a water treatment chemical used in steam engines. From a small manufacturing site in the Clearing Industrial District southwest of Chicago—in what is now Bedford Park—the young company supplied the chemical primarily to railroads to treat boiler feedwater. As the company grew and moved into new markets, the name was changed to Nalco Chemical Company in order to reflect the broader scope of its products and services.

Today, Nalco is a leading producer of specialty chemicals used in many applications of water, waste, and process treatment. Its customers come from all industries, including paper, pulp, chemical, steel, petroleum, metalworking, refining, electronics, municipalities, food, light to medium manufacturing, universities, and hospitals.

Nalco has more than 6,500 employees providing products and services to customers in more than 120 countries. Sales for 1996 topped $1.3 billion. More than 1,500 people are employed at the Clearing plant and at Nalco's facility at the Naperville Corporate and Technical Center.

The Nalco Corporate and Technical Center, located in west suburban Naperville, is the company's worldwide headquarters and major research facility (top).

Nalco is the world's leading boiler water treatment specialist, offering a variety of programs to improve boiler cleanliness, reduce operating costs, and extend boiler life. Sales representatives provide on-site expertise to help customers solve and prevent problems with their water systems and industrial processes (bottom).

COMMITTED TO BUILDING VALUE

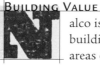

alco is committed to building value in all areas of operation. That commitment includes delivering shareholders a return on their investment; helping customers operate more efficiently; fostering a safe, pleasant work environment; and making a positive impact in the community.

Nalco uses the on-site expertise of its 3,000 worldwide sales engineers and its technically innovative products to help customers operate more efficiently and protect the environment while increasing their profits. Nalco's success in satisfying customer needs has helped it consistently meet or exceed aggressive financial goals of double-digit growth and increased profitability. That success has provided shareholders with unfailing dividends coupled with an attractive stock price.

Nalco builds value for customers through programs and services that consistently return more in long-term savings than they cost. A large U.S. paper mill that chose Nalco to boost its productivity saw a 35 percent gain in sizing efficiency. This, coupled with additional productivity improvements, netted a savings of $3 million. In Italy, improvements to a customer's boiler efficiency produced water and energy savings of $1.4 million with a return on investment (ROI) of 800 percent.

Innovative, patented technology helps Nalco solve and prevent customer problems. Its TRASAR® technology is in use in 4,000 locations worldwide. TRASAR helps customers to precisely measure volumes, locate water leaks and chemical loss, accurately determine flow rates, and trace chemicals for environmental control. Water-based ULTIMER® polymers used in water clarification, liquid-solid separation, and paper retention and drainage have been helping customers in the steel, refining, food and beverage, mining, and papermaking industries, with many recording ROIs in excess of 300 percent.

Unique, patented LAZON® technology—an advanced bioman-

agement program—offers enhanced microbiological control, reduced environmental impact, and improved operation of customer systems. LAZON customers report typical ROIs of 250 percent or more.

Nalco relies on its employees as heavily as it does technology. Thousands of sales and service representatives, as well as hundreds of researchers, are degree-bearing scientists or engineers. Working within a global support structure, they produce and deliver the solutions customers expect from Nalco. The company sees its employees as responsible for its success, and in return Nalco provides an exciting and rewarding workplace. Employees work in an environment that is safe, healthy, and fair in all aspects of work, pay, benefits, and career opportunities.

Nalco also builds value for the communities in which it operates. The Nalco Foundation donates more than $1.5 million to nonprofit organizations each year. The company adds to that with corporate contributions to various groups, a generous matching gift program, and strong support for the United Way. Recognizing that dollars are seldom enough, Nalco employees also volunteer their time and talents in their communities.

SCOTT MCDONALD/HEDRICH BLESSING

SCOTT MCDONALD/HEDRICH BLESSING

PROTECTING THE ENVIRONMENT

As a member of the Chicago community and the Chemical Manufacturers Association (CMA), Nalco is constantly working to improve safety and environmental performance. Through CMA's Responsible Care® initiative and by working with government agencies, Nalco strives to meet or exceed applicable laws and regulations at all of its operations worldwide. Nalco not only protects the environment during the development, production, and shipment of its chemical products, but it is also constantly developing innovative products and services that help customers safeguard the environment.

The PORTA-FEED® Advanced Chemical Handling System replaces traditional drums used to distribute chemicals. More than 100,000 PORTA-FEED units are in use worldwide. These stainless steel, reusable containers have eliminated the use of 3.5 million drums and the 35 million pounds of chemical waste from those drums.

Nalco's programs and services protect the environment by helping industry reuse and recycle water, cut energy use by operating more efficiently, clean wastewater, and reduce air pollution. In the paper industry—one of the largest markets it serves—the company's programs help customers cut waste by recycling paper.

For nearly seven decades in Chicago, Nalco Chemical Company has shouldered a serious responsibility to protect the environment and to build value for its shareholders, customers, employees, and communities. Standing firm on that commitment, Nalco is poised for continued success into the 21st century.

The Naperville research center includes process simulation laboratories where conditions in a customer's system are recreated in order to test solutions to the customer's problems.

Nalco's Zero Defect Delivery system combines training and equipment (including the company's patented PORTA-FEED® delivery units) to ensure proper deliveries—the right product, in the right quantity, at the right time, in the right tank—with no spills or contamination.

CHICAGO

1931 - 1971

1931	BAXTER INTERNATIONAL INC.
1932	PHOENIX DUFF & PHELPS CORPORATION
1932	RUST-OLEUM CORPORATION
1933	BARTON INCORPORATED
1934	BOZELL WORLDWIDE
1935	CHICAGO WHITE METAL CASTING, INC.
1935	COLUMBIA PIPE & SUPPLY CO.
1935	WILLIAM BLAIR & CO.
1936	RUDNICK & WOLFE
1944	QUERREY & HARROW, LTD.
1945	SARA LEE CORPORATION
1946	ATF, INC.
1947	CHICAGO TRANSIT AUTHORITY
1947	MAY & SPEH, INC.
1947	SCHUMACHER ELECTRIC CORP.
1948	BLOCK STEEL CORPORATION
1948	CAPITOL CONSTRUCTION GROUP, INC.
1948	WGN TV
1950	METRON STEEL
1952	EDELMAN PUBLIC RELATIONS WORLDWIDE
1954	BRITISH AIRWAYS
1955	MI-JACK PRODUCTS, INC.
1962	CRANE CARTON COMPANY
1962	FRANKEL & CO.
1964	DYNACIRCUITS MANUFACTURING COMPANY
1968	BANC ONE CORPORATION
1968	TELLA TOOL & MANUFACTURING CO.
1969	BROOKFIELD FARMS
1969	LAI
1969	QUIXOTE CORPORATION
1970	BOOK COVERS INC.

SINCE 1931, MEDICAL TECHNOLOGIES DEVELOPED BY BAXTER INTERNATIONAL HAVE HELPED SAVE THE LIVES OF COUNTLESS PEOPLE WITH KIDNEY FAILURE, HEART DISEASE, HEMOPHILIA, AND OTHER LIFE-THREATENING CONDITIONS. FROM ITS BEGINNINGS AS THE FIRST COMMERCIAL MANUFACTURER OF

intravenous (IV) solutions, the company has grown to become a global leader in the development and manufacture of a range of products and technologies related to the blood and circulatory system. Baxter has more than 38,000 employees in nearly 50 countries and does business in over 100 countries around the world.

PIONEER IN INTRAVENOUS THERAPY

efore Baxter introduced the first commercially produced IV solutions in glass containers in 1931, most hospitals considered IV therapy a treatment of last resort due to inadequate quality control in preparing their own solutions. In 1970, Baxter took the technology a step further when it introduced the first flexible, plastic IV container. Today, Baxter manufacturing plants around the world produce nearly 2 million containers of IV solutions a day. The company also manufactures a range of other IV and drug-delivery products, including electronic flow-control

Headquartered in Deerfield, Illinois, Baxter International Inc. is continuing to pursue innovative technologies to save the lives of people worldwide and expand its global presence.

pumps, automated pharmaceutical-dispensing systems, and anesthesia products.

LEADER IN PRODUCTS FOR TRANSFUSION MEDICINE

n 1939, Baxter introduced the first sterile blood collection and storage unit, making blood banking possible for the first time. Later, the company introduced the first plastic blood-collection container, making possible the separation of blood into its components, creating the field of blood-component therapy. The company remains the world's leading manufacturer of blood-collection and separation systems, extending its leadership to include automated systems for the collection and separation of blood.

Baxter also is a pioneer in the development of products to treat hemophilia. The company introduced the first commercially produced clotting factor in 1966, and in 1992, the first genetically manufactured clotting factor, virtually eliminating the risks associated with plasma-based products.

TREATING CARDIOVASCULAR DISEASE

axter's cardiovascular business also is responsible for a number of medical firsts: the first implantable heart valve, the first commercial heart-lung oxygenator, the first balloon-tipped catheter for vascular surgery, the first heart-monitoring catheter, and others.

The company remains a leader in all of these areas and continues to develop new products to treat late-stage cardiovascular disease. One recent innovation is an electronic, implantable pump that keeps blood circulating in people who are awaiting a heart transplant. The device has been approved in Europe as a long-term alternative to transplant.

BRINGING LIFESAVING DIALYSIS WORLDWIDE

axter also is a pioneer in the development of products to treat end-stage renal disease, or kidney failure. The company introduced the first artificial kidney machine in 1952, making lifesaving hemodialysis possible for the first time. In the late 1970s, Baxter pioneered peritoneal dialysis, which allows kidney disease patients to cleanse their blood at home rather than having to go to a clinic several times a week, greatly improving their quality of life. Baxter is the clear world leader in peritoneal-dialysis products.

THE FUTURE

eadquartered in Deerfield, Illinois, Baxter is continuing to pursue innovative medical technologies and expand its global presence. Building on more than six decades of leadership, the company is dedicated to saving lives around the world.

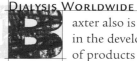

OLUMBIA PIPE & SUPPLY CO. HAS BEEN THE CHICAGO AREA'S PREMIER FULL-LINE PIPE DISTRIBUTOR FOR MORE THAN 60 YEARS. WITH MORE THAN $100 MILLION IN ANNUAL SALES, THIS PRIVATELY HELD COMPANY IS A LEADER IN THE DISTRIBUTION OF PIPE, VALVES, AND FITTINGS; PLUMBING SUPPLIES;

HVAC/hydronic supplies; pipe hangers and supports; automated valves and specialties; and industrial mill supplies.

Serving four core markets—construction, maintenance/repair/operations (MRO), capital improvement projects, and original equipment manufacturing (OEM)—Columbia Pipe & Supply is literally part of Chicago's infrastructure.

GROWTH

olumbia Pipe has strategically acquired similar companies, creating a distribution network that reaches from its Chicago headquarters at 1120 West Pershing throughout Illinois to Indiana and Wisconsin. Through membership in Affiliated Distributors (A-D), Columbia Pipe's coverage extends from coast to coast. A-D is North America's number one network of electrical, industrial mill supplies, and pipe/valves/fittings wholesalers, making it one of America's leading integrated-supply providers.

Columbia Pipe is renowned for its comprehensive inventory, which is expertly maintained through an automated warehouse management system. More than 700,000 square feet of warehouse space carries $20 million in inventory, ready for delivery. Columbia Pipe's fleet consists of more than 60 trucks and vans dispersed among its extensive network of branch locations, so customers have what they need when they need it.

QUALITY

olumbia Pipe strives to create a climate of cooperation to continually improve business processes while lowering costs for its customers. "Columbia isn't just about product," states Tim Arenberg, vice president of marketing and sales, "but about process as well." For instance, the company maintains

ISO 9002 registration through Underwriters Laboratories to ensure more efficient processes and services. "It is part of our TQM [total quality management] philosophy," Arenberg explains, "which is a systematic, disciplined approach to quality. All of our systems and procedures are continually pushed to be the best they can be to meet our customers' requirements."

SERVICE

o improve the bottom line for its customers, Columbia Pipe offers value-added services such as vendor-managed inventory, whereby Columbia Pipe personnel maintain stock in the customer's warehouse. "We can also be a complete outsource of customers' on-site procurement and material-handling functions," adds Arenberg. Columbia Pipe customers have several convenient options to conduct "electronic commerce" through the company's Web sites, on-line catalog, and other processes.

Columbia Pipe strives to add value to everything it touches—and that touches its customers. The company prides itself on listening to its customers' needs, then working hard to meet those needs. Contractors, industrial firms, institutions, and wholesalers have made Columbia Pipe their supplier of choice.

Bill Arenberg, president (on left), and Tim Arenberg, vice president marketing and sales, are among Columbia Pipe's leadership, positioning the company for growth in the next millennium (top).

The distinctive green trucks of the Columbia Pipe fleet are a familiar sight in the Chicago metropolitan area (bottom).

I N TODAY'S ROBUST INVESTMENT CLIMATE, MANY INVESTMENT MAN-
AGEMENT FIRMS CAN CLAIM THE DISTINCTION OF HANDLING LARGE
ACCOUNTS. FEWER MANAGEMENT FIRMS, HOWEVER, ENJOY A REPUTA-
TION FOR INTELLIGENT, INFORMED WORK BUILT UPON A ROCK-SOLID
FOUNDATION OF EXPERIENCE. AND FEWER STILL COMBINE BOTH THESE

attributes into one company.
One firm that has reached these
elite ranks is Chicago's respected
Phoenix Duff & Phelps Corporation.

Begun in 1932 as a research
service for financial institutions,
the company continues to make
a point of doing its homework
in order to make the best use of
clients' funds. This procedure is
just one sign of the sound and
sensible midwestern approach
that has characterized the institution since its beginnings.

Phoenix Duff & Phelps has
its roots in the respected Chicago
company of Duff & Phelps, which
joined with Phoenix Securities
in 1995. Although it is now headquartered in Hartford, Connecticut,
with offices around the country,
the company maintains a strong
local presence.

"A lot of our client base is in
Chicago," President Cal Pedersen
explains. "We manage a lot of money
for local pension funds. We're very
much a Chicago company."

Such commitment to civic
citizenship is also evident in the
company's strong participation
in community service projects,
including working with the United
Way and the Illinois branches of
the Leukemia Society of America,
the American Diabetes Association, and the Special Olympics.
In addition, many of the company's
approximately 150 Chicago-based
employees participate in the annual Chemical Bank Run.

THE DUFF & PHELPS UTILITY INCOME FUND

s a longtime presence
in the local financial
community, Phoenix
Duff & Phelps has many success
stories. Topping the list, however,
is the creation of the Phoenix Duff
& Phelps Utility Income Fund.
"Ask a hundred people on La Salle

Street at lunchtime what they
think of when they hear Phoenix
Duff & Phelps, and the majority
would name the Utility Income
Fund," Pedersen says. "We filed
in November 1986 with the SEC
for registration of a $100 million
mutual fund, and wound up with

$1.3 billion raised for the fund.
We closed the fund down because
it was so successful."

Not only was the Duff &
Phelps Utility Income Fund the
largest initial public offering in
the history of the New York Stock
Exchange, it was a ringing vote

of confidence in the company. And it was entirely justified: The fund's assets are now in excess of $2 billion. Pedersen says, "At the time we filed, we were confident, but we had no idea we would receive such a strong response. If there was an event that showed us people knew about our work, that was it."

A History of Excellence

The healthy condition of Phoenix Duff & Phelps throughout its history and into the present testifies to the vision of two men, George E. Phelps and William H. Duff. It was in 1932, while the United States was struggling through the depths of the Great Depression, that Phelps, a securities analyst, wrote to Duff, a utility-investment salesman, and suggested they join forces to provide banks, insurance companies, and individuals with background information on potential utility investments. Their agreement called for Phelps to write reports in his spare time, while Duff performed sales and client-contact duties.

Their work stood out from the start, in part because Phelps brought a broad base of firsthand knowledge to the endeavor. A graduate of Wisconsin's Marquette University, he had worked on rate cases at a Wisconsin electric power company. Moving to a securities company, he gained experience in analyzing bond and trust investments, eventually creating a research department within the company. By the time he and his partner had struck out on their own, Phelps had a thorough background in analysis.

As for Duff, the talented salesman traveled far and wide to gather the information that Phelps wrote into the meticulous reports that became the company's hallmark.

Initially, Duff & Phelps offered in-depth analysis of utility companies to institutional investors, who supported the firm via monthly, quarterly, or annual retainers. As its client list grew, its services expanded to include informed opinions on various types of financing, evolving from a sideline operation into the important field of financial consulting.

Duff & Phelps also pioneered such innovations as the practice of dividing credit ratings below Triple A into three categories each. In the 1970s, it initiated the D&P Watch List, which signaled potential credit rating changes. Both have been widely imitated.

Steady growth has led Phoenix Duff & Phelps to become a leading money management firm of institutional and retail assets. The firm offers several distinct investment management styles through a diverse product line, including open- and closed-end mutual funds, variable annuities, privately-managed accounts, and institutional accounts.

In 1995, Phoenix Duff & Phelps took pride in receiving the DALBAR Key Honors Award, conferred by the nationally recognized mutual fund industry rating organization.

That commitment to service remains firmly in place as Phoenix Duff & Phelps moves into the future. "One goal we've stated publicly is to be a premier, world-class investment organization," Pedersen says.

◀ VITO PALMISANO

Phoenix Duff & Phelps enjoys a reputation for intelligent, informed investment management built upon a rock-solid foundation of experience.

ODAY, THE NAME RUST-OLEUM® AUTOMATICALLY COMES TO MIND WHEN CONSUMERS WORLDWIDE AIM THEIR SIGHTS ON PREVENTING RUST ON METAL PRODUCTS. BUT BEFORE THE RUST-OLEUM LINE OF PROTECTIVE COATINGS FOUND ITS HOME ON THE SHELVES OF GARAGES AND HARDWARE stores everywhere, it was an idea forming in the mind of a 12-year-old cabin boy assigned the task of keeping his ship's metal rust-free.

Young Robert Fergusson noticed that where slow-drying, raw fish oil had spilled on the metal surfaces of his ship, further corrosion of the rusted areas was prevented. Over the years, this bit of knowledge stayed with Fergusson as he became a master mariner and sailed the world. Determined to turn what he knew about raw fish oil into a viable product, his challenge was to concoct a brew that would prevent rust and dry quickly—without leaving a fish odor.

At the end of World War I, Fergusson got the chance he'd been waiting for. Now a captain, he became custodian of a laid-up fleet of 100 ships for the U.S. Maritime Shipping Board. Using one of the ship's galleys as his test kitchen, and the ships as his experimental subjects, Fergusson combined the right fish oil resins heated to the right temperature to produce a coating that stopped rust, dried overnight, and did not leave a lingering odor.

In 1921, the captain retired from sea duty, set up the Anti-Rust Paint Company of New Orleans, and began crisscrossing the country in a Model A Ford painted in the four colors of his new paint line. In 1929, with $1,000 in his pocket, Fergusson moved to Chicago to expand the business. Three years later, Rust-Oleum Corporation began offering the rust-inhibitive product in nine colors.

Today, under the corporate ownership of RPM, Inc., Rust-Oleum is trusted by industrial end users around the world, and is a household name among more than 90 percent of do-it-yourself consumers across America. Its 2,200 products generate more than $200 million in annual sales in more than 80 countries worldwide. Timely delivery and service of industrial products is guaranteed through 1,000 authorized distributors and independent paint stores. And consumer products are sold at more than 30,000 retail outlets.

Whether it's coating every imaginable surface from metal deck furniture to outside storage tanks, or protecting everything from the space shuttle to concrete floors from harsh chemicals, Rust-Oleum has a solution. The reason for the success of Rust-Oleum is simple, says President Michael Tellor: "The product is of exceptionally high quality, and that has never been diminished. In other words, it works, so people keep coming back to it."

Today, the name Rust-Oleum® automatically comes to mind when consumers worldwide aim their sights on preventing rust on metal products.

STEADY GROWTH

That high quality explains why the story of Rust-Oleum is the story of growth. In 1933, the company sold coatings to a beverage company in Montreal, and Canada has been an important market ever since. In 1938, Fergusson built a plant in Evanston. After Fergusson's death in 1940, his sons, Donald and Robert, continued to grow the business. By 1948, the pair had organized 19 sales districts throughout the country, expanded into Central America, and increased the company's rust-preventive coatings to 20 colors.

In the 1950s, consumer demand for Rust-Oleum products exploded, and they quickly became staples in hardware and paint stores across the nation. At the same time, distributors were set up in the Middle East and Asia, and in 1960, a manufacturing facility was built

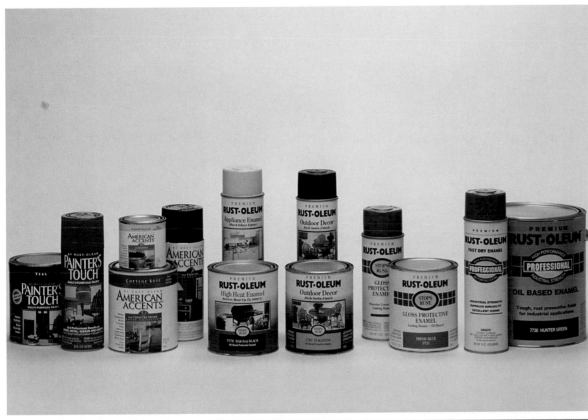

Rust-Oleum® consumer products are sold at more than 30,000 retail outlets.

Timely delivery and service of industrial products is guaranteed through 1,000 authorized distributors and independent paint stores.

in the Netherlands, marking the first time Rust-Oleum products were produced outside the United States. Consequently, international sales soon passed the $1 million mark annually.

Pioneering aerosol technology and high-profile advertising, particularly TV spots featuring comedian Jonathan Winters, made Rust-Oleum a household name by the 1970s, and continued plant expansion followed. In 1967, the Evanston facility was enlarged and in 1975, a manufacturing facility was built in Hagerstown, Maryland. Shortly before his death in 1976, Donald Fergusson, who had taken the helm upon his brother Bob's death in 1966, selected Vernon Hills, Illinois, as the site for the company's new international headquarters.

Donald Fergusson left behind a company that was producing more than 300 standard products and hundreds of special items sold in more than 80 countries by 1,300 distributors worldwide. In 1989, the Evanston plant was replaced by a 250,000-square-foot plant in Pleasant Prairie, Wisconsin, that houses manufacturing, research and development, and quality assurance facilities. Additionally, Rust-Oleum got into the business of manufacturing high-quality floor

coatings in 1991, when it purchased a flooring company in Tulsa.

New Owners Set Expansion Goals

PM, Inc., a publicly traded company consisting of more than 30 operating companies, purchased Rust-Oleum Netherlands BV and Rust-Oleum France SA in 1991. In June 1994, RPM purchased the entire Rust-Oleum Corporation, and record years of sales and profits have followed.

"We are aggressively expanding the scope of our business," says Tellor. "We are in the process of moving beyond the niche of just rust prevention to solving a variety

of problems where coatings can be a solution."

To that end, the company is launching products that can be used on all types of surfaces. "We are breaking outside the metal furniture market, moving indoors to wood surfaces and a variety of applications around the home," Tellor adds. "As for the industrial division, we now offer a complete maintenance package for a facility. We offer products that protect the roof, floor, and everything in between.

"We've set aggressive goals," admits Tellor. And why not? With a proven track record and phenomenal growth, Rust-Oleum Corporation will prosper well into the next century.

WHEN JIMMY BUFFETT GOES WASTIN' AWAY IN MARGARITAVILLE, HE NO DOUBT GETS HIS INSPIRATION FROM HIS CONCERT-TOUR SPONSOR, BARTON INCORPORATED, THE BEER AND DISTILLED SPIRITS MARKETER THAT HAS BECOME AN INDUSTRY MODEL

of energized growth, aggressive marketing, and management efficiency.

Barton Beers, Ltd., sponsor of the Buffett tour for more than 10 years, is the third-largest beer importer and largest non-brewery-owned beer marketer in the United States. Representing five of the top 20 imported beer brands and working with a nationwide network of roughly 850 beer distributors, Barton has repeatedly outpaced industry growth, which translates into annual sales of some 30 million cases nationally.

Barton Beers, Ltd. is the third-largest beer importer and largest non-brewery-owned beer marketer in the United States. Barton represents five of the top 20 imported beer brands, and sells some 30 million cases annually.

Barton Brands, Ltd. is the fourth-largest distilled spirits marketer in the United States, with brands selling in the top 10 in virtually every category of distilled spirits through a network of more than 250 distributors. While distilled spirits consumption has markedly decreased in the last 12 years, Barton has grown its business through acquisition and internal brand development.

"We are on an incredible roll," says Ellis Goodman, chairman and chief executive officer of parent company Barton Incorporated. "Our beer business has more than doubled in the last three years, and our spirits business is going through an extremely successful period of growth and diversification. We're now doing in excess of $800 million a year. In 1982, when we purchased Barton, it did $120 million. Profits are up some 1,200 percent over the period."

ADAPTABILITY AND STRATEGIC ACQUISITION

Adaptability to changing consumer preferences and markets, coupled with strategic acquisitions, has been the key to success, Goodman says. At Barton Beers, that philosophy has translated into a strategy of focusing on carving out market niches, with a targeted portfolio of leading

imported and specialty brands and craft brews.

Established in 1976 as ADP Liquor Imports, the company two years later introduced Corona Extra to the United States. Within eight years, Corona Extra was the second-best-selling import in America, and Goodman expects it to pass Heineken in 1998 as the top seller. In 1989, Corona Light was introduced, and quickly became the second-best-selling imported light beer. Barton also represents other Mexican beers—Modelo Especial, Negra Modelo, and Pacifico.

Barton Beers acquired Monarch Imports in 1987, the importers of Tsingtao Beer from China; became the importer in 1989 for Peroni, Italy's number one beer; bought Consolidated Pacific Products in 1990 (Pacifico beer); bought Associated Brands in 1993 (St. Pauli Girl from Germany and Double Diamond from the United Kingdom); and bought Stevens Point Brewery in 1992 (Point beers).

The same steady acquisition strategy has worked for Barton Brands, Ltd., including the 1989 purchase of the Ultra Brands Division from Hiram Walker (Ten High Bourbon, Imperial Blended Whiskey, Lauder's Scotch, Northern Light Canadian, and Crystal Palace Gin & Vodka). In 1995, the company acquired a major part

GREAT WITH CHOPS.

TSINGTAO BEER

of the United Distillers Glenmore business (Fleischmann's, Mr. Boston, Canadian Ltd., Chi Chi's, and Glenmore), virtually doubling the size of its spirits business.

Barton is the second-largest supplier of tequila (Montezuma) and Monte Alban, the number-one-selling mescal in the country. Most recently, the company extended its Chi Chi's line with Mexican Mudslide, Arctic Snowslide, and Caribbean Mudslide, which are light, cream-based drinks.

Barton Brands services its portfolio through its distilling and bottling plants and facilities in Bardstown and Owensboro, Kentucky; Albany and Atlanta, Georgia; and Carson, California.

NICHE MARKETING AND MANAGEMENT STABILITY

arton has capitalized on its diverse product lines through expert marketing. In addition to Corona Extra's sponsorship of the Buffett tour, St. Pauli Girl has sponsored jazz saxophonist Richard Elliot's national tour since 1995. A wide variety of promotional tie-ins and television, radio, and outdoor advertising support each of the Barton Beers brands in a coordinated marketing strategy groomed to enhance brand image, build brand loyalty, and boost sales. Barton Brands, Ltd. marketing includes outdoor advertising and sporting promo-

tions, TV cooking tie-ins, and magazine and news-paper ads.

Barton further believes that the stability of its senior management has been crucial to its success. The company's Chicago roots go back to 1933, when it was founded by the Abelson and Getz families after Prohibition. In 1970, Goodman founded Amalgamated Distilled Products Ltd. in the United Kingdom, parent company of ADP. Amalgamated bought Barton Brands, Ltd. in 1982, and ADP changed its name to Barton Beers, Ltd. In 1987, Goodman led a management buyout of Barton from its U.K. parent. In 1993, Barton merged with Canandaigua Wine Company, currently the second-largest wine supplier in the United States. Goodman; Alexander L. Berk, president and chief operating officer of Barton Incorporated; Edward Golden, president of Barton Brands, Ltd.; and Bill Hackett, president of Barton Beers, Ltd., have 114 years of combined experience within the liquor industry and have consequently built strong supplier/distributor relationships.

"We firmly believe that personal relationships are of the utmost importance in the development of our business," Goodman emphasizes.

As for the future, Goodman sees more of the same: "As the industry continues to consolidate, we can see more acquisition opportunities. I see us continuing to grow and getting better at what we do."

Clockwise from top left:
The Bardstown plant comprises 180 acres with 28 barrel warehouses, six bottling lines, and an annual bottling capacity of more than 4 million cases. The distillery has a production capacity of 150,000 proof gallons per week and a storage capacity of 550,000 cases.

The most recognized names in the Barton line—House of Stuart Blended Scotch Whisky, Barton Gin, Barton Vodka, Very Old Barton Bourbon Whisky, and Montezuma Tequila—all represent products with consistency, quality, and value in a rapidly changing environment.

The Fleischmann's brand family, produced at Barton's Owensboro, Kentucky, facility, includes nationally recognized, traditional spirits of the highest quality.

OZELL WORLDWIDE CONSISTENTLY DEMONSTRATES WHAT ADVERTISING, MARKETING, AND PUBLIC RELATIONS COMPANIES DO BEST: CHANGE ATTITUDES AND BEHAVIORS. BY WORKING WITH CLIENTS—AND THEIR CLIENTS' CLIENTS— BOZELL HAS MADE AN ART OF FINDING SOLUTIONS TO

tough problems such as taking ingrained public perceptions and turning them around.

What makes Bozell different from the other advertising agencies in town is that they take a media-neutral approach to building brands. Bozell's goal is to make something happen in the marketplace, not to create ads. Therefore, the company chooses the communications vehicle that best delivers the message. Whether it is an ad, a public relations effort, a direct mail piece, or point-of-purchase materials, the communication works to solve the challenge the brand faces.

"While people generally tend to think of us as an advertising agency, we've never had a client walk through the door asking us for an ad," says Tom Hayden, executive vice president and general manager of Bozell Worldwide's Chicago operation. "Marketers need solutions—to build their brands, to grow their businesses, to open a new store. They don't need ads, per se."

This media-neutral approach has been working for years for the

agency's clients such as the Milk Processors Promotion Board, Jeep, Weber Grills, and the "Pork. The Other White Meat®" campaign.

The pork campaign, surely one of Bozell's most notable, was born more than 10 years ago when the National Pork Producers Council and Bozell joined forces to reposition and reinvigorate a declining industry. The story of the pork campaign is now a Harvard Business School case study on how to achieve a successful turnaround.

Bozell is a global marketing communications organization with full-service operations in more than 90 cities. As a subsidiary of True North Communications, a global holding company also based in Chicago, Bozell ranks among the largest firms in the United States and is the fastest-growing agency in the United States top 20. Bozell was founded by Morris Jacobs and Leo Bozell in Omaha in 1921, and started in Chicago in 1934.

Today, Bozell Worldwide's Chicago office is located on North Michigan Avenue near the Tribune Tower and the Magnificent Mile. In addition, the offices house O'Connell, Norton & Partners and Bozell Public Relations.

O'Connell, Norton & Partners is the leading U.S. agency specializing in business-to-business food marketing, food processing, and grocery trade. O'Connell provides trade marketing support with a twist, recognizing that the consumer is the ultimate purchaser. Some clients need trade advertising alone, others need broader service support. This is where Bozell's integrated specialty comes on strong.

Bozell Public Relations is another important aspect of this unique company. It specializes in consumer marketing and has moved from 22nd to fourth in the Chicago rankings in the last five

Tom Hayden (on left) serves as executive vice president and general manager for Bozell Worldwide in Chicago and Dan O'Connell is general manager and senior vice president of O'Connell, Norton & Partners (top).

Bozell Worldwide's media-neutral approach has worked for clients such as Weber Grills (bottom).

years. This group helps manage the complex PR and event marketing for Kraft Foods, Quaker Oats, Harley-Davidson, Oscar Mayer, and Radio Flyer.

Bozell ranks eighth among the top 10 in the Chicago advertising market, thus reinforcing its position as a strong operating unit of a global company. Again this year, Bozell PR is poised to shine. Combining rapid growth, aggressive management, new business, strategic acquisitions, and cooperation across several marketing disciplines, the Chicago office is building strength and equity based on quality work supported by solid clients, a shared leadership vision, and an energized atmosphere.

CLOSE TO THE CUSTOMER

Close to the Customer, the company's credo, means being a physical presence that understands the client's business, its customers, and the ultimate customer.

"Being close to the customer to us means understanding a client's situation well enough to be able to provide a bigger solution. As such, we're not the first and foremost in the business of making ads or doing press releases; we're in the business of managing solutions," says Mark Williams, senior partner. Bozell's team strategy is based on redefining the traditional role of the advertising agency, on building campaigns from the client's perspective and the client's customer's perspective by offering services based on their needs.

Bozell's approach is unique in the advertising and marketing area. Employees from different departments organize their talents and pull them together into Primary Service Teams. The pork campaign is a perfect example. Bozell worked with the client and used public relations, marketing strategies, and media advertising to change the perceptions of the product in the general populace.

Bozell has won countless awards through the years. The Milk Mustache advertising for the National Fluid Milk Processor Promotion Board was named the most popular print campaign of 1996, based on a consumer poll. Bozell's campaigns for Jeep, Valvoline, and

Excedrin also have been award winners.

COMMUNITY FOCUSED

Bozell Worldwide has made a strong commitment to the community, especially to children. "We must pay rent for the space we occupy on this earth," cofounder Morris Jacobs once said. "Give back to the community." The company has always followed this idea.

Bozell supports programs for Off the Street Club, Junior Achievement, Juvenile Protective Association, Cristo-Rey High School—where Bozell pays the tuition for several children who, in return, work at Bozell once a week—and Catholic Charities, the city's largest social service organization.

With Junior Achievement alone, Bozell has made a significant impact. For the past years, the company has been instrumental in helping Junior Achievement persuade business leaders to devote their talents, time, and financial support to its programs, which encourage young people to cultivate an understanding of free enterprise.

With Junior Achievement, Bozell has made a significant impact.

These philanthropic endeavors coupled with an exemplary track record with Chicago-area businesses provide Bozell with the tools necessary to compete in an ever changing marketplace. Chicago's specialization of services will continue to distinguish the agency from its competition, says Hayden.

"The various parts that make up our whole consistently work as one to bring clients the right solution," he says. "It is this point of differentiation that will continue to make Bozell one of the fastest-growing, most-admired agencies in the United States."

"The Other White Meat®" campaign was born more than 10 years ago when the National Pork Producers Council and Bozell joined forces to reposition and reinvigorate a declining industry.

HICAGO WHITE METAL CASTING, INC., BORN IN THE BASEMENT OF A GERMAN IMMIGRANT'S HOME IN 1935, IS TODAY ONE OF THE MOST ADVANCED GLOBAL PRODUCERS OF DIE-CAST PRODUCTS IN ITS INDUSTRY, SHIPPING INTRICATELY FORMED COMPONENTS TO THE WORLD'S MOST DEMANDING COMPANIES.

FROM A BASEMENT TO ISO 9002

The story of Chicago White Metal Casting (CWM) began in the basement of a German immigrant to Chicago, Walter G. Treiber Sr.

In 1935, Treiber set about producing what were known as slush castings—designing bronze molds for coffin corners and lamp bases into which he poured molten zinc alloy, sometimes called white metal. Meeting with some success, Treiber and his partner, Sam Gullo, incorporated the business in 1937 and moved to a second-story loft on South May Street. On the heels of celebrating its 60th anniversary in 1997, CWM has a reputation as one of the world's leading producers of high-technology die-cast components.

Current President Walter Treiber, the founder's son, fondly recalls Saturday mornings spent at the plant. "If I did a particularly good job hand cleaning die castings, I'd be taken over to Barney's on Halsted and Randolph for one of their giant, 50-cent hamburgers," he says.

Later, the company moved to the corner of Des Plaines and Lake Street, behind the Fulton Fish Market. "In the summer," Treiber recalls, "the aromas were really memorable, even up on the third floor."

The purchase of a used automatic zinc die-casting machine (for $500) in 1940 moved the company squarely into the die-casting business, then a very young industry. Metal was uncertified and often metallurgically impure.

The postwar boom brought prosperity to die casters. Chicago White Metal purchased its first aluminum die-casting machine and its first mechanical trim press in 1954. The company by this time occupied three buildings on Chicago's Northwest Side, but began experiencing growing pains.

After seven years in sales positions outside the company, the young Walter Treiber joined CWM, visiting die casters worldwide for ideas on die-casting plant expansion. He proposed purchasing newly developed magnesium die-

Clockwise from top left:
Walter G. Treiber Sr.'s portrait hangs on the walls of Chicago White Metal Casting, Inc., the company he helped found in 1937. Today, his grandson Eric Treiber and son Walter Treiber operate the business.

The plant expansion from basement to Chicago loft in 1937 heralded the incorporation of Chicago White Metal Casting.

Today's Chicago White Metal facility is one of the best equipped in the industry.

casting machines for a new plant, capable of producing parts by the higher-performing hot-chamber mag process—little known to U.S. product designers. At the time, magnesium alloy was considered difficult to cast, with mag parts used by very few American companies.

A magnesium die-casting department was included in CWM's expansion plans, with a new plant constructed in the Chicago suburb of Bensenville in 1976. Sadly, although an office in the new building was designed for Walter Treiber Sr., he died in 1977 and was never able to occupy it.

In 1990, Eric Treiber joined his father in what is now a singularly successful third-generation family business, employing nearly 200 skilled workers from diverse ethnic backgrounds, manufacturing die castings on the cutting edge of the industry's capabilities.

The current Chicago White Metal facility is one of the best equipped in the industry, producing advanced die-cast parts in aluminum, magnesium, zinc, and ZA-8 alloys. The company's quality management system is ISO 9002-94 registered.

RECYCLABLE, NET-SHAPE COMPONENTS

aking a contribution to the world's environment, die-cast parts can be serviced, renewed, and finally recycled once they reach the end of their usefulness. All of the aluminum die castings produced by CWM are made from post-consumer recycled alloy.

Chicago White Metal has won numerous product awards in international competitions for computer, telecommunications, medical, and industrial applications. Walter Treiber has served an unprecedented three terms as president of the International Magnesium Association.

Because the company casts in all of the most widely specified alloys, designers can be assured of objective material recommendations for their applications.

CWM high-technology die-cast processing makes possible volume production of intricately featured products in high-strength metal. These parts are being cast to the net- and near-net-shapes required by product design engineers across all industries, routinely achieving exacting dimensional specifications, with no further machining or secondary operations. They are being shipped to customers throughout the world.

Early consultation with CWM engineers allows designers to achieve more intricate contours and closer tolerances in their die-cast parts, combining multiple parts into one and reducing costs even on shorter production runs.

Casting solidity can be assured with careful die design and the use of advanced vacuum technology. Thinner walls can be designed for added package space and reduced weight.

THE TECHNOLOGY FULL-COURT PRESS

tate-of-the-art CAD workstations, using the latest 3-D modeling software, are being used for CWM's dimension-driven execution of product and tooling designs. Electronic data access and transfer of component design data are routine.

For production as well as part prototype development and testing prior to tooling design, the latest CNC machining centers are in operation at CWM, in-house. And the newest CAD-integrated stereolithography technology is now being used for creating rapid prototype masters.

CWM's quality assurance has moved from production inspection to total management commitment and responsibility in all aspects of defect prevention.

Since qualified, well-trained, and motivated people are at the heart of any custom production system, CWM management is committed to an ongoing, comprehensive, and companywide education to assure that its employees are equipped to excel.

Today, Chicago White Metal takes turnkey responsibility for a company's complete product assembly, sourcing all of the parts required in addition to die castings, with final packaging to the customer's precise requirements.

The company's 136,000-square-foot facility houses one of the custom die-casting industry's largest hot-chamber magnesium departments, with three hot-chamber mag machines ranking among the world's largest (left).

State-of-the-art CNC machining centers are used for part prototypes and machining finished parts to precision tolerances where net-shape die-casting production is not feasible (right).

WILLIAM BLAIR & COMPANY IS AMONG A HANDFUL OF INVESTMENT FIRMS IN THE UNITED STATES THAT HAVE ENDURED AS INDEPENDENT, EMPLOYEE-OWNED ORGANIZATIONS FOR MORE THAN SIX DECADES. FROM ITS INCEPTION IN 1935, THE FIRM HAS BASED ITS

Clockwise from top left: Guiding today's William Blair & Company are CEO David Coolidge III (left) and Senior Director Edgar D. Jannotta.

William Blair & Company currently oversees more than $14 billion in investor funds.

The firm is dedicated to the fundamental principle of providing quality investment products and services to achieve outstanding long-term results for its clients.

operations in one main office. Even today, William Blair & Company remains dedicated to one fundamental principle: to provide quality investment products and services to achieve outstanding, long-term results for its clients.

"It's unique to have survived in the investment business for more than 60 years with the same employee ownership structure," says Chief Executive Officer E. David Coolidge III. "We've only had one name change, in 1944, and we've never merged with or acquired

other companies. We're a real rock of stability in an industry where firms change frequently."

A FIRM FOUNDATION AND HIGH STANDARDS

The key to the firm's success lies in its solid foundation. William McCormick Blair, who remained active in the firm until his death in 1982 at age 97, founded the company in 1935.

Bucking the odds, Blair and his partner, Francis A. Bonner, opened their general investment banking firm during the Great Depression in the aftermath of the 1929 stock market crash. The number of Chicago securities houses was dwindling, but Blair, Bonner & Company felt it could succeed by taking the high road in a field that was known for its shoddy practices. In fact, Blair and Bonner established a firm based on standards even more stringent than the newly formed Securities and Exchange Commission. The firm's reputation, then and now, was that of a conservatively financed organization that stood for honest dealings, sound corporate financial advice, unbiased investment

recommendations, and civic responsibility.

In addition to being driven by high goals, Blair was motivated by intense pride in Chicago and the Midwest, and by the desire to help finance the expansion of local companies. His firm rapidly grew in stature and size as he secured the financial backing of such local, notable names as Swift, Armour, Ryerson, and, of course, his own McCormick relatives of International Harvester fame.

INTERNATIONALLY KNOWN

Today, as a leading full-service investment banking firm that provides comprehensive financing, brokerage, research, and investment advisory services to corporations and investors, William Blair & Company enjoys an international reputation as one of the nation's most successful underwriters and research providers of high-quality growth companies. The firm's equity products are marketed to individual and institutional clients throughout North America, Europe, and the Far East. More than 20 full-time research analysts provide careful, in-depth knowledge

of more than 260 companies in industries that hold the promise of growth.

Several of Chicago's great growth companies, such as Safety-Kleen, Service Master, General Binding, Molex, and Oil-Dri Corporation, were introduced to the public by William Blair & Company. During the 1990s, the firm has managed initial public offerings for more than 91 companies, underwritten more than 112 secondary offerings, and raised more than $13.9 billion. The firm's clients include specialty retailing, business and consumer services, consumer products, technology, information services, health care, and manufacturing and distribution companies.

The firm currently oversees more than $14 billion in investor funds. Fee-based discretionary asset management is offered to pension plans, endowments, foundations, family estates and trusts, and individuals. Investors are able to select from all of William Blair & Company's products—including stocks, bonds, private equity, and mutual funds—on either a nondiscretionary or a discretionary basis.

In fixed income markets, William Blair has earned a national reputation for successfully raising debt capital for cultural institutions, including the Art Institute of Chicago, the Shedd Aquarium Society, the Lyric Opera of Chicago, the Museum of Contemporary Art, and the Museum of Science and Industry. The firm also serves traditional debt-issuing clients, such as private corporations and states, counties, municipalities, and school districts. The company has expanded its client base to encompass health care facilities, institutions of higher learning, and transportation authorities.

Employee Owned

he firm has more than 130 employee-owners, representing a significant percentage of the professional staff. Many of these principals have spent their entire careers with the company, and represent a wealth of experience and intellectual capital. William Blair makes a long-term commitment to its employees, and its broad ownership base is representative of the firm's inclusive culture.

The firm's commitment to Chicago is evident also in the charitable involvement of many of its employees and principals. Senior Director Edgar D. Jannotta

serves as chairman of the Lyric Opera of Chicago. He and Senior Director Edward McCormick Blair—son of William Blair—are past chairmen of the board of Rush-Presbyterian-St. Luke's Medical Center. Coolidge is a past president of the Better Government Association and Youth Guidance. In addition, the William Blair & Company Foundation supports many other charitable, civic, cultural, educational, and medical organizations in the Chicago area.

William Blair & Company continues to stake its claim as a leading player in the investment banking field. While the firm's national prominence can be attributed to underwriting highly successful companies and giving excellent investment advice, acknowledging and perpetuating company traditions in its day-to-day business have been equally important. As business leaders plan the long-range strategies that will shape the future of their companies, William Blair serves as a reminder that a sense of history and strong links to the past also have a place in America's corporate boardrooms. To its clients, this Chicago company is proof that tradition pays dividends.

William Blair's national prominence can be attributed to underwriting highly successful companies and giving excellent investment advice.

UDNICK & WOLFE'S HEART AND SOUL IS ITS ABILITY TO UNDERSTAND THOROUGHLY ITS CLIENTS' BUSINESSES, TO APPLY THE RELEVANT LAW, AND THEREBY TO DELIVER TOP-QUALITY, RESPONSIVE LEGAL SERVICE. THIS PHILOSOPHY HAS DRIVEN THE FIRM SINCE ITS FOUNDING IN 1936.

"Today, our clients demand more than technical proficiency," says Lee I. Miller, managing partner. "We believe the best lawyers are those who know the law and can provide business acumen to a transaction or to litigation."

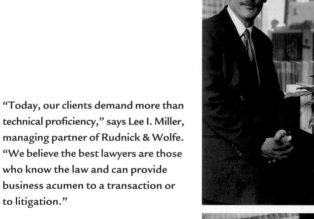

"Today, our clients demand more than technical proficiency," says Lee I. Miller, managing partner of Rudnick & Wolfe. "We believe the best lawyers are those who know the law and can provide business acumen to a transaction or to litigation."

Meeting this challenge requires a special kind of lawyer, the type Rudnick & Wolfe works hard to develop and retain. "We are committed to creating a work environment where quality, diversity, and collegiality are the cornerstones of our practice. We invest in our people by providing the optimal combination of training and mentoring of junior lawyers by senior partners of the firm. It is our belief that clients benefit from these relationships," says Miller.

"We also know the benefit of collaboration with clients," says Partner Peter C.B. Bynoe. "We strive to achieve measurable results for each client that we have the privilege to serve. We work closely with clients to understand the unique aspects of their businesses, their legal needs, and the industries and economic trends that impact their

businesses. It is our goal to build long-term strategic partnerships with each of our clients," says Bynoe.

Rudnick & Wolfe's approach to combining its insights into both business and the law has helped the firm grow to its current size of nearly 300 attorneys, with offices in Chicago; Tampa; Washington, D.C.; Baltimore; and Appleton. The firm continues to be a leader in the areas of real estate, franchising and distribution, litigation, and general corporate law. The geographic scope of the firm's practice is extensive, including both national and international representation of clients.

A REAL ESTATE LEADER

udnick & Wolfe distinguishes itself through the depth and expertise of its real estate law practice.

(From left) Tara A. Cope, associate; Stephen A. Landsman, partner; and Dorian R. Williams, partner, contribute to Rudnick & Wolfe's tradition of thoroughly understanding business and law.

The real estate practice is one of the most highly regarded and largest in the country. Its lawyers have expertise in virtually every aspect of commercial, industrial, and residential property—including financing, leasing, environmental compliance, construction, home building, affordable housing, shopping center development, workouts, tax increment financing, land use and zoning, and litigation arising from these transactions.

Effective Business Counsel

ver the years, Rudnick & Wolfe has also developed a very significant practice in the complex area of corporate law. The firm's corporate law practice includes advising clients on mergers and acquisitions, franchising and distribution, corporate finance, health care, intellectual property, estate planning, securities, employee benefits, taxation, and routine business matters. The firm's corporate lawyers bring considerable legal and business experience, as well as the capabilities of its attorneys in labor and employment law, ERISA, environmental, litigation, and other areas. At Rudnick & Wolfe, attorneys recognize that the tried and true approach may be suitable for one transaction, while a creative, cutting-edge structure may be best for another.

Commitment to Quality Litigation and Dispute Resolution

hrough its solid understanding of business, Rudnick & Wolfe provides superior services in the areas of litigation and dispute resolution. The firm's philosophy combines excellence, efficiency, and aggressive advocacy with skilled negotiation to deliver top notch counsel and vigorous representation for clients facing litigation. The firm's litigation practice has experienced tremendous growth. Today, the firm has more than 90 experienced trial attorneys. Firm attorneys work closely with clients to explore the feasibility of using alternatives to full-scale litigation, such as summary trials, arbitration, mediation, and other forms of alternative dispute resolution. The firm has handled a variety of mediation and arbitration cases before tribunals throughout the United States and in foreign countries.

Community Commitment

udnick & Wolfe has a long tradition of providing legal services on a pro bono basis to individuals and organizations in need. As an institution, the firm has adopted and provides pro bono, volunteer, and financial support to food banks in the cities where it has offices, and to Second Harvest, a national network of food banks.

In 1997, the firm was recognized for its numerous pro bono contributions. It received the Chicago Bar Association's Large Law Firm Pro Bono Legal Services Award and the Illinois State Bar Association's John C. McAndrew Award for Pro Bono Service. Litigation partner John Chen received the American Bar Association's Pro Bono Publico Award, only five of which are awarded across the nation annually.

As the new millenium approaches, Rudnick & Wolfe continues to invest in its people and the technology needed to consistently provide superior and efficient legal services to clients. The firm plans to do this by keeping an eye on the future, and remembering the wisdom and knowledge gained from the past.

UICK, EFFICIENT RESPONSE TO INCREASINGLY COMPLEX CLIENT NEEDS. AS ONE OF CHICAGO'S LEADING LITIGATION FIRMS, THAT'S WHAT QUERREY & HARROW HAS BEEN PROVIDING SINCE ITS INCEPTION 53 YEARS AGO. THE MULTISERVICE LAW FIRM, WHICH HAS REPRESENTED A WIDE RANGE OF INDIVID-

ual, industrial, financial, and commercial clients, currently is composed of 75 attorneys and five office locations in northern Illinois and New York City.

Querrey & Harrow's practice groups are experienced in handling litigation in both federal and state courts. The firm's transactional

lawyers include those with solid experience in banking, real estate, corporate law, health law, estate planning, and governmental relations. Widely regarded for its work in the insurance, transportation, and construction industries, Querrey & Harrow also provides service in the areas of professional liability, product liability, health care, employment, retailing, financial services, corporate/commercial law, and government practice.

"We feel that quality is our chief selling point," says Managing Partner Ronald Jerrick. "We promise quality and we stand behind it. And the result of that has been the long-term satisfaction of our clients. We don't just serve them once, we develop a relationship with them.

"The philosophy here is that, while we have attorneys broken into groups according to the areas

in which they have the most experience, we're still one firm—one that can handle multiple aspects of our clients' business. They can have a wide variety of their legal needs taken care of."

COMMUNITY AND PROFESSIONAL INVOLVEMENT

Partners of Querrey & Harrow are highly visible within the legal profession. Eileen Dacey has been reappointed to another two-year term on the Insurance Law Advisory Board for the Practicing Law Institute. Other partners serve as board members or officers of the Defense Research Institute and the Illinois Association of Defense Trial Counsel.

In addition, the firm's partners have served as faculty members for the National Institute of Trial Advocacy and have acted as

Attorneys at Querrey & Harrow often rely on teamwork to ensure quality service.

trial advocacy instructors for the Northwestern University School of Law and the Loyola University School of Law. Also, partners have taught many client seminars on the civil jury trial process, and have spoken to bar groups on trial skills and strategies.

The firm has made numerous contributions to the community outside the legal profession, as well. G.A. Finch, head of the corporate practice group, is vice president for urban emphasis of the Boy Scouts of America. Organizations that have received firm donations include Chicago's Jackie Robinson Little League, the Neighborhood Housing Services of Chicago, the Bears Care fight against breast cancer, DePaul University, and numerous hospitals, police, fire, and veterans organizations. Employees also have taken an active role in the Children's Miracle Network and, most recently, the Chicago Cares Day Serve-a-Thon.

A History of Steady Growth

Querrey & Harrow was founded at the end of World War II, when a shortage of lawyers had created a backlog of cases that stretched for years. At that time, Joseph Harrow was a Rhodes Scholar and author of *Harrow's Illinois Practice Manual*, which was widely recognized as the preeminent authority for Illinois civil procedure. At the same time, Corwin Querrey had an active insurance practice consisting primarily of claims involving auto liability. After exchanging referrals for some time, the two practices merged in 1944.

By 1948, Ed Gulanick and John Kennedy had become partners, and shortly thereafter, the firm was renamed Querrey, Harrow, Gulanick & Kennedy. During the 1970s, the firm experienced controlled growth, fueled by the changing and expanded needs of its client base, which included State Farm and Continental Insurance. By 1973, the firm had 23 attorneys.

Growth accelerated as clients expanded their businesses in the collar counties. The county seats of Wheaton and Waukegan were the first to get satellite offices, in 1968 and 1979, respectively. Offices in Geneva, Woodstock, Joliet, and Rockford soon followed, as well as offices in Racine and New York City.

The 1980s also saw a commitment to add a corporate legal capability to the firm's litigation practice. In the process, Querrey & Harrow began to reshape itself from a small- to mid-sized firm, primarily handling insurance defense cases, to a large firm with specific practice areas within almost every field of law. In 1993, needing space to grow, the firm moved into its present location in the Prudential Plaza.

With regard to the future of the firm, says Jerrick, "We will focus on continued growth in litigation and trial work because that is what we do best. Specifically, we want to continue to develop our employment law and coverage practice, and are considering embarking on intellectual property practice. We're also considering further development of commercial litigation in the area of retailers, product liability, and professional liability."

But in the process of growing, Jerrick assures, Querrey & Harrow will not lose sight of its primary mission: "Although we are now a large firm, we intend to maintain the integrity, professionalism, and personalized service to our clients that has characterized this firm for more than 50 years."

Querrey & Harrow attorneys know that client satisfaction is dependent on good communication (top).

Querrey & Harrow believes in using the latest technology to create an efficient workplace (bottom).

WITH A PORTFOLIO OF MAJOR BRANDS THAT INCLUDES SARA LEE, HILLSHIRE FARM, HANES, AND KIWI, CHICAGO-BASED SARA LEE CORPORATION IS A GLOBAL FOOD AND CONSUMER PRODUCTS COMPANY WITH $20 BILLION IN ANNUAL SALES. ■ A LEADING manufacturer of high-quality, brand-name products worldwide, Sara Lee Corporation has operations in more than 40 countries and markets its products in more than 140 nations. The corporation employs 141,000 people around the world.

Founded in 1939 as the C.D. Kenney Company, the name was changed to Sara Lee Corporation in 1985 to better reflect its consumer marketing orientation.

Under the leadership of John H. Bryan, chairman and chief ex-

ecutive officer for more than two decades, Sara Lee has successfully achieved its mission of building leading consumer packaged goods brands while creating long-term stockholder value.

The corporation's four major lines of business are Packaged Meats and Bakery, Coffee and Grocery, Household and Body Care, and Personal Products. In fiscal 1997, more than 40 percent of Sara Lee's total sales were generated outside the United States.

SARA LEE PACKAGED MEATS AND BAKERY

Sara Lee is the largest packaged meats company in the world, with leading market positions in the United States, Europe, and Mexico. The company holds number-one positions in categories such as hot dogs, smoked sausage, and breakfast sausage.

Examples of Sara Lee's well-known national brands include Jimmy Dean meats, Ball Park hot dogs, Hillshire Farm break-

fast and smoked sausage, and Sara Lee Premium meats. Leading regional brands include Bryan, Bessin, Kahn's, and Gallo Salame.

Chicago-based Sara Lee Bakery has operations and leading market shares in the United States, the United Kingdom, Australia, and Mexico. With products also marketed in France, Germany, Norway, Denmark, and Asia, more than 25 percent of Sara Lee Bakery's total sales are generated outside the United States. In fiscal 1997, the company began extensive distribution of Sara Lee baked goods in Continental Europe.

Sara Lee Corporation's foodservice business, PYA/Monarch, is the leading foodservice distributor in the Southeast and the country's fourth-largest foodservice company.

SARA LEE COFFEE AND GROCERY

Sara Lee is the number-two coffee company in Europe, with a stable of brands led by its 244-year-old flagship label, Douwe Egberts.

Clockwise from top:
John H. Bryan, chairman and chief executive officer of Sara Lee Corporation, has managed the company in achieving its mission of building leading consumer packaged goods brands while creating long-term stockholder value.

Sara Lee is the largest packaged meats company in the world, occupying leading market positions in the United States, Europe, and Mexico. Some of the company's well-known national brands include Jimmy Dean meats, Ball Park hot dogs, Hillshire Farm breakfast and smoked sausage, and Sara Lee Premium meats.

Chicago-based Sara Lee Bakery has operations and leading market shares in the United States, the United Kingdom, Australia, and Mexico. More than 25 percent of its total sales are generated outside the United States.

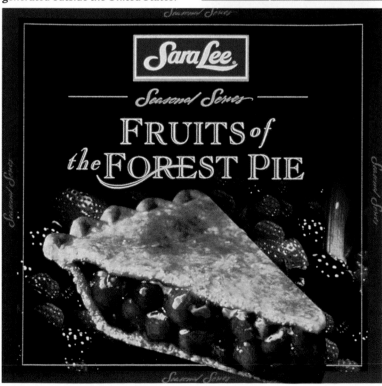

Other successful European coffee brands include Maison du Café, Marcilla, and Merrild. Pickwick tea holds leading positions in six European markets. Also under the corporation's Coffee and Grocery line of business is Chicago-based Superior Coffee, which distributes Superior and Metropolitan products to consumers throughout the United States through its successful foodservice operations.

Sara Lee markets grocery products in Europe under such popular brands as Duyvis, Lassie, Natreen, and Tijgernootjes. Product lines include sweeteners, as well as nuts, rice, and snack offerings.

SARA LEE HOUSEHOLD AND BODY CARE

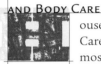

ousehold and Body Care is Sara Lee's most global line of business, with major brands such as Kiwi, Sanex, Duschdas, Badedas, and Ridsect. Its core product categories are shoe care, body care, and insecticides. Household and Body Care brands hold significant positions in key markets. Product innovations and expansion into new markets within Europe, Asia, Australia, Africa, and the Americas drive growth.

Sara Lee's Direct Selling division distributes a broad range of cosmetics, fragrances, toiletries, personal products, apparel, and jewelry through independent sales representatives in a number of international markets, including Mexico, Indonesia, China, Australia, and South Africa. Approximately 500,000 sales representatives distribute these products in more than 20 countries.

SARA LEE PERSONAL PRODUCTS

hrough its Personal Products line of business, Sara Lee markets intimate apparel and accessories, knit products, and hosiery to consumers worldwide.

Sara Lee's intimate apparel products hold the number one position in the United States, Canada, and Mexico. Domestically, the company markets a variety of intimate apparel offerings under the Playtex, Bali, Wonderbra, Just My Size, and Hanes Her Way brands. European intimate apparel is sold under such

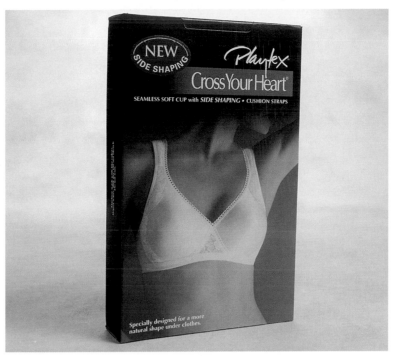

brand names as Dim, Lovable, Rosy, and Cacharel.

The leading marketer of men's and boys' underwear in the United States, Sara Lee sells underwear for adults and children under the Hanes and Hanes Her Way labels. In Europe, Sara Lee's various knit products brands hold leading men's and women's underwear positions with such brands as Dim, Abanderado, and Princessa.

As part of its worldwide legwear business, which includes sheer hosiery, socks, tights, and opaques, Sara Lee continues to broaden consumer choices in these categories with more value-added products. The U.S. leader in sheer hosiery, Sara Lee's top brands include Hanes, L'eggs, Donna Karan, and DKNY. The corporation also leads the U.S. market in socks, tights, and opaques.

COMMITTED TO COMMUNITY

ara Lee is committed to making lasting, positive impacts on the communities in which its employees live and work. To fulfill that promise, the company donates at least 2 percent of its pretax income—in cash and product contributions—to nonprofit organizations through the Sara Lee Foundation.

Each year, the Foundation designates 50 percent of its annual donations to organizations that help disadvantaged people in the community. Programs that tackle the immediate material needs of food, clothing, and shelter, or help

address unemployment, job discrimination, and substance abuse, are key priorities.

Recognizing that more than half of the corporation's employees and the vast majority of its consumers are women, the Sara Lee Foundation ensures that at least 25 percent of grants within the disadvantaged category are allocated for programs that help women realize their full potential, through services such as job training, health care, and legal assistance.

Forty percent of the Foundation's overall funding is dedicated to programs celebrating the human spirit through the arts. Grants are awarded both to established cultural institutions and to new and emerging arts organizations.

All divisions of Sara Lee Corporation administer their own local giving programs, with a similar goal to help local nonprofit organizations serve the needs within their own communities.

Clockwise from top left:
Sara Lee's intimate apparel products hold number-one positions in the United States, Canada, and Mexico. Domestically, the company markets a variety of intimate apparel offerings under the Playtex, Bali, Wonderbra, and Just My Size brands.

Household and Body Care is Sara Lee's most global line of business, with major brands such as Kiwi, Sanex, Duschdas, Badedas, and Ridsect.

Sara Lee is the number-two coffee company in Europe, with a stable of brands led by its 244-year-old flagship label, Douwe Egberts.

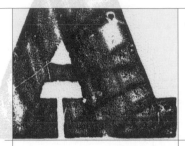

TF, Inc., a member of the Global Fastener Alliance "connecting the world," is a world-class manu-facturer of specialty fasteners and cold-formed parts. The company has strategic alliances in Europe and the Far East, and was one of the

first manufacturers to receive the QS 9000/ISO 9002 certification from its registrar, Underwriters Laboratories. ATF is also a Q1 sup-plier to Ford. Asyst Technologies—an alliance between ATF (which stands for Accurate Threaded Fasteners) and a German company, EJOT—manufactures assemblies and automotive forward lighting components in Kenosha, Wisconsin.

ATF, Inc. was established in 1946 as a privately owned distribu-tor of World War II surplus screws,

nuts, and bolts. It soon became a manufacturer and was acquired by Beatrice Foods in the early 1970s. In 1981, the company again became private when it was acquired by Donald E. Surber, who had been operating as the president under Beatrice. Since that time, ATF has grown from annual sales of $10 million to more than $60 million.

ATF's Lincolnwood manufac-turing facility, measuring nearly 200,000 square feet, employs more than 240 people from throughout

the northern Illinois area. They represent virtually every national-ity and religion, and the diverse cultures of its employees have as-sisted in developing a strong team orientation at ATF. Because of the stringent quality requirements of the ATF customer base, companies visit regularly to perform quality audits, to synchronously design new products, or just to visit a cold heading facility. ATF is strongly associated with Chicago and the vibrant commercial opportunities that exist in the Greater Chicago area.

ATF is located in a Chicago, Elgin, and Rockford corridor of fastener manufacturers, which, combined with the Cleveland, Ohio, and Detroit areas, produces more than 90 percent of the nonaero-space fasteners made in the United States.

Global Reach

Niche players in limited markets will find it increasingly difficult to survive in a world that knows no boundaries because of faxes, modems, instantaneous telecom-

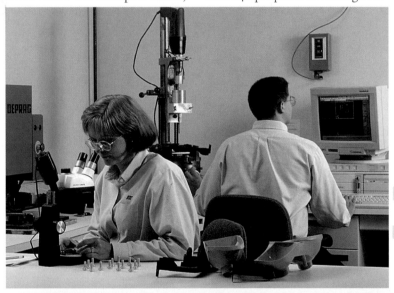

ATF's Lincolnwood manufacturing facility, measuring nearly 200,000 square feet, employs more than 240 people from throughout northern Illinois. The diverse cultures of its employees have contributed to the strong team spirit of ATF (top).

ATF manufactures specialty fasteners and cold-formed parts. With strategic alliances in Europe and the Far East, ATF was one of the first manufactur-ers to receive the QS 9000/ISO 9002 certification from its registrar, Under-writers Laboratories (bottom).

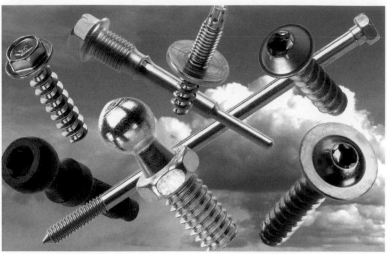

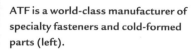

ATF is a world-class manufacturer of specialty fasteners and cold-formed parts (left).

Because of the stringent quality requirements of the ATF customer base, companies visit regularly to perform quality audits or to synchronously design new products (right).

munications, and electronic commerce. As these technological advances bring the world closer together, ATF is even more committed to being a true global supplier.

In addition to its European and Far Eastern strategic alliances, ATF has developed relationships in Canada, Mexico, and South America. Many ATF customers, particularly automotive manufacturers and their Tier I and Tier II suppliers, are global companies demanding the same of their entire supply chain. Many major automotive manufacturers have spread worldwide by either growth or acquisition. ATF intends to take a similar approach to having a worldwide manufacturing capability.

ATF, Inc. has continued to grow and profit because of its strategic focus. An annually updated, long-range plan, combined with an annual business plan, maintains a focus throughout the corporation. Although led by the management team, all employees participate to some degree in this process.

Four major product groups are critical to ATF's growth and success. These product groups, coupled with the sophisticated equipment to produce them, have resulted in an average double-digit growth over the last 10 years.

Strategic Products

he first product group, and one that has contributed significantly to ATF, Inc.'s growth, is the close tolerance, value-added, frequently safety-critical, larger-diameter, highly engineered fasteners. These parts are often used

in automotive and truck braking and suspension systems. They usually involve a number of secondary operations that may include trimming, shaving, grinding, drilling, tapping, broaching, or reaming. ATF, Inc. has the capability to do most secondary applications at its Lincolnwood plant.

Collar and ball studs, again used mostly in automotive applications, are major ATF products and are produced in a cell in the manufacturing facility. The collar studs are used for trim and fascia attachment, and usually include a machine thread on one end with a collar in the center and another thread design on the other end. The products are frequently used in plastic materials. Ball studs are used in adjustment or suspension joint applications.

ATF's proprietary products, of which the major fastener is the PT screw, are another significant portion of the company's sales. The PT®, which stands for plastic threadform, is used in many auto-

motive interior applications. As one of three manufacturers in the United States licensed by EJOT, ATF's share of the market ensures that the PT screw will continue to increase in sales as well as in percentage of total ATF sales.

The distribution market accounts for a significant portion of ATF's sales. Product sales are handled primarily through 15 distributors. As manufacturers continue to reduce their fastener supply base, they enter into contracts with distributors, who can buy from any number of manufacturers and provide all of a manufacturer's fastener requirements. The distribution portion of ATF, therefore, is expected to grow at a rapid rate.

ATF, Inc., through its Global Fastener Alliance, will continue to pursue major fastener opportunities worldwide. The Chicago-area headquarters in Lincolnwood will be the driving force in this rapidly growing privately held corporation.

ATF produces close tolerance, value-added, frequently safety-critical, larger-diameter, highly engineered fasteners. Secondary operations that may include trimming, shaving, grinding, drilling, tapping, broaching, or reaming are performed at its Lincolnwood plant.

WHETHER FOR WORK, SCHOOL, SHOPPING, OR FUN, CHICAGOANS COUNT ON THE CHICAGO TRANSIT AUTHORITY (CTA)—A TOTAL OF 1.4 MILLION TIMES A DAY. ■ AS THE NATION'S SECOND-LARGEST TRANSIT AGENCY, THE CTA SERVES THOUSANDS OF DESTINA-

tions in Chicago and 38 nearby suburbs. The agency operates nearly 1,882 buses over 129 routes, as well as seven rapid transit lines over 224 miles of track.

CTA destinations are as diverse as its customers. From parents with children, to busy executives, to students with armloads of books, to visitors from all over the world, everybody rides CTA.

Putting the Go in Chicago

Home of O'Hare International Airport, the world's busiest airport, Chicago was originally founded as a Great Lakes shipping port in 1837. Chicago's long history as a leader in transportation includes some impressive transit statistics.

In 1895, the first electric-powered transit train went into service here. The city's streetcar system was once the largest in the world with 1,100 miles of track. The elevated rail intersection above Lake and Wells streets was the world's busiest railroad junction.

Transit ridership flourished in Chicago throughout the 1920s. The depression cut into ridership, as did competition from automobiles. The CTA was formed in 1947 from two private companies. A massive transit modernization program followed, which included replacing streetcars with more flexible buses. Later, the CTA pioneered the practice of placing rapid transit lines in expressway medians. Park and ride facilities were also constructed.

The spirit of improvement lives on at the CTA. The Orange Line, opened in 1993, now provides the city's Southwest Side with rapid transit service. The CTA Green Line,

closed for a two-year rehab, was reopened in 1996.

CTA: An Agency on the Move

Chicago's skyline, regarded as one of the most impressive in the world, is symbolic of the dynamic changes taking place locally. The CTA is keeping pace with Chicago with many important initiatives.

The CTA's new Transit Card was introduced systemwide in 1997. More than 40 percent of CTA customers were using Transit Cards within three months of the launch date. The electronic cards streamline fare and transfer payments, and help customers avoid long lines.

The new fare system is making other services possible, such as the new $5 Visitor Pass. Perfect for out-of-towners, the pass is good for 24 hours of continuous CTA riding on every bus and train, and can be purchased at hotels and visitors centers.

New train station-specific timetables help customers plan their trips. A new toll-free customer ser-

Clockwise from top left:
The Chicago Transit Authority's elevated track above Lake and Wells streets is part of the city's rich transit heritage. It was once the world's busiest rail junction. The addition of subways would later reduce train traffic.

Within Chicago and 38 surrounding suburbs, a bus stop is never very far away.

CTA trains keep customers on schedule, even at rush hour.

RAY F. HILLSTROM/HILLSTROM STOCK PHOTOGRAPHY

RAY F. HILLSTROM/HILLSTROM STOCK PHOTOGRAPHY

RAY F. HILLSTROM/HILLSTROM STOCK PHOTOGRAPHY

The CTA's Library-State VanBuren station, which opened in 1997, blends in with its historic south Loop high-rise neighbors (left).

The CTA's Transit Card makes paying fares simple. The 24-hour Visitor Pass is perfect for out-of-towners (right).

vice hot line puts customer concerns on the fast track.

The CTA's neighborhood station improvement program is making neighborhood train stations friendlier, more inviting places with fresh paint, better lighting, and new benches.

INTERESTING DESTINATIONS

 Transit Card or one-day Visitor Pass is all someone needs to see the very best of Chicago. The Museum Campus, a must-see for a growing number of visitors, can be reached directly from North Michigan Avenue or State Street on the #146 Marine-Michigan bus.

Chicago's Navy Pier, which features three-quarters of a mile of continuous entertainment, can be reached by several routes from downtown and other areas of the city. Wrigley Field and Comiskey Park are both next to the Red Line train stations. The Museum of Science and Industry has fast service on either the #6 Jeffery Express or the #10 Museum of Science and Industry. And the Bulls and Blackhawks can easily be reached on the #19 Stadium Express to the United Center.

The CTA serves suburban attractions, too, such as the Frank Lloyd Wright Home and Studio in Oak Park. It's just a half-hour

trip on the Green Line from downtown.

The CTA itself is also recognized as a landmark. The Elevated, or 'L,' completed its 100th year of service in October 1997. The structure, which defines Chicago's central business district, provides efficient transportation for hundreds of thousands of daily commuters as well as spectacular views of the city along the way.

These and other Chicago landmarks can be easily reached by one or more CTA routes and lines. Whether it's a trip around the corner or across town, every customer is important to the CTA. The CTA's dedicated employees are proud to do their part in Putting the Go in Chicago.

A CTA bus heads south across the Michigan Avenue Bridge (left).

An entrance to the CTA's north-south Red Line trains on State Street invites customers to get on board (right).

NE OF THE BIGGEST CHALLENGES FACING COMPANIES IS HOW TO UNLOCK TECHNOLOGY'S POTENTIAL TO BETTER SERVE THEIR CLIENTS, IMPROVE THEIR OPERATIONS, AND PURSUE NEW MARKET OPPORTUNITIES. FOR 50 YEARS, MAY & SPEH HAS BEEN HELPING ITS CLIENTS TO HARNESS THE POWER OF

technology for business solutions that measurably improve their profitability.

Long before the days of microprocessors, personal computers, and the Internet, May & Speh helped pioneer the application of data processing to business needs. After leasing space in the back of a machine shop in 1947, Albert Speh and Roland May began selling tabulating services to Chicago-area companies. From its modest beginnings, May & Speh has grown into a leading provider of computer-based information management services for midsize to Fortune 500 companies. In recent years, the company has focused on two strategic, fastgrowing segments: database marketing and information technology outsourcing.

CLIENT FOCUSED

onsistently profitable since its first year, the Downers Grove-based company has grown to more than $90 million in revenues and nearly 600 employees. Since 1992 alone, revenues have grown at a compound annual rate of 24 percent while employment has more than doubled. The company also made a successful public offering in 1996.

"May & Speh has thrived because of our single-minded focus on clients," says Peter I. Mason, president and chief executive officer. "We develop long-term relationships with our clients, which includes a 50-year partnership with our first client, Sears, Roebuck and Co. Because of the depth of these relationships, we are able to work with our clients to develop innovative ways to apply technology to benefit their businesses and their customers."

For companies eager to build closer and more profitable ties to their customers, database marketing is increasing in strategic importance. Database marketing, which as an industry has been growing at a compound annual rate of 29 percent, allows companies in highly competitive consumer-based industries, such as financial services, retail, insurance, consumer products, and telecommunications, to develop direct marketing programs that are highly targeted and more relevant to the wants and needs of their customers. May & Speh designs, develops, and maintains customer and prospect management solutions that support the client's strategic marketing initiatives, including helping them acquire customers, retain them, make additional sales to customers, and even measure customer lifetime value and profitability.

DATABASE SOLUTIONS

ay & Speh recently introduced one of the industry's most comprehensive marketing information systems, taking database management to a new level. Developed with input from client review boards, Quiddity™ fully integrates the real-world database marketing process, taking marketers from the beginning to the end of their

Clockwise from top:
May & Speh is building a new, 200,000-square-foot headquarters office that will triple the size of the company's Downers Grove headquarters campus.

A member of the database product development team works on software upgrades for the new marketing database system launched by May & Speh in mid-1997.

"May & Speh has thrived because of our single-minded focus on clients," says Peter I. Mason, president and chief executive officer.

direct marketing programs. Specifically, it integrates the initial data analysis, campaign development and management, campaign execution, and postpromotion analysis phases of a direct marketing program into one system.

Quiddity is just one of many marketing database solutions that May & Speh has developed for direct marketers. Other services include systems consulting; strategic analysis and strategy management; data warehousing; modeling and analysis; and list processing. For each client, May & Speh leverages technical expertise with strong business knowledge to tailor a solution based on that company's specific business objectives.

TECHNOLOGY OUTSOURCING

May & Speh takes a similar solutions-driven approach to helping clients through its information technology outsourcing services. While computer systems are an essential corporate resource, a growing number of companies are finding that it is more cost effective to transfer responsibility for day-to-day management and operations of their systems to outsourcers. Companies turn to May & Speh to outsource data processing, to migrate from one processing technology to another (e.g. mainframe to UNIX), to manage data and voice networks, or to provide solutions related to information system operations. With May & Speh as an outsourcing partner, companies can concentrate on their core business, such as manufacturing aluminum packaging, operating a hospital, or providing financial services, while still benefiting from state-of-the-art technology and highly experienced computer professionals. Spurred by such advantages, the U.S. information technology outsourcing market is predicted to grow at a compound annual rate of 13.5 percent.

To deliver innovative solutions and superior client service, May & Speh has consistently invested in the latest technology. In fiscal 1997 alone, the company spent more than 10 percent of revenues on new hardware and software to support the technology solutions it develops for clients as well as

internal operations. Yet, the company's commitment to utilizing the most advanced technology began in its earliest years as a business. In 1954, May & Speh became the first midwestern company to buy a UNIVAC file computer. Today, that commitment continues. The company operates a state-of-the-art data center that includes the world's fastest IBM-compatible mainframe processor, as well as other high-speed mainframe and UNIX technology and advanced robotics and peripherals. Also within the data center, May & Speh maintains more than 8 trillion characters of data and more than 1 million computer files for its clients.

A key to the company's success is its ability to drive and manage growth in all areas of its business, while continuing to ensure world-class service and operations. To support this effort, May & Speh has been expanding its team at all levels, including senior management and the board of directors. Most

notably, May & Speh appointed Mason, the company's former outside legal counsel and a member of the board of directors, as president and chief executive officer in 1997 because of his leadership ability and previous success working with high-growth companies.

As May & Speh enters its next half-century in business, the company is committed to building its position as a premier provider of information management solutions. Through its business process improvement initiative, the company is strengthening its processes and operations to support the significant growth it is experiencing. It also is constructing a building that will triple the size of its headquarters campus in Downers Grove. Building on its strong heritage of investing in technology, expertise, and client relationships, May & Speh remains dedicated to delivering business solutions that ultimately help its clients be more competitive.

Clockwise from top left:
High-speed robotics is just one feature of the company's state-of-the-art Data Center.

More than a million records of data are stored on tapes within the Data Center tape library.

In the new command center, staff monitor data processing operations and provide client support 24 hours a day, seven days a week.

UPERCHARGED PERFORMANCE—FUELED BY DEPENDABILITY, GRIT, AND HIGH OCTANE—IS WHAT PROPELLED DON SCHUMACHER TO FIVE NATIONAL CHAMPIONSHIPS AND LEGENDARY STATUS ON THE FUNNY CAR DRAG-RACING CIRCUIT IN THE 1960S AND 1970S. AND THAT'S WHAT HAS PROPELLED THE SCHUMACHER

Electric Corp. to its championship position today as the world's largest producer of battery chargers.

Established 50 years ago in Chicago by Don's parents, Albert and Jean, Schumacher Electric now employs 745 people at manufacturing facilities in Rensselaer, Indiana; Hoopeston, Illinois; and north suburban Mount Prospect, home of the company's new corporate headquarters. Annually, Schumacher Electric brings in $70 million in sales, of which $60 million is from the sale of battery chargers.

Don, who joined the company full-time in 1976 and became president and CEO in 1991, attributes its success to maintaining the same high performance standards that made him a race car champion. "We know consumers recognize quality," Don Schumacher says. "First, we are committed to our customers by always delivering the best buy for their hard-earned dollar. Then, we attack our marketing plan with the same intensity as our racing. If you back up your mission in life with a relentless pur-

suit of perfection, you are bound to win, and even better than that, you will never disappoint anyone."

IMPRESSIVE CLIENTS, INNOVATIVE PRODUCTS

chumacher's all-star list of customers includes Sears, Roebuck & Co., for which it produces a 14-product line of DieHard battery chargers; Ace Hardware; Wal-Mart; Trak Auto; Western Auto; Home Depot; Mid-States Distribution; Central Tractor; Blaines Farm & Fleet; Price Costco; Sam's Club; Giant Auto; Advance Stores; AutoZone; Meijer; and Mills Fleet Wholesale.

Innovation has been a watchword at Schumacher Electric. The company was the first to offer a charger with digital readout and

touch pad control, features that make the product easier to use and more reliable. As for selection, Schumacher offers the broadest range of chargers available today. Its Consumer Products Division directly markets products to mass merchants/discounters and to the automotive aftermarket, while the Business Division manufactures custom transformers, ballasts, and coils. Customers include Motorola, Crown, Fender, Scientific Atlanta, Valmont, and more.

Schumacher's low-amperage chargers are ideal for people who don't use their car often, or who do a lot of stop-and-go driving. Metal, handheld, portable chargers for six-, 12-, 18-, 24-, and 36-volt systems can be used for a wide variety of car, light truck, motorcycle, and recreational vehicle needs, as well as in garden, farm, and marine applications. Schumacher's heavy-duty, professional wheel chargers—manufactured for fleet, farm, and industrial use—have built-in test modes and up to 300 amps of boost power. Schumacher also offers full lines of farm, ranch, and specialty chargers; welders; accessories; and merchandising support.

With a long history of service and a time-tested line of products, Schumacher Electric is racing toward continued success in the future.

Don Schumacher, president and CEO of Schumacher Electric Corp., insists that his company work as a top-notch team, incorporating the highest quality and the latest technology into its products (top).

Don Schumacher was a five-time NHRA National Event Champion and an IHRA and AHRA World Champion. Today, his racing legacy continues through his son Tony, IHRA's 1993 Rookie of the Year and the 1996 NHRA U.S. Nationals runner-up in his debut in the Top Fuel Dragster Category (bottom).

DELMAN PUBLIC RELATIONS WORLDWIDE, ESTABLISHED IN 1952, IS THE LARGEST INDEPENDENT AND FIFTH-LARGEST PUBLIC RELATIONS FIRM IN THE WORLD, WITH 34 OFFICES THROUGHOUT THE UNITED STATES, ASIA, CANADA, EUROPE, MEXICO, AND SOUTH AMERICA.

The company's 1,300 employees worldwide service a wide range of local and multinational clients. Edelman's specialty capabilities include government relations; corporate counsel; investor and financial relations; consumer, health care, business, and industrial marketing; technology; travel and tourism; environmental and public affairs; and crisis communications.

THE EDELMAN MISSION

delman supports its clients in their efforts to operate in the public interest; to communicate creatively the value of their products and services, and to counsel them on the measures needed to maintain a reputation for excellence with their key audiences.

Edelman strives to provide its staff with a working environment and career opportunity that is challenging and rewarding; that recognizes exceptional talent, but is based on encouraging teamwork; and that offers the opportunity and training to grow professionally and to develop and exercise management skills.

For the media, Edelman acts as a responsive, responsible, knowledgeable, and truthful resource, actively promoting its clients' achievements and views, and, when necessary, defending them against unjust criticism.

Edelman's corporate mission is to concentrate in the field of public relations; to manage the enterprise in a way that is rooted in high ethical and professional standards; to invest in growth internally and by specialist practice so that the company is represented by experts located at offices in all major markets of the world; to encourage innovation while exercising careful financial management; and to build retained earnings for reinvestment in growth of the company and enhancement of the equity in the Edelman brand name.

Daniel J. Edelman, chairman and founder of Edelman Public Relations Worldwide (left)

Richard Edelman, chief executive officer of Edelman Public Relations Worldwide (right)

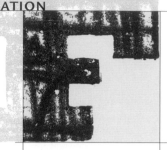

OR HALF A CENTURY, BLOCK STEEL CORPORATION HAS PROVIDED THE ESSENTIAL STEEL TO MANUFACTURE PRODUCTS FOR EVERYDAY LIFE, FROM AUTOMOBILE MUFFLERS TO BAKERY PANS. A FAMILY-OWNED BUSINESS THAT PRIDES ITSELF ON STRONG, LONG-TERM RELATIONSHIPS WITH CUSTOMERS,

suppliers, and employees, Block Steel has utilized the newest equipment and ISO 9002 quality methods to create and expand a successful niche while becoming the largest independent aluminized steel distributor in the country.

In addition, Samson Roll Formed Products Co., a division of Block Steel, is one of the nation's oldest and leading makers of custom-shaped steel products. Samson manufactures more than 2,000 shapes, and is the largest maker of the lockseam tubing used in both outdoor and indoor products, including residential flagpoles, badminton poles, patio torches,

towel bars, and shower rods. The newest and fastest-growing use for lockseam tubing is in closet organizer products, including shoe racks, garment bag frames, and ventilated shelving. Samson is also a major manufacturer of athletic flooring hardware.

Block Steel was founded in Forest Park, Illinois, in 1948 by Albert Block, his son Harvey, and his son-in-law Oscar Wolfson. The company started as a typical steel warehouse, with just 10 employees, and served primarily the Chicago metropolitan area. From the beginning, Block was committed to outstanding service, quality prod-

ucts, timely delivery, and competitive prices. Today, Block Steel and its Samson division have expanded into a 165,000-square-foot location in Skokie, employ more than 125 workers, and boast international sales that exceed $50 million.

RAPID GROWTH AND SPECIALIZED PRODUCTS

Since the early 1980s, Block Steel has grown at a rate unmatched by most of its competitors, expanding its market share in the United States, Central and South America, and the Far East. Sales have doubled in the last six years and are projected to double again in another five years.

The key to Block Steel's ongoing success has been the flexibility and personal service that are uniquely possible in a family-owned and -operated business, plus a long-standing policy of reinvesting profits. A third generation of the family is now in upper-management positions, and a fourth generation has joined the corporation.

Block Steel specializes in the distribution of two highly functional types of aluminum-coated carbon steel. The first is hot-dip

Clockwise from top:
Located in north suburban Skokie, Block Steel's headquarters occupies more than 165,000 square feet.

With more than 30 roll-form lines and an array of ancillary equipment, Samson, a division of Block Steel, can handle the most demanding metal-forming requirements.

An expansive, 15,000-ton inventory allows Block Steel to ship most orders immediately.

▲ JOHN WEINSTEIN

coated with an aluminum-silicon alloy. The second is hot-dip coated with commercially pure aluminum. Advantages of aluminized steel are its resistance to heat and corrosion and its ability to reflect heat. Block also sells a full line of galvanized products.

About 35 percent of Block's steel is used in the automotive market, where it is manufactured into mufflers, exhaust systems, water pump housings, and other parts. Another 30 percent is used in the HVAC (heating, ventilation, and air-conditioning) market and in fireplaces. The final 35 percent is used to manufacture such appliances as ovens, ranges, dryers, and barbecue grills, and for a variety of other uses, including pizza ovens, agricultural crop dryers, and home bread makers.

Typical of Block Steel's commitment to employing the latest technology to produce a better product, the company in 1992 invested more than $2.5 million in a fourth "slitter" for coil steel processing. It produces coils that are extra flat and tightly wound, without marring the coil's coating. It can handle 50,000-pound coils up to 72 inches wide, and was the first in the Chicago area to incorporate a shape-correction leveler.

THE ART OF ROLL FORMING

Because Block Steel is located in an adjoining facility, its Samson Division, founded in 1946 and acquired by Block in 1979, enjoys almost immediate access to a wide variety of material.

Roll forming is a highly productive, continuous process in which a strip of metal, usually in coil form, is passed through a series of roller dies and progressively shaped to a desired contour. Practically all metals can be successfully roll formed, and the ability to fabricate decorative parts from precoated, prepainted, or preplated metal is a distinct feature of the process.

Samson produces more than 2,000 shapes, an achievement in precision design made possible by experienced engineers capable of solving complex roll-forming tasks. With more than 50 years in the business, Samson believes roll

forming is as much an art as a science, and considers its older, more experienced employees to be true artisans.

Among the products manufactured by Samson are drawer slides for the furniture industry; cladding for wood windows and steel stiffeners for vinyl windows; parts for automotive applications, such as seating track and window frames; slotted channels for industrial storage shelving; and store fixture applications.

In addition to roll forming, Samson offers a full range of services, including pre- and post-notching, stamping, bending, assembling, and packaging. Because Samson has a large storage capacity and ready access to raw materials from Block Steel, deliveries are timely, and a customer's needs can be met on relatively short notice.

A COMMITMENT TO CHICAGO

Block Steel's dedication to the Chicago area has been solid and unflinching. Although courted by many other areas, the company has determined that Chicago is still the place to be. With the established infrastructure, key suppliers, transportation, skilled labor force, and cultural attractions the Chicago area offers, no other place can compare. Block's Skokie location is just minutes from O'Hare International Airport and downtown Chicago, providing easy access to shipping and the business district.

And Block's dedication to its employees and the community at large pays immense dividends in both productivity and economic

Block's 72-inch slitter with multi-roll shape-correction leveler provides a tight and evenly wound finished product to exact specifications (top).

The company's third-generation senior management team (from left) Larry J. Wolfson, president, Block Steel; Scott Boggs, president, Samson Division; Donald R. Morgan, vice president, Block Steel; and Joe Block, vice president, Block Steel (bottom)

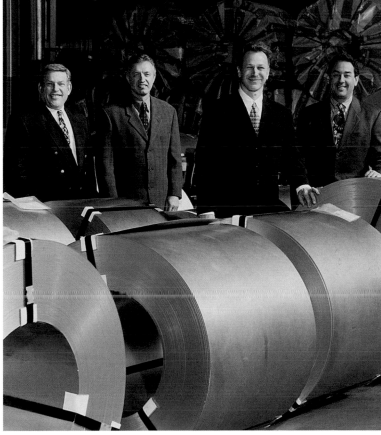

growth. With its progressive employment practices, Block Steel enables its employees to be productive and contributing stakeholders in Chicago's future.

The company's contributions to many community and charitable organizations help solidify the foundations of the social fabric, which in turn helps improve the quality of life for all.

For more than 50 years, Block Steel has been providing steel products that make all facets of life easier. From industrial and automotive customers to the home baker making muffins, Block Steel touches the lives of consumers in Chicago and around the world.

APITOL CONSTRUCTION GROUP HAS AMERICA COVERED— FROM VIACOM ON MICHIGAN AVENUE TO BATH & BODY WORKS IN SAN DIEGO TO WARNER BROS. IN ORLANDO. WITH ANNUAL SALES TOTALING MORE THAN $100 MILLION, THE WHEELING-BASED, DIVERSIFIED GENERAL CONTRACTOR builds more than 200 projects per year.

Celebrating its 50th anniversary in 1998, Capitol Construction Group has a long and proud history of excellence. Founded by Louis Freed as a supplier of fixtures to retailers in the Chicago area, the company expanded its focus to developing commercial properties, as well as building them. In 1948, Capitol became a separate entity under its parent company, Joseph J. Freed & Associates, currently the largest privately held shopping center developer in Illinois. Capitol has grown considerably from building shopping centers for the Freed organization to building a wide range of project types for a variety of national and regional clients. In fact, Capitol is ranked in *Crain's Chicago Business* as one of the top 200 privately held companies in the Chicago area.

DEDICATED TO EXCEEDING EXPECTATIONS

Since its inception, Capitol Construction Group has established itself as a company dedicated to exceeding client expectations on all phases of a project. "Our goal is to provide our clients with the best service possible at all times— from preliminary preconstruc- tion services including budgeting, scheduling, and value engineering, throughout the construction process, to project closeout and occupancy," says Thomas A. Donovan, president. "Capitol's strength lies in our employees, a team of highly skilled and technically trained managers, project managers, field superintendents, and support staff. Our employees are extremely knowledgeable in the construction of retail facilities, restaurants, hotels, office interiors, and theaters."

Each project manager undergoes a careful training process, which includes hands-on experience in estimating, field supervision, scheduling, and cost-control methods. Assisting the project managers is a staff of experienced administrative assistants, as well as field superintendents who are located on the job site full-time, directing the various subcontractors and ensuring conformity with the plans and specifications. In addition, Capitol's project managers are supported by a network of accounting professionals who provide job-cost reporting and analysis. Purchasing agents ensure the availability, quality, and delivery of materials, while data processing associates manage the company's information systems.

"In addition to being highly skilled, Capitol's employees are also very cognizant of their surroundings," Donovan notes. "That is, we are accustomed to completing projects without disturbing the operations of spaces in which we are working. For example, we remodeled each of the 361 rooms at the Ritz Carlton in Kansas City while the hotel remained open to guests." Capitol has received rec-

Capitol Construction Group is dedicated to exceeding client expectations on all phases of a project, from preliminary preconstruction services—such as budgeting, scheduling, and value engineering—through construction, project closeout, and occupancy (below).

◄ MARK SAMUELS

◄ STEVE HALL/HEDRICH BLESSING

Among the company's many projects across the country is Dive!, one of several Steven Spielberg and Larry Levy restaurant ventures.

ognition for this sensitive approach. *Shopping Center World* magazine lists it as one of the top 25 general contracting companies in the United States.

BUILDING CHICAGO, BUILDING AMERICA

n the Chicago area, the list of Capitol Construction's clients speaks volumes for the company's reputation. Its

many restaurant clients include Bistro 110, Bub City, Cafe Ba-Ba-Reeba!, Gino's East, Maggiano's Little Italy, foodlife, Scoozi!, Spiaggia, and Riva at Navy Pier. Capitol's retail projects include Viacom, Crate & Barrel, Galyan's Trading Company, Chernin's Shoes, Henri Bendel, Plaza Escada, Sears, and Carson Pirie Scott.

Capitol's hotel projects include Wyndham Garden Hotel in Chicago

and Oakbrook Terrace; the Drake Oak Brook; the Knickerbocker; and Homestead Village in Westmont, Naperville, and Schaumburg. Other notable projects include Argonne National Laboratory in Woodridge, Riverpoint Center at Fullerton and Clybourn in Chicago, Town Square in Wheaton, Chinatown Square in Chicago, and the restoration of Cafe Brauer, a registered national landmark at the Lincoln Park Zoo.

Throughout the country, Capitol counts as its projects such notable places as Dive! (Steven Spielberg's submarine sandwich eateries), McDonald's, T.G.I. Friday's, Starbucks Coffee, Brooks Brothers, Abercrombie & Fitch Co., Ghirardelli Chocolate Shop and Soda Fountain, Ann Taylor, Victoria's Secret, Warner Bros. Studio Stores, The Limited, and Eddie Bauer.

Capitol Construction Group has come a long way from its start as a fixture company. But it's still doing what it does best—providing customized service from start to finish.

Crate & Barrel is one of numerous local and national specialty retailers that rely upon Capitol's expertise (left and opposite right).

Capitol's hotel projects include Wyndham Garden Hotel in Chicago (below).

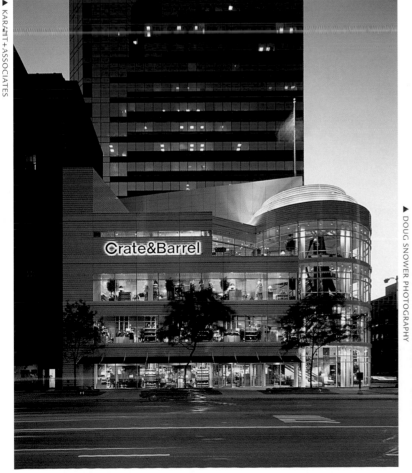

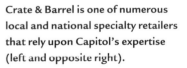

THERE HAS TO BE A STORY BEHIND A TELEVISION STATION WHOSE CALL LETTERS STAND FOR "WORLD'S GREATEST NEWSPAPER." AFTER ALL, WHEN TELEVISION FIRST BECAME WIDELY AVAILABLE, MOST NEWSPAPER PEOPLE REGARDED THE NEW MEDIUM WITH TREPIDATION, PERCEIVING ITS ability to usurp the print media's supremacy as a source of news, special features, and sports information.

But Colonel Robert McCormick, the fiercely conservative owner of the *Chicago Tribune*, welcomed television with enthusiasm. In television, he declared, "We have embarked upon another of America's adventures." From the beginning, the Colonel realized that there was room for both print and broadcast properties in his company.

The early days at WGN-TV (or Channel 9, as it's known locally) were much like those at every station exploring what the new medium could do. One thing it did very well was provide information quickly, especially when live was the only way to work, so WGN-TV began with the news. Today, WGN-TV remains committed to extensive local news coverage, producing on a weekday basis more hours of news programming than any other Chicago station.

From its very beginning, WGN-TV has been what its present-day slogan describes: Chicago's Very Own. As a superstation, WGN-TV is available to some 40 million homes outside Chicago, yet it remains unmistakably a Chicago station, delivering substantial local coverage in its news and continuing

to produce many programs on its own that feature local talent.

LEGENDARY TALENT, LEGENDARY STATION

Some of these programs and personalities are themselves legendary," says Peter Walker, the station's vice president and general manager. "As someone raised in the Chicago area, I grew up with WGN-TV. It wasn't until I began working here, though, that I came to realize how much the station means to the people of this community."

One of the city's passions—sports—is unimaginable without WGN-TV, whose first sports broadcast was the 1948 Golden Gloves boxing tournament. Soon

after, the station covered its first opening day at Wrigley Field, starting a relationship that has endured even longer than the Cubs' absence from postseason play. Generations of Chicagoans recognize the voices of Cubs broadcasters Harry "Holy Cow!" Caray and Jack "Hey! Hey!" Brickhouse as if they were part of their family. Brickhouse, who announced more than 5,000 Cubs games during a career spanning 34 years, has been inducted into the Baseball Hall of Fame and the Chicago Press Club's Journalism Hall of Fame. Caray, too, is in the Baseball Hall of Fame as a veteran of 50 years in sportscasting, and he continues to work as the voice of the Cubs.

Clockwise from top:
Skycam 9 is a TV studio in the air, providing live coverage of breaking news and daily traffic updates on WGN Morning News.

WGN-TV broadcasts more live sports programming than any other TV station in the country.

Colonel Robert R. McCormick was editor and publisher of the *Chicago Tribune* from 1914 to 1955.

WGN-TV, located in Chicago's near north side, has been broadcasting award-winning programming for 50 years.

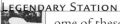

With WGN-TV's obvious interest in Cubs baseball, it was only natural that in 1981, when the Wrigley family put the Cubs up for sale, the buyer was none other than the Tribune Company, but there's more to WGN-TV's sports coverage than baseball. WGN-TV has brought Chicagoans Chicago Bears and Notre Dame football games; the last White Sox game at the old Comiskey Park; the first night game at Wrigley Field; and 20 years of Chicago Bulls basketball, including five championship seasons. The station has a long tradition of covering local college and high school sports as well, particularly basketball and football.

Equally legendary is the children's icon, Bozo the Clown. *Bozo* premiered on WGN-TV in 1961, starting a wait for tickets to join the studio audience that at one time lasted 10 years. Still one of the hottest tickets in town, adults who visited Bozo as kids, now bring their children to see the show. After more than 35 years and many

thousands of pies in the face, *Bozo* is the nation's longest locally produced, continuously running children's show.

In Touch with the Community

f course, there's a serious side to WGN-TV, too. It was the first station to offer hearing-impaired viewers closed-captioning on local news, and the first Chicago station to launch its own Web site at www.wgntv.com. The station's commitment to news and community service remains strong, with such features as a weekly profile of outstanding Chicagoland high school students. Many Chicagoans tune in to *Charlando*, the first and longest-running Spanish-language community affairs program on a commercial Anglo station. WGN-TV also produces special programs each year during Black History Month, Hispanic Heritage Month, and Asian-American Heritage Month.

Focusing on the need to better serve Chicagoland communities, WGN-TV supports a number of charitable causes, especially targeting those that help children. WGN-TV's Children's Charities offers grants through partnerships with many organizations, benefiting community resources like the Off the Street Club, a safe place for kids on the city's tough West Side. Another important station project is WGN-TV's Waiting Child Adoption Program. In its fifth year, this award-winning public service campaign has increased adoptions in Illinois more than 50 percent.

"We take our role as a Chicago broadcaster very seriously," Walker says. "Through news coverage, community affairs broadcasts, public service announcements, town hall meetings, educational programming, live coverage of citywide events—whatever the issue or concern—WGN-TV has been there for Chicagoans. We feel we must continue to earn the right to be called Chicago's Very Own."

Clockwise from top left:
The WGN News at Nine Team: (from left) Allison Payne, anchor; award-winning meterologist Tom Skilling; Steve Sanders, anchor; and Dan Roan, sports anchor.

Merri Dee, director of community relations, coordinates the efforts of WGN-TV's Children's Charities.

Harry Caray's famous broadcasting style is as much a part of Cubs baseball as the ivy that covers the walls of Wrigley Field.

WGN-TV's Bozo T. Clown entertains and educates Chicago's children every Sunday morning. (Bozo the Clown ™ ® 1997 Larry Harmon Pictures Corp. All Rights Reserved.)

THE WORD "METRON" REFERS TO BALANCE, AND METRON STEEL HAS STRUCK JUST THAT: A BALANCE OF PRODUCT, EXPERTISE, AND SERVICE THAT HAS MADE IT A LEADING DISTRIBUTOR, PROCESSOR, AND MARKETER OF STEEL COILS AND PLATES IN THE UNITED STATES. ■ "WE HAVE ACHIEVED A BALANCE OF quality, quantity, and variety of our products with the commitment, dedication, and knowledge of our people, and the strength, precision, and tight tolerances of our processing to provide our customers with the very best product and service possible," says Metron Vice President and General Manager John Swanson.

Metron's line of steel products includes hot-rolled coil, hot-rolled sheet, and plate and flame-cut steel parts. These products, along with custom services, are supplied to clients nationwide, including original equipment manufacturers, steel service centers, capital equipment manufacturers, shipbuilders, transportation and construction industries, and related services producers.

Metron is the largest of seven U.S. divisions and one South American division of Primary Steel, Inc. of Middletown, Connecticut, which distributes and produces more than 3,000 prime steel items. The other U.S. divisions include S & I Steel Supply in Memphis, and Gary Steel Company in California, Utah,

and Washington State. The president and CEO of the privately held corporation is Charles E. Pompea. The other officers are Vice President Mark L. Breckheimer and Treasurer Harcourt W. Davis III.

STEADY GROWTH AND PROGRESS

Metron was established in 1950 with a two-member workforce as a distributor of prime, hot-rolled steel products. In 1961, it moved from a tiny office to warehouse space on Root Street on Chicago's South Side. Six years later, Metron moved to the Lake Calumet region and began construction of two bays, from which hot-rolled bars and structural steel were distributed.

Over the next 12 years, two more bays were constructed, and plates and sheets were added to the product line. Shearing and shot blasting processes were added during this time, as well. In 1980, two more bays and a Paxson cut-to-length line were added. In 1987, Metron added a Bradbury cut-to-length line with edge-trimming capabilities, allowing the company to level 300,000 tons of steel coils

Clockwise from top:
Metron's workforce of 120 occupies 340,000 square feet of warehouse space and 15,000 square feet of sales/ support space, working three shifts.

To meet customer demand, Metron employs two cut-to-length lines.

A flame-cutting machine sizes steel to exact customer specifications.

RAY SCORY/INDUSTRIAL PHOTO SERVICE, INC.

per year. Today, Metron's workforce of 120 works three shifts and occupies 34,000 square feet of warehouse space and 15,000 square feet of office/support space.

Francosteel Corporation began acquiring interest in Metron in 1980, eventually achieving 100 percent ownership in 1990. Metron's assets were purchased in turn by Primary Steel, Inc. in 1995. Since then, Metron has achieved record production levels and operating efficiencies.

Metron's cut-to-length plate is what sets the company apart from its competitors. Customers required a hot-rolled product that exceeded mill specifications on flatness, and a stress-free product to reduce springback when burning or shearing. Consequently, Metron's unique coil processing cut-to-length lines produce the most consistently flat high-strength steel product in the industry.

Additionally, Metron is the only service center with its own electronically monitored mechanical descaling equipment on-site, and is one of the few with the capabilities to level floor plate to any size order.

TRAINING AND SERVICE ARE KEY

P roducts only begin to tell the Metron story. Its mission is to provide on-time quality products

and services in partnership with employees, customers, and vendors. Comprehensive, plantwide employee training is important to Metron. Statistical process control and safety instruction have resulted in virtually no lost-time accidents in company history.

Service is also key at Metron. The plant was recently redesigned to increase efficiency, reduce material handling, and cut down on lead times. All stock is readily available for immediate shipment, and Metron is able to ship 95 percent of its orders on-time or sooner. As a result, in the most recent

Jacobsen survey, Primary Steel, Inc. ranked fourth overall in customer satisfaction among all steel distributors in the United States.

In-house testing is another important element in Metron's success. An on-site testing laboratory is equipped with the industry's most advanced testing equipment and staffed by a team of experts using state-of-the-art techniques. Samples from every coil designated for end use are tested to ASTM standards. All tests are then recorded and maintained in a computer data system.

In addition, Metron recently received ISO 9002 certification, which is the world's newest international quality standard. "As a company, we are willing to go that extra mile, and then some, to provide the very best services to our customers," says Swanson.

RAY SCORY/INDUSTRIAL PHOTO SERVICE, INC.

Clockwise from top left:
By offering quality, quantity, and variety of inventory, Metron remains a leader in the steel industry.

The company's dedicated delivery fleet ensures timely delivery of finished product.

Metron's precision and tight tolerances are its keys to satisfied customers.

ITS NAME REFLECTS ONE LOCATION ON THE GLOBE, BUT BRITISH AIRWAYS' WINGS SPAN THE WORLD. THE CARRIER'S BOEING 747S FLY TO MORE THAN 160 DESTINATIONS IN SOME 80 COUNTRIES, INCLUDING A DAILY DOUBLE-RUN FROM CHICAGO'S O'HARE INTERNATIONAL TO LONDON'S HEATHROW AIRPORT, WHERE THE AIRLINE IS HEADQUARTERED.

To celebrate its global reach and herald the millennium, British Airways recently began a high-profile, three-year effort to adorn the tails of its 295 planes with the work of artists commissioned from around the world.

Known by its corporate slogan as "the world's favourite airline," British Airways also considers itself the world's most successful. The airline, owned by the British government until 1987, has made a profit every year since it was privatized. Fiscal year 1996-1997 saw a record profit of $900 million.

"We have remained profitable through 10 years of the most difficult challenges in the airline industry," says Eleanor Goodman, director of sales for the Midwest and a company employee for 24 years. "Even during the Gulf War, when other airlines were losing billions, we made a profit."

THE CUSTOMER'S CHOICE

Profitability is just one goal of British Airways. Two others are to be truly global and to be the customer's choice. In its quest to attain the latter, the airline recently refitted the business-class section of its aircraft with innovative cradle seats. When a passenger reclines, both the back and the bottom cushions shift comfortably into a reclining position, and a foot-rest extends for added comfort.

To promote its new seats, British Airways launched a successful radio ad campaign that drew chuckles from listeners and smiles from company officials. The ads proclaimed that if customers believed—for any reason—they had not sat in the industry's most comfortable business-class seat, they could register their complaints in writing and receive 25,000 bonus miles in the airline's Executive Club frequent flyer program. The promotion even featured a support group for liars who couldn't resist the temptation to earn free miles.

"Less than 1 percent wrote in," Goodman says. "And even if they lied, they got the miles."

Other airborne comforts in British Airways' business class include individual high-definition video screens, complimentary lip balm, eye compresses, and top-notch meals. Another innovation is the airline's "flying bed"—a six-foot, six-inch seat that folds out totally horizontal into a bed. Designed by a yachting company known for making the most out of small spaces, the flying bed is available to first-class passengers.

A COMMUNITY PLAYER

With a Chicago presence since 1954, British Airways builds goodwill, along with a future customer base, by sponsoring an annual essay contest open to local public-school children in grades four through eight. The entrant from each grade who best compares and contrasts Chicago and London receives an all-expense-paid week in London with a parent or guardian. Winners of the contest, now in its 11th year, are also honored at a luncheon in Chicago attended by local dignitaries.

As its shiny fleet continues to crisscross the world, British Airways approaches the millennium with plans to expand service still further, fulfilling its mission to be the undisputed leader in world travel.

Known by its corporate slogan as "the world's favourite airline," British Airways also considers itself the world's most successful. The airline, owned by the British government until 1987, has made a profit every year since it was privatized. British Airways recently began a high-profile, three-year effort to adorn the tails of its 295 planes with the work of artists commissioned from around the world.

TO CONSUMERS WHO HAVE EVER BOUGHT A BOX OF SALTINE CRACKERS, OR SWIFT BROWN 'N' SERVE SAUSAGES, OR TYSON CHICKEN BREAST PATTIES, BRUCE CRANE WOULD LIKE TO SAY THANK-YOU, AS THEY ARE HIS CUSTOMERS, TOO. CRANE IS CHIEF OPERATING OFFICER OF THE 36-YEAR-OLD

Crane Carton Company, a 200,000-square-foot operation on Chicago's West Side that produces folding cartons, primarily for the food industry. Crane Carton, whose 205 employees have produced double-digit sales growth each of the last five years, is at the cutting edge of industry technology. In the past decade, it has spent nearly $18 million upgrading its plant and equipment. "I don't think any folding carton company in the United States has spent nearly that much money on its operation as a percent of its annual sales," says Crane, proudly.

But Crane Carton's primary focus, according to Crane, "is our commitment to our employees—to their growth and to their dignity. That creates a climate of creativity and unsurpassed value for our customers."

ALL ARE DECISION MAKERS

Employee empowerment is not a slogan at Crane Carton; it's an indelible part of the culture—a legacy begun by Bruce's father, Alan. Alan Crane founded the company on the South Side in 1962 with two employees, and today remains active as chief executive officer.

"We have been training our employees in leadership, problem solving, and other skills necessary to work as a team, and as our employees have been participating in employee involvement teams, we have been continually impressed by the work they produce," says Bruce Crane. "Their point of view is indispensable to us to the point that their decisions are often more important than those of top management."

For example, a group of 14 hourly workers who had received special training recently chose a human resources manager from a field of four finalists approved by management. The group dynamic also has resulted in a redesign of equipment layout, which in turn has led to greater production efficiencies and improved workplace ergonomics. Line employees have been part of teams making capital acquisitions, too.

CREATING VALUE

An inclusive corporate philosophy benefits Crane employees in other ways, as well. An on-site training center offers computer training, literacy, and math classes. "We are committed to general skills rather than specific skills, so employees can grow within the company," says Crane.

Further, Crane employs a part-time psychologist to counsel employees looking for ways to get ahead within the company. And confidential, on-site health tests are offered annually. "Just as we want to prevent mistakes rather than react to them, the same is true for our employees' health. We want to prevent illness," says Crane.

There's a progressive profit-sharing program, too. Employees meet monthly by groups to share information about bottom-line profits, and annually, each employee gets a piece of those profits. "We take this year's profits and give them a check, whereas typical profit-sharing programs funnel the money into a retirement account," explains Crane.

"Our reason for doing all of this? To raise the bar. To get everyone—and it's a top-down thing—involved. All of this creates value, to the company, and to our customer."

Crane Carton manufactures cartons for a wide range of products and customers.

I N 1955 FROM HIS SOUTH SUBURBAN HOME IN DOLTON, JOHN LANIGAN, THEN A LINEMAN FOR THE CITY OF CHICAGO, ENVISIONED A BETTER WAY TO DO HIS JOB. HIS IDEA WAS A 360-DEGREE, REVOLVING BOOM TRUCK. FORTY YEARS LATER, THE RESULT IS A MULTIFACETED CORPORATION PROVIDING MACHINERY AND SOLUTIONS FOR THE MATERIAL

handling industry worldwide.

Although Mi-Jack—named for two of Lanigan's sons, Michael and Jack Jr.—no longer manufactures the 360-degree, revolving boom truck, it is recognized worldwide as an industry leader and innovator. Corporate headquarters remains in Hazel Crest, and the company maintains four regional operations headquarters, five sales offices, eight equipment distribution centers, 55 intermodal terminals, and nearly 2,000 employees. The 17 divisions and companies comprising Mi-Jack are supported by 24-hour-a-day, seven-day-a-week access to a $24 million-plus inventory of spare parts through a nationwide on-line computer network.

Clockwise from top:

John Lanigan's idea in 1955 for a 360-degree, revolving boom truck was the basis for Mi-Jack, a multifaceted corporation providing machinery and solutions for the material handling industry worldwide.

Mi-Jack's Construction Equipment (CE) Division distributes other manufacturers' forklifts, scissor lifts, aerial work platforms, and hydraulic truck, rough terrain, and industrial cranes. CE also operates regional distribution centers, including Walter Payton Power Equipment Inc. of Schaumburg, a joint venture with the football Hall of Famer.

Mi-Jack's corporate headquarters remains in Hazel Crest, and the company maintains four regional operations headquarters, five sales offices, eight equipment distribution centers, 55 intermodal terminals, and nearly 2,000 employees.

Today, John Lanigan is chairman of Mi-Jack, which remains privately held. His sons Jack Jr., Mike, Bill, and Dan are all executives within the Mi-Jack corporate family.

CUSTOMER SATISFACTION IS A KEY GOAL

Mi-Jack has been described as a friendly, little, aggressive company. Truth is, we've grown into a pretty big, aggressive company, with worldwide distribution of products and services," says John Lanigan. "But we're still friendly, and our commitment to customer satisfaction hasn't faltered since day one. Our goal is still to provide the most efficient material handling equipment available, and then back it up with the largest parts inventory and best-trained professional service personnel."

Early on, Mi-Jack distributed self-propelled rubber tire gantry (RTG) cranes, and focused on the railroads and ports of the United States. As Lanigan pioneered new methods and technologies in intermodal transportation, other industries soon found the RTG crane equally effective in increasing productivity.

Lanigan knew that keeping old customers was as important as finding new ones. Attentive service became a hallmark of the company's approach to customers. Mi-Jack expanded its business to include providing operating services, and then manufacturing and distributing construction equipment. In the early 1980s, Mi-Jack purchased the manufacturing rights to the cranes it had been selling, which helped open up new national and international markets.

A LIFT FOR EVERY NEED

Mi-Jack's Hazel Crest headquarters is an ISO 9001-certified facility, and produces Translift and Travelift RTGs. Now in use on six continents, Travelift cranes have capacities ranging from 15 to 325 tons, with dimensions tailored to customer applications.

Mi-Jack's Construction Equipment (CE) Division distributes other manufacturers' forklifts, scissor lifts, aerial work platforms, and

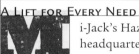

HATS
OFF
TO

the world's
most versatile
BOOM!

With In-Terminal Services Corporation as the premier intermodal terminal services provider and Mi-Jack Products as the leading intermodal equipment manufacturer, a strength in synergy is created, providing world-class terminal operations, 24 hours a day, seven days a week (top).

Mi-Jack believes that good customer service helps maintain relationships with existing customers, as well as earning the loyalty of new customers (bottom).

hydraulic truck, rough terrain, and industrial cranes. In 1972, the CE Division was instrumental in altering the way construction crews work by introducing the aerial work platform into the marketplace, replacing cumbersome ladders and scaffolding.

Today, CE operates regional distribution centers, including Walter Payton Power Equipment Inc. of Schaumburg, a joint venture with—and named after—the football Hall of Famer. CE's in-plant services division provides fleet management expertise to manufacturing facilities under the philosophy: "We do what we do best, so you can do what you do best."

Mi-Jack Intermodal is the undisputed leader in providing equipment to the railroad and port intermodal industry. Complementing that equipment is Mi-Jack's In-Terminal Services Corporation, a turnkey management package providing 14 services to virtually every major railroad in the United States. Those services include transportation consulting, such as terminal design; design and manufacture of equipment, parts, and service;

lift on and lift off; product support; maintenance; inspections; clerical operations; and personnel.

GOING GLOBAL

Mi-Jack has long recognized the importance of the global marketplace. International sales have grown annually, creating a network of 27 dealers servicing 53 countries. Joint ventures include Terminales Portaris Argentinas, operators at the Port of Argentina, known for their expertise in handling unusual cargo; Terminals Intermodals in Mexico, the leading privatized intermodal operators in Mexico; and the Panama Canal Railway.

Mi-Jack is preparing for the next century, too. Lantech Logistics is dedicated to the utilization of new technologies that will increase productivity in the transportation industry. Q Sales and Leasing is the leading supplier of thermal protection products in the shipping industry. Technical Services International brings advances in operations and maintenance practices to customers worldwide. And

Waste Transfer Technologies is taking on the nation's growing problem of solid waste disposal.

As Mi-Jack continues to grow, its goal will not be forgotten. "Our business philosophy is simple," Lanigan says. "We want to be the leader in any market. And we will do that by providing superior products and superior service." Nor will its roots be lost, he adds. "We treat our old customers like new ones. If you always give the customer a little more than what they came for, they tend to come back."

WHEN BUD FRANKEL ENTERED THE SALES PROMOTION BUSINESS 35 YEARS AGO, A "PROMOTION AGENCY" DID JUST THAT: IT PRINTED BANNERS, CARDBOARD DISPLAYS, AND BROCHURES WHEN ITS CLIENTS NEEDED TO PROMOTE A NEW PRODUCT OR SERVICE. IF THE CLIENT

needed personalized key chains as a trade show giveaway, the agency would order them. Part print shop, part product wholesaler, the agency essentially was just another vendor to its clients.

Such ventures bear little resemblance to the types of projects Frankel & Co. has worked on recently. The company designed a retail presence for longtime client McDonald's Corp. at the 1996 Summer Olympics site in Atlanta—a project that included the designing, constructing, and staffing of foodservice locations. It created a state-of-the-art World Wide Web site for cellular-phone provider 360 Communications. On behalf of client Amoco Corp., it negotiated the rights for a blockbuster tie-in campaign with the Warner Bros. film *Batman & Robin*.

That's some leap from cardboard displays—and Frankel's newest initiative, subsidiary Siren Technologies, may even make those

old-fashioned signs obsolete with its revolutionary digital signage system.

It's no surprise, then, that Frankel & Co. today calls itself the brand contact agency whose mission is to become "our clients' most valuable marketing partner."

SELLING THINKING

he company's mission statement comes directly from Bud Frankel's original vision. He believed that within the marketing world, sales promotion was the catalyst. But for promotion to reach its full potential, it must blend professional expertise and creativity. An agency, Frankel realized, must sell clients its thinking, not just products.

Frankel decided that to realize that vision, he had to strike out on his own. He teamed up with a former colleague, Marv Abelson, and in 1962 opened the doors to

Abelson-Frankel Inc., located in a two-room office on East Ontario Street. The first client, recruited on the first day, was Zenith. The first big on-premise client meeting took place around a piece of drywall that served as a tabletop.

PERSEVERANCE THROUGH INNOVATION

he first few years were tough, with the agency frequently operating on a shoestring. But Frankel forged ahead with his innovative ideas. To reinforce his focus on strategic thinking, the agency began charging clients on an hourly basis, instead of making money by marking up its key chains and cardboard displays. That shift was the first of many significant Frankel legacies to the promotion business.

Another was the agency's idea in 1968 to have client Clark Gum Co. contribute 2.5 cents to UNICEF for each empty gum package con-

Frankel & Co.'s newest initiative, subsidiary Siren Technologies, introduced a revolutionary new digital signage system.

Although Bud Frankel (left) relinquished day-to-day operational duties in 1988, he has remained an active force in the 1990s, as the agency has continued its growth record while enjoying impressive industry recognition. Frankel relinquished day-to-day operational duties to 20-year agency veteran Jim Mack (center), who as president runs the agency alongside Chief Operating Officer Dave Tridle (right).

sumers returned to a clearinghouse. In the years since, cause-related promotions have become a mainstay of the marketing business.

But Frankel's agency really came into its own when it teamed up with another legendary Chicago company. Frankel survived a review of 55 agencies and was named to handle promotions for McDonald's Corp. in 1973.

The Frankel-McDonald's partnership made its first headlines—and reinvented the boundaries of sports marketing—with its When the U.S. Wins, You Win campaign developed for the 1976 Summer Olympics. Another magic moment occurred when the team came up with the idea of prepackaged meals for kids: Happy Meals, perhaps the most successful promotion ever. Frankel also was there when McDonald's launched its huge breakfast initiative, and helped McDonald's "Dino-size" its products during a tie-in with the blockbuster movie *Jurassic Park*—a promotion that sparked a supersizing trend in the entire fast-food industry. The Frankel-McDonald's alliance not only has led fast-food marketing, but also has made Chicago the center of that activity.

A PROMOTIONS BOOM

When Abelson left in 1980 to start an ad agency, Frankel reiterated his commitment to the promotion business. During the 1980s, the renamed Frankel & Co.

rode the wave of an incredible boom in the promotion industry.

When it relocated to East Wacker Drive in 1981, Frankel had nearly 100 employees, with revenues rising above $5 million for the first time. By the end of the decade, it had doubled the staff, with revenues pushing $20 million and companies including United Airlines, Visa International, Target Stores, and Amoco joining the client roster. It was a decade when marketers—especially packaged-goods manufacturers—shifted substantial chunks of their marketing budgets out of traditional advertising like network TV commercials, and into consumer and trade promotion.

While its core promotion business was booming, Frankel was readying itself for the next phase of its growth. Since the late 1980s, Frankel has aggressively expanded into new service areas. What the company calls its Integrated Services groups now boast 110 staffers in eight related areas, from sports and event marketing to direct marketing, licensing, digital marketing, and retail design. The agency now expects the growth rate of those once-ancillary services to outpace that of its core promotion business.

In 1988, Frankel relinquished day-to-day operational duties to 10-year agency veteran Jim Mack, who as president runs the agency alongside Chief Operating Officer Dave Tridle. But Frankel has remained an active force in the 1990s,

as the agency has continued its growth record while enjoying impressive industry recognition.

Frankel & Co. headed into its 35th anniversary year as winner of the promotion industry's coveted Super Reggie award for the year's most effective promotion—a multifaceted, cause-related promotion for Visa called Read Me a Story. In early 1997, the company was celebrating again when it was named Agency of the Year by trade magazine *Promo*.

The stream of plaudits comes as Frankel continues to post remarkable financial numbers. Its revenues have grown to nearly $66 million, as it has added to its portfolio of blue-chip clients. The agency that started with two partners and a spouse-cum-secretary has expanded to more than 700 employees. A Detroit office, which opened in mid-1997 to serve new client Oldsmobile, joins Frankel's other two network offices in southern California (opened in 1986) and San Francisco (1995).

Despite all the changes, though, the basic challenge remains the same: to look at the full range of marketing options and communications channels—from coupons to catalogs to the World Wide Web—and, with no bias toward any one medium, to select the best solution for a client. That's what Frankel & Co. has specialized in for the first 35 years of its life. Its expanded toolbox promises only to make Frankel an even more valuable marketing partner for the next 35 years.

RIVING DOWN THE EXPRESSWAY AND DROPPING SOME COINS IN THE TOLLBOOTH OR PULLING INTO THE DRIVEWAY AND PRESSING THE GARAGE DOOR OPENER MAY SEEM LIKE SOME OF LIFE'S MOST COMMONPLACE TASKS. BUT THESE AND OTHER EXAMPLES OF TODAY'S CONVENIENCES DEPEND ON

the use of printed circuit boards— ubiquitous copper-clad panels that have been finely etched to exacting specifications with electronic pathways for the transmission of information.

Of the roughly 800 circuit board manufacturers in the United States, Dynacircuits Manufacturing Company in Franklin Park is among a select group to receive the highest of quality ratings. Dynacircuits is a custom manufacturer, producing high-volume, single-sided, printed circuit boards based on designs and blueprints provided by its customers.

Dynacircuits' custom-made boards are used by Motorola's lighting division, in Coin Acceptors, and by White-Rodgers, as well as for major garage door opener com-

panies, including Whistler-Stanley, Chamberlain, and Genie.

In addition, Dynacircuits produces circuit boards for most manufacturers of smoke detectors and security systems, and many suppliers of industrial control devices, heaters and air conditioners, thermostats, and other appliances. "We are successful because we do it better than anybody else. As a result, we are the largest supplier of single-sided circuit boards in the United Sates," says company president Dick Golden.

A HIGHER LEVEL OF QUALITY

ynacircuits is one of only six circuit board companies designated as a Q1 supplier to Ford Motor

Company. Even more significantly, Dynacircuits was the first circuit board manufacturer to receive the coveted QS 9000 rating, granted through ANSI/RAB, an international quality certification board.

The relatively new QS 9000 designation was instigated by the Big Three automotive manufacturers, who dictated that all of their suppliers must meet stringent quality controls. "We didn't have to change any of our processes," explains Golden. "But we did have to demonstrate and document control over our processes and all facets of the business to prove that everything is done exactly the same way every day."

In order to keep its quality high and prices reasonable, Dynacircuits relies heavily on the work of quality improvement teams made up of cross-functional individuals who work to improve a particular aspect of the company's business, such as the printing or etching processes.

The company has also worked extensively in employee training, providing, for instance, English-as-a-second-language classes for its Hispanic employees. Overall good working conditions have contributed to an outstandingly low rate of turnover. Dynacircuits'

Clockwise from top:

The Dynacircuits staff includes (standing, from left) Lil Asbury, sales manager; John Gulino, director of manufacturing; John Holmquest, direct of quality assurance and engineering; (seated, from left) Dick Golden, president; Charlotte Kelly, accounting manager; Ivonne Alzate, director of human resources; and John Ozag, chairman of the board and treasurer.

The company's printed circuit boards are used in a variety of applications, including garage door openers, toll collection booths, lighting systems, and coin acceptors in vending machines.

Dynacircuits relies heavily on the work of quality improvement teams, made up of cross-functional individuals who work to improve a particular aspect of the company's business. The hospitable work environment contributes to an outstandingly low rate of employee turnover.

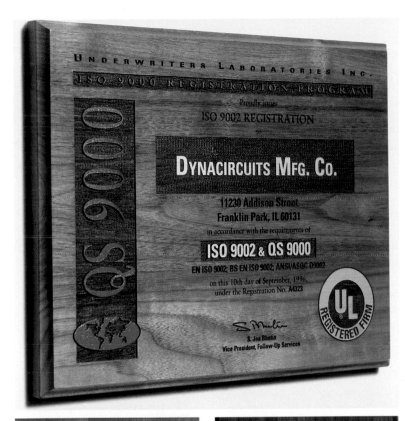

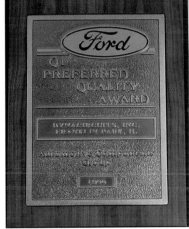

Dynacircuits is one of only six circuit board manufacturers designated as a Q1 supplier to Ford Motor Company. The company also was the first circuit board manufacturer to receive the coveted QS 9000 rating, granted through ANSI/RAB and dictating stringent controls for quality.

All photos by Beach & Barnes Photography

employees—today numbering 220—stay with the company an average of 11 years.

Dynacircuits keeps up with its clients' needs with annual customer surveys, which are used to plan improvements. "We have a set of measurables we've identified for the success of the company, such as a low rate of returns, delivery performance, productivity, bookings, and training," Golden says. "Each month we have targets that drive our continuous improvement. When we are successful, we celebrate. That has proved very successful for us."

VALUE-ADDED SERVICES

D ynacircuits has stayed ahead of the pack by also offering value-added service, highlighted by fast turnaround time when necessary.

Clients have been known to call on Friday and request 10,000 boards by Monday, even though the usual turnaround time is two weeks. Dynacircuits typically delivers zero defects and 100 percent on-time deliveries.

Another value-added service offered by the company is a design staff available to troubleshoot for the client. "If our customers have a problem, usually it is a design problem or an internal problem with their production line," Golden says. "But no matter what the cause, we will assist them in solving it. Our goal is to satisfy them 100 percent."

With Dynacircuits' producing some 250,000 circuit boards every day, sales volume has been growing at approximately $2 million a year, with 1997 sales projected to reach $22 million.

LOOKING TO THE FUTURE

N ot only is Dynacircuits flourishing where others have failed, it is also planning for substantial growth in the future. Among the company's goals are plans to increase sales volume to about $28 million annually, expand its facility, and continue forming alliances with manufacturers of double-sided circuit boards.

"Many customers are looking for one-stop shopping," Golden explains. "Through these alliances we can supply all of our customers' needs." But first and foremost, Dynacircuits plans to continue producing high-quality circuit boards made by dedicated, well-trained employees, whose commitment to quality will help keep Dynacircuits high on the list of the world's primary users of circuit boards.

HROUGH ACQUISITIONS AND CUSTOMER GROWTH, BANC ONE HAS BUILT A NATIONAL FRANCHISE THAT CONTINU-ALLY ADDS TO EARNINGS AND SHAREHOLDER VALUE. BANC ONE HAS THE FOURTH-LARGEST RETAIL BANKING DISTRI-BUTION SYSTEM IN THE COUNTRY. IT IS ONLY NATURAL FOR

BANC ONE to be operating in Chicago since the city is a major financial market with a dynamic and robust economy.

BANC ONE is an aggressive, high-performing organization that has aligned itself by lines of business, or customer types, to enable it to focus on the needs of each customer in a more effective manner. These include retail, commercial, private banking, credit card, investment management and trust, and capital markets. Employees in Chicago operate under one of the lines of business and increase their expertise in the unique products and services to be able to provide financial solutions to people and businesses.

Corporate Banking

BANC ONE uses a range of products and services developed specifically for middle-market com-

panies. These financial options include treasury management, trade banking, interest rate risk management, loan syndications, foreign exchange, leasing, and investment management.

BANC ONE is the second-largest bank in the United States for companies with sales between $5 million and $50 million. Some of the new developments in its Corporate Banking division include The One Connection, which enables businesses that use cash management services to conduct much of their financial management from their office using a desktop PC. BANC ONE has also made it easier for larger businesses with operations across the country to conduct their banking by utilizing its interstate depository network, enabling the customer to deposit funds into one master banking account from operations in multiple states.

Chicago businesses working in the international markets will benefit from BANC ONE's automated Letter of Credit issuance through its United States or Hong Kong operations. Plus, BANC ONE's automated wire and drafts systems are being installed at customer sites. BANC ONE's recent

acquisition of Delphos International in Washington, D.C., allows it to provide more complete and broader access to international trade and investment financing programs made available by the U.S. government or supplied by foreign governments. And BANC ONE intends to provide global cash management capabilities to track international payments and provide automated global collections services.

Real Estate Lending

 Chicago is regional headquarters for BANC ONE's real estate lending activities, and the organization is quickly becoming a major player in the market. Financing is provided for all property types with loans ranging primarily from $5 million to $50 million.

Small-Business Banking

 This one-stop approach to financial services is also available to small businesses through BANC ONE's Business Banking unit in Chicago. In 1996, BANC ONE was ranked nationally as the third-largest lender to small businesses as measured by the dollar volume

BANC ONE focuses on the needs of each customer to provide personalized service (left).

In 1970, BANC ONE was the first to introduce and install plastic card automated teller machines. Today, the bank continues to be a leader in ATM distribution (right).

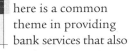

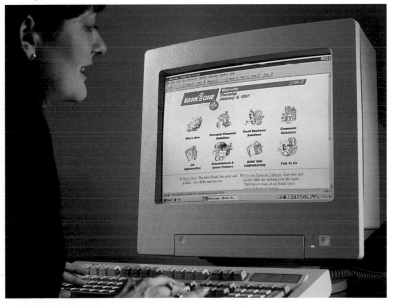

of commercial loans under $1 million. BANC ONE's strong retail distribution system, aided by aggressive marketing and the right products, has earned it a place as the fourth-largest retail banking distribution system in the country.

Business customers can take advantage of BANC ONE's Telephone Tax Payment Service, which allows businesses to pay their federal and state taxes electronically over the telephone. Other aids that help small-business owners save time include BANC ONE's Business Loan by Phone, which allows business owners to apply for loans up to $100,000 over the phone, and ATMs, which businesses can now use to make deposits.

CONSUMER BANKING

he average Chicagoan has most likely been exposed to BANC ONE through the retail bank that provides products and services to individual consumers. Bank One banking centers are spread throughout Chicagoland from downtown Chicago to Evanston, Wilmette, Aurora, Elgin, LaGrange, Arlington Heights, Orland Park, and Winnetka.

The consumer bank operates by providing one-to-one financial solutions. In 1970, BANC ONE was the first to introduce and install plastic card automated teller machines. Today, many of the newest solutions use technology such as computers and the telephone in addition to ATMs.

One of BANC ONE's latest innovations is on-line banking. The bank's customers in Chicago

can access their accounts via their own computers, as well as over the telephone, 24 hours a day. If someone is looking for a mortgage, that too can be secured on-line or over the telephone.

At the same time, one of the fastest-growing bank products is the checking or debit card. A debit card enables a customer to make purchases anywhere a credit card is accepted; however, the purchases are automatically deducted from the customer's checking account. BANC ONE's The One Card features the customer's photo and signature on the front for added protection and identification.

Other popular customer services include credit cards, check cards, and ACH transactions. Through its acquisition of First USA, BANC ONE is now operating the third-largest credit card company in the United States and is the largest issuer of Visa check cards in the country. BANC ONE is also the second-largest organization in the nation in origination of ACH transactions, a service that provides an automatic transfer of funds into or out of a customer's account.

INVESTMENT MANAGEMENT

anc One Investment Management Group has broad capabilities to provide both personal and business clients with the most appropriate investment consultation and service at each stage of the financial life cycle. In addition, the One Group Family of Mutual Funds, managed by Banc One Investment Advisors Corpo-

ration, continues to grow and earn a reputation as one of the premier mutual fund families in the nation.

GIVING TO THE COMMUNITY

here is a common theme in providing bank services that also crosses over to the community—the need to provide one-to-one solutions. BANC ONE in Chicago continues to be a contributor to many nonprofit organizations, and many of its employees volunteer for various organizations.

BANC ONE's corporate vision says it all about its commitment to Chicago and its customers: "We will settle for nothing less than to be a national leader in providing financial services to the people and businesses of America. We are committed to the relentless pursuit of ideas that enable those we serve to prosper and achieve their goals."

BANC ONE provides one-to-one solutions for the community and customers. This includes sponsoring local activities (left).

Customers benefit from BANC ONE's individual attention and expertise (right).

One of BANC ONE's latest innovations is on-line banking. Customers in Chicago can access their accounts via their own computers, as well as over the telephone, 24 hours a day.

YOU CAN HAVE A GREAT PRODUCT, TERRIFIC EMPLOYEES, AND EXCELLENT BUSINESS PRACTICES, BUT A TRULY SUCCESSFUL COMPANY MUST ALSO HAVE A LEADER WITH GREAT BUSINESS INSTINCTS. AT TELLA TOOL & MANUFACTURING IN LOMBARD, YOU'LL FIND ALL THESE TRAITS. A TOOL-

and-die company founded by Dan Provenzano in 1968, Tella Tool posts impressive sales gains every year—a noteworthy feat in an industry that has plenty of competitors, and one that has been seeing business steadily trickle overseas.

Provenzano attributes the company's continued success to the fact that Tella Tool offers a full range of tooling capabilities all in one shop. Says Provenzano, "We are a good company eager to please and serve our customers."

A FULL RANGE OF SERVICES

Tella Tool was scarcely a glimmer in Provenzano's eye when he took a tooling class in order to accumulate enough credits to graduate from high school. After graduation, he apprenticed at a now closed tool-and-die firm in Franklin Park and then, at the age of 19, bought a few pieces of basic tool-and-die equipment, using a loan from his dad.

Provenzano set up shop in his dad's garage in Melrose Park. His

first account was with an Addison company that made antennae for CB radios. He then gained Western Electric Co., located in Cicero, as a client.

At first, Provenzano only built stamping dies for others in the manufacturing business. "Stamping is still a major part of our business," he says, "and tooling supports that." But now, Tella Tool uses punch presses and multislide equipment to produce, among other things, speaker baskets for

the automotive industry; chassis for a variety of industries; deep drawn cases for the food service and electrical industries; and springs, washers, brackets, flanges, and keyboard panels for a variety of industries. And the company has expanded far beyond its original scope to include design, fabricating, machining, assembly, polishing, toolmaking, hardware insertion, and MIG/TIG/spot/robotic welding.

Fabrication, another main service, uses press brakes, computer

Tella Tool & Manufacturing Co. main headquarters is one of four manufacturing facilities that produces a wide variety of products ranging from aerospace components to telecommunications equipment.

Tella Tool's high-speed stamping division with presses ranging from 60 tons to 200 tons is capable of running at speeds up to 600 strokes per minute.

numerical control (CNC) turrets, welders, and laser equipment to produce such things as card cages and card cage assemblies for the telecommunications and electronics industries; cosmetic stainless steel enclosures for food services, cosmetic panels made of plastic and metal; and brackets, hinges, chassis, covers, and housings.

Machining, both prototype and production, is accomplished using state-of-the-art CNC machining centers as well as three-axis CNC turning equipment. The process is used at Tella Tool to produce precision shafting for the aerospace and material-handling industries; valves for automotive and industrial use; heat sinks, housings, and screws; electronic connector housings; bushings; and spacers.

Tella Tool high power 2600 watt laser is designed to cut a variety of metals, ranging from aluminum to stainless steel. With this technology, the requirement for specialized tooling is reduced and competitive pricing is achieved.

GREAT BUSINESS INSTINCTS

nlike most companies, which garner new business and then scramble to accommodate it, Tella Tool has expanded in anticipation of new business coming in.

"The banks think I'm crazy," says Provenzano, "but if you get loaded up on business and can't handle it, you will lose it. Right now, for instance, we have purchased another building. At the moment, I can't justify it, but I think I know what is coming down the road. It's rolling the dice, but that's what you do when you are a small company."

Those same instincts led Provenzano in 1989 to open a 17,000-square-foot facility in Dallas. "We've always done a lot of business in Texas," he explains, "but Texans think there is no world outside Texas. Down there, it's Be Local or Be Replaced. That was a smart move for us." The Lombard-based company has also expanded several times at home and now has a 65,000-square-foot building next door to a 10,000-square-foot facility used for design-and-build projects.

Tella Tool is currently seeking its ISO 9000 certification. "I didn't do that necessarily for our customers, but for our business," Provenzano says. "It's a good way to run a small business with a documented system. Using ISO

Tella Tool CNC fabrication department consists of seven turret presses of precise short run to mid-range production requirement.

9000 practices will allow us to run our business a lot more effectively."

Provenzano believes that Tella's recent business surge, including a one-third increase in sales from 1996 to 1997, can in part be attributed to the fact that clients can find the whole gamut of tool-and-die services under one roof at Tella.

"Besides a traditional tool-and-die area, we are the equivalent to four or five different businesses," says Provenzano. "We also offer precision sheet metal fabricating, CNC machining, welding, riveting, assembly capabilities, high-speed small stamping, multislide, and large stamping. So it's worthwhile for clients to come here for all services."

Recently, the company has acquired some excellent new customers that take Tella Tool up a notch. "Though we anticipate really good volume in the next fiscal year, it's really only a stepping stone to doubling again," says Provenzano. "We expect to see growth at 40 to 50 percent a year for the next five years, if we do everything correctly."

Yet Provenzano refuses to rest on his laurels, adding, "We have to get better and better, and do the impossible more and more often. If we don't, we have a bunch of competitors who are more than happy to do that. Continuous improvement and total customer satisfaction are our goals."

A

S CONGLOMERATES GROW LARGER AND LARGER, MANY SMALL AND MEDIUM-SIZED COMPANIES MUST BECOME NICHE PLAYERS TO COMPETE AND SURVIVE IN THE MARKETPLACE. BROOKFIELD FARMS, WHICH EMPLOYS 120 PEOPLE, IS ONE OF THOSE COMPANIES, HAVING CREATED

a niche for itself in the meat processing industry by becoming one of the largest suppliers and processors of fresh corned beef, pork, chicken, and beef products.

Like many other companies affected by changes in technology, the economy, and the laws of supply and demand, Brookfield has tailored its products to meet the changing needs of its customers. The company was established in 1969 as a breaker of sides of beef under the auspices of its parent company, Nationwide Beef, which was cofounded by Frank Vaia and Frank Swan, who is still chairman of the board. When the industry moved west, the company began boning pork loins, becoming a specialist in boneless pork and baby back ribs for the supermarket and food service industries. The company decided that another product line was necessary to support the pork business, and Brookfield Corned Beef was introduced in the marketplace. As the pork business

The Brookfield Farms' management team includes (from left) Chuck Burkley, George Kordyak, Brian Fleck, Joe Pirelli, Robbie Robinson, Gene Gunsberg, Frank Swan, Dennis Gleason, and Pat Keable (top).

Brookfield Farms serves as a custom manufacturer of value-added portion-control products for specialty markets in all 50 states, the Caribbean, and the South Pacific. Brookfield produces all its products under the Brookfield name as well as under many private labels manufactured for a variety of its customers (bottom).

has slowed in recent years, the corned beef operation has become the backbone of Brookfield Farms. "Our foresight and dedication to the changes demanded by the marketplace have allowed us to prosper in an industry where simply maintaining status quo is comparable to putting yourself out of business," says Swan.

Staying on top of the industry means upgrading equipment on a regular basis. Brookfield Farms

is proud of its state-of-the-art slicing equipment, portion-control process, packaging, and newly upgraded refrigeration and computer systems.

Brookfield Farms also serves as a custom manufacturer of value-added portion-control products for specialty markets in all 50 states, the Caribbean, and the South Pacific. Brookfield produces all its products under the Brookfield name as well as under many private labels manufactured for a variety of its customers. Currently, Brookfield is expanding its product line by offering new pork, beef, and chicken specialty items. Because of its array of products, the company is able to fulfill its customers' needs by providing high-quality, competitively priced products to its customers. "And that," says Executive Vice President Gene Gunsberg, "translates into savings for our customers."

IMAGINATION, QUALITY, AND SERVICE

C hanging with the market has reaped tremendous financial benefits for Brookfield. In the last five years, the company has experienced more than double-digit growth and above-average profit for the industry. To get to that point, Brookfield employs a strategy called IQS (imagination, quality, and service). Employees use their imagination in coming up with high-quality food items designed to fill their customers' needs and tempt the palate of the ultimate end user—the shopping public. Products are produced under strict quality control guidelines and delivered to the customer in a timely manner as ordered.

"We look at our customers as joint partners," says Gunsberg. "We involve them in the process of determining what new products to offer. We're able to provide quick response time. We can take an idea or concept to final product in 30 days."

Brookfield's efforts have not gone unnoticed. Shurfine International Inc., a billion-dollar marketing company and one of Brookfield's private label customers, named Brookfield a Supplier of the Year in 1996.

EMPLOYEE LOYALTY

Gunsberg and CEO Dennis Gleason credit Brookfield Farms' operational structure for the company's success in meeting customer needs. "We have few layers of management," says Gleason. "We communicate directly to employees at every level. We have excellent quality control in all areas of operations and sanitation. Our accounting and engineering departments are constantly being upgraded to keep us competitive going into the next century. Management meets at least twice a week and often daily with employees. We get everyone involved."

Such involvement is rewarded by a low turnover rate. Many of Brookfield Farms' employees have been with the company for a long time—some for more than 20 years. And that's just fine with Gunsberg and Gleason, who value the dedication and hard work put in by their employees. Brookfield's personnel come to work from all parts of the Chicago area, many by public transportation. "There is a direct correlation between the quality of our workforce and the success of our company," says Swan. "Their input into many facets of this business has been instrumental in making us the company we are today."

"We frequently operate up to 20 hours a day," says Gunsberg. "We close down long enough for cleanup and sanitation, then reopen to begin production at 5 a.m. the next morning. Our workforce is made up of virtually all ethnic groups in the Chicago area. With its multicultural mix, Chicago is one of the greatest cities in the country to operate a business. It has a great employee base, a great workforce. Chicago used to be the center for meat processing, but not now. That hasn't stopped us from staying here. The city offers good transportation, raw materials, and services."

The decision to stay in its present location has meant Brookfield Farms' leaders have had to stand their ground in the face of gentrification. Located at 219 North Green Street in the colorful Fulton Market area, the company is surrounded by trendy new restaurants and lofts that once housed industries such as Brookfield's. As a member of the newly formed Randolph Fulton Market Association, Gleason is heading the fight to keep the area unique.

Both Gleason and Gunsberg hold steady to the company's credo, "Taking new products and ideas into the 21st century." "We pioneer, not follow," says Gleason. If he has his way, Brookfield Farms will be leading the industry from North Green Street for many years to come.

JOHN BEDESSEM

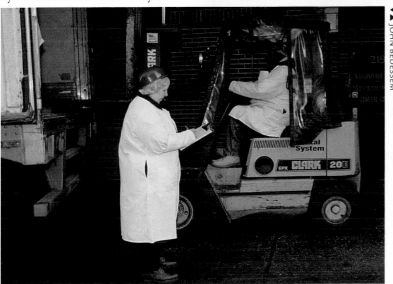

JOHN BEDESSEM

Keeping quality standards high is critical for Brookfield Farms and its staff including (top) Irineo Castro, production supervisor, and quality assurance staff members Andrew Bender and Elvis Asker; (bottom right) Enrique Guzman, production supervisor, portion control, and Robbie Robinson, vice president of operations; and (bottom left) Linda Sheehy, curing supervisor, and Pete Hardy, shipping and receiving supervisor.

EADERSHIP. COMPANIES BUILDING LEADERSHIP TEAMS WOULD BE WISE TO LOOK TO LAI, WIDELY CONSIDERED ONE OF THE FASTEST-GROWING EXECUTIVE SEARCH FIRMS IN THE UNITED STATES. *Executive Search Review*, A LEADING INDUSTRY PUBLICATION, LISTS LAI AS THE FIFTH-LARGEST FIRM OF ITS kind in the nation, serving clients that range from Fortune 50 companies to emerging market players.

LAI was founded in 1967 in Cleveland, and opened its Chicago office in 1969. The local office has a staff of 40. The firm also has offices in Atlanta, Boston, Cleveland, Dallas, Houston, New York, Los Angeles, San Francisco, and Tampa. Through its connection with Amrop International, a global executive search partnership, LAI is linked with a worldwide network of some 250 professional consultants in 81 offices in 48 countries, including Great Britain, China, the Philippines, Australia, Germany, and the former Soviet Union. LAI also maintains a European practice headquarters in Geneva.

LAI seeks out middle- and upper-level senior managers and executives for placement in the communication and entertainment, consumer, financial services, biotechnology and pharmaceuticals, industrial, professional services, energy and natural resources, real estate, and information technology industries. The average annual compensation of executives placed by LAI in fiscal 1997 was $242,000.

"We fulfill our clients' needs by identifying, evaluating, assessing, and recommending qualified candidates for senior-level positions," says Managing Partner John Rothschild. LAI's success at executive search and placement has earned it an enviable 70-plus percent repeat business rate.

MAKING A MATCH

bility. Matching an executive with a company can be a delicate business. "Different expectations have to be fulfilled," explains Rothschild. "The candidate has personal and professional growth expectations, and the client has corporate growth expectations. You have to match the company's expectations with the individual's expectations." For example, a company that is content to maintain the status quo would be ill-served hiring a manager who is growth-oriented. A mismatch of expectations could lead to serious problems.

The key to LAI's success is the caliber of its employees. Most of LAI's recruiters have years of managerial and executive experience in industry. Among its professionals are former chief operating officers, human resources and finance executives, and partners in professional services. With extensive experience managing business, LAI recruiters can effectively assess what customers are looking for in a management prospect. A wide range of contacts and developed networking skills are also useful assets for recruiters.

LAI's knowledge-based practice also involves extensive use of research and technology. LAI maintains a proprietary database containing professional information on hundreds of thousands of executive candidates. More than 60 associates, researchers, and information technology professionals support consultants by gathering and analyzing information obtained from numerous electronic databases, trade journals and directories, the Internet, and other sources.

BUILDING LEADERSHIP TEAMS

ntegration. The end result is the pride LAI takes in building leadership teams. "We help companies become more successful. We helped make PepsiCo, Compaq, Enron Energy, AlliedSignal Corp., Bristol-Myers Squibb, and GTE industry lead-

Managing Partner, Chicago and Global Technology Practice Leader John S. Rothschild

ers in the markets they serve," Rothschild says. Other clients include Grand Metropolitan, Cooper Industries, Lucent Technologies, UAL, Andersen Consulting, and Arthur Andersen.

Overall, the executive placement industry has grown at an 11 percent annual rate, from $1.6 billion in 1985 to $4.4 billion in 1995. Industry revenues are projected to reach $7.4 billion by the year 2000. LAI performs an average of 1,200 searches annually.

"In our first year, which was 1967, we had revenues of $51,000. We've been growing at a 30 percent rate for the last five years," says Rothschild. "Revenues in fiscal 1997 were $60 million, with significant future growth expected."

LAI went public in July 1997, making it the only publicly traded executive search firm in the United States. Although strategic acquisitions have not historically been an important part of its growth, the company intends to expand

its client base, industry coverage, and geographic reach through selective purchases.

"In the near future, LAI plans to develop broader and deeper relationships with clients," Rothschild says. "We are embarking on providing management planning and succession services, outsourced strategic staffing, merger and acquisition, and employee retention consulting. These are new and innovative services our clients desire."

Companies building leadership teams would be wise to look to LAI, widely considered one of the fastest-growing executive search firms in the United States and located in the heart of the Loop.

ESTERDAY'S NEWS IS GOOD NEWS FOR THOSE AT BOOK COVERS, INC. (BCI). THE PAPER ON WHICH NEWSPAPERS ARE PRINTED PROVIDES THE RAW MATERIAL, ALONG WITH OLD CORRUGATED BOXES, FROM WHICH BCI MANUFACTURES ITS PRIMARY PRODUCT—LAMINATED, RECYCLED PAPERBOARD

that is then sold to manufacturers of books, loose-leaf binders, photo albums, and game boards for use as the basis for their products.

A division of The Newark Group, Inc. in Cranford, New Jersey, BCI started operations in 1960 on the East Coast and established itself in Chicago in April 1970 in a 47,000-square-foot facility. In 1982, the company moved to its current location, a 188,000-square-foot facility located at the corner of 16th Street and Kilbourn Avenue in the North Lawndale area. The building, erected in 1919, housed a manufacturer of air valves for the Pullman Standard Corporation until the mid-1930s. It was then home to a book manufacturing plant until BCI took occupancy.

BCI, which started with 12 employees, now has about 550 nationwide. BCI's other plants are located in Newark, Los Angeles, Dallas, and Franklin, Ohio—all cities that put BCI in close proximity to raw materials suppliers and major customers. The Midwest, particularly, is a strong area in the manufacturing of loose-leaf binders and hardbound books because it is rich in the necessary raw materials, says Jay Curtis, vice president of BCI-Chicago.

In 1982, Book Covers, Inc. moved to its current location, a 188,000-square-foot facility at the corner of 16th Street and Kilbourn Avenue in the North Lawndale area.

INNOVATIVE AND SUCCESSFUL

e owe our total growth to innovation," Curtis says. In fact, the company's tag line is "Innovators in Fiber Components." In the paperboard industry, that translates in large part to employing the most up-to-date, efficient laminating and slitting equipment. Innovation also means using the latest and best processing techniques. In this area, BCI has what

BCI, which started with 12 employees, now has about 550 nationwide. BCI's other plants are located in Newark, Los Angeles, Dallas, and Franklin, Ohio.

Curtis calls a "full store" of many processes it has patented, while competitors occupy just a "department in a store" when it comes to supplying clients with state-of-the-art processing methods.

BCI, for example, uses a patented microfluting process called Maxite, which was developed as an improvement over and replacement for solid fiberboard. Because of such innovation, the company has grown 37-fold since 1970, Curtis says. The BCI division manufactures more than 140,000 tons of product each year.

Curtis also credits his company's success with its ability to work directly with clients in developing a concept or method that reduces client costs, yet still offers the maximum in quality. By modifying its manufacturing processes, BCI is able to offer customers exactly what they need.

"We have many loyal, faithful customers, and we learn from them," Curtis says. "We have to and we want to." The industry has changed. To do well, a company must be cost efficient. There's a demand for quick turnover time and exact specification of product. "Because paper and paperboard products are always in demand, the industry is relatively stable, no matter what the state of the economy," says Curtis. "We don't have the sudden ups and downs that other industries experience. People still want books, loose-leaf binders, and Bibles."

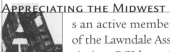

APPRECIATING THE MIDWEST

As an active member of the Lawndale Association, BCI has witnessed a resurgence of business activity in its neighborhood. "Where once there were empty buildings, now not one is unoccupied," Curtis says. Through working with community organizations and other businesses located in the Lawndale area, Curtis has seen an overall improvement in its socioeconomic status.

Curtis and others at BCI are involved in many civic organizations and donate to a variety of charities. The company also sponsors athletic teams for its employees.

BCI's low turnover attests to employee satisfaction. "Many of our employees come to work here and don't leave," says Curtis, who has been with BCI in Chicago since it began operations in 1970. A few of his employees have been there almost as long.

BCI's employees know that if they develop and manufacture good products and provide superior service, the customers will be there to buy them. That philosophy will continue to serve the company well as it turns the page on a new century.

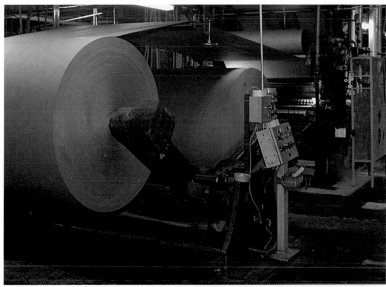

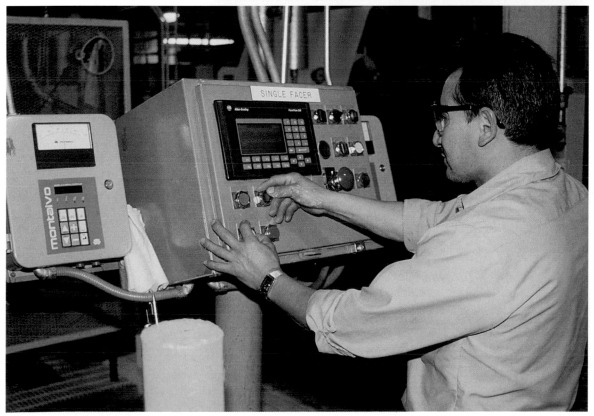

The BCI division manufactures more than 140,000 tons of product each year.

QUIXOTE CORPORATION, THROUGH ITS WHOLLY OWNED SUBSIDIARY, ENERGY ABSORPTION SYSTEMS, INC., IS THE WORLD'S LEADING DEVELOPER AND MANUFACTURER OF IMPACT-ABSORBING HIGHWAY AND TRUCK-MOUNTED CRASH CUSHIONS AND RELATED TRANSPORTATION SAFETY PRODUCTS. SINCE 1969, its crash cushions have saved an estimated 28,000 lives worldwide—more than the seat belt and air bag combined—and are in use in all 50 states and exported to 44 other countries.

Quixote Corporation was founded in 1969 by Philip E. Rollhaus Jr., its chairman and chief executive officer, and his associates in Chicago. The company's first product was a patented energy-absorbing bumper for vehicles. In an innovative twist, Quixote's founders decided to reformat that technology and, accordingly, developed the first crash cushion to place in front of roadside hazards that errant vehicles periodically run into.

With this decision, the highway crash cushion was born, ranging from the now familiar yellow, sand-filled barrels in front of roadside obstacles to the sophisticated QuadGuard® System, the latest in an ever evolving line of crash cushions that protect motorists from the dangerous ends of guardrails and concrete median barriers, using advanced, energy-absorbing technology. This same technology has been adapted for use on the back of work vehicles in the form of truck-mounted attenuators to protect drivers and workers from potentially fatal rear-end impacts. Other innovative safety products include the revolutionary Triton® water-filled barrier, a cost-effective and easy-to-use protective barrier for highway contractors and work crews. The Triton is easily transported when empty, yet is an effective crash barrier when filled with water. The BarrierGate® is an automatic gate that allows emergency vehicles, by operation of a wireless remote system, to pass between sections of concrete median barriers. All of these products make roadways safer by preventing serious crashes and by reducing the severity of those high-speed crashes that do occur.

Quixote has expanded over the years to embrace new solutions and technologies and to meet the manufacturing demands placed upon it by its growing product lines. Safe-Hit Corporation, an Energy Absorption subsidiary, manufactures and markets flexible guideposts and portable sign systems. These products play an important role in preventing collisions and helping to control traffic flow.

Another subsidiary, Spin-Cast Plastics, Inc., makes the plastic components for Energy Absorption's crash cushions and also manufactures a diverse range of plastic products for the automotive, marine, and home markets. Quixote operates manufacturing facilities in South Bend, Indiana, and in Pell City, Alabama. A third facility in Rocklin, California, is an engineering and research center that has an on-site test track, allowing Energy Absorption to conduct its own full-scale crash tests. Quixote's headquarters is in Chicago and the company is proud of its Chicago heritage.

"Chicago is the birthplace of many inventions, such as the adding machine, zipper, lie detector, and computer browser," notes Rollhaus. "Quixote is proud to have its energy-absorbing crash cushions take their place alongside such life-enhancing innovations and inventions."

Quixote thrives today as a global enterprise, continuing to introduce new products around the world to meet the rising public demand for greater roadway safety. The company and its products are successfully meeting the challenge of achieving a safer, more cost-efficient infrastructure system for future generations by making its goal—Saving Lives by Design—a reality.

Quixote Corporation is the world's leading developer and manufacturer of impact-absorbing highway and truck-mounted crash cushions and related transportation safety products. Its crash cushions have saved an estimated 28,000 lives worldwide, and are in use in all 50 states and exported to 44 other countries.

SAVING LIVES BY DESIGN

CHICAGO

1971 - 1998

1971	Podolsky Northstar Realty Partners, LLC
1973	The Chicago Board of Options Exchange
1974	Giordano's Enterprises, Inc.
1974	Hyatt Regency Chicago in Illinois Center
1974	Russell Reynolds Associates
1975	Norrell Corporation
1975	Sundance Homes Inc.
1976	Corporate Travel Management Group, Inc. (CTMG)
1976	MCL Companies
1977	Quality Screw & Nut Co.
1978	DraftWorldwide
1978	Marketing Innovators International Inc.
1981	ESi
1982	Aon Corporation
1982	National Futures Association
1983	US Can Company
1984	Ameritech Corporation
1984	CDW Computer Centers
1984	CenterPoint Properties
1985	Habitat Corporate Suites Network, LLC
1986	Allscripts
1986	UGN Incorporated
1987	ABC Rail Products Corporation
1987	The Fairmont Hotels
1987	Firstar Bank of Illinois
1988	Jordan Industries, Inc.
1988	Technology Solutions Company
1989	Andersen Consulting
1991	TMB Industries
1993	Oakwood Corporate Housing
1994	Bank of America
1994	Illinova Energy Partners
1995	Favorite Brands International
1996	Westin River North

GROUP OF RISK TAKERS, INNOVATORS, AND INDUSTRY LEADERS IS WORKING TO DEFINE THE FUTURE OF CHICAGO-AREA COMMERCIAL REAL ESTATE. CALLED PODOLSKY NORTHSTAR REALTY PARTNERS, L.L.C., IT MANAGES ALMOST 10 MILLION SQUARE FEET OF COMMER-

cial real estate, and in 1997 completed transactions that exceeded $500 million. The firm's expertise lies in commercial real estate brokerage, leasing, property and facilities management, and design-build construction for ownership or lease.

In 1996, Podolsky and Associates made a major leap toward increasing its strength in all areas of commercial real estate when three new partners, Lynn E. Kunde and brothers Mark B. Goode and Steven J. Goode, joined the team. With their arrival, the firm changed its name to Podolsky Northstar Realty Partners, L.L.C. That addition more than doubled Podolsky's business in 1997, and the partners

anticipate further growth. Steven Goode states that he expects the firm to develop more real estate in the next few years, and to be on the cutting edge of the real estate development and brokerage business. "Our business has grown from a local niche player to one with national and international representation," says Randy D. Podolsky, managing partner. "We are an exciting, entrepreneurial group that is industry involved and growth oriented."

A COMBINATION OF TALENTS

 odolsky Northstar is a consolidation of two dynamic groups of real estate professionals. The Podolsky company was founded by Milton Podolsky, who first ventured into commercial real estate in 1957. He served as a partner in Nardi & Podolsky in the 1960s, and in 1971, established Podolsky and Associates, Ltd. At the time, the firm specialized in industrial brokerage and leasing, but it soon developed a sound reputation for property management.

Randy and his brother Steve took over leadership of the firm in 1986. At that time, 80 percent of the firm's business was in industrial properties; today, it is more

evenly split between office and industrial. In 1992—for the first time—nonfamily members joined the firm's leadership when John Musgjerd and Richard Levy, both then with the firm, became partners with the brothers as Podolsky and Associates L.P.

The second group, whose former company, Corporate Realty Advisors, Inc. (CRA), was started by Irving Goode, Mark Goode, Steven Goode, and Kunde in 1987, had its foundation dating back to 1961. CRA's primary focus was on industrial and investment brokerage. CRA was known for its creative brokerage techniques and had won national awards from both the Society of Industrial and Office Realtors (SIOR) and the Certified Commercial Investment Members (CCIM) for the most creative deal of the year.

Together the principals have branched out from their Chicago roots and have been active in brokerage transactions in every major city throughout the United States.

REAL ESTATE PIONEERS

 n the mid-1980s, sensing a need for office space in the Oak Brook area, after millions of square feet of successful industrial and office develop-

Clockwise from top:
Orchard 88 Business Park is a mixed use development for industrial and office users to be developed by Podolsky Northstar Realty Partners, L.L.C. soon. Properties managed by Podolsky average an occupancy rate greater than 97 percent, and a renewal rate of more than 90 percent.

Podolsky Northstar's brokerage professionals consummated a build-to-suit/lease for this specialty metals fabrication and distribution facility.

Podolsky Northstar has grown from a local niche player to one with national and international representation.

ment, Podolsky ventured into its largest commercial development to date with its first large-scale, Class A office building project: Westbrook Corporate Center. Made up of five 10-story towers, the complex was a risky venture, given that of the initial $69 million development cost, $20 million needed to be privately financed. "It was soon fully leased by tenants who were lured by the building's unbeatable near-west suburban location and such attractive amenities as the nation's first speculative on-site day care center, a fitness center, a full-service bank, Federal Express service, and three restaurants, including the renowned Morton's Steakhouse," says Musgjerd.

By the late 1980s and into 1994 and 1995, commercial real estate activity plummeted in the Chicago area. Although many companies were hard hit by the industry depression, Podolsky and Associates stood strong. "We prospered because we dramatically increased our third-party business," says Randy Podolsky. "We took on assignments for institutions and others that were not performing and successfully turned them around to where they could either be disposed of or positioned for long-term growth."

Significantly, Podolsky and Associates was the first company in the Chicago area to build speculative office space in the suburbs or the CBD in the early 1990s. The firm opened the fifth tower at Westbrook in early 1996, bringing the corporate campus to more than 1 million square feet. To complete the investment cycle, Podolsky

recently sold its flagship Westbrook project through an UPREIT transaction. Due to the property's high profile and success, it is likely to be a further acquisition catalyst in the future.

In addition to Westbrook, the firm has also developed the Rosemont/Chicago Industrial Park, O'Hare International Industrial Plaza in Schiller Park, Tower Industrial Park in Alsip, Oakwood Industrial Park in Westmont, and Triton Industrial Center in Elk Grove Village, as well as many other office and industrial buildings in the Chicago metropolitan area, Detroit, Cleveland, Milwaukee, and Florida. According to industrial veteran Levy, "Our firm's success in industrial real estate goes back to the early 1960s and is even stronger in our 'second generation.' "

CORE STRENGTHS

Podolsky Northstar's core strengths lie in its proven abilities to sell, lease, and manage office, industrial, and investment properties. According to Mark Goode, "The new Podolsky Northstar team expects to also be recognized quickly as an industry leader in the national/international brokerage business."

To achieve that goal, Podolsky Northstar has become affiliated with various organizations, including CORFAC® International, a global brokerage network cofounded by Steve Podolsky in 1987. CORFAC allows Podolsky and other brokers around the globe to network on projects of a national or international scope. Podolsky Northstar is also active in SIOR, with seven

of the its partners as active members, while the company's total number of members is the second most of any single office in the country.

In property management, Podolsky Northstar measures its success in various ways, including the ability to maintain positive tenant relationships, control and reduce operating expense costs, and exceed its owners' objectives. And the company can unequivocally quantify its success. Podolsky Northstar-managed properties have an overall occupancy rate greater than 97 percent, and a renewal rate of more than 90 percent.

"We embrace each of our projects with a 'why not?' attitude and address problems with creative solutions," Kunde says. "It's our combined imaginative problem solving over three decades that has earned us a reputation as an industry leader, and that will carry us into the next millennium as a progressive, forward-thinking partnership."

Clockwise from top left:
Westbrook Corporate Center, made up of five 10-story towers, offers attractive amenities such as the nation's first speculative on-site day care center, a fitness center, a full-service bank, Federal Express service, and three restaurants, including the renowned Morton's Steakhouse.

Podolsky Northstar orchestrated this build-to-suit industrial facility development for an Illinois firm. All facets of this design-build construction were coordinated through the Podolsky team.

To accommodate a critical need, Westbrook's early childhood playgrounds became the state of Illinois' first rooftop daycare facility.

ELEBRATING ITS 25TH ANNIVERSARY IN 1998, THE CHICAGO BOARD OPTIONS EXCHANGE (CBOE) REVOLUTIONIZED OPTIONS TRADING AND WORLD STOCK MARKETS ON APRIL 26, 1973, WHEN IT INTRODUCED STANDARDIZED, LISTED OPTIONS ON THE STOCKS OF 16 COMPANIES. SINCE THEN, USAGE OF

the options product has grown dramatically, and CBOE has become the second-largest listed securities exchange in the country and the world's largest options marketplace. Today, CBOE lists options on the stocks of approximately 1,200 companies and on the most actively traded index options in the world.

Options are risk management tools used by investors to hedge market positions or protect portfolios, to capitalize on market opportunities, or to enhance income. Their versatility—the fact that there is an options strategy appropriate for almost any market situation—is one of their most compelling features. The utility of the options product has been recognized the world over, with CBOE as the global standard for offshore markets that now include more than 55 exchanges.

In addition to the emergence of options exchanges throughout the world, the award of the 1997 Nobel Prize for Economics to

Myron Scholes and Robert Merton for their groundbreaking work in stock options is further evidence of the global recognition of the utility of the options product. Beyond acknowledging the accomplishments of these men in developing a formula for the valuation of stock options, this award underscores the importance of options to the world of equities and finance in general.

The broad appeal of options may be attributed to both the flexibility of the instrument and the range of options products available to investors. Since its inception 25 years ago, CBOE has been a pioneer in product innovation. Ten years after the first trades took place in equity options, CBOE again revolutionized the securities industry with the introduction of index options in 1983. Although other exchanges have since introduced index options products, CBOE remains the industry leader, commanding a 92 percent share of the U.S. index options market. Home

to the three most actively traded index options in the country—options on the world-renowned S&P 100, S&P 500, and Nasdaq 100—CBOE recently expanded its index options complex to include options on the Dow Jones Industrial Average™.

The launch of Options on The Dow™ on October 6, 1997, marked the first time in the 101-year history of The Dow that the world's most recognizable index was made available to investors through listed securities options. The new product generated tremendous enthusiasm in the global investment community, and Options on The Dow quickly became the most successful new product introduction in the history of the U.S. options industry.

LEAPS® (Long-term Equity AnticiPation Securities®) represent another groundbreaking options product engineered by CBOE. LEAPS, which were introduced in 1990, are longer-term options that allow investors to take a position

The CBOE's world-class trading facility is the forum where its market makers meet the needs of their customers. Today, 70 percent of all orders are entered electronically at CBOE, where speed, accuracy, and efficiency in all aspects of trading make the Exchange one of the most dynamic trading environments in the world.

Chicago Bears Hall of Famer Walter Payton and Chicago Bulls star John Paxson ring the opening day bell at CBOE in a confetti-filled launch of Options on The Dow. They are joined by (from left) John Stroger, Cook County board president; Peter Kann, chairman and CEO of Dow Jones & Company; U.S. Senator Carol Moseley-Braun; William J. Brodsky, CBOE chairman and CEO; Chicago Mayor Richard M. Daley; Charles J. Henry, CBOE president; and Thomas A. Ascher, CBOE vice chairman.

in the stock market at a fraction of the cost of buying stock. The LEAPS concept has proved so popular among investors that CBOE now lists LEAPS on more than 100 stocks and on several stock indices, including DOW LEAPS, OEX LEAPS, and SPX LEAPS.

CBOE's FLEX® (FLexible EXchange®) Options illustrate another example of how the Exchange has responded to investors' needs through product development. The options were pioneered by CBOE in 1993 to provide institutional customers with an alternative to the over-the-counter market. FLEX Options allow institutions to place large-scale portfolio hedges and to select certain terms of the options contract while securing the benefits of an exchange setting, such as competitive price discovery and the financial backing of the only SEC-regulated clearing entity rated AAA by Standard & Poor's Corp.

Since its inception, CBOE has been dedicated to educating the growing number of potential options users, and in April 1985, formed the Options Institute. The recognized leader in options education, CBOE's Options Institute conducts classes around the world. Its international alumni number more than 40,000, including account executives, brokers, branch office managers, institutional money managers, pension fund sponsors, public customers, regulators, and staff from other exchanges. CBOE each year offers hundreds of seminars for new and current options users that highlight the versatility of the options product in protecting and enhancing portfolios in nearly any market condition.

Today, CBOE also communicates with and educates investors through its award-winning home page on the World Wide Web (www.cboe.com). CBOE's Internet site, which has grown to 3 million hits per month, offers a vast range of data, tools, and educational materials. Popular features include a virtual visit to the CBOE, market data summaries, E-mail news alerts, and a stock and index option pricing calculator. Investors can also register on-line for options seminars and order free options literature, videotapes, and software.

CBOE's world-class trading facility is the forum where its market makers meet the needs of their customers. Today, 70 percent of all orders are entered electronically at CBOE, where speed, accuracy, and efficiency in all aspects of trading make the Exchange one of the most dynamic trading environments in the world. One of CBOE's latest technological innovations is the handheld market-maker terminal, which today is used by a rapidly increasing number of traders at the Exchange. These nine-ounce devices were developed by CBOE to provide market makers with trade capture, position analysis, immediate price reporting, and stock execution capabilities, while storing records of trading activities. CBOE also recently introduced the Booth Automated Routing System (BART). Also known as the "electronic runner," this latest form of user-friendly technology enables member firms to execute orders with a push of a button. Currently, CBOE is in the midst of a multiyear plan to revamp its infrastructure to create the ultimate client-server environment, which promises to define the standard for trading floor technology well into the 21st century.

CBOE is a membership organization that employs approximately 900 people in the Chicago area, and is composed of approximately 1,400 members and their support staff. The Exchange is governed by a board of directors and is subject to the oversight of the SEC. Ongoing efforts to advance product development, trading technology, and options education have made CBOE the industry leader and, in turn, have helped make Chicago the risk management center of the world.

IN THE PIZZA-CRAZY CITY OF CHICAGO, IT TAKES SOMETHING SPECIAL TO STAKE OUT NEW TERRITORY. A SUBTLE CHANGE TO SAUCE OR SAUSAGE, A NOVEL TOPPING, A TWIST IN THE TOSS OF A CRUST—ANY OF THESE CAN MAKE OR BREAK A HOPEFUL RESTAURATEUR'S FUTURE IN A TOWN THAT COUNTS PIZZA AS A BONA FIDE FOOD GROUP.

Pizza makers must, in short, offer a pie that competes. And that is what crowds have been finding for more than 20 years at Giordano's. From its start as a small but singular pizza place on the city's South Side, Giordano's has grown to today's successful group of 40-plus restaurants, spreading from the Gold Coast flagship at 730 North Rush Street to city and suburban locations throughout the metropolitan area. Giordano's has also established outposts in other towns where hungry, homesick Chicagoans congregate, all the way from Milwaukee to Florida.

AN OLD-COUNTRY RECIPE

Giordano's offers customers a pie with plenty of everything pizza lovers love: gutsy tomato sauce; lots of gooey, chewy cheese; and a substantial crust that stands up to both. A Giordano's pizza has character and origins that lie in recipes handed down from one generation to the next.

The Chicago-based chain takes its name not from its founders, brothers Efren and Joseph Boglio, but from their culinary muse— their mother—who was born a Giordano. Efren brought his mother's recipes to the United States from the small town near Turin where she was an accomplished cook known far and wide for many specialties.

Of all her recipes, the Boglio family was most fond of their mother's deep-dish, double-crusted pizza, which she made with ricotta cheese and served at Easter. Efren loved it so much, in fact, that when he came to America in 1967, he found a job in a pizza restaurant to be close to his favorite food. But he found the pizza just ad-

equate, not the mouthwatering treat his mother made.

On further exploration, and much to his dismay, Efren found nothing but pallid pizza all over town, and he decided to do something about it. The result was his first Chicago restaurant, Roma, a pizza place that was a predecessor to today's company.

A MATTER OF TASTE

It was with the arrival in Chicago of his brother Joseph that Efren got serious about pizza. The brothers worked for months adapting their mother's recipe to commercial preparation and, just as important, to American tastes. The generous amount of garlic that agreed with the brothers, for example, overwhelmed their new customers and had to be reduced (although the sauce that today's customers adore remains good and garlicky).

At last, in early 1974, the pair opened the first Giordano's. "The pizza was very well accepted right from the beginning," says President John Apostolou, who joined the company as a restaurant operator in 1980. "Giordano's is a unique product—the original and the best. The taste is unique; there's nothing filler or artificial about this pizza. Everything is made fresh, according to the original recipes. From time to time, we'll change our pastas and other things on our menu, but we never alter the pizzas."

THE IMPORTANCE OF TRADITION

Another Giordano's tradition that never changes is its warm relationship with the surrounding community. "Anyone who sends in, we give them certificates," says Apostolou. "Churches, universities, schools, clubs, people working for a cause. We give donations,

The Giordano's Chicago Gold Coast location, a block from world-famous Michigan Avenue shops, was chosen for its exposure to a large international clientele.

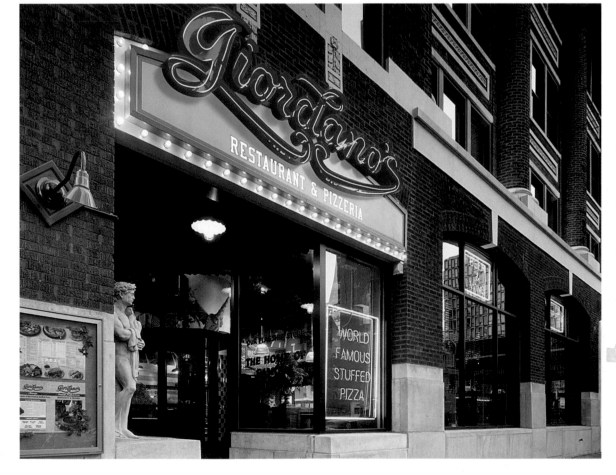

Chicago's "Big Shoulders" fame can be appreciated in Giordano's main dining room. Off-the-shelf furnishings were chosen to create a comfortable replica of a classic, early-Chicago interior.

in money or in pizzas. We always help."

To convey the city's spirit in its restaurants, the Giordano's decor uses an old-Chicago theme. First installed in its Rush Street restaurant and now in the process of reaching the chain's other locations, the look makes use of dark wood, comfy booths, and lots of Chicago memorabilia. Reproductions of vintage posters, newspaper pages, and advertisements make up an archive chronicling more than 100 years of local, national, and international life. A glance around the walls shows an ad for the architecture competition that resulted in the Tribune Tower; a promotion for the *Chicago Daily*

News foreign bureaus; travel posters for the North Shore and South Shore railroads; newspaper coverage of the White Sox pennant victory in 1959; and front pages blaring news of "Nazi Surrender Terms" and the end of World War II.

The decor—together with great food, value for money, and a friendly attitude—creates the

warm, welcoming atmosphere that is the pride of Giordano's. "We don't have a commercialized attitude," Apostolou says. "We like our community, whether that's in Chicago or Florida. Over the years, Giordano's is like family. People come as kids, as teens; they bring their friends and their families. That's the atmosphere we want."

The upper level VIP room at the Giordano's Gold Coast location was made clubby with wood paneling, carpeting, fabric upholstery, linen tablecloths, and upscale artwork (left).

Giordano's offers customers a pie with plenty of everything pizza lovers love: gutsy tomato sauce; lots of gooey, chewy cheese; and a substantial crust that stands up to both (right).

THE HYATT REGENCY CHICAGO IS THE LARGEST HOTEL IN BOTH THE WINDY CITY AND IN THE HYATT CHAIN, BUT THAT IS NOT ITS ONLY CLAIM TO FAME. THE 36-STORY, TWIN-TOWER LANDMARK OPENED IN 1974 AND RECENTLY UNDERWENT A $21 MILLION RENOVATION. ITS AMENITIES

include 210,000 square feet of meeting space; 2,019 guest rooms, including more than 175 suites; and a walkway that connects the hotel to Illinois Center, one of the largest urban retail, commercial, and residential developments in the country. The Hyatt's 4,000-square-foot, 3.5-story lobby features

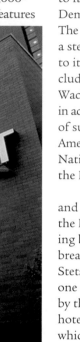

a glass-enclosed atrium furnished with comfortable seating in a natural setting that includes two lagoons, 27-foot-high Washington palm trees, a 14-foot ficus tree, seasonal plants, and prairie grass.

Another of the hotel's claims to fame was its hosting of the 1996 Democratic National Convention. The Hyatt Regency Chicago attracts a steady convention crowd, thanks to its wide variety of facilities, including the 70,000-square-foot Wacker Hall. The hall was designed in accordance with the specifications of such regular exhibitors as the American Medical Association, the National Medical Society, and the Hardware Show.

The Hyatt houses six food and beverage facilities, including the Big Bar, the largest freestanding bar in the United States, with breathtaking views of the city; and Stetson's Chop House, considered one of the city's best steak houses by the *Chicago Tribune*. Also at the hotel are the All Seasons Cafe, which serves American favorites; Knuckles Sports Bar, decorated with sports memorabilia and 15

television sets operated by satellite to show sporting events in many countries; and the Big Brasserie and Bar, which features bar fare and an impressive view of the city.

THE HYATT TOUCH

All these amenities are to be expected from a hotel chain that promises and delivers the Hyatt Touch. The Hyatt Touch means employing a diverse staff that speaks 24 different languages. It includes room check-in by telephone and video checkout by television. To its 1,500 employees, the Hyatt Touch means treating each individual as a person, not a number. The hotel advocates the "five and 10 rule": If you're five feet from another person—whether he or she is a guest or a coworker—say hello. If you're 10 feet away, smile.

The Hyatt Touch also extends into the community. Each employee is asked to spend a certain number of hours doing community service work, coordinated by the hotel's human resources department. Recently, employees planted flowers and hosted a barbecue at Maryville Academy, the largest emergency shelter for children in Illinois. The Hyatt also built a kitchen in Roberto Clemente High School, located in the inner city, where Hyatt chefs teach culinary classes. Graduates of the program are often hired by Hyatt. And, in 1988, the Hyatt became the first hotel in the Windy City to start a comprehensive waste reduction and recycling program.

Since Hyatt Regency Chicago opened in 1974, the hotel has become one of the most well used and valued establishments in the city. Its high occupancy rate and solidly booked facilities ensure its continued high profile as a place to meet, eat, and enjoy all that Chicago has to offer.

The twin-tower Hyatt Regency Chicago is the largest member of the Hyatt Hotel chain, and recently completed a $21 million renovation of all guest rooms and meeting, reception, and ballroom space.

The "glass house" lobby of the hotel was designed by renowned architects A. Epstein and Sons, and reflects a parklike conservatory with fountains, palm trees, and flowering plants.

USSELL REYNOLDS ASSOCIATES IS ONE OF THE WORLD'S LEADING EXECUTIVE RECRUITING FIRMS, SERVING CLIENTS IN ALL MAJOR MARKETS. ■ WITH A TEAM OF MORE THAN 600 PROFESSIONALS WORKING TOGETHER IN A GLOBAL NETWORK OF 33 OFFICES, RUSSELL REYNOLDS ASSOCIATES ANNUALLY

conducts an average of more than 2,000 recruiting assignments. The majority of these assignments are at the very highest levels—chairmen, chief executive officers, chief financial officers, chief operating officers, and directors.

Founded in New York in 1969, Russell Reynolds Associates established its Chicago office in 1974, convinced that a Midwestern office was crucial to serving clients not only in the American heartland, but across North America. Russell Reynolds Associates has grown to become the largest executive recruiting firm in the Midwest, with a client list that mirrors the area's wide range of businesses.

THE CHANGING GLOBAL MARKET

assive structural shifts in business globally have fueled a demand for business leaders with an entirely new portfolio of skills. Boards of directors are taking a more active role in matters relating to corporate governance, and hands-on international experience by senior executives is more important than ever. Because the international business environment is intensely competitive, successful enterprises require objective information, intelligence, and insight on a continuous basis. Only a truly global firm such as Russell Reynolds Associates, with its specialized industry knowledge and consistently high standards of quality, can meet this need.

At the same time, many of the assignments Russell Reynolds Associates conducts are for local organizations—whether in London, Tokyo or Chicago—where firsthand knowledge and familiarity with the local business community are essential. The firm shares with its clients a thorough knowledge of the local market, and encourages its associates to participate in local

civic, charitable, and cultural organizations. By doing so, Russell Reynolds Associates strives not only to be a good corporate citizen, but to create further links for its clients. Members of the firm serve on the boards of the United Way, the Urban League, the Art Institute of Chicago, and the Chicago Children's Museum.

WIDE-RANGING EXPERTISE

t Russell Reynolds Associates, teams of professionals provide expertise in more than 40 industry and functional specialties. Among the industry specialties are consumer markets, financial services, health care, industrial manufacturing and distribution, natural resources, and technology. Functional specialties include nonexecutive

directors and financial officers. By concentrating its activities in specific industries, the firm comes to know its clients' businesses exceedingly well, and can best advise them on growth opportunities and strategies—and the executives they need to maintain a competitive advantage.

Throughout its history, Russell Reynolds Associates has emphasized the importance of long-term client relationships. The firm's success in this area is demonstrated by its high ratio of repeat and referred business—more than 70 percent in recent years. Over time, most of Russell Reynolds Associates' clients come to view the firm as a strategic partner, helping them face the business challenges of today—and tomorrow—through the recruitment of outstanding executive talent.

Andrea Redmond and Charles A. Tribbett III jointly manage the Russell Reynolds Associates Chicago office.

ORRELL CORPORATION CHAIRMAN AND CEO DOUG MILLER USES CHAMELEONS TO MAKE A POINT. "THESE CREATURES HAVE AN ADAPTABILITY THAT WOULD BE USEFUL TO AMERICAN BUSINESS," HE SAYS IN THE PETER DRUCKER FOUNDATION'S *The Future Organization*. MILLER

should know. Like the sensitive chameleon, Norrell has seamlessly adapted to the changing environments of its clients, transforming itself from a supplier of temporary staffing to a strategic workforce management company.

In the early 1990s, while a mild recession and corporate downsizing shook up some of the nation's largest corporations, a little-noticed industry began to expand: the tem-

porary staffing business. Large companies needed to reduce built-in costs and adjust the size of their workforces to meet market needs. Temporary agencies supplied the labor that enabled companies to maintain their flexibility.

Like the ever morphing lizard, Norrell Corporation pioneered changes in the industry by following the needs of its clients. Norrell led the field by developing the con-

cept of Strategic Workforce Management. Out of the more than 7,000 staffing services in the United States, Norrell has risen to the top 10, primarily because of some visionary thinking in Chicago.

In 1961, Guy Millner of Atlanta established Southeastern Personnel to place college graduates in their first jobs. By 1965, Southeastern had acquired Norrell Personnel Services and reached its first $1 million in revenue. During the next decade, the renamed Norrell Corporation marketed franchises and ran company-owned branches. By the late 1980s, Norrell had revenues of more than $100 million and had opened franchises in Canada.

CHICAGO: NORRELL'S CITY OF OPPORTUNITY

he year 1990 saw a shift in focus for the company. When Sears hired Norrell to provide staff for its corporate offices, Norrell faced a challenge. Sears not only wanted people to answer the phone and

A major challenge today's businesses face is how to find a capable, productive workforce, and once they find these people, how to retain them and keep them effective. One of Norrell's core competencies is finding a workforce with the necessary skill base. With Norrell as a partner, businesses can focus on their core functions and are more able to adapt to the rapidly accelerating pace of change.

Norrell's emphasis on diagnosing a client's needs has fueled its leadership position in strategic workforce management.

work in the mail room, but it wanted to delegate all noncore employee functions to one source: a company that would be accountable for all aspects of the administrative staff, while slashing staffing costs.

This concept, later termed outsourcing, would rescue the balance sheets of many large corporations facing cash crunches during the recession. Norrell adapted to this client-driven environment, and the company realized that instead of just providing staff, it now had the chance to supply solutions to large businesses. Norrell can cut staffing costs by cross-training employees and increasing efficiency.

Two years later, another large Chicago presence, IBM, asked Norrell to assume administrative operations for 1,000 jobs nationwide. Norrell formed a specialized operation to handle this $100 million account. Again, Norrell consolidated tasks so that IBM could focus on critical core personnel and leave support work to Norrell. Norrell's on-site managers supervised staff while suggesting innovations and streamlining strategies.

Norrell developed a further innovation: Master Vendor Partnering (MVP). Through the MVP Program, Norrell gives clients a single "vendor" who is accountable for all aspects of screening, hiring, and staffing. Plus, as a single vendor, Norrell can leverage discounts and save clients paperwork and administrative costs. The MVP Program has opened the door to many other clients, including UPS, Ernst & Young, MCI, and Prudential.

PINPOINTING SOLUTIONS

Norrell's emphasis on diagnosing a client's needs has fueled its leadership position in strategic workforce management. Norrell tracks employee performance and can consult with clients on ways to fine-tune their businesses.

In Chicagoland, these include specialists in administrative, customer service, light industrial, and financial positions. Norrell provides accountants, bookkeepers, and even chief financial officers through Norrell Financial Staffing. Punch press operators, electronic assemblers, and other factory workers

Norrell provides employees the opportunity to take personal responsibility for acquiring the training and development they need to enhance their skill base.

Norrell's services range from traditional and managed staffing (including financial and information technology staffing) to complete outsourcing and information technology project management and consulting services.

are assigned through the company's Light Industrial Operations. The Office Services branches in Chicago and the suburbs supply administrative staff, desktop publishers, call center operators, customer service personnel, and other clerical staff. HR Services offers large volume workforce selection options to clients.

Although a tightening labor market provides challenges for all staffing services, Norrell takes advantage of the rise of the nontraditional work life. "Employees can work when they want to, and where they want to, while continuing to meet requirements of both their career choices and our clients' needs," says Miller.

Norrell has been recognized by other industry leaders. In 1995, the company received the Arthur

Andersen Enterprise Award for Best Business Practices. The Ford Q1 Quality Supplier Award was also given to Norrell that same year. Sears has named the company a "Partner in Progress" for service quality in 1996 and 1997. Norrell Services, Inc.'s Chicago region received the Illinois Lincoln Award for Commitment to Excellence in 1997.

Miller envisions meeting the needs of even more companies as the focus changes to harnessing the workforce as a competitive advantage. For American workers, adaptability is also crucial. "The challenge for workers," Miller says, "is to take personal responsibility for acquiring the training and development they need to enhance their skill base. Norrell can be an important resource in providing that opportunity."

INNOVATION, DIVERSITY, AND COMMITMENT—THAT'S WHAT SUNDANCE HOMES INC. IS ALL ABOUT. AS ONE OF ILLINOIS' TOP FIVE HOME BUILDERS, THE CHICAGO-BASED COMPANY HAS DESIGNED MORE THAN 30 RESIDENTIAL COMMUNITIES AND BUILT MORE THAN 8,000 HOMES IN THE CHICAGO AREA. "SUNDANCE DELIVERS GREAT VALUE IN THE

marketplace by offering location, quality, price, design, and on-time delivery that are unmatched in the industry," says Maurice "Mickey" Sanderman, chairman, founder, and CEO.

Since 1975, the company has delivered what customers want with a solid record of dependability and service. Sundance achieves this record by partnering with its customers to determine their thoughts and visions regarding a new home. Sanderman believes

that to be successful, a business must intimately understand what the customer needs and wants, and then deliver it quicker and better than anyone else.

Sundance's eye-catching homes consist of classic designs that embrace living, pay close attention to detail, and are filled with light and space. In addition to being recognized for its superb design capabilities, Sundance Homes Inc. has received numerous awards for the overall design of its communi-

ties. The company's 124 employees are proud of and are committed to delivering the desirable living spaces that fit their many customers' diverse lifestyles.

SATISFYING EVERYONE'S NEEDS

As an award-winning company, Sundance Homes Inc. maintains several divisions designed to satisfy home buyers from a wide variety of lifestyles and income brackets, as well as those with diverse design preferences. Because each division specializes in a specific market, customers from all walks of life can find what they need.

For value-conscious buyers who are unwilling to compromise on function or design, the Sundance Homes division offers houses with high-quality construction and functional designs in convenient, suburban locations. "We care about people's satisfaction and well-being more than any other builder," says Tom Small, president of the division. "Sundance instills quality and value into every step of the construction process, from materials and floor plans to amenities and service."

Customers looking for a more customized building experience can turn to Rembrandt Homes, which features homes that exude quality and luxury. The versatility of the Rembrandt home invites customers to become partners in the planning process, ensuring that the structure is designed around the customer's tastes and needs. Rembrandt Homes provides flexibility for people who want a home designed for their lifestyle. These homes include such luxuries as ceramic and wood floors, fireplaces, and high-end appliances, along with many other amenities. Jogging trails, golf course views, and ponds are just a part of the idyllic surroundings included in many Rembrandt communities.

TILLROCK

The firm's Chicago Urban Properties division is developing this residential site at 1515 Michigan Avenue (top).

The Alcott, another Sundance property, boasts an efficient dining area and sunny living room (bottom).

DOUGLAS FOGELSON

Finally, customers who prefer ▸ an urban location can look to Chicago Urban Properties for homes with unique architectural style, panoramic views, and unprecedented attention to detail. Chicago Urban Properties selects distinctive city properties for development and makes them architecturally unique and significant. All include innovative design, uncompromising quality, lasting value, and incredible location. Customers can choose from condominiums, lofts, and town houses in buildings of all sizes, as well as a variety of floor plans, building materials, finishes, and custom detailing. "We transform urban sites and structures into beautiful, elegant living spaces. We add vibrancy to this great city," says John Mullen, president of Chicago Urban Properties. "There are scores of restaurants within blocks of your door, and the incredible views, terraces, and balconies make these dwellings the epitome ▸ of urban living."

DOUGLAS FOGELSON

CREATING STRONG COMMUNITIES

Sundance is committed to the growth and well-being of Chicago and the metropolitan area. In addition to creating communities, the company is involved in them, working hand in hand with community leaders and groups to deliver the best possible product. Sundance employees are not only active participants in the company's villages and municipalities, but many live in communities and homes built by Sundance. "We aren't deal makers who build one property and move on. We're committed to this region and our customers," Sanderman says.

As evidenced by the homes it builds and its commitment to community, Sundance cares about people. And the innovative company plans to stay on the leading edge of home building by continuing to focus on the customer. Says Jon Tilkemeier, executive vice president of Sundance Homes Inc., "With our tenacity, team energy, and continued focus on what customers need and want, we can raise, set, and exceed current industry standards and customers' expectations."

BILL KILDOW

DOUGLAS FOGELSON

From top:

For value-conscious buyers who are unwilling to compromise on function or design, the Sundance Homes division offers houses with high-quality construction and functional designs in convenient, suburban locations.

Chicago Urban Properties offers condominiums, lofts, and town houses with unique architectural style, panoramic views, and unprecedented attention to detail.

Sundance's eye-catching suburban homes consist of classic designs that embrace living, pay close attention to detail, and are filled with light and space.

A t CORPORATE TRAVEL MANAGEMENT GROUP, INC., TRAVEL IS A PASSION, AND THE COMPANY HAS PARLAYED TRAVEL MANAGEMENT INTO A ROLE AS ONE OF THE INDUSTRY'S LARGEST INDEPENDENT FIRMS. ACROSS THE UNITED STATES AND THROUGHOUT THE WORLD, CTMG IS WELL positioned to provide consolidated travel services and consultation.

CTMG's worldwide headquarters, including a 24-hour service center, are in west suburban Lombard, with regional headquarters in Chicago, Dallas, and New York, and satellite locations throughout the country. International affiliates are located throughout Europe, the Middle East, the Americas, and the Pacific Rim.

Founder and CEO Bonnie Lorefice opened her doors as Corporate Travel Consultants in 1976 with three employees. Today, she oversees a $220 million organization and was named one of the top 100 women in travel by *Travel Agent* magazine. CTMG operates through several divisions—corporate travel management, meetings and incentives, travel management consulting, leisure travel, and travel industry education.

THE TRAVELING CUSTOMER

C TMG is and has always been focused on customer-centered corporate travel management. Its distinctive aspects include consultation, account management, steady client-base growth, technological development, and long-term partnerships. Clients represent a wide diversity of industries, travel management requirements, and size.

GTE Directories has repeatedly recognized CTMG as a Quality Service Vendor in its own successful bid for the Malcolm Baldrige Award. Among CTMG's other clients are Volvo, SOFTBANK FORUMS, Telephone & Data Systems, Turtle Wax, the Field Museum of Natural History, Phoenix Duff & Phelps, and the Joint Commission on Accreditation of Healthcare Organizations. As one of the first in the industry to conceive and implement

At Corporate Travel Management Group, Inc., travel is a passion, and the company has parlayed travel management into a role as one of the industry's largest independent firms.

◄ BEACH & BARNES

◄ BEACH & BARNES

CTMG knows that successful travel management depends on putting the right people in the right places; ensuring accessibility, especially at the executive level; accurately measuring strategies and performances; and supporting it all with good resources.

CTMG operates through several divisions—corporate travel management, meetings and incentives, travel management consulting, leisure travel, and travel industry education.

a full-service, 24-hour, 365-day-a-year capability, CTMG is ready no matter what the hour, whatever the circumstance.

Throughout its history, CTMG has partnered with its clients to bring distinctive service and recognizable value. Its Client Development department helps clients streamline travel management programs, thereby providing a competitive advantage. "Policy review, traveler orientation, vendor negotiations, report and trend analysis, and process improvement are just a few areas of involvement," says Sharon Calvo, vice president of Corporate Development.

Technological Efficiency

hile developing its travel program, CTMG conceived and helped to develop several software programs for travel documentation, travel history records, and policy implementation. When the firm saw a need for automated quality control, Lorefice originated the idea for Auto COP®, a PC-based software program that checks and adjusts travel records at multiple

levels. CTMG pioneered development for another PC-based reporting tool, AutoTECH®, that provides clients with detailed travel management reports.

In 1996, CTMG took another step in its technological commitment by helping launch SABRE BTS (Business Travel Solutions), a total integrated solution for travel booking, policy adherence, expense reporting, and decision management tools, available for desktop PC applications. In 1997, the company announced alliances with several other third-party software providers, bringing capabilities such as expense management and automated booking options to its clients.

CTMG's strategic partnerships also provide a leading-edge international service framework. International capabilities include 24-hour service, international faring, program consolidation and consistency, and global information exchange. Assistance is available with governmental regulations; currency manipulation; business culture and cross-cultural training; and destination information, including state department travel

advisories, climate data, entertainment information, and security. A worldwide cellular telephone service is also available. CTMG's long-term, strategic partnership with FIRST Travel Management International offers a complete travel management resource for multinational clients.

In the community, CTMG participates in numerous events for charity. The company and its employees have participated in activities for the Anti-Hunger Federation, the Anti-Cruelty Society for Animals, and the American Cancer Society, as well as taking part in a multiple sclerosis walk-a-thon and working in soup kitchens for the homeless.

CTMG knows that successful travel management depends on putting the right people in the right places; ensuring accessibility, especially at the executive level; accurately measuring strategies and performances; and supporting it all with good resources. And by doing all of that, CTMG has ensured the client corporation and the traveler will have a consistent, reliable partner.

COMBINE DYNAMIC, FORWARD-THINKING COMPANY LEADERSHIP WITH A PLEASANT, HIGH-TECH WORK ENVIRONMENT; ADD A COMMITMENT TO QUALITY THAT ASSURES THE FIRM OF ISO 9002 RECOGNITION; AND PACK IT IN WITH 20 PERCENT ANNUAL GROWTH, AND WHAT HAVE YOU GOT? ■ A UNIQUE COMBINATION

of just-in-time manufacturing and total logistic distribution—Quality Screw & Nut Co. (QSN), headquartered in Bensenville, Illinois.

With branches in Phoenix, Tucson, Nogales, Atlanta, Dadeville, Detroit, Buffalo, El Paso, McAllen, and Monterrey and Aguascalientes, Mexico, QSN operates as a tightly knit organization that is highly responsive to its marketplace. QSN was founded in a garage by president Art Wondrasek in 1977 as a fastening specialty distributor. In 1990, to enhance the support capabilities to its customers, QSN became a manufacturer with the purchase of National Threaded Fasteners. That acquisition added 42 employees and 120 pieces of production equipment, and prompted

the company to relocate production to a new, 80,000-square-foot facility a few miles from headquarters.

"That acquisition gave us better control of our product line and our future," Wondrasek explains, "because we now have total traceability and certification of the fasteners we produce and supply to our OEM customer base."

Today, QSN makes screws in all sizes to all specifications, and distributes washers, plastic fasteners, nuts, rivets, socket products, pins, and clips. The company also stocks and sells the products of other leading fastener makers, and buys, stocks, and ships a variety of nonfastener components to assist its customers with vendor reduction programs. Both purchased parts and manufactured

parts are held to the same high-quality standards. QSN tends to deal with a select group of suppliers that have been evaluated and rated. The company specializes in custom-designed parts. "Our CAD-CAM abilities," Wondrasek says, "along with our in-house facilities department, can design and produce anything a customer might require. Our volume is five times greater than it was a few years ago and our quality has only gotten better as our volume has increased."

The company also has its own 150,000-square-foot packaging facility, where parts are sorted manually or electromechanically. Kits and bagging of component parts, including literature and video packs, further complement the

Quality Screw & Nut Co. makes screws in all sizes to all specifications, and distributes washers, plastic fasteners, nuts, rivets, socket products, pins, and clips.

company's role as a partner with its customers. With the earned achievement of ISO 9002 and QS 9000, QSN is poised for the future. In fact, QSN endeavors in every way to be an integral part of its customers' businesses. QSN's procurement group, for example, becomes an integral arm of a customer's purchasing operation.

"We provide total logistical support," Wondrasek says, "by providing inventory management, just-in-time deliveries, or consigned deliveries, and by being a single-source supplier for our customers."

QSN sometimes even receives the customer's production schedules, integrates them with QSN's understanding of the company's requirements per unit, and transforms that schedule into QSN's own production and acquisition schedule.

As part of QSN's just-in-time delivery process, the company maintains a substantial inventory so that customers can defer deliveries and reduce operating costs, without sacrificing production schedules.

QSN's systems are all computerized with EDI, bar coding, SPC, and other sophisticated electronic programs that make serving customers easier.

QSN's main office building in Bensenville is crowned with a large stainless steel QSN on top. Inside, visitors are greeted by a 10-foot-tall European wind chime (which employees call the doorbell) in the company's signature colors of red and black. All office workers share a large, open space framed in total-glass window walls. Perhaps due to the pleasant working environment, the company has almost no turnover.

Wondrasek takes great pride in the company's relationship with its employees. "We are a company without an organization chart and without titles," he says. "An organization chart only limits a person's growth and scope of the job. I believe what distinguishes us is that we believe in the dignity of employees and give them tremendous empowerment to act in their areas of responsibility.

"QSN is fortunate," he adds, "to have been founded in a culture of distribution. We know our products and we are attuned to customer needs. Servicing those customers, as well as exceeding their expectations, remains our top priority. We have the flexibility to manufacture the quality threaded fasteners our customers need and to function as an outsourcing specialist on other components."

Among the firm's more well known clients are such companies as Lucent Technologies; Maytag Manufacturing Group, which includes Hoover, Admiral, Maytag,

Magic Chef, Jenn-Air, and Dixie Narco; Motorola; Zenith; Mercury Marine; Mirro Products; McCullough Corporation; and Chamberlain Manufacturing. The company's astounding growth in recent years has called for an additional 140,000-square-foot manufacturing facility.

Wondrasek expects QSN to continue to expand with new facilities in high-growth areas. A newly opened branch in Mexico will likely be followed in the next few years by branches in Europe and perhaps South America. "The 21st century will see even more globalization of business," Wondrasek says. "We want to position ourselves to be a global supplier and the best in our class."

To that end, the company welcomes and endorses change. Wondrasek says, "We don't do business today the way we did it years ago, and we won't be doing it five years from now the way we do it today. That attitude gives us a great deal of confidence in the future."

IN A TOWN KNOWN AS THE BIRTHPLACE OF DIRECT MARKETING, DRAFTWORLDWIDE IS WRITING THE LATEST CHAPTER IN WHAT HAS BECOME THE FASTEST-GROWING SEGMENT OF THE ADVERTISING FIELD. SPECIALIZING IN BRAND-BUILDING, DIRECT, AND PROMOTIONAL ADVERTISING, DRAFTWORLDWIDE IS THE THIRD-LARGEST AGENCY OF ITS

kind, employing 1,400 people in 36 offices throughout the world and reporting annual billings of more than $1.3 billion.

A leader in multidiscipline advertising, DraftWorldwide has never lost its focus on the premise inherent in its direct marketing roots: that advertising must be actionable and accountable. That principle has guided DraftWorldwide through expansion of its service offerings. DraftWorldwide is committed to an analytical, research-driven approach, backed by breakthrough creative work. Quantitative methodologies govern the strategic planning process, from product positioning to prospect analysis, behavioral modeling, and results tracking.

Clients who enlist Draft-Worldwide in a marketing part-

nership are leaders in their own fields: Anheuser-Busch, American Express, Bell Atlantic, Christian Dior, Hertz, Home Box Office, Philip Morris, PrimeStar Satellite, Sprint, and the U.S. Postal Service, to name a few. By working with clients who want to establish marketing partnerships, DraftWorldwide forms collaborative, enduring relationships that are centered on the creative art of selling.

A HISTORY OF SUCCESS

DraftWorldwide's dynamic growth parallels major advertisers' demands for greater accountability and measurability in their advertising. What began as an in-house marketing department at Bankers Life & Casualty became an independent agency in 1978, and soon

developed a diverse roster of consumer and business-to-business clients.

In 1982, a New York office opened that was headed by Howard Draft. One of the first accounts was a direct marketing project for HBO, which celebrated 15 years with DraftWorldwide in 1997. The agency began to expand overseas, opening offices in Madrid, London, and Paris, as advertisers abroad clamored for accountability in their advertising. As new markets such as China opened their doors, Draft opened offices to service clients' marketing needs. Today, the DraftWorldwide network spans 36 offices in North America, South America, Europe, the Middle East, Asia, and Australia.

In 1996, the agency became part of The Interpublic Group of Companies, the third-largest organization of advertising agencies and communications companies in the world. DraftWorldwide became the fourth component in a network that includes such powerhouses as McCann Erickson, Ammarati Puris Lintas, and Lowe & Partners.

The 1997 acquisition of Lee Hill, Inc., a Chicago-based promotional marketing firm noted for its outstanding creative product, had a profound impact on DraftWorldwide. For the first time, the agency was able to offer promotional and direct marketing services working in tandem under one roof. The seamless integration of these disciplines has redefined the agency and helped chart its course for the future.

SPECIALTY SERVICES

Understanding the customer's needs, wants, reactions, and behavioral patterns is central to effective advertising. The complexities of today's commercial environment demand intense knowledge of the

Headquartered in Chicago, Draft-Worldwide specializes in brand-building, direct, and promotional marketing.

STEVE HALL/HEDRICH BLESSING

Success with a direct/relationship marketing program for Cadillac DeVille led Cadillac to name DraftWorldwide the agency of record for direct marketing on all its brands.

product category and the factors that govern users. To this end, DraftWorldwide established specialty divisions, such as Healthcare Marketing Services and Minority Marketing Services. Staffed by experts in the field, these divisions are innovators in their own right. Minority Marketing Services, for example, issued the first study of Hispanic consumers' attitudes toward and preferences in direct marketing techniques. Healthcare Marketing Services developed the first program-length announcement—or infomercial, as it is commonly called—for Rogaine, which was then a prescription product.

D.L. Blair, Adler Boschetto Peebles & Partners, and the MCA Marketing Agency round out the agency's complement of services. D.L. Blair is one of America's oldest, largest, and most respected sales promotion agencies, and develops and executes more sweepstakes, games, and contests than any company in America. D.L. Blair is responsible for many of the innovations in the category, including scratch-off games, preselected-number games, matching-half games, and TV Watch & Win®.

Adler Boschetto Peebles & Partners is a full-service agency specializing in brand-building, direct response, sales promotion, and point-of-sale marketing. The agency's core philosophy is to provide creative, memorable advertising that generates measurable results for clients and builds distinctive brands that become category leaders. Founded in 1916, the agency is a charter member of the American Association of Advertising Agencies.

EXECUTIVE CLUB
BRITISH AIRWAYS

Miles de

Millas

los Martes.

Oferta exclusiva para los Socios del Executive Club de British Airways en Chile.

7.500 Millas para los socios del Executive Club que vuelen los martes en First.
5.000 Millas para los socios del Executive Club que vuelen los martes en Club World.

MCA Marketing Agency has prospered by following the principle that "our success depends upon our client's success." "Creative ideas that sell" has been the cornerstone of this vision. Loyalty marketing, new brand introductions, special event promotions, brand marketing programs, and marketing partner alliances form the bulk of the agency's special expertise.

Volunteerism is deeply ingrained in DraftWorldwide corporate culture. The agency demonstrates its commitment to charitable causes, particularly those that affect children, by encouraging involvement in two specific causes: Pediatric AIDS Chicago and Birch Summer Camp, a special camp for families affected by AIDS. Employees who wish to volunteer as counselors are flown at company expense to Birch camp. A similar arrangement is in place for employees who wish to volunteer for Pediatric AIDS Chicago activities.

As the call for accountability in advertising continues, DraftWorldwide remains focused on strategic planning backed by creative selling. Whether drawing from direct, promotional, or other marketing disciplines, research-driven, actionable advertising continues to be the hallmark of the DraftWorldwide brand.

Clockwise from top:
International clients are served from 36 offices around the globe.

DraftWorldwide is one of the world's largest buyers of direct response TV.

Work for the American Express Consumer Card division called on DraftWorldwide to make complex programs easy to understand.

MARKETING INNOVATORS IS A FULL-SERVICE PERFORMANCE IMPROVEMENT COMPANY AND A LEADER IN THE INCENTIVE INDUSTRY. WITH INNOVATION AS ITS CORNERSTONE, THE FIRM WORKS CLOSELY WITH BUSINESSES TO DEVELOP PERFORMANCE SOLUTIONS THAT reward the heart and soul of every company—its employees.

Under the leadership of Lois M. LeMenager, chairman and CEO, Marketing Innovators provides customer-driven solutions through quality consultation, products, and services. Founded in 1978, the company has been recognized by *Crain's Chicago Business* for several consecutive years as one of the 10 largest woman-owned businesses in Chicago. With a staff of 56, Marketing Innovators is able to work closely with its clients, which include both large and small businesses, to improve employee performance and enhance customer loyalty.

From concept to conclusion, Marketing Innovators works with clients to develop performance ideas with a creative flair. The company offers clients assistance in program development, program implementation, creative design, high-impact communications, and fulfillment.

"In order to be successful, businesses must focus on people," explains Rick Blabolil, Marketing Innovators' executive vice president. "We understand that the key to success is improving the performance of your people—because companies don't change, people do."

Clockwise from top:

Under the leadership of Chairman and CEO Lois M. LeMenager, Marketing Innovators provides customer-driven solutions through quality consultation, products, and services.

From concept to conclusion, the firm works with clients to develop performance ideas with a creative flair, and offers assistance in program design and high-impact communications.

Marketing Innovators offers a complete line of travel services, including incentive travel; meeting planning; and corporate, individual, and group travel.

A TRUE INNOVATOR

True innovation is more than developing new products—it is developing new applications for existing products and services. Borrowing an idea from the consumer market, LeMenager was one of the first to use gift certificates in the business-to-business market. She and her team created the Freedom to Choose® network of more than 200 national, regional, and local retail merchants for award fulfillment. The program was considered to be the first genuinely new concept the incentive industry had seen since its inception.

Today, retail gift certificates are the most popular nonmonetary award option used by businesses to improve performance. "Companies like to offer gift certificates as incentives because they can be redeemed in local stores for a virtually unlimited selection of merchandise," explains LeMenager.

Marketing Innovators was also one of the engineers in orchestrating an application for retail gift certificates beyond the corporate market. Through its not-for-profit fund-raising program, thousands

of nonprofit associations, schools, churches, and civic groups have raised millions of dollars in the last five years.

In addition to being a merchant access provider for gift certificates, Marketing Innovators' many products and services include merchandise awards, debit cards, creative communications, training seminars, database management, and program evaluation, plus a complete line of travel services.

TRAVEL DIVISION

riginally founded as an incentive travel company, Marketing Innovators continues to play an important role in the industry, offering a multitude of travel services, including incentive travel; meeting planning; and corporate, individual, and group travel. To ensure successful results from each program, the company provides program management for all of the essential travel services, including site and transportation logistics, meeting planning, registrations, special functions, leisure activities, pre-trip materials and communications, and program evaluation.

Marketing Innovators separates itself from others who merely process airline tickets and make hotel reservations. "Travel is a hospitality service," states Sherry Blabolil-Das, executive vice president, operations. "We see it as an opportunity to demonstrate our creativity and flexibility, while providing personalized services."

STAYING AHEAD OF THE MARKET

echnology is the gateway to evolution and innovation in performance systems. As Marketing Innovators celebrates its 20th anniversary, the company continues to move forward with advanced technology. Marketing Innovators prides itself on its ability to keep up with the fast-growing incentive industry and is exploring new applications involving virtual incentive systems, CD-ROM programs, and the World Wide Web.

In recent years, Marketing Innovators has developed several information system modules for the strategic and tactical management and tracking of incentive programs. The MIBANC personal account system allows employees to accumulate program earnings and decide when to redeem their earnings. It also permits them to choose which certificates they want and how much to withdraw from their account. MIBANC tracks earnings, redemptions, and all related activities easily and efficiently. Another module, the MIPERC performance tracking system, allows program participants to measure their results against established goals and objectives.

"Metrics have become increasingly more important for corporations," states Blabolil. "Our clients are looking for tools that enhance program integration, provide database management, and then evaluate the results."

Marketing Innovators strives to be a catalyst and facilitator of individual performance improvement, by providing workplace incentive performance solutions that motivate, educate, and communicate. Such programs enhance the performance of corporations through the positive impact they have on the people who are the heart and soul of the company— an impact felt both in the workplace and in people's personal lives.

Today, retail gift certificates are the most popular nonmonetary award option used by businesses to motivate or recognize employee performance and enhance customer loyalty (top).

Marketing Innovators continues to be an innovator within the incentive industry, moving forward with advanced technology and exploring new applications in performance improvement systems (bottom).

IN TODAY'S RAPIDLY CHANGING WORLD, DISCUSSIONS OF HEALTH CARE TYPICALLY REVOLVE AROUND COST. AND WHEN PEOPLE TALK ABOUT REDUCING HEALTH CARE COSTS, THEY OFTEN TALK ABOUT ENTERPRISE SYSTEMS (ESi). ■ ENTERPRISE SYSTEMS WAS FOUNDED IN 1981 TO HELP HEALTH CARE ORGANIZATIONS, PRIMARILY IIOSPITALS, OPERATE

efficiently. ESi promoted a strong focus on cost management with its first product, a materials management system. Its success led the company to create a solution for operating room logistics and an integrated financial program.

Enterprise Systems developed an excellent reputation for quality service, responsiveness, solid products, and great people, which led to an industry leadership position and continuing profitability.

MANAGED CARE ACCELERATES COST PRESSURE

By 1995, the world of health care was changing in some very dramatic ways. With the advent of prepaid managed care, health care organizations were under tremendous pressure to reduce costs. In addition, the industry was going through a major consolidation.

Health care organizations were forming integrated delivery

systems, which included not just acute care hospitals, but clinics, surgical centers, and physician practices as well. These large, integrated delivery networks required a new level of powerful, sophisticated software designed to manage complicated, ever changing, geographically dispersed networks.

A NEW DIRECTION FOR A NEW WORLD

The company had reached a strategic inflection point. The decision was made to bring in a new CEO to build upon the successes of the past, and to make the changes necessary to position ESi to succeed in this new world of health care. As Glen Tullman, the newly appointed CEO, recalls, "Transitioning from an entrepreneurial environment to a professionally managed growth company is tough enough. When the entrepreneurial environment you are

trying to change has enjoyed a healthy amount of success, creating an impetus to change can be even more challenging."

FROM ENTREPRENEURIAL TO GROWTH COMPANY

The first objective was to define the business strategy. The future presented dramatic challenges for ESi's customers: defining quality care while reducing the cost of delivering that care. The centerpiece of this strategy was ESi's NOVA materials management system as a substitute for the expense- and transaction-laden materials systems used by most hospitals. Combined with operating room and financial systems offered by ESi, the strategy developed into the resource management solution that ESi offers today.

A second objective was to accelerate sales. In a small software company, incremental sales fall directly to the bottom line, so the objective was to increase growth to fund investments and prepare for a public offering. Steve Katz, chief operating officer responsible for sales and marketing activities, notes, "There was a tremendous amount of pressure to accelerate sales, to educate the sales force for a new type of sale, and to reposition the company." Katz delivered, with sales increases of 35 percent in 1995 and 57 percent in 1996.

The next stage in the company's growth was to prepare for an initial public offering (IPO). Dave Mullen, the company's chief financial officer, was a veteran of a previous IPO for one of *Inc.* magazine's fastest-growing companies. "While ESi had great prospects, we knew that in order to compete successfully, to invest in research and development, and to make the necessary acquisitions to complete the vision, we needed a larger source of capital," says Mullen.

ESi's dedicated staff of more than 400 associates has helped secure the company's future as the leader in enterprisewide resource management. The client services group, pictured here, builds and maintains the strong client relationships integral to ESi's success.

The ESi management team includes (from left) Joe Carey, Steve Katz, Bob Rook, Stanley Crane, Glen Tullman, Dave Carlson, Dave Mullen, and Jim Ray.

The company's initial public offering of stock in October 1995 was priced above the range, and the stock was soon selling at $30, almost twice the IPO price.

With those tools in place, Tullman recruited Stanley Crane, a veteran of Silicon Valley, to be chief technology officer. Crane was responsible for developing the design and implementation of the Windows-based, distributed client/server software that powers the company's solutions today, while at the same time enhancing the existing DOS-based offerings and releasing three new products.

Crane comments, "To redesign the architecture and convert the products in a short time frame, while at the same time adding world-class documentation and quality assurance groups, speaks to the quality of our people and also demonstrates what teams, working together, can accomplish."

Along the way, two veteran executives helped manage the entire transition. Joe Carey, president of the company, maintained responsibility for all operations. "The real goal of managing through change is to keep people focused on what's important and to teach them the process of constantly questioning how to improve without being defensive. In the past two years, we changed the management lead-

ership and direction in every operating area. And yet, during that process, we successfully retained our frontline, most experienced people," says Carey.

Dave Carlson, one of the founders of the company, had the vision that was the basis of ESi's integrated resource management approach. Carlson notes, "I've seen each of the stages of the company, from the initial entrepreneurial start, to a 'best-of-breed' provider, to a publicly held growth company offering an integrated resource management suite. Every stage presented unique challenges that we had to address." Tullman continues, "Flexibility and humor, two of Dave's strengths, helped pull the company through some pretty difficult transitions."

The final ingredient to sustaining ESi's emerging growth culture was the addition of Bob Rook, executive vice president of human resources. Rook's previous experience in both large and small corporate environments, as well as consolidating physician practices, helped him understand the need to create a culture capable of thriving under the demands of constant change. Rook explains, "Creating and articulating a strong foundational theme and developing a people strategy was the first order of business."

Results

The results speak for themselves. ESi's team of more than 400 dedicated associates delivered two record years. Infrastructure investments enabled record growth, helping position the company as the leader in enterprisewide resource management in an industry that clearly can use the company's help. Carey says, "Our strategy is to have fun and keep learning. We believe that if we follow both of those objectives, we will be rewarded for it. And while we have talked about the executive team, it's the people on the front line that make it happen every day. They are our eyes and ears, and have the strong client relationships our success is built upon."

With an energized workforce, a strong strategic plan, and a continued emphasis on meeting client needs, Enterprise Systems is well positioned to continue its record of growth and success, and to do its part to help solve the nation's health care cost problem.

In June 1997, ESi was acquired by Atlanta-based HBO & Company (HBOC), the world's largest provider of health care information systems. ESi continues its resource management strategy as a separate business unit of HBOC.

On Corporation, headquartered in Chicago, is the world's premier insurance and consulting services organization. Derived from a Gaelic word, the Aon name connotes unity, oneness, and coming together. The name embodies the unique culture and the company's innovative way of conducting business throughout the world.

Through an extensive distribution network, Aon offers commercial insurance, reinsurance and wholesale brokerage; risk management services; consulting solutions for commercial and industrial businesses and insurance organizations; and consumer insurance products for individual policyholders.

What truly sets Aon apart is the powerful combination of entrepreneurship and interdependence that unites its professionals and motivates them to provide exceptional client service.

The Aon Culture

Interdependence—two or more Aon companies working together on behalf of clients—is fundamental to Aon's culture.

Aon professionals capitalize on the synergies that exist in Aon's businesses, working together to deliver the expertise that clients need anywhere, anytime. They solve client problems intelligently, with innovation and flexibility. Whatever the business specialty may be, Aon professionals can call upon the exceptional knowledge and experience of colleagues throughout the company to address clients' most basic and most complex risk management and consulting requirements.

Interdependence allows every Aon professional to draw upon Aon's unparalleled resources to provide clients with a distinct advantage. By striving to ensure that clients have convenient and easy access to Aon's vast network of experts, Aon professionals bring tangible value to a client's bottom line.

Entrepreneurial Spirit

Entreprenuerism is personified in Patrick G. Ryan, the chairman, president, and chief executive officer of Aon Corporation. A man of strong vision, he has been called by those who work with him "the ultimate strategy guy."

In only three decades, Ryan has built one of the most successful and dynamic companies in the global insurance services marketplace. At the core of his leadership is his capacity to translate vision into reality. Where others have seen difficulties and seemingly insurmountable challenges, Ryan has found and capitalized upon opportunities. His actions have made an impact well beyond the boundaries of his own company. His leadership and vision have triggered a succession of changes, creating a momentum that has affected the entire insurance services industry.

Aon's culture of interdependent teamwork and entrepreneurial spirit generates the energy that powers the organization.

Strategic Growth

Ryan initiated Aon's explosive growth in August 1982 when he merged his Ryan Insurance Group, Inc. with Combined International Corporation. Just months later, Aon purchased broker Rollins Burdick Hunter Co., which significantly increased its insurance brokerage and consulting business.

Through the remainder of the 1980s and throughout the 1990s, Ryan continued to spearhead the consolidation of the insurance and reinsurance brokerage industry by a series of strategic acquisitions and organic growth that fueled

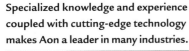
Specialized knowledge and experience coupled with cutting-edge technology makes Aon a leader in many industries.

in key acquisitions, including the Bain Hogg Group; Alexander & Alexander Services, Inc.; Minet, Inc.; Sodarcan, Inc.; Martineau Provencher & Associates, Ltd.; and Jauch & Hübener KGaA.

While Aon is a leader in virtually every market it serves, size is not its primary goal. Though size is important, Aon aims to be the world's highest-quality, most responsive insurance and consulting services company.

CLIENT ADVOCACY

s client advocates, Aon professionals take a consultative rather than a transactional approach to risk management. They are dedicated to working in partnership with their clients, listening, understanding, and responding effectively, making the client's interest their top priority. They find or, if necessary, create the solutions clients seek.

Today, clients face challenges and uncertainties that result from an ever changing business environment cutting across local, regional, and global economies. Aon's extensive experience with the commercial customs and practices in countries it serves around the world adds a valuable dimension to its approach to business and client service.

GLOBAL DISTRIBUTION

n most every area of its worldwide business, Aon controls the distribution of its products and services. Aon's distribution networks assure

Entrepreneurism is personified in Patrick G. Ryan, the chairman, president, and chief executive officer of Aon Corporation.

Aon's expansion in the global insurance marketplace. In 1991, Aon acquired Hudig-Langeveldt, a Netherlands-based brokerage and consulting company founded in the 17th century. The following year, the businesses of Frank B. Hall, a major brokerage and consulting organization, were acquired.

A strategic redirection of the company in 1995 led to the sale of two of Aon's domestic life insurance businesses and the deployment of those proceeds into a broader range of specialized insurance brokerage and consulting services. Throughout 1996 and 1997, combined with internal growth, Aon invested significantly

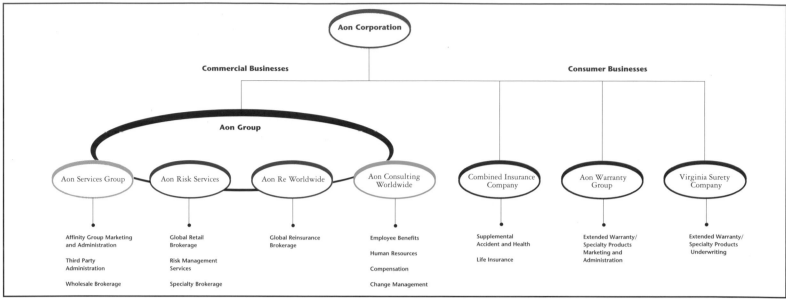

Aon Corporation organizational chart:

Aon Corporation

Commercial Businesses — **Aon Group**

- **Aon Services Group**
  - Affinity Group Marketing and Administration
  - Third Party Administration
  - Wholesale Brokerage
- **Aon Risk Services**
  - Global Retail Brokerage
  - Risk Management Services
  - Specialty Brokerage
- **Aon Re Worldwide**
  - Global Reinsurance Brokerage
- **Aon Consulting Worldwide**
  - Employee Benefits
  - Human Resources
  - Compensation
  - Change Management

Consumer Businesses

- **Combined Insurance Company**
  - Supplemental Accident and Health
  - Life Insurance
- **Aon Warranty Group**
  - Extended Warranty/Specialty Products Marketing and Administration
- **Virginia Surety Company**
  - Extended Warranty/Specialty Products Underwriting

Interdependence—two or more Aon companies working together on behalf of clients—is fundamental to Aon's culture.

clients that they are receiving the most innovative products, as well as the most effective and cost-efficient services, and are accessing the best professionals in the business.

Aon professionals work on six continents in more than 500 offices in some 100 countries. Virtually all of Aon's offices are company owned, ensuring that clients are provided with seamless, quality service anywhere in the world.

MARKET LEADERSHIP

Specialized knowledge and experience coupled with cutting-edge technology make Aon a leader in industries such as aviation, marine, construction, energy, financial services, health care, media, entertainment, sports and leisure, public entities, utilities, fine arts, transportation, and high-tech.

Aon experts offer a broad spectrum of specialized products such as errors and omissions, professional liability, directors' and officers' liability, workers' compensation, property, catastrophic risk, and alternative risk financing. Aon leads the industry in developing innovative capital market products by tailoring financial risk management services as an alternative to risk transfer.

Aon's insurance, reinsurance, and wholesale brokerage operations are the largest in many parts of the world. The company is the leading specialty broker in London. Aon is a unique provider of underwriting management expertise to insurance companies. Its consulting arm is one of the world's preeminent employee benefits, compensation, human resource, and change management firms, linking people strategies with business strategies

for improved performance.

Aon's consumer businesses reach a loyal customer base of more than 5 million policyholders. It is a leading underwriter of supplemental accident, health, and life insurance products sold directly to individuals and through work-site marketing programs. Aon companies are among the world's largest underwriters of extended warranties on automobiles, electronics, and appliances.

Aon's insurance underwriting operations complement its focus on brokerage distribution and services, providing a strong financial presence that enhances cash flow. Through new products and distribution relationships, the insurance underwriting companies seek opportunities to work interdependently with Aon's brokerage and consulting operations to better serve clients.

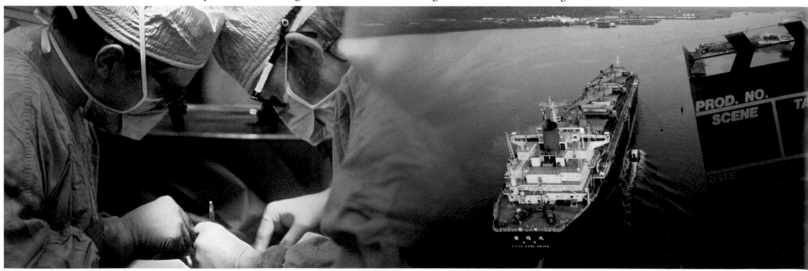

Argentina	Denmark	Jamaica	Oman	Switzerland
Aruba	Dominican Republic	Japan	Panama	Taiwan
Australia	Ecuador	Kazakhstan	Papua New Guinea	Tanzania
Austria	Estonia	Kenya	Peru	Thailand
Bahamas	Fiji	Kuwait	Philippines	Trinidad and Tobago
Bahrain	Finland	Lebanon	Poland	Tunisia
Barbados	France	Lesotho	Portugal	Turkey
Belgium	Germany	Lithuania	Puerto Rico	Turks and Caicos Islands
Bermuda	Greece	Luxembourg	Romania	U.S. Virgin Islands
Bolivia	Guadeloupe	Macau	Russia	Uganda
Botswana	Guam	Malawi	St. Lucia	Ukraine
Brazil	Guatemala	Malaysia	Saipan	United Arab
British Virgin Islands	Haiti	Malta	Saudi Arabia	Emirates
Canada	Honduras	Mexico	Singapore	United Kingdom
Cayman Islands	Hong Kong	Namibia	Slovak Republic	United States of
Channel Islands	Hungary	Netherlands	Solomon Islands	America
Chile	India	Netherlands	South Africa	Vanuatu
China	Indonesia	Antilles	South Korea	Venezuela
Colombia	Ireland	New Zealand	Spain	Vietnam
Cyprus	Isle of Man	Nigeria	Swaziland	Zambia
Czech Republic	Italy	Norway	Sweden	Zimbabwe

Aon offers clients creative insurance brokerage and consulting solutions through local representation supported by an extensive network of offices.

CUTTING-EDGE TECHNOLOGY

 on's investments in the latest technology in new software and communications have benefited clients and employees alike by providing instant access to vital information.

AonLine, Aon's network of electronic services, integrates a client's complete risk management needs. Aon's Internet-based catastrophe modeling network delivers detailed forecasting of major catastrophes around the world directly to the client's desktop.

Aon's Risk Management Information Systems are tailored to a client's specific needs.

Aon was also a founder of and investor in the Worldwide Insurance Network, helping to revolutionize the insurance industry as it moves to full electronic commerce.

AON'S GREATEST ASSET

 he creative, diligent employees of Aon have made it one of the most successful companies in the insurance services industry. Their hard work, knowledge, and dedication to providing the very best products and services are key to that success.

Aon attracts and retains the best professional talent in the industry—people who are empowered with responsibility, authority, and accountability in a challenging, entrepreneurial, and interdependent environment. Aon encourages employees to develop groundbreaking solutions on behalf of clients, and rewards them for their efforts.

Aon employees own more than 30 percent of the company's common stock. That clearly indicates the confidence they have in Aon and increases their motivation to do their best at all times. They share the same financial objectives as other Aon investors.

AON OUTLOOK

 or 46 consecutive years, Aon has provided stockholders with annual increases in the common dividend. Aon Corporation (symbol: AOC) is listed on the New York, Chicago, and London stock exchanges. The company is proud of its dividend record, matched by only a select few public companies. Aon also continues to emphasize its strong balance sheet, significant cash flow, high equity, and balanced earnings from a diverse business mix.

Aon Corporation looks to the future with confidence that it will continue to excel for its clients, employees, and stockholders.

UCKED BETWEEN THE CHICAGO BOARD OF TRADE AND THE CHICAGO MERCANTILE EXCHANGE IS NATIONAL FUTURES ASSOCIATION (NFA), THE INDUSTRYWIDE SELF-REGULATORY ORGANIZATION FOR THE NATION'S COMMODITY FUTURES MARKETS. CHARGED IN 1982 WITH RESPONSIBILITY FOR

protecting the interests of participants in the marketplace, NFA has proved that with vision, strong leadership, and appropriate financial support, an industry can successfully regulate itself.

The commodity futures industry, which traces its Chicago roots back to the mid-1800s, was originally established by agricultural producers as a vehicle for managing risk. However, in the early 1970s, a number of new and innovative futures contracts were introduced that brought a whole new set of participants to the marketplace. As a result, in 1974, the U.S. Congress enacted legislation to create the Commodity Futures Trading Commission (CFTC), an independent federal regulatory agency with direct and exclusive jurisdiction over the futures industry. That legislation, the Commodity Exchange Act, also authorized the creation of registered futures associations, which gave the futures industry an opportunity to develop an industrywide self-regulatory organization that would standardize business practices and work in conjunction with the CFTC.

In 1976, seven founding fathers, representing diverse segments of the industry, formed an organizing committee and began NFA's development process. But it wasn't until 1978, when Congress amended the act, that one of the factors critical to the organization's success was finally addressed. "The original act didn't actually require membership," explains Laura Oatney, director of public affairs and education for NFA. "There was no assurance that everyone who needed to belong would belong. The 1978 amendment made membership mandatory for firms and individuals who sell futures to the public."

By 1981, the committee had finalized its operating plan and incorporated National Futures Association. In 1982, NFA began

Chairman Hal T. Hansen (left) and President Robert K. Wilmouth help NFA achieve its mission to provide innovative regulatory programs and services that ensure futures industry integrity, protect market participants, and help members meet their regulatory responsibilities.

operation in Chicago. It is still headquartered in the Windy City, where the bulk of futures trading takes place, but maintains a branch office in New York City.

Today, anyone who conducts futures business with the public must belong to NFA, which is primarily funded by assessment fees paid by market users. NFA is a not-for-profit, membership organization, staffed by 275 employees and governed by a diverse group of industry representatives who are committed to the success of the self-regulatory process.

NFA's mission is to provide innovative regulatory programs and services that ensure futures industry integrity, protect market participants, and help members meet their regulatory responsibilities.

PROBLEM SOLVING

hile NFA's original objectives were to eliminate regulatory duplication and enable the indus-

try to more effectively police itself, the need for investor protection in the industry really drove the early development of our programming," says Oatney. "How we screen and license prospective member firms and individuals, scrutinize their business activities, administer our dispute resolution forum, and develop our educational materials all reflect our commitment to investor protection."

NFA took on some big challenges in its early years. Beginning with an entire group of market participants who had never been subject to direct oversight, NFA brought all of the diverse industry components into the self-regulatory fold.

The organization also has had to cope with the fallout from a number of commodity-related investment fraud schemes. And while most were perpetrated by non-NFA member firms, they clearly had a negative impact on the industry. "This is not to say that there have never been problem firms among NFA's membership," says Oatney. "But this industry wants no part of unacceptable business practices, and has worked very hard to eradicate bad players."

PLAYING BY THE RULES

FA members must comply with a variety of rules that govern all aspects of futures business practices, such as advertising, telemarketing solicitations, record keeping, supervision, and disclosure documents. The organization has some 125 compliance auditors who monitor the activities of a membership that totals about 4,000 member firms and 45,000 associate members.

NFA has the power to enforce its rules and take appropriate disciplinary actions against its members when warranted. Depending upon the nature of the violations, sanctions can range from fines to expulsion from the industry.

INFORMATION ACCESS

FA operates a toll-free information center with a hot line, known officially as the Disciplinary Information Access Line or DIAL. By calling DIAL, investors can gather background information on a

company or individual involved in the futures industry. NFA members frequently use DIAL to check on other members they are considering doing business with, or people they are thinking of hiring.

"Prior to DIAL's introduction in 1991, the industry had no central resource for such inquiries," Oatney says. "To get the full picture, you had to call us, the CFTC, and each of the exchanges. We consolidated all of the information. It has been a tremendously useful service."

SUCCESS AND THE FUTURE

he continued strength and vitality of the futures industry depends on the confidence of the investing public in the integrity of the marketplace. The contributions NFA's self-regulatory efforts

have made to customer confidence in the industry are most clearly demonstrated by a 60 percent drop in customer complaints received during the 1986-1996 decade. During this same time period, the volume of futures contracts traded doubled.

The need for market integrity is not unique to the United States. Because of NFA's accomplishments and effectiveness, financial leaders from around the world turn to NFA for regulatory guidance and insight, making it an international model for self-regulation.

As the futures industry continues to evolve, so must the self-regulatory process. NFA remains committed to providing innovative programs and services that both meet its organizational goals and contribute to the success of the futures industry.

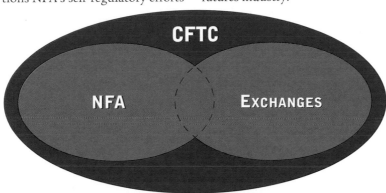

Clockwise from top left:
Although the various regulatory organizations in the futures industry have their own specific areas of authority, together they form a regulatory partnership that oversees all industry participants. The Commodity Futures Trading Commission provides government oversight for the entire industry. Each U.S. futures exchange operates as a self-regulatory organization, governing its floor brokers, traders, and member firms. And NFA regulates every firm or individual who conducts futures trading business with public customers.

NFA's Web site (www.nfa.futures.org) serves as an information resource for members and the investing public.

Conducting periodic audits of member firms is just one of the ways NFA maintains the integrity of the futures markets.

I N A DECADE AND A HALF, U.S. CAN COMPANY HAS EVOLVED FROM A FLEDGLING DOMESTIC CAN MAKER INTO A WORLD-CLASS MEMBER OF THE PACKAGING COMMUNITY. ROOTED IN THE SOLID TRADITIONS OF AMERICAN MANUFACTURING, THE OAK BROOK, ILLINOIS-BASED COMPANY HAS BUILT ON ITS INHERITED STRENGTHS AND AT THE SAME

time moved ahead in new directions.

U.S. Can was established in 1983 when veteran packaging executive William J. Smith, drawing on his 32 years of experience with American Can Company, led an investment group that purchased the three can plants of the Sherwin-Williams Corporation—one in the northwest suburb of Elgin, the home of the current flagship plant, and one each in California and Ohio. It was a classic leveraged buyout that formed a modest platform for the can industry's newest entry. Sales volume was $100 million.

With a commitment to grow by acquisition, but only in areas related to its core businesses, the new company moved quickly to acquire Southern Can Company. It then acquired Continental Can's general packaging business, and later, American National Can's aerosol and general line assets. In the process, U.S. Can became the nation's leading supplier of metal containers for personal care, household, automotive, paint, and industrial products. More recently, the company has moved aggressively into the specialty container field,

and has entered the European aerosol market in a significant way.

All told, U.S. Can has made 22 acquisitions, including eight in 1995 and 1996. Today, the company serves more than 3,000 manufacturers/marketers of consumer and industrial products, and holds either the number one or number two market position in each of its product lines, as annual revenues move into the $700 million to $800 million range.

U.S. Can's move into Europe came in 1996 when the company bought five strategically placed

can manufacturing locations from Crown Cork & Seal in the United Kingdom, France, Germany, Spain, and Italy—strong growth markets for aerosols.

The purchase of Crown Cork & Seal's facilities paralleled the completion of a new, fully integrated U.S. Can manufacturing plant in Merthyr Tydfil, South Wales. These moves gave U.S. Can the number two position in the European aerosol market.

AEROSOLS A MAINSTAY

W ith aerosol containers as the company's bread-and-butter business, it seems natural that Chicagoland should be home to U.S. Can's headquarters. Illinois has more aerosol-related jobs than any other state, and the Chicago area is considered the aerosol capital of the nation.

The domestic aerosol market is big, in Chicago and nationwide, with 3 billion cans a year made and sold in the United States, more than half of them produced by U.S. Can. Americans use more than 1,500 different kinds of aero-

Fully formed aerosol containers march toward the shipping department at U.S. Can's Elgin plant. The company supplies better than one of every two aerosol cans produced in North America.

Suburban Oak Brook is headquarters for U.S. Can, which has 35 manufacturing plants in the United States and Europe.

At U.S. Can's Elgin plant, some 500 employees produce more than 1.5 million cans every working day.

sol products, from shaving cream and hair spray to oven cleaner and insect repellent.

Major U.S. Can customers include Gillette, Procter & Gamble, Sherwin-Williams, Dow Brands, Reckitt & Colman, and Chesebrough-Pond's.

In Europe, the market for aerosols shows greater potential for growth than in the States. Already larger than the U.S. total—hovering at the 4 billion-unit level—aerosol can production there is at an all-time high. More than half of the European volume is in personal care products, with shaving cream, hair spray, and deodorant alone accounting for more than 2 billion cans annually.

PAINT AND GENERAL LINE CANS

ound paint cans, familiar to generations of amateur and professional painters, are a mainstay of U.S. Can's "general line" business, a term originally applied by the industry to any metal can not used for food or beverage products.

Supplementing the traditional round can, which is made in sizes ranging from a half pint to one gallon, is U.S. Can's line of resealable, injection-molded plastic pails, used increasingly by house painters. The company also makes an oblong metal can, long associated with such products as charcoal starter, paint thinner, and varnish.

SPECIALTY PRODUCTS

easuring its customers in the thousands and with an almost endless variety of metal products, the Custom and Specialty Group is unique among U.S. Can's businesses. With five plants from coast to coast, it is the leader in its field and has significant potential for growth. The Custom and Specialty Group was essentially put together at U.S. Can in 1994. Since then, heavy investment in equipment, tooling, and infrastructure has enabled the group to produce superior results.

Throughout its network of plants and support facilities, U.S. Can operates with five important concepts in place: quality, service, safety, housekeeping, and inventory management. These concepts are in keeping with the midwestern work ethic of this solid, no-frills company that has stayed close to its roots.

In spite of its remarkable story of growth, U.S. Can's objective never was to be the biggest, just the best. Building on its strengths, and with its traditional focus on quality and service, the company looks forward to the demanding days ahead.

These lithographed sheets of tinplate will be trimmed to size and formed into cans. The company processes more than 400,000 tons of steel annually.

ALL ROADS LEAD TO CHICAGO. IN FACT, THE COMMUNITY HAS ENJOYED CENTURIES OF ECONOMIC PROSPERITY THANKS TO TRANSPORTATION NETWORKS INTEGRATING WATER, RAIL, ROADWAY, AND AIR ROUTES. IN THE 19TH CENTURY, FOR EXAMPLE, THE CITY WAS THE CENTRAL

point on the nation's network of rail lines. Chicago could not have become "hog butcher for the world" without the railroads that provided the essential link between farmers and the marketplace.

Today, Chicago relies on other networks that play just as fundamental a role in ensuring its economic vitality. The trader buying and selling futures contracts, the manufacturer creating consumer products for foreign markets, and the researcher in the city's world-class universities all depend on an advanced communications network built, managed, and enhanced by Ameritech, one of the world's 10 largest communications companies.

NETWORKING CHICAGO

 meritech has invested billions of dollars building networks for the Chicago metropolitan area. The company continues to make

significant investments to ensure that it meets the growing needs of the community. In 1996, for example, Ameritech invested $300 million in the local telephone network alone.

Massive, comprehensive, and complex, these webs of fiber-optic, coaxial, and copper cables and advanced digital switches integrate homes, businesses, and institutions

throughout the Midwest with the global marketplace. Transmitting voice, video, and data signals, these networks serve as the platforms for an arsenal of new and exotic communications services.

Ameritech uses its networks to deliver distance learning that brings the world into the classroom, telemedicine that helps doctors diagnose patients in faraway communities, and videoconferencing that enables managers of global corporations to hold meetings with their far-flung operations— even though no one has traveled farther than the coffee machine. Whether they are used to jump on the Internet or to make a phone call to Australia, Ameritech's networks are the gateway to the world.

This communications infrastructure is one of Chicago's most valuable assets. Advanced communications capabilities are essential to retaining and attracting healthy businesses—in fact, it is one of the first things companies examine when they make location decisions. The most competitive companies today are those that have the fastest and most efficient access to the right information. And Ameritech works diligently to provide Chicago—its headquarters city—with state-of-the-art communications.

A GLOBAL REACH

Just as Chicago is the center of vast communications networks, it also is the center of Ameritech. From its base in the city, this global information company conducts business in all 50 states and more than 40 countries from New Zealand to Norway. It provides local telephone service to more than 23 million customers worldwide and prints 40 million directories every year. Ameritech serves 3 million cellular customers and 1.4 million paging customers.

More than 3,700 libraries use products from Ameritech, the world

This "city of big shoulders" and its spectacular buildings require robust cellular services. Introduced first in Chicago, Ameritech ClearPath℠ delivers improved voice clarity and advanced features such as Caller ID (top).

A world capital, Chicago is headquarters city for one of the globe's 10 largest communications companies, Ameritech, which conducts business in all 50 states and more than 40 countries. Ameritech's joint venture with Deutsche Telekom holds a two-thirds stake in MATAV, which provides local, long-distance, and cellular services in Hungary (bottom).

leader in automated library systems. The company's SecurityLink℠ delivers security monitoring services to more than one million customers throughout North America. In fact, Ameritech is the second-largest security monitoring company in North America.

In addition, Ameritech is swiftly taking a leadership position in the cable television and Internet industries. The company has reached dozens of cable TV franchise agreements with cities and towns in Ohio, Illinois, and Michigan. Ameritech, along with other communications companies, is in a joint venture with the Walt Disney Company to create innovative and imaginative video programming and interactive services, and to deliver superior choices to customers.

Ameritech is swiftly becoming a force on the Internet, thanks to an access service known for ease of use, reliable network connections, and round-the-clock customer service. Ameritech.net℠ features 24-hour-a-day, 7-day-a-week assistance with experienced customer service and technical support professionals.

INNOVATIVE COMMUNICATIONS

Demonstrating a consistent willingness to lead the communications industry during this period of revolutionary change, Ameritech is a company of firsts. It was the first in the industry to call for full competition and an end to market barriers. Committed to providing customers with a complete range of services, Ameritech was the first of the former Bell companies to enter the security monitoring business. It was also the first to successfully compete on a broad scale with existing cable companies by building its own networks in their service areas.

According to a J.D. Power survey, Ameritech is ranked number one in customer satisfaction among U.S. cellular companies. That seems particularly appropriate since Ameritech was the first in the nation to introduce commercial cellular service in the early 1980s.

All of these firsts are based on a single fact: Ameritech's insistence on making customers paramount. In 1993, the company initiated a rigorous process of transformation in support of its commitment to putting the customer at the center of its operations.

Ameritech took aggressive action to stake its claim on the future and to embrace a vision that drives fundamental change on three levels. First, the company rebuilt itself from the ground up to develop a flexible structure and ensure that all decisions are based on customer needs. Second, the company began to pursue an assertive external agenda to foster regulatory reform to create an environment flexible enough to accommodate changing customer demands. Third, and most important, the company initiated an ongoing effort to radically change its corporate culture to focus its efforts more rigorously on the customer.

These strong actions have paid ample benefits to share owners, as well as customers. The company with the industry's best financial results, Ameritech is number one in total return to investors and is the only U.S. communications company with a positive total return for 1994, 1995, and 1996. It also is the most productive local communications company, and, in 1996, reported the strongest-ever revenue growth and posted the largest dividend increase among the former Bell companies since 1992.

Financially strong, technologically nimble, and customer focused, Ameritech makes the city of big shoulders a communications powerhouse.

Ameritech provides a broad range of services for home offices, including its new Internet access service, Ameritech.net℠ (top).

Families in dozens of Illinois, Michigan, and Ohio communities enjoy leading-edge cable TV services from Ameritech. One popular feature is Red Jr., a kid-friendly remote that helps children get to their favorite channels easily and enables parents to maintain positive control over their children's channel selections (bottom).

A S COMPUTER USERS INCREASINGLY BECOME MORE PROFICIENT WITH PC TECHNOLOGY, THEY ARE TURNING TO DIRECT MARKETERS TO PURCHASE THEIR PRODUCTS. FEW OF THESE MARKETERS ARE AS OVERWHELMINGLY SUCCESSFUL AS VERNON HILLS-BASED CDW COMPUTER CENTERS.

Founded in 1984 by Michael Krasny, the company today employs more than 1,000 people and logs more than $1 billion in annual sales.

What began in the 1980s as a computer configuration and repair business has become one of the most successful computer direct marketers in the industry. Today, the company enjoys explosive growth and a sterling reputation. In 1993, CDW made an initial public offering, and its shares are now traded on the Nasdaq under the ticker symbol CDWC.

THE RIGHT PRICE, THE RIGHT ADVICE

C DW sells only name-brand computers, such as IBM, Compaq, Toshiba, and Hewlett-Packard. It also sells name-brand accessories, peripherals, and software, and offers up-to-the-minute competitive pricing on all products. Notebook and desktop computers remain the company's largest product category, representing more than 38 percent of net sales.

CDW reaches its customers through telemarketing and direct-mail catalogs. The company distributes more than 80 million catalogs annually. Since 1996, business from the company's Web site (www.cdw.com) has grown to more than 5 percent of the overall sales volume, and the company expects Internet sales to increase proportionally. The CDW site was developed in close conjunction with Microsoft as part of the Microsoft Trophy Site program, and incorporates advanced technologies and features.

When CDW's corporate customers call for the first time, they

CDW Computer Centers President Greg Zeman (left) and Chairman and CEO Michael Krasny

Founded in 1984 by Michael Krasny, CDW Computer Centers today employs more than 1,000 people and logs more than $1 billion in annual sales.

are assigned an account manager, who becomes their liaison every time they do business with the company. Recognizing that building rapport and good customer relationships is required in order to maintain repeat business, CDW requires its sales staff to undergo up to four months of training in product knowledge and selling techniques at CDW University. All CDW department heads are required to produce a daily one-page report on their key activities, so that other managers can review these reports and spot new and emerging trends.

As a result, CDW has a reputation for its highly qualified account managers, and its emphasis on training makes the company unique in the industry. This customer-oriented service helps CDW fulfill its motto: The right price. The right advice.

REMARKABLE GROWTH

One measure of the company's remarkable growth is its sales volume, which has increased at a compound annual growth rate of 50 percent from 1992 through 1996.

Growth has been so great, in fact, that CDW is considered an operations role model in the industry for sales and profit growth.

With this financial success has come a rapid need for more space. To accommodate this need, CDW has moved twice in the past four years. In 1994, the company moved from its offices in Northbrook to double the space in Buffalo Grove. By 1997, facilities were splitting at the seams, and CDW had to move again, purchasing 28 acres in Vernon Hills that offered room for future expansion.

The new, 218,000-square-foot facility, which became operational in July 1997, features a state-of-the-art phone system and an automated warehouse distribution center for receiving and shipping goods. The new location also includes a product showroom similar to one located in downtown Chicago. The new facility provides the capacity necessary for CDW to execute its cost-efficient operating model while continuing the company's growth.

Despite the company's busy year in 1997, CDW still had time and energy left for charitable con-

cerns. CDW is a supporter of numerous children's charities and is well known for its annual challenge gift of $25,000 to Children's Memorial Hospital's annual telethon. CDW employees have also given generously, donating some $23,000 of their own money in 1996.

CDW also donates to the Center for Enriched Living, an organization that provides essential life skills development for the mentally disabled. And for the past two years, the company has participated in a new function, the Charita-Ball, which harnesses the fund-raising strengths of three area computer-related businesses that donate the proceeds to three different charities.

"We've always taken an aggressive posture toward helping charities, especially those for children who cannot help themselves," Krasny explains. "We try hard to be the best company in the computer sales business, and I believe it is important to put that same amount of effort into helping the community. We are in a position to help move mountains, and it is not only our duty, but our pleasure to do that."

HICAGO EARNED ITS REPUTATION AS THE CITY OF BIG SHOULDERS AND MAINTAINS IT BY BEING THE LARGEST INDUSTRIAL PROPERTY MARKET IN NORTH AMERICA, WITH 1.2 BILLION SQUARE FEET, STRETCHING FROM WISCONSIN THROUGH NORTHWEST INDIANA. ■ IN KEEPING WITH THIS TRADITION,

CenterPoint Properties' mission is starting to be realized by becoming the landlord of choice for industrial property users within a 150-mile radius of Greater Chicago. The city's diverse industrial tapestry of warehouses, manufacturing facilities, airports, and railroads represents a perfect market for the acquisition, new construction, and rehabilitation of industrial space.

With its 25 million-square-foot industrial property portfolio, CenterPoint is Chicago's largest industrial property owner and manager, serving local and national tenants alike. In Greater Chicago, CenterPoint buildings are "Where Industry Works."™

SERVING CLIENT NEEDS

he typical CenterPoint building is a $3 million to $5 million industrial facility with a flexible floor plan, highway and rail access, and ample loading docks. The firm's goal is to provide the right space at the right time in the right place, serving any of the wide and varied occupancy needs of its broadly diverse tenant base.

One of CenterPoint's strategies is the purchase of industrial sites with the intention of leasing part or all of the space back to the seller, a practice called sale/lease-back transactions. Not only does this allow the selling company to free up needed capital and seamlessly maintain operations in whatever space is necessary, but it frequently allows CenterPoint to redevelop buildings into multi-tenant facilities, serving yet additional tenant needs. In keeping with this strategy, CenterPoint purchased the 60-acre campus of Honeywell in suburban Arlington Heights, and then leased the office space back to the company on a long-term basis, while converting and releasing the balance of the 360,000-square-foot warehouse space to multiple tenants.

Attention to detail and client satisfaction in another recent transaction led to a deft reshuffling of six different tenants within 60 days. CenterPoint upgraded five buildings, acquired a sixth, and initiated two more as build-to-suit developments. As evidence of tenant satisfaction, CenterPoint retained 96 percent of its tenants in 1997 and 94 percent over the four-year period between 1993 and 1997.

The firm has also found a niche in meeting the needs of air cargo shippers in and around O'Hare International Airport. CenterPoint is the developer of O'Hare Express Center, a 1 million-square-foot airfreight development with direct ramp access to O'Hare's South Cargo area, and the only such private development on airport property. Tenants include airfreight carriers Burlington, DHL, Air Canada, and Alliance Airlines, all of which have quick access to planes.

Continuing to work with air cargo shippers, CenterPoint is

Alliance Airlines is just one of the many tenants in CenterPoint's O'Hare Express Center development.

currently redeveloping space located across from O'Hare, which the company purchased from Montgomery Ward in 1995. The 677,000-square-foot facility is being prepared for other cargo and distribution tenants.

SEEING POTENTIAL

edevelopment projects are an area in which CenterPoint prides itself. Seeing possibilities, which others have often overlooked, in fitting industrial space to meet clients' needs is a keystone of CenterPoint's success. A top-to-bottom rehabilitation of a former defense plant was accomplished in just 87 days—quick enough to meet the tight scheduling demands of Fortune 500 steelmaker Wheeling Pittsburgh. The refurbished, 65,300-square-foot facility is now the home of Wheeling Corrugated. Wheeling recently initiated a third project with CenterPoint.

Custom construction of a client's future home requires having an understanding of the client's needs and designing a project that still is flexible enough for future tenants. Most of CenterPoint's new construction projects are 100 percent preleased before construction is completed. Long-term client relationships are sustained by designing and building cost effectively, on time, and in the right location. In 1997, CenterPoint added approximately 9 million square feet to its industrial property portfolio, including projects for such clients as General Tire, Playboy Enterprises, and Ameritech.

"CenterPoint made an initial public offering in December 1993 and was first traded on the New York Stock Exchange in June 1996. The company's impressive 1997 results were driven by the huge size and diversity of the Greater Chicago market," says John S. Gates Jr., president and CEO of CenterPoint.

"Our approximately 1.5 percent market share leaves us enormous opportunities for additional growth, and our strengths—deep market penetration, creative solutions, and the ability to respond quickly—position us to succeed this year and beyond."

The Ameritech building in Elgin, Illinois, is yet another CenterPoint redevelopment (top).

CenterPoint is the developer of O'Hare Express Center, a 1 million-square-foot airfreight development with direct ramp access to O'Hare's South Cargo area (bottom).

USINESS IS BOOMING FOR THE SHORT-TERM HOUSING INDUSTRY AND FOR HABITAT CORPORATE SUITES NETWORK, LLC, AS WELL. HABITAT CORPORATE SUITES WAS CONCEIVED IN 1985 BY THE HABITAT COMPANY, A 25-YEAR LEADER IN CHICAGO REAL ESTATE, AND WHILE THE CORPORATE SUITES

division is now a solely operated enterprise, the relationship with the Habitat Company has provided the Corporate Suites division with a framework that keeps it thriving amid fierce competition. Occupancy remains high in the 500 fully furnished apartments that Habitat Corporate Suites rents on a temporary basis, a fact that doesn't surprise David Flando, chief operating officer of the company, which has its headquarters in Presidential Towers, one of its six Chicago sites.

"We know Chicago and property management well," Flando says. "Most of our employees come from the hospitality industry and are steeped in the tradition of service, service, service. We're big enough to accommodate corporate requirements of housing several employees at one time, yet small enough to extend one-on-one service to all of our guests."

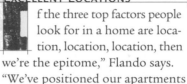

Excellent Locations

f the three top factors people look for in a home are location, location, location, then we're the epitome," Flando says. "We've positioned our apartments in areas that are close enough for residents to walk to the Loop in one direction, and in any other direction to restaurants, shopping, entertainment, and nightlife."

Habitat Corporate Suites are located in strategically positioned sites, offering studio and one- or two-bedroom units. (Three bedroom units are available upon request.) Columbus Plaza, just off Michigan Avenue, offers views of Lake Michigan and the Chicago River. Cityfront Place is located on the river, a stone's throw from Navy Pier. Huron Plaza, situated

Clockwise from top left:
Habitat Corporate Suites employees are selected for their attitude and experience. They understand the nuances of managing a corporate suites facility and know instinctively how to help people.

The New York, a Habitat Corporate Suites property located on Lake Shore Drive, offers residents a stunning view of Lake Michigan.

Habitat Corporate Suites' spacious, fully furnished apartments range in size from 600 to 1,300 square feet, with weekly maid service, color TV with cable, fully equipped kitchens, direct-dial phones with voice messaging, 24-hour guest service desk, parking, fitness center, swimming pool, grocery store, dry cleaners, and much more.

The Presidential Towers is also Chicago headquarters for Habitat Corporate Suites Network.

on the Gold Coast, is close to Rush Street, Michigan Avenue, Water Tower Place, and Oak Street Beach. The New York, near Lincoln Park, offers tenants a view of Lake Michigan from their balconies. Presidential Towers is located near the heart of the financial district in the west Loop area.

Wheaton Center apartments are located in a tranquil suburban community, due west of downtown Chicago, with easy access to the METRA train station directly across the street from the apartment complex. Habitat Corporate Suites also offers convertible, one, and two bedroom apartments in the Iroquois Club of Naperville. Naperville, a western suburb located in a high-tech corridor, is rated as one of the finest suburban communities in the country.

PERSONALIZED SERVICES

In addition to great locations, Habitat prides itself in offering the finest accommodations and personalized services to best satisfy the needs of those requiring extended stays of 30 days or more. For half the price of a hotel room, clients receive a spacious, fully furnished apartment, ranging in size from 600 to 1,300 square feet, with weekly maid service, color TV with cable, fully equipped kitchens, direct-dial phones with voice messaging, 24-hour guest service desk, parking, fitness center, swimming pool, grocery store, dry cleaners, and much more. The suites are expertly maintained for quality and comfort, including systematic replacement of apartment furnishings, redecorating as needed, and replacement of carpeting. The staff, which caters to many Fortune 500 companies, their employees, and employees' families, can easily make arrangements for providing such items as cribs and extra beds, as well as other amenities to add to the guests' satisfaction.

Habitat Corporate Suites employees are selected for their attitude and experience. They must understand the nuances of managing a corporate suites facility and know instinctively how to help people. "You cannot teach someone to be customer service oriented," Flando says. "You either want to

Clockwise from top left: Habitat Corporate Suites are located in strategically positioned sites across the Chicago area.

Second City is one of Chicago's nightspots close by Habitat Corporate Suites locations.

All Habitat Corporate Suites locations offer the same amenities available in an upscale hotel, with the comforts and security of a homelike setting.

help people or you don't. All our employees do. If you have the right personality, you can learn the mechanics. We hire nice people—people who care."

The Chicagoland Apartment Association apparently agrees. It gave Habitat Corporate Suites awards for excellence in 1993, 1995, and 1996. Sports stars, celebrities, dignitaries, and CEOs regularly make a Habitat Corporate Suite their home away from home.

The demand for corporate suite accommodations by extended stay travelers is still growing, and Habitat Corporate Suites Network is growing right along with it. The company has set its sights on further expanding its services in the Chicago area. Eventually, the company hopes to go national. "But we want to make sure we're prepared to provide service at the level that is expected from Habitat Corporate Suites," Flando says.

Habitat Corporate Suites is well aware that with all the choices

available to Chicago-based clients, providing service and flexibility is what is most needed to maintain a successful corporate suites program. In that venue, Habitat Corporate Suites is right at home—and so are its guests.

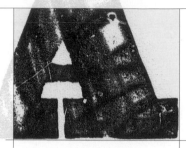

ALLSCRIPTS WAS FOUNDED IN 1986 BASED ON A SIMPLE IDEA: ALLOWING PHYSICIANS TO DISPENSE COMMONLY PRESCRIBED MEDICATIONS DIRECTLY TO PATIENTS. WHAT FOLLOWED WAS THE COMPREHENSIVE MEDICATION MANAGEMENT SOLUTION THAT ALLOWS PHYSICIANS TO address the increasingly complex world of managed care.

With the goal of simplifying access to medications, Allscripts developed a manual dispensing system designed to work in the physician's office. The ability to deliver chronic medications by mail and through a retail pharmacy network followed soon thereafter. The Allscripts solution offered patients convenience, confidentiality, an opportunity to begin treatment immediately, and a more cost-effective process. Based on this comprehensive offering, Allscripts has experienced solid growth, with 1996 revenues exceeding $75 million. With more than 15,000 physicians dispensing medications at the point of care, representing more than 3,600 practices, Allscripts has become the industry leader in point-of-care dispensing and distribution.

However, virtually every aspect of health care is undergoing dramatic change and the pharmacy component is no exception. Allscripts has been quick to respond to the changing needs of its clients and the marketplace. The growth of managed care has forced health care organizations to reexamine their costs. While this focus first centered on hospitals and physicians, it quickly progressed to other areas, including pharmacy costs, which were out of control in many areas and in need of improvement. In this new world of managed care, the physician's need for more information and support to effectively manage his or her practice has expanded dramatically. As the physician's practice moved from a cash reimbursement model to one increasingly influenced by managed care, reimbursements, co-payments, and formulary com-

pliance became key parts of the physician's responsibility. In many cases, physician compensation incentives are tied to performance and in every case pharmaceutical management has become a time-consuming part of the physician's day. Allscripts needed to provide software to simplify prescribing and dispensing in this complicated environment—sophisticated software to handle all the new demands of managed care, including prescribing the most cost-effective medications, submitting prescription claims electronically, and checking for potential adverse drug reactions. The physician also was developing a new requirement for more and better objective information on newly released and ever changing pharmaceuticals.

Based on these changes in the environment, Allscripts redefined its mission to provide innovative, point-of-care medication management and distribution to its clients, who are primarily physicians working directly with patients. The focus was on developing state-of-the-art software that would simplify a complicated part of a physician's life, while at the same time provide benefits to patients, physicians, and health care insurers.

"Our goal is to be a trusted, objective adviser to physicians, providing information at the point of care, which helps them make more informed and cost-effective decisions, which lead to better outcomes for the patient," said Glen Tullman, Allscripts' chief executive officer. "Everyone wins. In addition, our team of pharmacists spends hours consulting with physicians to keep them up to date on the latest drug data in the fast changing pharmaceutical world."

Given that many physicians had not previously dispensed medications on-site, Allscripts had a

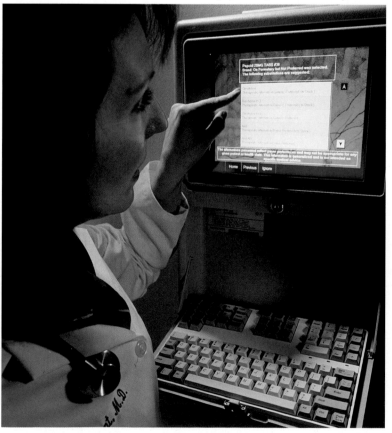

Allscripts' innovative touch screen technology puts the power of informed prescribing at the doctor's fingertips.

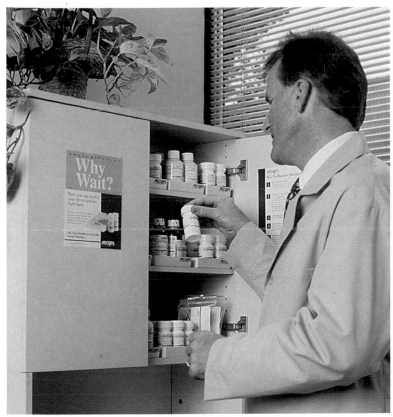

recently, we have created compelling reasons why a physician would want to use the Touch*Script* system," comments Michael Cahr, chairman of Allscripts. "Touch*Script* saves physicians substantial time and provides valuable information when they most need it."

While strategy and vision are an important part of the business, the task of making it happen every day is the responsibility of Dave Mullen, Allscripts' president and chief financial officer. Coordinating logistics to deliver millions of prepackaged pharmaceuticals to thousands of offices on a just-in-time basis is no easy task. "We're fortunate to have a brand new facility that we designed along with great people who make it happen every day. While software is important to our business, we really consider ourselves to be in the service business," comments Mullen.

This concentrated focus on people and service, paired with a new and innovative approach to a process that has been around for years, positions Allscripts to continue its growth and to play an important role in changing the way America receives its medications.

four-part task: to change a process with which physicians were comfortable; to make the new process easy for the physician; to provide new and added value for the physician as a reason to change; and to build in safety features and protections that make both the physician and the patient comfortable with the process.

In 1996, Allscripts released version 1.0 of Touch*Script*™, its touch screen prescribing and dispensing medication management software. By incorporating unique touch screen technology, Touch*Script* enables a physician to both prescribe and dispense pharmaceuticals with only seven touches of the screen, making this process no more difficult or time consuming than writing a prescription on a pad. The system also saves time and aggravation for physicians by eliminating callbacks from pharmacies with suggested changes or questions on prescriptions. Touch*Script* enables a physician to electronically transmit a "script" to a local pharmacy of the patient's choice, or to directly enroll a patient in a mail-order program offered by Allscripts or by another provider.

Allscripts has also engineered a unique dispensing process with prepackaged pharmaceuticals that includes a bar code and two-step safety procedure that results in fewer errors than a typical pharmacy would experience and useful printed patient information.

"Since we started dispensing on-site, we've always understood the benefits to the patient, but

Dispensing is the key to improving the process for patients and for the physicians (top).

TouchScript reinforces strong doctor/ patient relationships and the confidentiality so important to patients today (bottom).

HE OPEN ROAD LOOKS A LOT BETTER THAN IT SOUNDS, BUT MOST OF THE HONKING AND REVVING ON THE AVERAGE HIGHWAY CAN BE SHUT OUT BY CLOSING A WINDOW. THIS LITTLE MIRACLE OF QUIET IS DUE TO THE EFFORTS OF UGN INCORPORATED. FOUNDED IN 1986 TO SUPPLY THE

transplant auto industry, UGN today designs and manufactures sound-deadening materials for the largest Japanese automakers, including Toyota, Honda, and Mitsubishi.

"The business of silencing the sound of speed is little more than 30 years old," says company CEO Gary Jamison, who recalls first seeing the advantages of a quiet ride on television in 1965. "A commercial for the 1965 Ford LTD showed a guy rolling up the window of the car; there's a guy mowing the lawn, and as the window goes up it gets very quiet."

Though the LTD's sound barriers were invisible, the materials insulating it from the noisy lawn mower could be seen on the top of any house. Jamison explains, "The first sound-deadening materials were asphaltic sheet products that were similar, if not identical, to roofing products." Seizing upon

this innovation, Globe Industries, a Chicago-based roofing company, shifted easily from roofs to cars until the early 1970s, when the sound-deadening industry faced new challenges driven by the energy crisis.

Although the asphaltic products produced quiet cars, these sound-deadened cars weighed hundreds of pounds more than other cars. The solution lay in lighter-weight asphaltic materials and new types of insulators made from poly-urethane foam and cotton fibers.

"Over the years, we were able to improve acoustics by reducing the relative weight contribution of the sound-deadening material," Jamison says. "The vehicles that we designed in conjunction with Japanese manufacturers have excellent acoustic performance, but they are not penalized by excess weight. We've discovered the best of both worlds."

THE FOUNDING OF A POWERHOUSE

In 1986, the owners of Globe Industries were approached by emissaries from Nihon Tokushu Toryo Co. Ltd., a Japanese corporation involved in the acoustic auto parts industry in Japan. A joint venture was formed between the Americans and the Japanese; Globe would continue to serve the domestic carmakers in North America, and UGN would supply the Japanese transplants.

One of the first actions of the new company was to open its first plant in Chicago Heights. In 1989, Globe decided to divest itself of its roofing businesses. By focusing on the design and manufacture of sound-deadening materials, Globe and UGN established a notable presence in the industry, each serving its respective clients. UGN is now headquartered in Chicago, with additional manu-

UGN Incorporated, a world leader in automotive acoustics, has its corporate offices in Chicago.

UGN, Inc. operates manufacturing facilities in Chicago Heights (left) and Valparaiso, Indiana (below).

facturing facilities in Chicago Heights and Valparaiso, Indiana.

In 1995, Globe Industries was purchased by Rieter Holding A.G. of Zurich. When Globe became part of Rieter's automotive systems division, it was renamed Rieter Automotive North America, and Globe's shares in UGN were transferred to Rieter Automotive. While the ownership of UGN remained evenly split between the Japanese and American shareholders, the addition of Swiss investors added a new dimension. Rieter has long been regarded as a technology leader for automotive acoustics in Europe and has worked with Nihon Tokushu Toryo Co. Ltd. through licensing and joint ventures in Japan and the Pacific Rim for the past 30 years. This established business relationship between UGN's new shareholders has brought opportunities to grow and expand the company's business.

REACHING OUT TO CHICAGO

Committed to a philosophy that stresses employee involvement, the 700 employees of UGN have successfully made their factories safe and comfortable environments. Every day, they take UGN's corporate philosophy beyond the walls of the factory and into the surrounding community.

Of the numerous community outreach organizations formed by UGN's employees, Jamison is most proud of the Care Bears and the Waste Busters. Care Bears is an annual drive to donate toys and clothing to underprivileged children during the Christmas holidays, while Waste Busters actively spreads the word about the importance of cleaning up hazardous waste.

While the company provided money for the inception of Waste Busters, Jamison is quick to point out that the project was the brainchild of UGN employees. "They distributed fliers, bought radio ads, and worked with the Illinois Environmental Protection Agency and the city of Chicago Heights to set up a station for the disposal of hazardous materials," he explains. Nearly 800 Chicago residents came to UGN's station to dispose of waste materials with the help of officials from the Illinois EPA and volunteers from UGN.

AWARD-WINNING SERVICE

Throughout the years, the auto industry has bestowed numerous awards on UGN, the most recent of which was presented in 1997 by the president of Toyota. "We were one of four suppliers to receive this superior-level award out of

a supply base of 1,600," Jamison says, "so it's really very special."

UGN's product line has expanded beyond sound to vision. "Anything that's visible in the car is called trim," Jamison says, "Acoustics have expanded to include interior trim." Interior trim, while decorative, also performs the function of quieting the car. UGN makes package trays, the shelves that sit behind backseats under the rear window, and headliners that insulate the ceiling of the car. UGN also supplies a special sound-damping material based on unique, proprietary technology.

Through new products and a commitment to the communities it serves, UGN will continue to make its presence known—locally, nationally, and internationally—for many years to come.

ROM THE INVENTION OF THE STEAM LOCOMOTIVE IN 1797 THROUGH THE ADVENT OF HIGH-SPEED RAIL, AMERICA HAS HAD A FASCINATION FOR RAILROADS. THOSE TWIN RIBBONS OF STEEL AND THE GREAT, FIRE-BREATHING LOCOMOTIVES THAT RODE THEM VIRTUALLY DEFINED OUR NATION IN THE

19th century. And even today, though there is far less track being laid in the United States than during the golden age of railroads more than a century ago, trains continue to carry heavier freight loads than trucks, planes, and barges combined.

As one of America's largest manufacturers of rail products, ABC Rail keeps those trains on the move. It's a job that has become more challenging over the years as the amount of rail has shrunk, while the amount of rail traffic has continued to grow. Since modern railcars are heavier than those of the past and more traffic is running over the rails, rail support systems need more maintenance and repair than before. As a result, railroads have turned to ABC Rail.

As one of America's largest manufacturers of rail products, ABC Rail keeps trains on the move.

HISTORY

In the 1860s, the American landscape was being wrapped in steel. Foundries in the East were forging miles of rail to feed the nation's ravenous appetite for westward expansion, and entrepreneurs and other risk takers were gambling vast fortunes in the iron and steel industry. One such man was William Wait Snow, who started a foundry in Hillburn, New York. From the manufacture of railroad castings, Snow expanded his business into brake shoes in the 1880s and moved the foundry to Mahwah, New Jersey, where he passed the company on to a relative, Elmer J. Snow.

Elmer Snow bought several other brake shoe companies and in 1902 created the American Brake Shoe and Foundry Company. The business grew as the nation grew, acquiring plants from Baltimore to Chicago and eventually branching out into rail-related products.

With deep roots in the Midwest, the company is also a citizen of the world—supplying track, wheels, switches, and other related products that move passengers and freight around the globe.

The company manufactured switches, wheels, specialty track, and "frogs," which are specially designed pieces of trackwork that keep trains running on the proper rails at intersections and switching points.

In the 1960s, the company was purchased by the IC Industries conglomerate and became the Rail Products Group of Abex Corporation, a division of IC Industries. By 1981, it had moved its headquarters from Mahwah to Chicago, which had been the railroad hub of the nation for much of the 20th century. In 1987, the company was incorporated as ABC Rail Products Corporation.

TOTAL QUALITY FOR THE 21ST CENTURY

uality and reliability are integral parts of the corporate strategy at ABC. Soon after the company opened its doors, it instituted a total quality system to ensure accountability for problem solving. Under the system, each worker is responsible for sending a high-quality product up the line to the workstation. The result has been a consistent improvement in quality and reliability of ABC products, and a growing reputation in the industry for providing outstanding value and unsurpassed customer service.

With Chicago as the nation's railroad center, it's only natural that ABC Rail should have three plants in the area—all of which have differences symbolizing the progression of the rail industry. The trackwork plant is one of the oldest railroad factories still in use, housing forges where metal is heated white-hot and then pounded by massive machines. The flying sparks and the glowing light of molten steel offer a glimpse into an earlier age when men, not machines, bent and shaped steel with nothing but strong backs and sturdy hammers.

By contrast, ABC's rail mill is a manufacturing facility for the 21st century. Here, computers are in control, instantly transmitting instructions to the milling machines that produce rails at a rate soon to exceed that of several current milling plants combined. In keeping with such advances in technol-

ogy, and in support of its workers, ABC is currently offering retraining to its employees in the older plant, teaching them the skills they'll need to operate the new rail mill system.

As part of its strategy for growth in the 21st century, in addition to growing its own business, ABC Rail is constantly evaluating high-performance companies that will fit into its line of rail products and services. In 1996, ABC Rail acquired American Systems Technologies (AST) of Verona, Wisconsin. AST supplies signal installation and maintenance services to short lines, regionals, commuter lines, and Class I railroads.

With 19 operating facilities strategically located throughout the United States, ABC Rail is able to offer railroads high-quality products at low cost and with value-added services.

ABC AROUND THE WORLD

The company's roots run deep in the Midwest, and its values and work ethic are those of the heartland. But in a larger sense, ABC Rail is also a citizen of the world—supplying track, wheels, switches, and other related products that move passengers and freight around the globe. That citizenship carries with it a large and growing responsibility. But as a company with more than 120 years of experience in designing, manufacturing, and maintaining America's rails, it's a responsibility that ABC Rail is uniquely equipped to handle.

With 19 operating facilities strategically located throughout the United States, ABC Rail is able to offer railroads high-quality products at low cost and with value-added services.

SINCE THE ORIGINAL FAIRMONT OPENED ON SAN FRANCISCO'S NOB HILL IN 1907, THE HOTEL'S NAME HAS BEEN SYNONYMOUS WITH LUXURY AND ELEGANCE—BOTH IN THE UNITED STATES AND ABROAD. WITH HOTELS IN DALLAS, NEW ORLEANS, SAN JOSE, BOSTON, AND NEW YORK, THE FAIRMONT HAS STEADILY MOVED

toward its goal of being one of the world's most-talked-about grand hotels. And with plans to open one or two grand hotels each year, the Fairmont path seems clear.

Likewise, the Fairmont Hotel at Grant Park in Chicago, which opened in 1987, strives to be the most desirable site to hold business, social, and civic events, year after year—a hotel with a name so prominent that it comes to mind first when people think of Chicago hotels. The Fairmont also aspires to be the most glamorous, most elegant hotel in the city, featuring the greatest restaurants, the most exciting entertainment, and the

most magnificent ballrooms and luxurious accommodations.

TOP-NOTCH AMENITIES

Owned by a partnership of Saudi Arabian royalties and the Swig family of San Francisco, Chicago's Fairmont easily meets its goals, offering elegant, European decor; 692 luxurious rooms, including 66 suites; 24-hour room service; modem hookups; fax machines; extra-long mattresses in every guest room; and antiques and original artwork throughout its pink Spanish granite tower.

The Fairmont's two restaurants, Primavera and Entre Nous, are top-

notch establishments. Entre Nous has won various awards, including the Mobil four star, the AAA four diamond, and America's Finest Restaurant from the Chefs of America, as well as recognition from the Distinguished Restaurants of North America and the International Wine & Food Society.

The Fairmont also boasts two grand ballrooms, 12 smaller rooms for social and business functions, and such state-of-the-art audiovisual facilities as teleconferencing, projection rooms, closed-circuit television, and built-in sound and light equipment.

Its convenient location and wide variety of amenities attract many families to this world-class hotel. "We provide a theatrical display in terms of events—events to remember," says Ken Todd, general manager of the hotel. "And we make it interesting enough so children and parents want to return. For example, we put a teddy bear in a child's crib, and send up milk and cookies at bedtime. We have a children's menu at Primavera Ristorante."

But the high-quality service also lures discerning business executives and luminaries, including Hillary Rodham Clinton, Joseph Cardinal Bernardin, Bob Dole, French President Jacques Chirac, Henry Kissinger, U.S. Secretary of Defense William Perry, and Sarah Ferguson, the former Duchess of York. Recent celebrities to stay at the Fairmont include members of the Orlando Magic and the Utah Jazz NBA teams, Martha Stewart, Lassie, Hootie and the Blowfish, Captain Kangaroo, Ivana Trump, Joe Frazier, Mrs. Fields, and Tony Bennett.

Major social events that have been held at the Fairmont include the Chicago Academy of the Arts Ball, the St. Joseph Hospital Cornette Ball, the Chicago House Art of Caring Gala, the Goodman Theatre

The Fairmont Hotel is one of Chicago's most exciting grand hotels.

Women's Board Ball, the Cystic Fibrosis Grand Chef's Gala, and the American Civil Liberties Union Ball. Other prominent functions held at the Fairmont include those sponsored by the Arthritis Foundation, Anti-Defamation League, Erikson Institute, Options for People, Special Children's Charities, Test Positive Award, Spertus Institute of Jewish Studies, and Rita Hayworth Alzheimer's Gala.

Employee Happiness

erhaps the Fairmont's customers are happy because its employees—referred to as colleagues—are happy. With its motto "What I do today creates a memory for guests tomorrow," the Chicago staff of 700 operates as a team, and Todd heads a seven-member executive staff that oversees 20 department heads.

"We have an open-door policy—anyone can talk to anyone," says Todd. "A lot of current colleagues have been here since day one. We have probably one of the lowest employee turnover rates in the industry." He credits several managerial tactics for his staff's contentment. An extensive training program starts with an orientation and an apprenticeship, and continues in regularly held seminars. Monthly roundtable discussions serve as an open forum at which colleagues can ask questions and voice their concerns. Colleagues are frequently switched around to fill other positions temporarily so they know the ins and outs of the whole operation. And

high expectations—from both management and clientele—ensure that Fairmont colleagues are working at their peak performance.

A Member of the Community

ocated in Illinois Center overlooking Lake Michigan, the Fairmont enjoys a prime location in the Windy City. It is close to—but not on top of—one of the city's most desirable streets, Michigan Avenue, and it is merely a swing away from the MetroGolf Facility, a public nine-hole golf course and driving

range designed by the renowned Dye Designs International. Hotel guests also enjoy privileges at the tony Athletic Club Illinois Center, which is a 116,000-square-foot, complete health and fitness facility featuring a full European spa and a 98-foot rock climbing wall.

Fairmont management cares about its hometown. "We provide leadership for the city," Todd says. "Chicago is one of the greatest cities in America. It's the center of the Midwest. The Fairmont wants to be in major cities."

The hotel gives back to the Chicago community by supporting many charitable and service organizations, which is part of the Fairmont vision to be the foremost leader in service to the community and to have an unwavering commitment to charitable causes.

To that end, the Fairmont donates food regularly—and sponsors an employee food drive—to the Greater Chicagoland Food Depository. In addition to food, the hotel also donates soap, shampoo, linens, and furniture to those in need, and open guest-room amenities to many of the city's homeless shelters.

The Fairmont donates gift certificates for approximately 250 Chicago-area fund-raisers each year

The Lobby Lounge is the perfect spot to meet or to be seen. Cocktails, afternoon tea, or after dinner drinks are served daily.

Entre Nous Restaurant combines an intimate atmosphere with an award-winning menu and wine cellar.

and sponsors its team of fund-raising employees for the March of Dimes Walk-A-Thon and for AIDS Walk Chicago. It also participates in Mayor Richard Daley's Clean Sweep program, the United Way Campaign, the EarnFare welfare hiring program, and the LifeSource blood drive.

THE RECOGNITION IT DESERVES

t's very, very unusual for a small company to have this kind of exposure. It's due to word of mouth, and it multiplies through the years," says Todd of the Fairmont. "We're one of the leaders in occupancy. An independent survey showed that 98 percent of those who stay at the Fairmont say they would return."

The Fairmont's annual gross sales of more than $50 million bear out its success rate, as do the awards it has won, including a position on the *Condé Nast Traveler* Gold List; the Executive Choice, given by *Sales and Marketing Management Magazine*; and the Gold Key Award, given by *Meetings & Conventions Magazine*, as well as the review in the 1997 *Zagat's Guide* that praises

the modern high-rise for "up-to-the minute luxury," "style and class all the way," and having "every detail in place."

"We have shown the industry how you can be a large hotel but still have high standards and a noncommercial look," Todd says, referring to the Fairmont's individually appointed guest rooms. "We've received almost every award to be won."

Sustaining high standards necessitates spending a great deal in capital improvements. A recent,

$3 million upgrade involved installing new carpeting, redoing upholstery, and repolishing the marble in the lobby and all rest rooms. Clients, some of whom reserve one of four $3,500-per-night suites, notice such things.

But such high standards have become a hallmark of Fairmont Hotels over the years. They have attracted thousands to the grand hotel in Grant Park and will continue to lure families, business-persons, and celebrities alike for many years to come.

The adjacent Athletic Club Illinois Center offers guests of the Fairmont state-of-the-art health, athletic, and spa facilities.

The Fairmont Hotel guest rooms are luxuriously appointed with spectacular skyline and lakeshore views.

AKWOOD APARTMENTS, A LUXURY HIGH-RISE ON CHICAGO'S WEST HURON STREET, IS A HOME AWAY FROM HOTELS FOR HUNDREDS OF PROFESSIONALS WHO ARE BASED TEMPORARILY IN CHICAGO. ONE OF THE MAIN JEWELS IN THE CROWN OF OAKWOOD CORPORATE HOUSING (OCH), AN EXTENDED-STAY

residential services company with locations nationwide, Oakwood provides all the conveniences of home, as well as the atmosphere and amenities found in only the finest hotels. Extended-stay guests enjoy extra touches, including concierge services, 24-hour security, an indoor pool with skylights, and a sundeck with a 180-degree view of the Chicago skyline.

Oakwood Apartments is one of 70 buildings owned and/or managed by R&B Realty Group, a Los Angeles-based, full-service real estate company and the nation's 10th-largest apartment management company. From 130 offices, R&B manages 33,000 furnished and unfurnished apartments in more than 1,000 cities, and leases apartments in many other buildings for its clientele.

ONE CALL DOES IT ALL

CH takes care of everything from the time customers book an apartment in an Oakwood community to the day of their departure. One call to OCH's national toll-free reservations line allows clients to book temporary housing anywhere in the country, and to request the amenities and services that meet their specific needs.

Oakwood also has an interactive Web site that profiles its services and provides information about accommodations anywhere in the country. To make the Web site more user-friendly, the company continually updates the information, lists the advantages over hotels, and supplies answers to frequently asked questions. OCH also has developed the Web site to allow clients to pre-reserve apartments on-line at www.oakwood.com.

MEETING A NEED

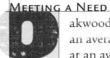

akwood clients stay an average of 60 days at an average cost of $55 per night. Most are business professionals on out-of-town assignments; many work for Fortune 500 companies. An increasing number of clients from other areas and with other needs, however, seek out OCH: bands, theater troupes, film crews, and other entertainment groups on location or touring; disaster victims without inhabitable homes; transferees looking for permanent housing; government employees on special assignment; seniors going to warmer climates; and home owners who are remodeling or are between homes.

Oakwood meets a client's housing needs by providing furniture, televisions, linens, and kitchen utensils. Clients also can custom-order accessories and furnishings, such as small kitchen appliances, telephone answering machine, fax machine, baby furniture, and a complete home office package with an IBM-compatible computer.

As the company's motto says: Oakwood—simply put—the most trusted name in corporate housing™.

Clockwise from top:
The indoor rooftop pool with skylights is enclosed in glass, offering residents 180-degree views of the Chicago skyline.

Oakwood's downtown location offers immediate access to mass transportation, shopping, restaurants, and entertainment.

Oakwood Chicago offers an inviting atmosphere with all the comforts of home.

AS ONE OF THE 10 LARGEST BANKS IN CHICAGO, FIRSTAR BANK ILLINOIS PLAYS AN ACTIVE ROLE IN THE FINANCIAL LIFE OF THE CITY AND ITS RESIDENTS. FIRSTAR BANK ILLINOIS HAS 42 BRANCHES THROUGHOUT THE STATE, MOST OF WHICH ARE IN THE CHICAGO AREA, WITH

locations as far north as Crystal Lake, as far west as Geneva, and as far south as Park Forest. To Firstar, the Chicago area offers diversity, opportunity, and growth potential.

Firstar Bank Illinois is part of Milwaukee-based Firstar Corporation, a $20 billion, multistate holding company that provides competitive investment, banking, and insurance products and services. Founded in Milwaukee in 1853 as Farmers and Millers Bank, Firstar Corporation primarily serves the upper Midwest, and is now active in Wisconsin, Minnesota, Iowa, and Illinois. In addition, the bank has other specialized offices in Omaha, St. Louis, and Kansas City, as well as locations in Arizona, Florida, and northern Indiana.

Since its beginning, Firstar Corporation has grown steadily, earning many distinctions, includ-

ing Small Business Lender of the Year. Firstar was ranked at the top of a cash management services survey by *Cash Management* magazine. The bank provides comprehensive financial services for 1.2 million households and currently has consumer deposits totaling $10.8 billion.

The bank offers extensive commercial financial services to assist its business clients. Firstar provides loans and asset-based lending, commercial real estate lending, and other capital market products. The bank also offers correspondent banking services and cash management services, and has one of the largest check collection operations in the Midwest.

For both individuals and institutions, Firstar offers comprehensive trust and investment management services. Firstar Investment Research & Management Company, LLC (FIRMCO) was established in 1986 and has become

nationally recognized as an investment adviser. FIRMCO manages the Firstar Funds (formerly known as Portico) family of 16 mutual funds, which range from aggressive to conservative investments in stocks, bonds, and money market funds. Of the $18 billion in assets currently managed by FIRMCO, $4.2 billion is invested in Firstar Funds.

A FAVORITE WITH THE PUBLIC

Firstar Corporation has spent a lot of time talking with customers— from individuals to families to small businesses—to determine what they want from their banking company. The answers have led to major restructuring and streamlining at the bank, including many new and redesigned products and services, simplified pricing, and better accessibility. New services include 24-hour banking, a site on the World Wide Web, electronic banking, and an expanded ATM network. This restructuring aims to make Firstar Corporation one of the most competitive financial services companies in the country.

The new Web site makes Firstar's products and services more accessible, and is designed to be used by consumers and businesses to access account information and to receive pertinent articles and other investing and financial information. The site incorporates an educational component in its overall design to encourage customers to become more involved in their own financial decisions.

The Goal Planner Program is another new, customer-focused product. This free service is a great way to walk customers through financial goals and help them examine the impact of different financial decisions. When completed, the program produces a printout for further study. The Goal Planner

From banking and investments to insurance, loans, and retirement planning, Firstar offers complete financial strategies that help customers reach their goals.

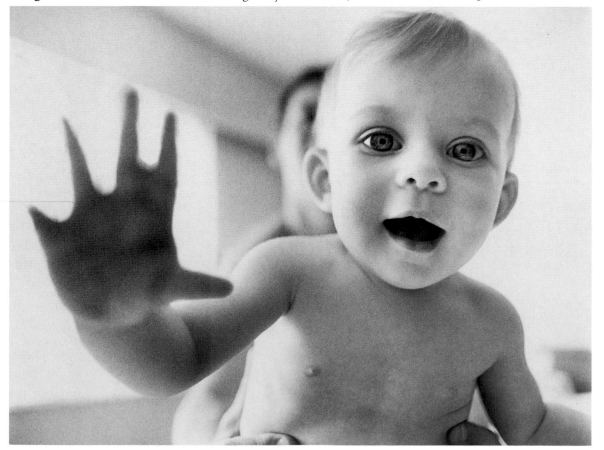

Firstar Bank offers complete financial strategies for small businesses.

also offers one-on-one, 20-minute discussions based on the three most frequently asked customer questions: How much house can I afford? How do I plan for a child's education? and How do I plan for retirement? The program breaks down this potentially intimidating process into easily digested segments so the customer can find the most beneficial answers and make well-informed decisions.

A Community Partner

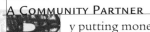

By putting money back into the communities it serves, Firstar Corporation demonstrates its responsibility and commitment to each. To that end, Firstar contributes to the well-being of these communities by reinvesting customer deposits in local enterprises and by offering both time and money to support a wide variety of regional philanthropies. Each year, Firstar Corporation contributes more than $6 million to such causes.

In the Chicago community, Firstar Bank Illinois is active in several charitable concerns. The Firstar Foundation gives a majority of its grants to businesses in the low- to moderate-income neighborhoods in which it does business. Firstar also supports Brian's Run, a 5K race that is held annually on Father's Day in memory of former Chicago Bears running back Brian Piccolo. Proceeds go toward cancer research. And Firstar is involved in various family-focused local charities.

Banking for the Future

Since the beginning of 1998, banks have been allowed to operate on an interstate basis. Firstar prepared for this move by developing streamlined customer access and record keeping, and a well-developed wealth management team. In Illinois, the teams have a package of financial services and products that will be ready for each market segment: commercial, trust, investment, and private banking. Most competitors do not offer this complete package, and Firstar has teamed its employees to give customers the entire picture.

Firstar will spend the next several years building on its new structure and creating more efficient services. The bank is dramatically increasing the amount of training and information that employees receive, which Firstar believes is a significant way to add value at every interaction. The development of new and better products will pave a path for future business and better prepare consumers for the marketplace.

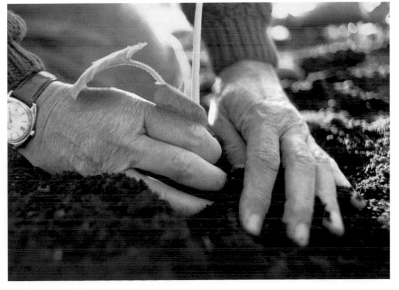

Planning for retirement is one of the many services available at Firstar.

ORDAN INDUSTRIES, INC. IS A PRIVATE HOLDING COMPANY THAT ACQUIRES ENTREPRENEURIAL COMPANIES AND HELPS THEM GROW. ■ ESTABLISHED IN 1988 BY NOTRE DAME ROOMMATES JOHN "JAY" JORDAN, CHAIRMAN AND CEO, AND THOMAS H. QUINN, PRESIDENT AND COO, JORDAN INDUSTRIES, INC. (JII)

runs its international operations from offices in suburban Deerfield, Illinois.

Unlike many acquisition firms of the late 1980s that used sophisticated financial arrangements to dismantle and sell off assets of acquired companies, JII targets and acquires companies for growth. By deploying its business expertise and capital, JII helps its constituent companies to achieve and expand market opportunities, improve plants and facilities, and achieve greater distribution of their products. Nine years after its founding, Jordan Industries owns more than 50 of the nation's top privately held companies.

Chicago is a strategic location for Jordan Industries. As a transportation hub, Chicago is a gateway city for national and international travel. Also home to some of the best business and graduate schools in the country, Chicago has provided well-educated and experienced talent necessary to fuel JII's growth. At JII's Deerfield headquarters, a staff of 20 commits resources and expertise to advance aggressive growth strategies for JII's constituent companies, actively positioning those companies for long-term growth both domestically and internationally. "We can do this with a small, efficient corporate

staff because we let the companies run themselves, while we concentrate on expanding opportunities for our individual companies. By not imposing a corporate hierarchy on our constituent companies, they're free to run their businesses. We provide a high level of expertise they access as needed," says Tom Caffery, senior vice president of business development.

Partners for Progress

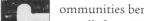

Communities benefit, as well, from JII's focus on developing and improving the capabilities of all its businesses. Only through growth are jobs created in communities where JII operations are located. More than half of Jordan's companies are in small towns that count on the jobs and taxes created by these successful companies. Jordan values and nurtures each of its constituent companies for the long term, enabling these companies and communities to realize their greatest potential.

An excellent example of JII's commitment is its partnership with Dura-Line Corporation, in Middlesboro, Kentucky, a manufacturer of innerduct polyethylene

Clockwise from top left:
Dacco is America's number one rebuilder of torque converters, and a Jordan acquisition since 1988.

The customer service center at Riverside Book and Bible

Imperial Electric designs, engineers, and manufactures specialized electric motors.

Dura-Line has been expanding internationally since the early 1990s to take advantage of the worldwide expansion in telecommunications infrastructure.

plastic pipe that houses fiber-optic cables. JII has helped Dura-Line grow from $8 million in sales in 1988 to $75 million in 1996 by identifying and creating opportunities in Eastern Europe, and in many emerging markets including China, India, and South America. With these opportunities and hard work, Dura-Line has become a major player in the telecommunications market internationally. Increased demand means more jobs, more raw materials, and more local taxes—all a benefit to the community.

Jordan assisted Dura-Line with the capital, organizational expertise, and long-term international business strategy necessary for Dura-Line's management to achieve its goals. "With JII acting as our banker and helping us build and implement an international strategy, we were freed up to concentrate on projects rather than proposals. JII shares our view of taking advantage of key business opportunities as soon as they arise, and they were there every step of the way to ensure we had what we needed to get the job done," says John Shoffner, Dura-Line president.

ACQUISITION CRITERIA THAT UNIFY DIVERSE BUSINESSES

t first glance, Jordan Industries is a diverse group of companies, in differing markets and manufacturing settings, offering a unique array of products and services. However, a closer look reveals a tightly focused set of characteristics that define all Jordan acquisitions. To a very large extent, these companies share much in common.

Jordan Industries seeks companies with a revenue of $5 million to $150 million that fit one or more of the following profiles: companies that enjoy high margins through proprietary products or services and have excellent growth prospects; well-managed private companies with a track record of consistent sales and earnings growth; a company synergistic or complementary with one or more of JII's current businesses or industry groups; and subsidiaries and divisions of larger corporate entities, the industries and products of which coincide with JII's strategic objectives.

"Companies meeting our profile will realize the greatest growth potential under our unique approach to business. Those businesses, overall, represent the greatest growth potential to our national economy as well. They are nimble, innovative, and successful before we acquire them. We simply build on those assets in ways they couldn't," says Quinn.

LEADERS ARE HONORED, NOT REPLACED

nother cornerstone of JII's philosophy is that quality management at the company level is critical. Equally important is the chemistry that exists between managers of the constituent companies. JII's businesses are based on the fundamentals of good judgment, planning, fiscal discipline, experience, and common sense, and these factors inform as many of Jordan's success stories as any factor in industry. Jordan, therefore, values leaders who share and appreciate this perspective.

Even more important to Jordan is the fact that constituent companies sustain this philosophy, not from JII, but as a lasting imprint of the entrepreneurs who founded them. To that point, JII works with company leaders, and fosters a personal and collaborative style that allows company managers to address issues and formulate answers within the framework of their own businesses. This is especially true with regard to the planning process, the devising of

Beemak is the designer, injection molder, and distributor of plastic point of sale pamphlet and literature holders (top).

Parson Precision Products of Parsons, Kansas, specializes in the manufacture of hot-formed titanium parts for the aerospace industry (bottom).

growth strategies, the strengthening of organizational structures, and appropriate responses to abrupt change.

"Jordan Industries is committed to sustaining the excellence achieved by the founders of its constituent companies, and to sustaining continuity in the communities and industries in which these businesses work," Caffery says.

Jordan Industries is positioned to grow through excellence and the continuation of the entrepreneurial spirit that built the companies it owns. That energy and drive, combined with Jordan's ability to assist its companies with strategic acquisitions, plant and equipment needs, new product development, and market opportunities, give this spirit the strength and stamina to thrive.

ECHNOLOGY SOLUTIONS COMPANY (TSC) IS A LEADING
INTERNATIONAL MANAGEMENT CONSULTING AND SYSTEMS
INTEGRATION FIRM. ITS MISSION IS SIMPLE: TO PROVIDE
GLOBAL ORGANIZATIONS WITH INTEGRATED BUSINESS AND
TECHNOLOGY SOLUTIONS, HELPING THEM MAXIMIZE BUSI-

ness benefits of information technology. TSC specializes in delivering a unique blend of technology expertise and business consulting services across multiple industries and around the world. Its innovative ideas and proven project management expertise have helped clients revolutionize the way they interact with their customers, business partners, and employees as they compete for global leadership.

In the rapidly expanding professional services industry, TSC stands apart from its competitors due to its success in attracting world-class professionals to the organization. With more than 1,500 professionals deployed glo-

bally, the company boasts a workforce of exceptional knowledge and expertise. Explains John T. Kohler, president and chief executive officer, "Clearly, the difference is our people."

As the company enters its 10th year, TSC remains committed to its core values: a relationship-driven approach, world-class professionals, and, above all, delivery of high-impact, innovative business solutions worldwide.

BUILDING MOMENTUM

SC went public in 1991, as the U.S. market for professional information technology services

was approaching $24 billion. The worldwide market for those services grew to $187 billion in 1997, according to Dataquest. TSC's growth has been equally admirable, with projected annual revenues nearing $250 million.

The company began in 1988—organized around three core areas of industry emphasis: Financial Services, Consumer Products, and Manufacturing—and grew successfully through its expertise in client/server and systems integration work. TSC has continued its forward momentum by identifying key areas where technology can provide the highest business value to clients, specifically in its Call Center and Enterprise Applications business units.

TSC quickly gained market recognition in both areas. Enterprise Applications, responsible for the large-scale implementation and integration of third-party application software packages, created significant market impact by internally developing specialized implementation approaches and methodologies that generated quick results for its clients. Growing from a small team in 1994, TSC's Enterprise Applications area represented its fastest-growing business unit based on successful partnerships with the premier packaged application providers. Today, the group continues to grow and provide clients with highly successful implementations delivered efficiently and within budget.

TSC also became a leading provider of enterprise customer management consulting, with a strong emphasis on call center technologies. This practice area has been a significant source of growth for TSC, and continues to provide its clients with a strategic vision for their customer service needs, creates a robust architecture

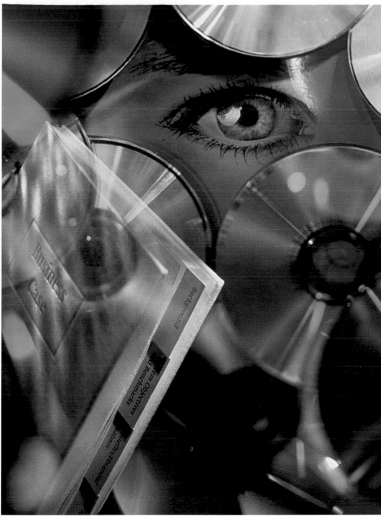

to support its vision, and integrates the various complex components to create a sophisticated call center environment. Leading companies have turned to TSC to build world-class customer management solutions throughout the United States, Canada, and Europe.

GOING GLOBAL

Moving into the global arena, the company launched TSC Europe with an initial focus on customer relationship management consulting, taking advantage of Europe's growing need for state-of-the-art call center and customer management solutions. To gain an even stronger foothold in this market, TSC acquired Aspen Consultancy, a respected call center and communications consulting firm based in London.

In other areas of global expansion, TSC de Mexico, TSC's initial foray into Mexico, has focused on the growing enterprise applications market there, leveraging investments that Mexican companies were making, and continue to make, in technology. TSC's Latin American operations are also a key contributor in global expansion, and are also initially leveraging its Enterprise Applications expertise. TSC has established an office in Bogotá to support growth in Latin America.

Additionally, TSC identified other key capabilities that would enable the company to offer a broader set of technology-enabled business solutions, and therefore acquired McLaughlin & Associates, now the TSC Strategy Group, a high-end strategy consulting firm specializing in telecommunications.

This acquisition helped TSC strengthen its strategy consulting capabilities and its telecommunications expertise. In a separate move, TSC also formed its Change & Learning Technologies unit to provide multimedia, Internet/intranet services, change management programs, and education and training.

TSC has further expanded its expertise through strategic relationships. The company merged with HRM Resources, Inc., a technology implementation firm that specializes in large-scale enterprise software solutions, and also with The Bentley Company, a strategic consulting and systems integration firm focused on helping companies enhance their internal support and operations through help desks and customer-driven applications. These strategic acquisitions, mergers, and internal start-ups have helped to broaden TSC's service offerings and geographic reach, enabling the company to offer the highest-quality service to its clients.

A COMMITMENT TO QUALITY

In addition to a strong commitment to its clients, TSC has made a significant commitment to its community, as well. Recently, TSC developed and sponsored an award program with The Computerworld Smithsonian to honor 21st-century pioneers. TSC's sponsorship gives it the unique opportunity of working with the Smithsonian Institution to influence the archiving and recording of history around the significant human and cultural impact of technology.

The company also is committed to service. As a member of the Summer Intern Program of Chicago, it provides educational support for economically and socially disadvantaged young adults who wish to obtain a college degree and work toward a career in business. TSC sponsors and mentors interns in its domestic and international offices. Several of these interns have subsequently joined TSC as full-time employees, joining the ranks of TSC's talented, self-motivated, team-oriented professionals.

Today, TSC, located at www.TechSol.com on the World Wide Web, is a full-service solutions provider to clients worldwide, offering high-end strategic consulting, end-to-end implementation and integration, and comprehensive education and training services. As the company celebrates its 10th anniversary, TSC looks forward with enthusiasm to solving the challenges that lie ahead for its clients and its growing community.

NDERSEN CONSULTING TRAVELS THE WORLD HELPING CLIENTS CHANGE TO BE MORE SUCCESSFUL AND CREATES MUCH SUCCESS AT HOME IN ITS CHICAGO HEADQUARTERS. ■ A LEADING GLOBAL MANAGEMENT AND TECHNOLOGY CONSULTING FIRM, ANDERSEN CONSULTING NOW EMPLOYS

nearly 51,000 people, with more than 5,000 of those in the Chicago area. Revenues in 1996 were $5.3 billion, up 26 percent from 1995, marking one of the largest and healthiest growth rates in the industry. Originally an arm of Arthur Andersen, the management consulting unit became independent of the parent in 1989.

CHANGE AND INNOVATION

his fast-growing, high-profile organization practices what it preaches by aggressively shaping the organization into its vision of the consulting firm of the future. This means Andersen Consulting is meeting the needs of the market-

place by changing and innovating. As one of its own tenets states: "We must continue to have enough pride in Andersen Consulting to have the courage to change it."

Change and growth have been swift for Andersen Consulting. In Chicago, a major move and space redesign is under way that will be in progress until 1999. Eventually, the firm's operations will include four sites in the Chicago metro area, and an internal training facility, the Center for Professional Education, based in St. Charles. With new facilities and a contemporary layout, Andersen Consulting expects to create the "office of the future," which will provide a great variety of work settings: open and private,

formal and informal, individualized and team-oriented.

"In years past, Andersen Consulting's Chicago Metro office was recognized as the flagship office," says Ken Bergren, office managing partner. "Our midwestern can-do determination and hard work earned the Chicago Metro office a reputation as being an innovator and a doer. Although we have become a truly global firm, we continue to carry on our flagship heritage in spirit. Just as Chicago has the reputation of the 'city that works,' Andersen Consulting's Chicago Metro office is a successful operation, but we're never satisfied with the status quo. To be the consulting firm of the future, we must provide an environment that lends itself to meeting that objective, and that meets the needs of our consulting professionals and our clients."

ACHIEVING THE BEST BUSINESS PERFORMANCE

Distinguishing Andersen Consulting from other consulting organizations is the integrated approach it uses to deliver valued results for its clients. Andersen Consulting's approach aligns an organization's people, processes, and technology in support of its overall strategy—harnessing the total power of that alignment to achieve the best business performance.

Andersen Consulting has helped thousands of organizations shape themselves for leadership by embracing change as an ongoing opportunity. Its integrated approach empowers an organization for change by focusing on execution as strategy, maximizing human performance, developing technology-enabled strategies, and building process excellence. Integrating these catalysts for change is far more important than any single initiative, no matter how far reaching.

Andersen Consulting professionals take an integrated approach to helping a financial services client improve a customer billing function.

ROBERT TOLCHIN

Bringing Value to Clients

In all that it does, Andersen Consulting's focus is on bringing value to its clients. It does this through integrated teams that specialize in specific competencies and virtually all industries, ranging from financial services to products to communications. The real key to the firm's success, however, is its ability to share information, expertise, access to the best technology, and the best management thinking.

Andersen Consulting continually explores new, creative ways for delivering value to clients. For example, its Business Integration Centers, each tailored for a specific industry, encourage out-of-the-box thinking and long-range planning. Its Centers for Strategic Technology in Palo Alto and Sophia Antipolis, France, help translate research into results. Its Solution Centers provide a new model for creating valued, reusable answers to client needs, and its Knowledge Xchange® system enables its professionals to share information and ideas.

In these ways, Andersen Consulting consistently delivers value to its clients in Chicago and around the world—value that can improve business performance and be passed on to customers.

Partnering with the Best

Andersen Consulting is fortunate to have the opportunity to partner with clients who are among the world's most successful companies and most innovative government organizations. It works with three-quarters of the world's 100 largest public companies. Organizations are asking Andersen Consulting to help them make fundamental changes to their entire businesses, and the firm is successful because it is able to deliver quantum improvements and bottom-line benefits. More organizations are finding value by working with Andersen Consulting, in Chicago and worldwide.

Community Involvement

Community service and volunteerism are important components of Andersen Consulting's presence in the Chicago marketplace. Since 1989, a wide array of civic, economic development, education, arts, and social service organizations have benefited from an inherent commitment to give back to the communities in which Andersen Consulting does business.

The philanthropic focus of Chicago Metro is to strike a balance in the giving of funds and of volunteer time, delivered through programs dedicated to the education, training, and development of Chicago youth. This emphasis on youth provides the opportunity for Andersen Consulting people to listen, diagnose, teach, and transfer knowledge—the basics of client work—and to make a difference in the communities where the education, training, and development of youth is faltering or nonexistent. To that end, organizations such as Cabrini-Green Tutoring Program, Chicago Cares, Junior Achievement of Chicago, Information Technology Resource Center, and Lawndale Community School have benefited from Andersen Consulting's significant support.

"Andersen Consulting," says Bergren, "has always been dedicated to giving back to the cities in which we do business. It's a constant reminder to us that our time and commitment to the community are often more valuable than money."

▶ JOAN HACKETT

An Andersen Consulting employee spends time at a local school for a volunteer activity designed to develop mentoring relationships (top).

Andersen . . . At Your Service helps employees achieve a better balance between work and personal commitments (bottom).

▶ JOE GINEX

AT ANY GIVEN MOMENT ON ANY GIVEN DAY, SOMEONE IS LIKELY USING A PRODUCT MANUFACTURED BY ONE OF THE MANY COMPANIES OWNED AND/OR OPERATED BY TMB INDUSTRIES, INC. ALL OF FORD'S REAR-WHEEL-DRIVE SPORT UTILITY VEHICLES AND LIGHT TRUCKS HAVE

castings in their transmissions made by DuPage Die Casting Corp. of Niles, a Chicago suburb. The brackets for the exhaust system on many cars are made by Heckethorn Manufacturing Co. of Dyersburg, Tennessee. All seat belt extractors in Chrysler's automobiles are made by Flint Manufacturing in Michigan.

Commonwealth Edison uses coal cars produced by Johnstown America Corp. to take coal from mines in Montana to its power plants in Illinois. About half of all tractor trailer trucks have drivers' seats made by Bostrom Seating Inc. And Accura Tool & Mold of Crystal Lake makes the tools that are used to produce the plastic caps on many cosmetic and drink bottles.

In 1989, Thomas Begel, who had been chairman and CEO of Pullman Company from 1982 through 1988, founded TMB Industries, Inc. Through his leadership, the entity that began as an empty shell created to acquire and operate manufacturing entities has become the parent company of a variety of businesses. TMB's enterprises cover a wide range of industries that employ almost 5,000 people and generate

annual revenues of close to $900 million.

HELPING PEOPLE

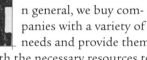

"In general, we buy companies with a variety of needs and provide them with the necessary resources to grow," says Begel, chairman and CEO. "Sometimes we sell them, and sometimes we take them public, and sometimes we just own them, depending on what the economy is doing. Typically, we are driven by outside forces as opposed to internal ones."

The end benefit, Begel explains, has both an economic and a societal impact: "By adding life to sick companies and resources to growing companies, we have saved and created many jobs that otherwise would have been exported to foreign manufacturers. The effect is that we buttress local economies. For example, take the wire mill we bought in Johnstown. Bethlehem Steel shut it down on a Friday, and we took it over on a Monday. Within two years, we had tripled its size."

As for the business point of view, Begel says, "We're providing high-yield returns for investors, but we don't look at ourselves as just giving people yields. We really see ourselves as operating investors

with an emphasis on increasing a company's profitability, which in turn increases the value of the businesses."

TMB made its first purchase in 1989, acquiring Dayton Superior, a construction products company which went public in 1996. In 1991 came the purchase of the freight-car division of Bethlehem Steel, which TMB renamed Johnstown America Corp. Today, that operation is a leading manufacturer of aluminum and steel gondolas—open-hopper and covered-hopper railroad freight cars used for hauling coal, agricultural, and mining products. Johnstown also produces steel freight cars used for hauling inter-modal containers and highway trailers.

Clockwise from top:
Johnstown America Corp. is a leading manufacturer of aluminum and steel gondolas—open-hopper and covered-hopper railroad freight cars used for hauling coal, agricultural, and mining products. Johnstown also produces steel freight cars used for hauling intermodal containers and highway trailers.

Each Heckethorn clamp is inspected for defects during the assembly process to ensure that the final shipment is 100 percent free of defects.

Gunite brake drums for a class 8 truck have a major market share.

In 1993, Begel formed a publicly traded holding company called Johnstown America Industries, Inc., which acquired several truck component and iron castings businesses in 1995. In addition to Johnstown America Corp., it now includes Gunite Corp., the leading North American supplier of wheel-end components, including brake drums, slack adjusters, and spoke wheels; Bostrom Seating, Inc., a leading manufacturer of air-suspension and static seating for the heavy-duty truck industry; and Fabco Automotive Corp., which sells steerable drive axles, gear boxes, and related parts. Johnstown America's portfolio also includes Brillion Iron Works, a producer of complex iron castings used as components in many types of light- and heavy-duty equipment; JAIX Leasing Co., which provides lease financing and fleet management services on new and rebuilt railroad freight cars; and Freight Car Services, Inc., which rebuilds and repairs railroad freight cars. The holding company had more than $600 million in revenues in 1997.

STEADY GROWTH

In 1995, TMB Industries purchased DuPage Die Casting Corp., a $50 million leading manufacturer of aluminum die castings for automotive and light-truck transmissions. The following year, TMB acquired Heckethorn Manufacturing, a prominent manufacturer of exhaust-system support brackets that has about $50 million in annual revenues.

In early 1997, TMB bought Accura Tool & Mold, a tool-and-die shop with $10 million in annual revenues. In addition, DuPage acquired Indiana Metal Works in Angola, Indiana. Most recently, TMB formed Automotive Systems International Inc., which then purchased Flint Manufacturing Corp. and DynAmerica Manufacturing Corp., both metal stampers with annual revenues of $40 million. Today, Automotive Systems revenues are approaching $100 million.

In January 1998, Global Metal Technologies, Inc. was formed as the parent company for DuPage and Accura. GMT signed a definitive agreement to acquire the Precision Die Casting Division of ITT Automotive at the same time. The combined companies will have revenues in excess of $225 million.

Begel, originally from Peoria, moved TMB headquarters to Chicago in 1991, and he has made a point of ensuring that the company has a significant presence in Illinois. Gunite is in Rockford, Freight Car Services is in Danville, JAIX Leasing is headquartered in downtown Chicago, DuPage is in Niles, and Accura Tool is in Crystal Lake.

Begel expects TMB's future to mirror its past, concentrating on the purchase of $20 million to $200 million manufacturing companies in industries related to transportation, machinery, and material-handling equipment, as well as companies that produce forgings, castings, plastics, and stampings.

"We will continue to search for acquisitions that fit into our overall strategy," Begel says. "We also will continue to focus on our leadership in research and development, and technological innovation, as well as on our ability to deliver a high degree of customer satisfaction."

Clockwise from top:
Heckethorn has been designing and manufacturing clamps for automotive exhaust systems since 1974.

In 1995, TMB Industries purchased DuPage Die Casting Corp., a $50 million leading manufacturer of aluminum die castings for automotive and light-truck transmissions.

Brillion Iron Works, a subsidiary of Johnstown America Industries, Inc., produces complex circular castings used as components in many types of light- and heavy-duty equipment.

Coal gondola car manufactured by Johnstown America Industries

I N 1994, TWO BANKING GIANTS WITH LONG AND SIGNIFICANT HIS-
TORIES MERGED. TOGETHER THEY CREATED A SOPHISTICATED,
FAR-REACHING INSTITUTION WITH A FUTURE AS AN INTERNATIONAL
POWERHOUSE, DETERMINED TO MAXIMIZE SHAREHOLDER VALUE
WHILE STRIVING TO BE THE BEST PLACE TO BANK, WORK, AND INVEST.

This merger of Continental Bank and Bank of America, 137 years after the founding of Continental Bank in the heart of downtown Chicago, was celebrated much like a wedding. Thousands of employees and clients gathered on Chicago's LaSalle Street for a huge block party, toasting the convergence of two powerful and successful financial institutions into an even more dynamic organization.

Today, Bank of America employs more than 3,500 people in the Midwest and approximately 90,000 worldwide.

BANK OF AMERICA IN THE MIDWEST

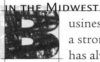usiness banking with a strong client focus has always been the foundation of Bank of America's operations in the Midwest. Several major business groups with international reach are headquartered at its LaSalle Street location. The U.S. & Canada Group provides sophisticated financial and advisory services to more than 3,000 large corporate clients in the

United States and Canada with annual revenues of $250 million and above, including most companies on the Fortune 1,000 list. The Midwest Commercial Bank serves midsize corporations with annual revenues greater than $10 million.

The Global Private Bank provides an array of products, services, and expertise for high-net-worth

individuals, entrepreneurs, and business-related wealth. Services include investment management, estate planning, charitable management, family business services, and credit.

Global Equity Investments, the bank's private equity investment group, has a $1.5 billion portfolio of U.S. and international investments.

Clockwise from top:
Several major businesses with international reach are headquartered at Bank of America's LaSalle Street location, including U.S. & Canada Group, Midwest Commercial Bank, Global Private Bank, and Global Equity Investments.

Bank of America is involved in the New Homes for Chicago project, which has provided 23 new, single-family homes in the North Kenwood/Oakland neighborhood, and a similar effort for 40 new homes in Austin.

The 1994 merger between Continental Bank and Bank of America was celebrated with thousands of employees and clients gathered on LaSalle Street for a huge block party.

Other major business groups have operations in Chicago. BancAmerica Robertson Stephens, a premier global financial services organization, offers the expertise of a leading underwriter of debt and equity securities, and the strength of one of the nation's largest financial institutions.

Bank of America's Midwest Community Finance Group offers loans, investments, and grants to community-based businesses, nonprofit organizations, and real estate developers and investors. Global Payment Services is the Midwest arm of one of the largest cash management operations in the nation. BA Futures, the bank's exchange-traded futures and options risk management broker, provides clearing and execution of exchange-traded futures and options on approximately 30 exchanges worldwide.

The Commercial Banking division provides services to more than 1,500 middle-market clients and offers sophisticated corporate finance products, including private placements (debt and equity), asset securitization, and risk management.

In the U.S. & Canada Group, expertise, financial strength, and teamwork are the foundation of the group's approach to finance, because meeting today's business needs takes more than size alone. It takes a willingness—and an ability—to understand clients' business issues, try new approaches, develop better financial solutions, and set ever higher standards for corporate banking performance. The Global Private Bank provides the same kind of sophisticated financial solutions for the owners and executives of these companies.

Working with BankAmerica's investment banking subsidiary, BancAmerica Robertson Stephens, the U.S. & Canada Group client teams concentrate on finding the most appropriate capital-raising solutions for their clients' specific needs. Together, the U.S. & Canada Group and BancAmerica Robertson Stephens have the ability to identify emerging financing opportunities—and to originate, underwrite, and place a broad range of flexible, low-cost public and private debt securities with institutional investors.

BancAmerica Robertson Stephens' capabilities and advisory services include investment-grade to high-yield public market debt; loan syndications; domestic and international private placements; money market/short-term financing; public and private asset-backed finance; medium-term notes; mergers and acquisitions; tax/accounting structuring products; mortgages; municipal bonds and U.S. treasuries and agencies; expertise in equity underwriting; depth in securities and industry research; experience at bringing new issues and issuers to public and private markets; equity securities primary and aftermarket support; and a high-performing suite of mutual funds.

As a key player in the banking industry, Bank of America recognizes its responsibility to its clients, employees, shareholders, and its community, and embraces this philosophy: to be the best place to bank, work, and invest.

A Tradition of Community Service

 omplementing the business strategies designed to keep Bank of America as a world leader well into the next century, the company strives to be a good neighbor at the local level.

Bank of America is involved in more than 100 nonprofit organizations, boards, and committees in Chicago and the Midwest, and serves as a community partner with a number of them by providing grants, executive support, credit, and financial expertise.

Bank of America understands that it must also be located in a city that is the best place it can be. With a 140-year history of corporate and community leadership in Chicago, the bank is poised for the great successes still ahead and gratefully salutes its home city in the Heartland, which has contributed to its reputation of excellence.

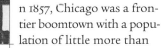
n 1857, Chicago was a frontier boomtown with a population of little more than 100,000. It was home to more than 1,500 businesses when the first stock certificate for Merchants' Savings, Loan and Trust Company, the predecessor of Continental Bank and today's Bank of America in Chicago, was issued to business-

Bank of America is the fifth-largest bank holding company in the United States, and has offices in 37 countries abroad (top).

Bank of America employs more than 3,500 people in the Midwest and approximately 90,000 worldwide (bottom).

man and philanthropist Walter O. Newberry.

When in 1924 Continental Bank moved into its current building, an architectural gem designed and built by Chicago's best tradesmen, it was the largest bank under one roof in the world. Today, still in the landmark building at the heart of Chicago's financial district, directly across from the Chicago Federal Reserve Bank, the headquarters provides one million square feet of office space.

Bank of America's rich story unfolds with many parallels in the Midwest and along the western seaboard, as the bank's wholesale strengths were fostered in Chicago simultaneously with a powerful and illustrious retail presence in California.

A.P. GIANNINI: A MAN AND HIS VISION

Amadeo Peter "A.P." Giannini was born in 1870 in San Jose, California, to an immigrant couple. At age 12, Giannini joined in his stepfather's wholesale business handling fresh produce. A few years later, he began traveling up and down California, meeting with ranchers, growers, and dairy farmers to sign contracts for bringing their goods to market, offering fair prices and respectful treatment. Most of all, he honored his word. Giannini said he got his best training from farmers, stevedores, teamsters, peddlers, and small merchants. In 1902, he joined the board of a San Francisco bank, but discovered that banks cared more for the carriage trade and that the little fellows and small-business proprietors had to hide their savings under a mattress and borrow from loan sharks at high rates.

Giannini launched his own venture, opening the doors of a remodeled San Francisco saloon as Bank of Italy (later renamed Bank of America) on October 17, 1904. Giannini and his employees went door-to-door explaining to people what a bank could do for them, and inviting them to become clients. Immigrants, farmers, and wage earners, struggling to make something of their lives and willing to back their dreams with hard work, responded. Bank of Italy grew from these small accounts.

Christmas in April (top left) and NeighborWorks Day, sponsored by Neighborhood Housing Services (top right), are two of the many projects that Bank of America participates in through its employee volunteer network, TeamAmerica. BofA was the recipient of the 1996 Award for Corporate Community Service from the Points of Light Foundation, due in large part to its volunteer activities.

BofA brings together a network of 13 schools with resources to provide a community-based approach to educational improvement in the West Humboldt Park neighborhood. Here, students at Muñoz Marin Primary Center, one of the school partners in Bank of America's Urban Education Initiative, perform during an assembly (bottom).

Meanwhile, Chicago's first mayor, William B. Ogden, along with agricultural industrialist Cyrus Hall McCormick and North-western University founder Grant Goodrich, had established the Merchants' Savings, Loan and Trust Company, and they were building its reputation as a reliable and trustworthy bank.

The Bank built on its solid reputation with Chicagoans by providing assistance during the great fire of 1871 that raged for two days and engulfed and demolished four square miles of the city; 500 lives were lost, and the property loss from 18,000 buildings downtown and northward came to more than $200 million.

Because no bank records survived the blaze, all accounts were verified on the basis of the customer's word alone. Solomon Smith, then Merchants' president, reopened the bank for business in his own basement. Contrary to what other local bankers were suggesting—paying out as little as 25 cents on the dollar for lost balances—Smith made full payment on all accounts. By doing so, he gained the public confidence needed to spur recovery in much the same way that Giannini did three decades later.

Both the Illinois and the California banks grew rapidly in the following decades, as commercial and trust banking expanded; each gained strong personal deposit bases and built successful bond departments. Investment offices were opened in many new cities throughout the western states and in other major cities by each of the banks, and each served a nationwide client base.

BUILDING BRIDGES TO THE FUTURE

As Continental Bank was creating lasting partnerships with industry and building its 23-story skyscraper, Giannini was expanding his branch banking system to Italy. Domestically, when women finally gained the right to vote in 1921, BofA established a Women's Banking Department. Late in the 1920s, Bank of America began participat-

ing in bonds outside California—for a school district in Dallas, parks in Chicago, a hospital in Boston. Also, it lent financing expertise and capital to the fruit, vegetable, and wine industries, becoming a premier agricultural lending institution.

The Great Depression brought a rash of bank runs and failures. In a scenario that would be revisited a half-century later (in 1984), the government had to rescue Continental by pumping in $50 million. In facing the effects of the depression, Giannini, with his usual optimism, urged people to break the cycle of self-defeat. Bank of America launched a public campaign called "Now, all together, on to good times," and Giannini used the slogan Put Your Money to Work! Bank of America bought millions of dollars of state and local bonds across the country,

contributing to many communities as they recovered from the economic collapse.

It is said that the Golden Gate Bridge would not have been built without Giannini, because engineer Joseph Strauss had to fight his way through 2,000 lawsuits filed by skeptics and special-interest groups.

Asked how long the bridge would last, Strauss answered, "Forever," and Giannini replied, "California needs that bridge. We'll buy the bonds."

This and subsequent neighborhood loans right up through the present day spread prosperity. Bank of America continues to help people help themselves. The power of this commitment is evident in Giannini's axiom, "Banks will grow in direct relation to their service to the public, and the smart banker will recognize that the way to grow is to serve."

Clockwise from top:
Continental Bank began as the Merchants' Savings, Loan & Trust Company, and survived the Civil War, the Great Fire of 1871, the Great Depression, and two world wars.

Bank of America's home in Chicago, the Continental Bank Building on LaSalle Street, was built in 1924 and offers one million square feet of office space.

A.P. Giannini, 1870-1949, founded Bank of Italy in 1904. By 1920, the bank had added branches in several locations throughout California, had expanded to sites in New York, and had developed a branch banking system in Italy. In 1930, Giannini renamed his company Bank of America to reflect his vision of bringing "helpful banking" to communities across the nation.

N AN ERA WHEN THE ENERGY INDUSTRY IS GOING BACK TO ITS ROOTS—TO A TIME WHEN CUSTOMERS HAD A CHOICE, AND ENTREPRENEURIAL SHOPS TAILORED PRODUCTS AND SERVICES FOR CLIENTS—ILLINOVA ENERGY PARTNERS IS MAKING QUITE A NAME FOR ITSELF. AND IT IS DOING IT THE OLD-FASHIONED WAY—BY PROVIDING CUSTOMIZED ENERGY

solutions to fit the unique needs of its wholesale and retail customers.

Since its inception in 1994, Illinova Energy Partners has climbed into the ranks of the top 10 power marketing organizations in the country; it is the third largest in the western United States, with expected sales of approximately $600 million in 1997. The company is part of Illinova, an international Fortune 1,000 corporation with combined assets of $5.7 billion, which gives it the financial strength to cover a broad array of energy management information, energy, and energy service, products. Illinova has been in the electric and natural gas business for more than 100 years. This experience, combined with the financial

strength to cover products and with talented employees drawn from around the country, has contributed to the rapid rise of Illinova Energy Partners.

The Illinova family also includes Illinova Generating, an independent power producer that invests in, builds, and operates independent power projects worldwide; Illinois Power, which delivers electricity, natural gas, and energy products to 600,000 customers in Illinois; and two partnerships—Tenaska Marketing Ventures, which enables Illinova to market natural gas supplies, and North American Energy Services, which operates and maintains power projects. With holdings in nine countries and offices in 12 U.S. cities, including Chicago,

Illinova helps businesses improve productivity and profitability.

CRAFTING ENERGY SOLUTIONS

Illinova Energy Partners' first step is to listen and learn about a client's operational needs. It then analyzes a customer's energy use and acts as an extension of its staff to manage and, if necessary, finance energy projects. Illinova then leverages its capabilities and experience to craft bankable energy solutions, which range from energy services and energy supply to resource management and development of independent power projects and financing packages. It manages energy supply portfolios in a way that reduces risks while

Illinova Energy Partners follows in the tradition of the early utility companies, which were market-focused shops that tailored energy solutions for their customers. Pictured is a utility company located in the Midwest circa 1920.

saving time and money. Illinova's customer-focused approach to solutions means there is no bias toward a particular fuel source, equipment manufacturer, or vendor.

"Deregulation of electricity is the driving issue now," says Robert Schultz, president of Illinova Energy Partners. "We provide energy information and energy products to businesses, plus offer a range of energy services that help clients improve their operations or save money. In this way, businesses are prepared to extract savings today and have a strategy for saving in the new marketplace."

In Illinois, Illinova's customers include Target, Home Depot, Ford Motor Company, Kerr McGee Chemical Company, Decatur Memorial Hospital, Eastern Illinois University, and a host of correctional facilities and schools. The company also serves clients that have many sites across the country, such as the Hughes Electronics family of companies.

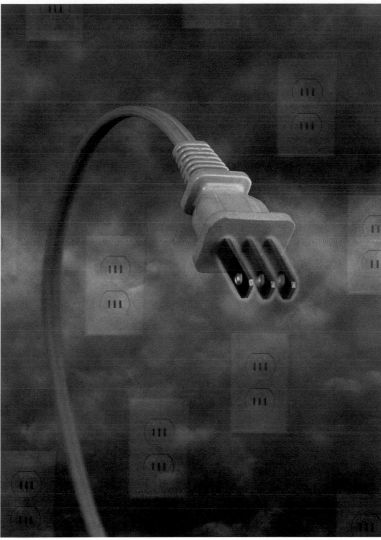

EVALUATION IS KEY

leader in providing customer-focused energy products, Illinova Energy Partners helps clients evaluate their position in three key ways. The first is by employing The Utility Manager, EQ Network, the EQ Service Bureau, or EQ Energy Audits, a combination of software and hands-on services that provide management information on all utilities electricity, solid waste, water, natural gas, recycling, and sewer—and help clients assess and control utility costs. Illinova's partner with The Utility Manager is Utility Cost Management, a Washington State-based company that owns the program.

With these energy information services, customers can tell where utility resources are going, their costs, and uses that need attention. The software can also be used to benchmark, check billings, budget, analyze performance, build consumption patterns, and forecast purchasing requirements.

With information generated by one of the energy management

services just mentioned, customers can better manage their use and determine what to purchase in a deregulated energy market. With Illinova's help, they can get more from the rate they're on, negotiate a better rate, and evaluate what they should pay in the future.

These evaluation tools can include outsourcing a customer's utility accounting and dramatically reducing headaches. For example, the EQ Service Bureau is a service bureau approach to managing utilities, streamlining the accounting process, and forecasting purchasing needs. With its 47 verification checks, the EQ Service Bureau assures billing accuracy and locates savings opportunities.

Another evaluation tool offered by Illinova Energy Partners is the EQ Energy Audits, which involves inspection of a customer's facilities to identify ways to increase energy efficiency and reduce energy costs. Each audit report includes a complete energy inventory and a range

of recommendations, cost options, and payback periods.

Illinova is a single contact for improving energy efficiency, upgrading equipment, or outsourcing operations. In addition, the company relieves budget pressures and distractions from a client's core business by providing customer service, turnkey engineered solutions, project management, system operation, and flexible financing tools. Experienced staff can design, engineer, acquire equipment, and manage construction of energy-related projects, as well as plan, design, and install energy management systems to maximize productivity and minimize energy costs. Illinova also offers expertise in gas distribution systems and devices.

Illinova's portfolio of services helps customers develop their energy consumption and supply strategies, and then extract financial benefits from both the supply and demand sides of their energy requirements equation.

Illinova's portfolio of services covers a broad array of energy management information, energy, and energy service products.

OUNDED IN 1995, FAVORITE BRANDS IS ONE OF THE LEADING NON-CHOCOLATE CONFECTIONERS IN THE WORLD, SPECIALIZING IN MARSHMALLOWS, FRUIT SNACKS, GUMMIES, AND GENERAL LINE AND SEASONAL CANDY. THE COMPANY OFFERS HUNDREDS OF HIGH-QUALITY CANDIES—AT A GREAT VALUE.

Favorite Brands International—led by Al Bono, chief executive officer and president—is one of the leading non-chocolate confectioners in the world, specializing in marshmallows, fruit snacks, gummies, and general line and seasonal candy. The company offers hundreds of high-quality candies—at a great value.

Favorite Brands, led by Al Bono, chief executive officer and president, has a strong track record in the food industry. The company was founded with the purchase of Kraft Foods' confectionery business, including Jet-Puffed Marshmallows, Caramels, Peanut Brittle, and Butter Mints.

The company grew quickly, initially by acquisition, establishing itself as the manufacturer of many of the most popular varieties of candy in the important non-chocolate confections category. Favorite Brands' acquisition of five candy companies within fewer than 18 months catapulted it from industry newcomer to the fourth-largest confectioner in the country.

According to Bono, "Each of our acquisitions was strategic, keeping us focused on the confections industry. Our first acquisition was Kidd & Company, a marshmallow manufacturer. Since then, we've acquired Farley Foods, a general line candy manufacturer with strong sales in the grocery category; Sathers, a general line candy company with a strong convenience store business; Dae Julie, a manufacturer of gummi and jell candies; and Trolli, an innovator in the gummi candy business."

Bono said that he initially thought Favorite Brands would "get the Kraft business up and running . . . and look at acquisitions a bit later." But opportunities to acquire great companies began to appear—and Favorite Brands "simply couldn't walk away from them."

Favorite Brands' decision to compete in the non-chocolate confections category was a strategic one. Candy consumption is growing—in fact, per capita consumption is up to 25 pounds per year. While per capita consumption of chocolate has been flat over the past few years, non-chocolate candy sales have been rising.

"Non-chocolate candy is fat-free, and as such, it's been embraced by baby boomers seeking the great taste of a sweet treat without the guilt," says Bono. "They're looking for small indulgences—and a simple piece of hard, jellied, or gummi candy fills the bill."

Today, Favorite Brands manufactures and markets non-chocolate candy to virtually every supermarket, mass merchandise outlet, and convenience store in the country. As an industry leader, Bono has charged his team with driving and growing the non-chocolate candy category. They're doing that by marketing existing products to new sales channels, as well as creating new and innovative variations of their popular marshmallows,

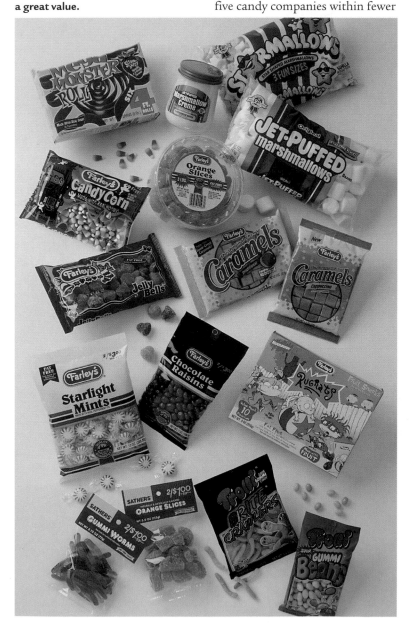

fruit snacks, gummies, and general line and seasonal candies.

Never before has there been such an array of sizes, shapes, and flavors. Favorite Brands leads the industry, offering a host of new tastes and textures. Offering candy flavors such as peach, watermelon, and kiwi, its products go far beyond the traditional favorites, such as root beer barrels, starlight mints, and orange slices. At the same time, the company is finding new uses for these products as ingredients in other popular foods.

MAKING MOUNTAINS OF MARSHMALLOWS, CARAMELS, AND MORE

The foundation of Favorite Brands' business was marshmallows, caramels, and other confections manufactured by Kraft Foods. These timeless treats are enjoyed by people of all ages, who have memories of eating them as an ingredient in favorite recipes as well as straight out of the bag.

Creamy, soft, and fluffy . . . nothing tastes like a marshmallow, which is why it continues to be one of America's favorite foods. Favorite Brands offers marshmallows in all shapes, sizes, and flavors, including the Original Jet-Puffed® Marshmallow, Jet-Puffed® Miniature Marshmallows, Jet-Puffed® Toasted Coconut Marshmallows, Jet-Puffed® Marshmallow Creme, and seasonal-shaped marshmallows. In addition to the branded marshmallows, Favorite Brands is the leading manufacturer of private label varieties, sold by retailers nationwide.

Of course, from Memorial Day through Labor Day, most Americans prefer their Jet-Puffed marshmallows lightly toasted and "smashed" between two graham crackers and a chocolate bar, creating that rite of summertime, "S'mores" (as in "I want some more"). And around the winter holidays, it's hard to calculate just how many batches of Fantasy Fudge—the gold standard recipe for fudge—are created using jars of the company's Marshmallow Creme. Year-round, consumers scoop out hundreds of marshmallows to make Crispy Treats, made from rice cereal lightly coated with

melted marshmallows. Finally, the delicious, soft, and creamy confections maintain a significant following from loyal consumers who enjoy simply eating them as a snack right out of the bag.

When it comes to caramels, "Who could imagine the fall and Halloween season without Favorite Brands' original chewy caramels?" asks Bono. This delicious ingredient and snack has been around for more than 60 years. Favorite Brands' Farley's caramels are known on sight because of their unique, square shape and special individual cellophane wrappers. "Our caramels are synonymous with homemade caramel apples, and are called for as an ingredient in a variety of desserts," Bono says.

The crinkly sound of the caramels' cellophane wrapper being opened has long been a giveaway

for someone sneaking a treat. And, as a special surprise, several Fudgie caramels are always included in each bag. For families throughout America, these delectable chocolate fudge treats have been an exciting taste inside the bag—and no doubt the topic of extensive negotiations to decide "who gets it"—since their introduction more than 40 years ago.

LONG ON FLAVOR: FRUIT SNACKS AND FRUIT ROLLS

riginally introduced in 1988, Farley's Fruit Snacks are the top-selling fruit snacks. Available in soft, chewy pieces and long, flavorful rolls, Farley's Fruit Snacks are made with fruit and fortified with vitamins C and E, and beta-carotene. Fruit snacks are popular with kids,

Farley's Fruit Snacks are the top-selling fruit snacks. Available in soft, chewy pieces and long, flavorful rolls, Farley's Fruit Snacks are made with fruit and fortified with vitamins C and E, and beta-carotene. Fruit Snacks are popular with kids, who like the fun flavors and shapes, and with moms, who appreciate the convenience and "better for you" ingredients (left).

Favorite Brands offers marshmallows in all shapes, sizes, and flavors, including the Original Jet-Puffed® Marshmallow, as well as Jet-Puffed® Miniature Marshmallows, Marshmallow Creme, and seasonal-shaped marshmallows (right).

who like the fun flavors and shapes, and with moms, who appreciate the convenience and "better for you" ingredients.

Produced on long sheets of waxed paper that needs to be peeled away before eating, fruit rolls practically beg kids to play with their food. Favorite Brands has even created fruit rolls that come with a "stamper," which lets kids have fun stamping the shape of their favorite characters right onto the roll.

Favorite Brands makes its fruit snacks and rolls available nationwide, through grocery and mass merchandise outlets. "We keep consumer excitement for these products alive by introducing a variety of new shapes and sizes each year," Bono says. "For example, Farley's Fruit Snacks are available in the shapes of popular licensed characters like Nickelodeon Rugrats, Teenage Mutant Ninja Turtles, Street Sharks, and Power Ranger fruit snack rolls, as well as snacks shaped like traditional favorites—Dinosaurs and Zoo Animals." Popular fruit roll varieties include the MegaMonster

Roll—four feet of fruit snack fun—and the traditional 30-inch rolls of strawberry, cherry, and Trolls in Trouble. The packaging is integral to the allure of these products, and each box boasts lively graphics and bright colors.

"GIMME THOSE GUMMIES"

Gummi-type candies have been produced for at least 100 years, but have recently experienced a boom in popularity. Gummi Bears became popular in Europe in the 1940s, and spread to the United States in the 1970s. While the bear shape and the delicious taste of gummies were compelling to American consumers, companies like Favorite Brands—and in particular, its Trolli division—are recognized as innovators because of the wide range of shapes and flavors they have introduced over the past few years. "Trolli has introduced so many unique gummies in exotic shapes and sizes that the bear shape isn't even one of its top five sellers. Its wild worm, dinosaur, caterpillar, octopus, and other fun shapes are enjoyed by kids and adults alike," Bono says.

One way Trolli has made gummies more appealing to adults is by introducing more sophisticated flavors like raspberry, grapefruit, and fruit salad. Packaging is also targeted to the adult—featuring drawings of fruit and highlighting that the gummies are fat-free.

For kids, gummi products and packaging feature vibrant colors and intense flavors like neon gummi

worms and sour gummies. Trolli captured the attention of the candy industry and the public when it introduced BriteCrawlers, a worm-shaped gummi. These treats were unique because of their appearance—brightly colored with a "sugar sanding"—as well as their sour taste. They quickly became a best-seller for Trolli, and raised consumer awareness of gummies in the process. Another Trolli innovation is Gummi Beans, delicious bean-shaped candies with a crunchy sugar shell and a soft, tart, and tangy gummi center. This mouthwatering sweet-and-sour combination offers a distinct taste with a "long chew." Like their gummi counterparts, Gummi Beans are fat-free.

In addition to Trolli, Favorite Brands' Dae Julie, Farley, and Sathers divisions also market gummi treats. The combined sales of Favorite Brands gummi products make it one of the leading U.S. gummi manufacturers.

ALL THE FAVORITES FROM THE TRADITIONAL CANDY STORE AND A WHOLE LOT MORE

From starlight mints to candy corn; from jelly beans to spice drops, Favorite Brands offers a wide assortment of general line candies to a variety of retail outlets. Its strong brand names—Farley's, Sathers, and Dae Julie—offer high-quality traditional candies at a great value to supermarkets, mass merchandisers, convenience stores, and drug stores.

When it comes to general line candy, there isn't much Favorite Brands doesn't manufacture. Its hard candies include starlight mints, root beer barrels, sour fruit balls, lemon drops, butterscotch discs, and lots of lollipops. Other favorites include Boston baked beans, French burnt peanuts, panned chocolates, jujus, spearmint leaves, orange slices, spice drops, jelly rings, and more. For those on restricted diets, Favorite Brands also offers some of its best-selling candies in sugar-free (with Nutrasweet®) versions, including starlight mints, butterscotch discs, root beer barrels, and sour fruit balls.

Packaging plays an important role in marketing Favorite Brands'

Similar to jelly beans, Trolli's Gummi Beans are delicious bean-shaped candy with a crunchy sugar shell and a soft, tart, and tangy gummi center. The mouthwatering sweet-and-sour combination offers a distinct taste and long-lasting chewing satisfaction. They're fat-free, too (left).

The company keeps consumer excitement for its fruit snacks and rolls alive by introducing a variety of new shapes and sizes each year. Fruit Snacks are available in the shapes of popular licensed characters as well as more traditional favorites (right).

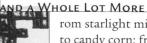

general line candies. The best-selling varieties are packaged in a number of styles to make them appealing to Favorite Brands' wide range of customers. Small boxes of candy are offered at the checkout counter to consumers who like to enjoy a little treat. The company's "2 for $3" program offers the opportunity to purchase two bags of candy for $3, and is primarily offered to grocery stores; a "2 for $1" program appeals to shoppers on the run at convenience stores. Tubs of candy are sold through mass merchandise and club stores, for customers who like to purchase larger quantities of their favorite sweets.

WHAT ARE THE HOLIDAYS WITHOUT CANDY?

easonal candy is finding new ways to get consumers into the spirit of the season—whether it's conversation hearts for Valentine's Day, jelly beans for Easter, individually wrapped treats for back-to-school/Halloween, or stocking stuffers for Christmas. In fact, Favorite Brands makes the country's best-selling lines of jelly beans for Easter and mellow cremes for Halloween. Favorite Brands offers a variety of seasonal candies including traditional candy dish candy, novelty candies, and other confections that can be used as ingredients to make holiday treats.

Retailers are finding that by offering holiday treats to consumers earlier, they can establish themselves as a headquarters for seasonal products. This is important, because once a store establishes that thought in consumers' minds, their customers will return for other seasonal shopping needs, such as ingredients and specialty products. To help retailers market seasonal products, Favorite Brands offers a wide range of items as well as package options.

LEADING A DOUBLE LIFE— AS INGREDIENTS

onsumers would be surprised to learn that marshmallows, caramels, gummies, and fruit snacks lead double lives as confections with a strong ingredient market. Favorite Brands has a staff dedicated to creating new varieties of

these versatile confections, and is the only ingredient supplier that specializes in both caramels and marshmallows.

The experts in the Favorite Brands technology center work year-round to create new confection varieties that can be offered as ingredients to industry. While most of the group's sales are in the cereal and confectionery areas, applications are growing. Its products can be found in many cereals, cocoa mixes, candy bars, and ice creams.

Among Favorite Brands' unique concoctions are the patented melt-restricted marshmallow as well as caramel chips that retain their shape and texture when heated. These are being incorporated into cookies, brownies, pies, and casseroles. Other creations include a host of variegates—marshmallows and caramels that are created to swirl through ice cream and remain creamy even at subzero temperatures.

Beyond marshmallows and caramels, Favorite Brands is offering its other candies—and variations on them—to industry. For example, consumers' interest in gummies

is motivating more manufacturers to ask Favorite Brands for suggestions for how they can be incorporated into other foods, like cake mixes, yogurts, and ice creams. Other variations of Favorite Brands' candies are being reformulated as ingredients, too, because of the unique taste and fun that candies can add.

A SWEET FUTURE

t seems that everyone has a favorite candy—and a special memory to go along with it. Bono says he can remember playing in his grandparents' general store in New York—and being rewarded for good behavior with candy from the many jars that lined the countertop. And still today, the eyes of children and adults alike light up when a package of candy is pulled from the grocery bag, or when mom refills the candy dish. Favorite Brands understands the universal appeal of candy and is focused on creating high-quality products and offering them to consumers at a great value. That should ensure that the company's treats wind up in every home's candy jar.

Packaging plays an important role in marketing Favorite Brands' general line candies. For example, the best-selling varieties of its Farley's line of candy are packaged in a variety of styles —boxes, bags, tubs, and more— to make them appealing to Favorite Brands' wide range of customers.

OUR-STAR HOTELS CERTAINLY EXIST IN CHICAGO, BUT HERE OR ANYWHERE, THERE'S NOTHING QUITE LIKE THE WESTIN RIVER NORTH. THIS CORPORATE SIBLING OF TWO OTHER CHICAGO GEMS, THE WESTIN O'HARE AND THE WESTIN MICHIGAN AVENUE, HAS ITS OWN PERSONALITY AND ITS OWN

perks. From its riverside location to its sophisticated sushi bar to its luxurious rooms and suites, the Westin River North offers everything a traveler needs to feel rested, relaxed, and pampered.

Of course, the Westin River North is more than a four-star hotel. Its further accolades include ranking as a four-diamond luxury property, and it is a recipient of the High Excellent rating by Zagat's valued customer review for U.S. hotels, resorts, and spas. Recently, for the third year in a row, the Westin hotels have been named as the number one upscale hotel chain by the Corporate Meeting Planner, an honor resulting from a sampling of frequent travelers.

CATERING TO BUSINESS TRAVELERS

Frequent travelers tend to be business travelers, and the Westin River North caters happily to them. Meetings and other groups can take advantage of four conference parlors, 14 meeting rooms, the dramatic Executive Room (ideal

for that top-level caucus), and even the Grand Ballroom, which opens onto an outdoor terrace with spectacular views. Business travelers also find their practical needs anticipated, with the Executive Business Center's computers, fax machines, and other helpful equipment. And all guests can take advantage of the Fitness Center's workout options, even if they've forgotten their workout clothes—the hotel provides these, too.

Whether they've come for business or pleasure, visitors are sure to notice an air of serenity throughout the Westin River North. That's because, prior to its incarnation in January 1997 as a Westin property, the hotel spent a decade as the Hotel Nikko, a Chicago outpost of a Japanese chain that provided guests who were so inclined with a stay as authentically Japanese as possible in this all-American heartland. Several suites were appointed with tatami mats and other Japanese furnishings, and one of the hotel's restaurants offered the option of one's own tearoom for dinners.

Though many of these features were rarely used and have not remained as standard offerings at the Westin River North, General Manager Gary Sieland believes their aura lingers. "There will always be an Asian accent, an Asian feeling, to this hotel," Sieland says. "We will be redoing all the rooms, however, to give them a more residential feeling, to lighten them up a bit. We're bringing in several top interior designers to work on it."

While an inviting appearance is important, the comfort level of the Westin River North's rooms already ranks as superb. Each of the 422 luxurious rooms provides such business services as multiple telephones with voice mail, dataport, and fax machines. Refreshment centers and televisions are standard equipment, and each room's enormous marble bath is ready for guests to make themselves comfortable—perhaps wrapped in the cozy terry robe that awaits every guest.

The hotel's restaurants are equally impressive. The Celebrity Café specializes in American food,

The Westin River North is located just west of the State Street and Michigan Avenue shopping areas, adjacent to entertainment, art galleries, trendy nightclubs, top restaurants, snug cafés, and chic boutiques. Guests can walk easily to the Merchandise Mart, State of Illinois Building, Daley Center, Dirksen Building, and Quaker Tower (left).

The Westin River North's presidential suite offers luxurious comfort in a spacious setting (right).

The Celebrity Café specializes in American food—prepared and served with sophistication in a sumptuous setting that overlooks the Chicago River—and features a popular Sunday jazz brunch.

prepared and served with sophistication in a sumptuous setting that overlooks the Chicago River. On Sundays, the Celebrity Cafe's jazz brunch attracts fans from the city and suburbs, as well as from the guest roster. Jazz is also featured nightly in the Hana Lobby Lounge, where a Japanese garden soothes guests observing the cocktail hour (from 5 to 9 p.m. each weekday evening) with drinks, sake, and an assortment of exquisite sushi.

PREMIER LOCATION

When guests venture forth from their elegant Westin River North surroundings, they're pleased to find their hotel is situated perfectly for just about any downtown destination. Its location is just to the west of the State Street and Michigan Avenue shopping areas, placing the hotel in one of the hottest entertainment neighborhoods in town. Art galleries are especially prominent in the area, but there's no shortage of trendy nightclubs, top restaurants, snug cafés, and chic boutiques. And travelers here on business can walk easily to the Merchandise Mart, State of Illinois Building, Daley Center (where "The Picasso Scupture" lives), Dirksen Building, and Quaker Tower (which is adjacent to the hotel).

Like the rest of his staff and the entire Westin Corporation, Sieland is proud of the Westin River North's commitment to the good of the city and its citizens. "We're phenomenally good corporate citizens," Sieland says. "I speak for all the Chicago hotels in saying that I don't think there is a more generous industry anywhere. We receive probably 25 letters a day asking for help for a specific cause, and we respond positively to an amazing number of them. Each of our hotels has specific charities, as we do; but we always try to be open to deserving organizations."

The Westin River North, Sieland believes, is just hitting its stride, as exemplified by its parent chain's current national advertising program. "The tagline is 'Choose your travel partner wisely,' " Sieland explains. "It's very sophisticated, and very, very upscale. We think it speaks directly to the extraordinary levels of quality and service that are rooted throughout this culture at Westin. It is a truly upscale place to stay."

The Westin River North caters to business travelers, providing a number of conference rooms and meeting facilities.

HOWARD E. ANDE, a self-taught photographer from Oakville, Connecticut, specializes in agricultural and industrial photography, as well as his passion, railroad photography. In addition to calendars and greeting cards, his images have appeared in numerous trade publications, children's books, coffee-table photojournals, and magazines. Ande lives in Streamwood with his wife and his pet Airedale terrier.

STEVE BAKER is an internationally published photographer who has contributed to more than 100 publications. With a degree in journalism from Indiana University, he is the proprietor of Highlight Photography, specializing in assignments for such clients as Eastman Kodak, Nike, Budweiser, the U.S. Olympic Committee, and Mobil Oil, which has commissioned seven exhibitions of his work since 1994. Baker is the author and photographer of *Racing Is Everything*, and he has contributed to two other Towery publications, *Indianapolis: Crossroads of the*

American Dream and *Nashville: City of Note*. Currently, Baker resides in Indianapolis.

MARK BALLOGG, the co-owner of Steinkamp/Ballogg Photography, specializes in architectural, lifestyle, and fine-art photography. An honors graduate from Chicago's Columbia College who continued his studies during a 13-month scholarship at l'École Nationale Supérieure des Arts Décoratifs in Paris, Ballogg has worked extensively as a dye transfer technician and studio photographer. His images have been featured in several group and solo exhibitions, as well as in such publications as *Artweek*, the *Chicago Tribune*, the *Chicago Sun-Times*, the *New York Times*, *Smithsonian*, *Interior Design*, and *Chicago Magazine*, to name a few. Originally from St. Petersburg, Florida, he enjoys gourmet cooking, gardening, coaching basketball, and riding bikes.

JOHN BOOZ, originally from Pittsburgh, moved to Chicago in 1979. He specializes in documentary photography and

photojournalism, and his work has been featured in *Boxing Illustrated* and *International Boxing Digest*, as well as the *Chicago Tribune Magazine*, the *Chicago Sun-Times*, and *People* magazine. In December 1996, Booz traveled to Chernobyl to document the cancerous effects of radiation on children. Currently, he is working on *La Charriada*, a book about Mexican rodeo in the city of Chicago.

ROY CAJERO, a self-employed freelance photographer who lives in Memphis, specializes in photojournalism and capturing local music, especially the blues, on film. In addition to being regularly featured in the *Memphis Flyer*, Cajero's work has been published in the *New Yorker*, the *Washington Post*, and *Spin* magazine, as well as in Towery Publishing's *Memphis: New Visions, New Horizons* and Hyperion Books' *Dear Dr. King*.

MITCHELL CANOFF is a lifelong Chicagoan who owns and operates Mitchell Canoff Photography. A self-taught

▼ CHARLES ESHELMAN

photographer, he specializes in people and black-and-white photography.

JANET CENTURY has been producing black-and-white and color photography for a wide range of corporations, publications, agencies, and universities for more than 15 years. Her images have been published in *Images from the Heart: A Bicentennial Celebration of Cleveland and Its People*; *To Heal a Nation*, a book about the Vietnam Veterans Memorial; *The Beacon* magazine, in a story about Vietnam veterans returning to Vietnam; and Towery Publishing's *Cleveland: Continuing the Renaissance*. The recipient of numerous industry awards, Century recently was commissioned to photograph workers for USS *Kobe's Steel Town Story*.

CHURCHILL & KLEHR, a Chicago-based studio owned by self-taught photographers Winsoar Churchill and Alan Klehr, specializes in editorial, corporate, travel, architectural, location, and stock photography, as well as environmental portraits. Their images have been published in *Forbes*, *Business Week*,

and *Wine Spectator*, among others, and their clients include IBM, AT&T, Norwegian Cruise Line, DuPont, and Hyatt Hotels.

JAMES CRUMP, a native of Leamington, Ontario, moved to Chicago in 1989. The recipient of a bachelor's degree in communications from the University of Windsor, he is currently the owner of Rolled Steel Photography, Inc. Crump specializes in concert photography and digital imaging, and his work has been published in *Rolling Stone*, the *Chicago Tribune*, and the *Chicago Reader*. He enjoys traveling, cooking, and participating in sports.

TOM CRUZE grew up in Fort Wayne and received his bachelor's degree from Indiana University in 1979. Currently, he works as a staff photographer for the *Chicago Sun-Times*, covering national political conventions, major sports competitions, and other events of community interest. Cruze has received several awards from the Chicago, Indiana, and Illinois press photographers associations.

ROBERT DAVIS works for the *Chicago Sun-Times* and freelances for several national magazines. Born and raised in Chicago, he became interested in photojournalism during high school, when he gained an understanding of the power of photography. Then, while studying at Columbia College in Chicago, Davis began his career as a photojournalist. He has covered a wide range of stories—from the homeless in the heart of downtown to people repainting the antennae atop the John Hancock Center to the Bulls' last five NBA championships.

GEOFFREY ELLIS is a native Californian who moved to Memphis in 1997 after spending a total of 11 years in Miami, Gainesville, and Jacksonville, Florida. A graduate of the University of North Florida with a degree in graphic design, he currently works for Towery Publishing as an art director. Ellis specializes in graphic design, freelance photography, and Super 8mm film, and he enjoys collecting 8mm and 16mm films, cameras, and LP records. His work has been published in

Towery's *Jacksonville: Reflections of Excellence*.

CHARLES ESHELMAN, a self-taught photographer from South Bend, resides in Chicago, where he heads Charles Eshelman Photography. His work includes editorial, corporate, portrait, and publicity photography. In addition to appearing in *Chicago Magazine*, *Publisher's Weekly*, *Wine & Dine*, and the *Chicago Tribune*, Eshelman's photography has been exhibited at the Hubbard Street Gallery.

LEE FOSTER is a veteran travel writer and photographer who lives in Berkeley. His work has been published in a number of major travel magazines and newspapers, and he maintains a stock photo library that features more than 250 worldwide destinations. Foster's full travel publishing efforts can be viewed on his World Wide Web site at http://www.fostertravel.com.

BLAINE HARRINGTON III calls Colorado home when he is not traveling around the globe. For 10 weeks in the fall of

▲ JAMES NEWBERRY

1996, he journeyed 36,000 air miles to 11 countries on photo shoots. In addition, he has worked for a variety of magazines, including *Business Week, Forbes, Time, Newsweek, National Geographic Traveler*, and *Ski*. Harrington has also completed assignments for National Geographic and Time-Life, and has taken cover photos for such travel guides as *Fodor's, Frommer's, Insight Guides*, and *Real Guides*.

HEINZ JUERGEN HESS, a native of Frankfurt, is a Cleveland-based, freelance photographer who specializes in editorial photography. The son of a commercial photographer, Hess has had a lifelong interest in taking pictures, especially those of technical events, railroads, and trains. Some of his first images of Cleveland were featured in the Faces of Cleveland contest. He also contributed to *Cleveland: Continuing the Renaissance*.

HILLSTROM STOCK PHOTO, established in 1967, is a full-service stock photography agency based in Chicago. Its largest files consist of images of architecture, agriculture backgrounds, classic autos, gardens, and high-risk adventure/sports.

KAREN I. HIRSCH is an award-winning commercial and editorial photographer based in Chicago. Her images have been featured in numerous publications, including the *Chicago Tribune*, the *Chicago Sun-Times, Graphis, Communication Arts, Adweek, Advertising Age*, and *Sail*. Other books featuring her photos include *Lake Michigan* and Towery Publishing's *New York: Metropolis of the American Dream*; *The Towery Report on DuPage County, Illinois*; *Colorado Springs: Rocky Mountain Majesty*; and *Chicago: Second to None*. Hirsch's honors include two photography grants from the Chicago Department of Cultural Affairs and national awards from competitions sponsored by Eastman Kodak and the Professional Photographers of America. She serves on the board of directors of the Chicago/Midwest chapter of the American Society of Media Photographers. Hirsch lived and studied in France and Spain for two years while earning bachelor's and master's degrees from the University of Illinois.

JOHN D. IVANKO, an award-winning photographer and writer, resides in Browntown, Wisconsin, on a turn-of-the-century organic-farm-turned-bed-and-breakfast. Ivanko's images have been published in *Fodor's* guidebooks, *Wisconsin Trails*, and *Sky* magazine, and his work is featured in *Children from Australia to Zimbabwe: A Photographic Journey around the World*, a book sponsored by SHAKTI for Children, a nonprofit organization dedicated to helping bridge children's understanding of and respect for the diversity of cultures. Ivanko's clients include United Parcel Service, Red Wing Shoe Company, Wilderness Travel, and Johnnie Walker brands from Schieffelin & Somerset. He is represented by the 11th Hour Stock Photography Agency in Chicago.

HOWARD N. KAPLAN graduated with a master of fine arts from the Rochester Institute of Technology, where he studied photography and furniture design. Specializing in architectural and underwater images, he opened HNK Architectural Photography, Inc. in 1977. Kaplan's work has been published in *Architectural Digest, Chicago Magazine, Interior Design, Newsweek*, and *Time*, among others. He also has taught photography at his alma mater, as well as museum and curatorial practices at Columbia College.

DANIEL KURUNA, originally from Pennsylvania, moved to Chicago in 1992. He received a master's degree from the Institute of Design at the Illinois Institute of Technology. Currently employed at D4 Photo, Kuruna specializes in documentary photography. His clients include Doblin Group, Design Research, Firstar Bank, Chicago Humanities Festival, and Nature Conservancy.

MAYUMI LAKE, a native of Osaka, moved to the Windy City in 1992 and earned a bachelor of fine arts from the School of the Art Institute of Chicago in 1997. She currently lives in Providence, where she is working toward a master's degree in photography from the Rhode Island School of Design. Lake primarily experiments with still life photography, videography, and 16mm filmography. Her work has been featured in *Chicago Magazine*.

JAMES A. MILTON graduated from the Commercial Photography program at Hennepin Technical College. Specializing in scenic and nature photography, as well as portraits, Milton works for Ritz Camera, serves as head photographer for *Lavender Magazine*, and does freelance work out of his own studio, Flames Photography, in Minneapolis. In July 1997, Milton won the Northern Lights photo contest sponsored by *Minnesota Monthly*. His work

is included in another Towery publication, *Minneapolis-St. Paul: Linked to the Future*.

KEVIN O. MOONEY, a native of Salt Lake City, moved to Chicago in 1963. Specializing in editorial magazine work, as well as advertising, travel, landscape, people, and panoramic photography, he manages his own studio, Kevin O. Mooney Photography. His clients include the State of Illinois Department of Tourism and the Chicago Office of Tourism. His work has been published in *National Geographic, Life, Outside, Parenting Magazine*, and *Forbes*.

JAMES NEWBERRY, a graduate of Columbia College who studied photography and filmmaking, enjoys taking pictures of music personalities. A native Chicagoan, he has worked for American Recordings, Atlantic Records, Children's Television Workshop, Jive Records, and *Spin* magazine, among others. Newberry's photo gallery can be accessed through his Web site, www.skyparlor.com/photo.

VITO PALMISANO, originally from Chicago, is a corporate advertising photographer whose most memorable assignment required him to climb an antenna atop the John Hancock Center. An avid runner with a black belt in tae kwon do, Palmisano has worked for such clients as American Airlines, Edison, McDonald's, Motorola, Owens Corning, Gateway 2000, and Michigan Travel Bureau. The owner of Vito Palmisano Photography, based in

his favorite subjects include religious life, processions, rituals, and the rich cultural life of Latinos in the United States and Mexico.

MARTY PEREZ, a self-taught photographer, has lived his entire life in Chicago.

JAMES PURDUM, a native of Des Moines and a graduate of the University of Iowa, moved to Chicago in 1992. The

KAREN I. HIRSCH

Holland, Michigan, he contributed to Towery's *Greater Detroit: Renewing the Dream.*

ANTONIO PEREZ, a native of South Chicago, is currently employed at *¡Exito!,* the *Chicago Tribune's* Spanish publication. Specializing in documentary photography and photojournalism,

owner and operator of his own studio, he specializes in alternative people photography, primarily for the magazine, entertainment, and advertising industries. Purdum's work has been featured in *Us, Guitar Magazine, Better Homes and Gardens,* and *Forbes,* as well as on several record albums.

MARK REINSTEIN has lived in Washington, D.C., and Bethesda, and presently calls Alexandria, Virginia, home. A self-employed photographer, he specializes in taking pictures of fireworks, as well as in travel, news, and wedding photography.

RON SCHRAMM specializes in photographing architectural elements within the environment, as well as taking many pictures of his native Chicago. His images can be seen in numerous newspapers, brochures, exhibits, commercial products, and advertising pieces; on wall murals and magazine covers; and in the book *Chicago: A Pictorial Guide.* A member of the American Society of Media Photographers, American Society of Picture Professionals, and Chicago Convention & Visitors Bureau, he owns Ron Schramm Photography, a stock agency that maintains a comprehensive file of images.

ART SHAY, a Chicagoan since 1950, has worked as a freelance photographer and writer for the *Washington Post* and as a staff photographer for Time-Life. He has had more than 30,000 photographs published—including some 1,000 covers—in *Time, Life, Fortune, Sports Illustrated,* the *New York Times, Forbes, Business Week,* and many others. Shay has worked on annual reports for 3M, National Can, and Baxter Labs, and his photographs have been included in more than 80 books. In 1959, his shot of Nikita Khrushchev on an Iowa farm won *Life* magazine's Picture of the Year award. Most recently, Shay has written a play called *Nelson, Simone, and Gad,* which was entirely produced in Chicago and which opened in 1998.

STEVE SHAY, a freelance photographer for more than 18 years, was influenced at a young age by his father, a Time-Life photographer. At age 18, Shay traveled in Asia and the South Pacific, taking pictures of what he saw. His work has appeared in the *Chicago Sun-Times,* the *Chicago Tribune,* the *New City* newspaper, and the *New York Times,* to name a few. His clients include the Archdiocese of Chicago, the Chicago Theological Seminary, Barat College, Highland Park Hospital, the Highland Park Strings, and the Chaine des

Rotisseurs, a gourmet food and wine tasting group that hires him to capture photogenic meals with his camera. Shay also enjoys taking pictures at weddings and bar mitzvahs.

ALAN SHORTALL was born in Dublin, Ireland, and move to New York in 1983. He parlayed his degree in photography into assisting jobs for established photographers before opening his own studio in 1986. Since his move to Chicago in 1988, Shortall's clients have included *Chicago Magazine;* the Statue of Liberty Foundation; Continental Bank; Scott, Foresman; and numerous design firms and advertising agencies. His work has appeared in *Graphis, Communication Arts,* and a guide to Chicago commissioned by the American Institute of Graphic Artists.

JAMES STEINKAMP, is a native of Chicago, is the co-owner of Steinkamp/Ballogg Photography. Specializing in architecture, aerial, interior/exterior, and fine-art photography, he has been the feature photographer in several books, including *Skyscrapers,* and his images have been displayed at O'Hare International Airport and Navy Pier. Steinkamp is also the recipient of numerous awards from the American Institute of Architects.

DEVON WHITMORE graduated from Columbia College with a degree in photography. After working in Vail, Colorado, as a commercial photographer for the ski resort, Whitmore returned to the Windy City, where he is currently employed by *Chicago Magazine.* Also a freelance photographer, he has worked for the Lutheran Family Mission, Virgin Records, and Zeinabu Davis Films. In addition to specializing in commercial, fashion, and landscape photography, Whitmore enjoys taking pictures of tire shops, which he finds to be beautiful and unique.

Other organizations and photographers who contributed to *Chicago: Heart and Soul of America* include Chris Barret, Scott Barrow, Michael Brosilow, Chicago Historical Society, Chicago Symphony Orchestra, Blair Jensen, Mark Lind, and Steppenwolf Theatre Company.